CW01651879

3D Graphic Programming in BASIC

Jennrich
Massmann
Schulz

A Data Becker Book

Published by

Abacus

Second Printing, February 1989
Printed in U.S.A.
Copyright © 1989, 1990 Abacus
5370 52nd Street, SE
Grand Rapids, MI 49508

Copyright © 1987, 1988, 1989 Data Becker GmbH
Merowingerstrase 30
4000 Duesseldorf, West Germany

This book is copyrighted. No part of this book may be reproduced, stored in a retrieval system, or transmitted in any form or by any means, electronic, mechanical, photocopying, recording or otherwise, without the prior written permission of Abacus or Data Becker GmbH.

Every effort has been made to ensure complete and accurate information concerning the material presented in this book. However, Abacus can neither guarantee nor be held legally responsible for any mistakes in printing or faulty instructions contained in this book. The authors always appreciate receiving notice of any errors or misprints.

Amiga 500, Amiga 1000, Amiga 2000 and Amiga are trademarks or registered trademarks of Commodore-Amiga, Inc. AC/BASIC Compiler and AC/BASIC are trademarks or registered trademarks of Absoft Corporation. Cray is a trademark or registered trademark of Cray Incorporated. AmigaBASIC is a trademark or registered trademark of Microsoft Corporation.

Library of Congress Cataloging-in-Publication Data

Jennrich, Bruno, 1958-
Amiga 3D graphic programming in BASIC / Jennrich, Massman, Schulz.
p. cm.
"A Data Becker book."
ISBN 1-55755-044-1 : $19.95
1. Computer graphics. 2. Amiga (Computer)--Programming. 3. BASIC (Computer programming language) I. Massman, Andreas, 1960- . II. Schulz, Peter, 1964- . III. Title.
T385.J46 1989
006.6'765--dc20 89-18559

Table of Contents

1. Introduction 1

2. The Basics of Ray Tracing 5
2.1 Natural Objects 7
2.2 In the Computer 8
2.2.1 Light and Darkness 8
2.2.2 Shadows 9
2.2.3 Reflection 9
2.2.4 Transparency 10
2.2.5 Limitations 10
2.3 Presentation in the Computer 11
2.3.1 Data Structure 16
2.4 Simulating Perception 19
2.4.1 What Do You See? 22
2.4.2 What You Should See 31
2.4.3 The Dark Side of the World 37
2.4.4 Reflection 38
2.4.5 Bringing Color to the Screen 40
2.5 Optimization 44

3. The Tracer Program 49
3.1 Wire Models 51
3.1.1 From 3D to 2D 51
3.1.2 Objects and Surfaces 61
3.2 The Editor 74
3.2.1 Why an Editor? 74
3.2.2 The Tasks Required of the Editor 75
3.2.3 Individual Components of the Editor 78
3.2.3.1 The Input 78
3.2.3.2 The Output 86
3.2.3.3 The Graphics 89
3.2.3.4 Data Operations 92
3.2.3.5 Disk Operations 96
3.2.3.6 Mouse and Gadgets 98
3.2.4 Tips on Writing an Editor 102
3.3 The Main Program 104
3.3.1 The Remaining Tracer Routines 104
3.3.2 Merging Tracer Modules into one Program 141

4. Using the Program 143
4.1 Editor Documentation 145
4.1.1 Input—General Information 145
4.1.2 Entering Object Data 146
4.1.3 The Operations Menu 152
4.1.4 The Material Editor 152
4.1.5 The Transform Menu 153

4.1.6 The Disk Menu 154
4.2 Tracer Documentation 155
4.2.1 After Starting 155
4.2.2 Amiga Menu 156
4.2.3 File Menu 156
4.2.3.1 Loading and Saving Objects 156
4.2.3.2 Loading Materials 157
4.2.3.3 Background 157
4.2.3.4 Saving Graphics 158
4.2.3.5 Printing Graphics 158
4.2.3.6 Setting New Colors 159
4.2.3.7 Leaving the Program 159
4.2.4 The Editor Menu 159
4.2.5 The Parameter Menu 160
4.2.6 The Draw Menu 161
4.2.6.1 Shadows 161
4.2.6.2 The Wire Model 162
4.2.7 Keyboard Program Control 163

5. Program Enhancements 165

6. 3D Tricks and Tips 171

7. Mathematical Basics 177
7.1 Vectors 179
7.2 Using Vectors 182
7.3 Angles Between Two Vectors 184
7.4 Intersecting Lines and Planes 187

8. The Optional Disk 191
8.1 Compiling the Programs 194
8.1.1 Compiling the Editor 194
8.1.2 Compiling the Tracer 196

Appendices 201
A. Modules of the Tracer 203
B. The Tracer Program 207
C. The Editor Program 302
D. The SetPoint Program 345
E. Tracer Error Messages 356

Index 357

1. Introduction

1. Introduction

The Amiga is a truly amazing machine, especially when it's used for graphics. Most Amiga users, when asked why they bought their Amiga, reply, "Great graphics." The picture on the cover of this book was generated using the editor and tracer programs listed at the end of this book. This shows some of the Amiga's graphic capabilities. This book will help you explore programming 3D graphic ray tracing on your Amiga, using the computer language that came with your Amiga —AmigaBASIC.

There is one thing we should mention before starting. Programming three dimensional graphics requires a knowledge of mathematics. Therefore, this book has a mathematical basis. If you don't know much about math, don't panic. We'll do our best to explain the subject to you in understandable terms. When you finish reading this book you'll know more about the subject than you did before you read the book.

You'll need basic math skills to use this book—but you won't need a PhD in math. Many of the equations involved in computing three dimensional figures may not make much sense to you. To help these make sense, we've placed many explanations of the mathematical equations alongside the sample programs and program descriptions.

The programs presented in this book, tracer and editor, are very large. A complete listing of each of the programs can be found in the appendices. Ray tracing requires many math calculations, which can be very slow when done in BASIC. We recommend that the programs presented in this book be compiled for maximum speed. The programs should only be compiled after complete testing has been done in BASIC. Chapter 8 describes the changes required to compile the programs using the AC/BASIC® compiler.

The optional disk available for this book also contains the complete program modules in ASCII format and versions compiled using AC/BASIC®. The disk also contains two example pictures created with the programs. The important individual routines are described through the course of the book, but you should refer to the complete listing when entering the programs.

Before going on to the main part of this book, there are two terms you'll see throughout this book—*ray tracing* and *algorithms*. These may not sound familiar to you if you're studying 3D graphics for the first time, so we'll define the two of them now:

Ray tracing defined

There are a number of methods used in generating three dimensional graphics on computers. Ray tracing traces the effects of light rays which shine on an object or group of objects. Since ray tracing has its basis in actual light and optical calculation, it reproduces the object's surfaces and qualities (e.g., shadows, colors, reflectivity, transparency).

Many programmers consider this the best method of 3D graphic reproduction, because ray tracing produces very lifelike effects. The photograph on the cover of this book is a result of ray tracing, and the entire book discusses the subject of ray tracing in AmigaBASIC.

Algorithms

This is a common buzzword in computing. An algorithm describes a plan for solving a problem, usually using a computer program. This book, for example, lists algorithms for performing such tasks as drawing geometric figures on a computer screen, then adding data to these figures that will implement shadows, color, etc.

2.
The Basics of Ray Tracing

2. The Basics of Ray Tracing

Hidden line algorithms

Computer graphics of any kind look great on the Amiga. But three dimensional computer representations of familiar objects are fantastic. String art graphics are a very simple example of 3D graphics. A computer can go one step further and display only the visible lines of a 3D graphic. Hidden line algorithms display the visible surfaces only. The results achieved using hidden line algorithms are very good. However, hidden line algorithms make it difficult to remove objects or to display objects covered by other objects.

Hidden surface algorithms

Hidden surface algorithms are used when you want more realistic graphics. The object is represented by many small triangles. These triangles can be arranged so the the ones furthest away are shown first and the closest are shown last. This gives a display with invisible surfaces. The best presentation occurs when the triangles are a very small distance apart. Hidden surface algorithms also can display the illusion of shadows (e.g., when a bright light is shone on an object's surface).

Ray tracing algorithms

Ray tracing algorithms are a step beyond hidden surface algorithms. Ray tracing gets its name from tracing the effects of light rays shining on an object. Unlike hidden surface and hidden line algorithms, ray tracing allows the calculation of shadows, reflection and transparency of objects. The result of a graphic generated from ray tracing requires more calculation time than hidden line or hidden surface graphics, but the finished graphic looks much more realistic.

The basics of ray tracing are pretty simple. You won't have to devote your life to the study of mathematics to understand and use them.

2.1 Natural Objects

Before we go on to develop a ray tracing algorithm, we must first take a look at objects and how they appear in the real world. Imagine a green cube lit by the sun. The cube absorbs all light rays in colors other than green, and reflects all the green light rays back to your eyes.

As each light ray enters your eyes, you see a green point of light coming from the direction of the cube. Because the sun (the light source) sends out light rays that reflect off the cube, your eye receives an image (graphic) of how the cube looks.

2.2 In the Computer

To duplicate the green cube as a computer generated 3D object, you must get past some obstacles. First, your computer has only one visual receptor (the screen) to replace your two eyes. In addition, the light source is very low powered—it simulates light as a small group of pixels on the screen. Our own sun sends out an extremely large number of light rays: So many that all the computers on this planet couldn't reproduce this phenomenon in a reasonable amount of time.

Your eye sees the visible light rays coming from the green cube. The visible light rays reflect the cube's color, and send this information to your eyes. You see this information because your eye is sensitive to light rays and can receive the reflected colors.

Visual rays

The computer screen uses visual rays rather than the visible light rays available to us. The computer must calculate each visual ray and determine whether this ray came from the surface of an object, and from which direction the visual ray came. If the ray bounced off an object, the computer must determine the color. The ray then appears on the screen as a pixel, just as a retina reads light rays. Your eyes receive light rays through lenses. The following figure shows the eye's concept of an image, then a computer's ray tracing view of the same image:

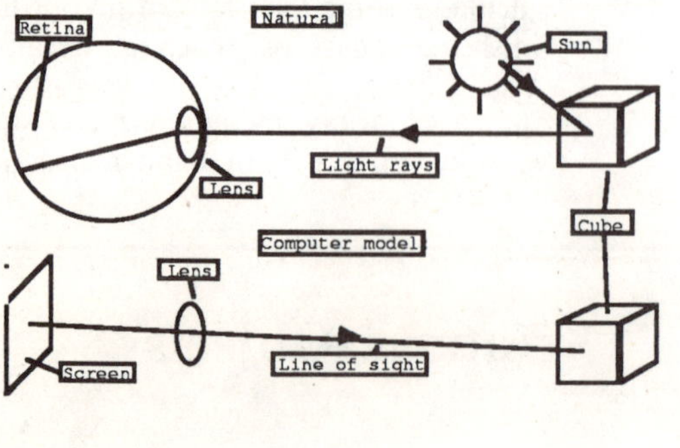

Figure 2.1

2.2.1 Light and darkness

Think of our imaginary green cube in the form of a computer image, based on the data presented so far. Right now all you really have on the screen is the green outline of what could be a cube. One important factor in ray tracing makes an image three dimensional: Shading. If you think of a real cube lit by the sun, the sides most directly exposed to light are brighter than those sides less directly lit. The more perpendicular that you place a light source to a side, the brighter that side appears.

It isn't hard to program the computer to understand the brightness of a side. The same calculations can determine whether the side of an object faces toward or away from the light source.

2.2.2 Shadows

The computer model becomes really interesting if it includes shadows that a real object might cast. Shadows occur when an object blocks the path of light rays. Imagine our sunlit cube again. The cube interrupts the sunlight's path as it travels toward the base on which the cube stands. This interruption appears on the base as a shadow.

Visual rays calculate the computer model instead of actual light rays. Therefore, we need to tackle the problem in a different manner. Imagine that you are wearing a light source placed at the same location and pointing in the same direction as your line of sight. Viewing the cube with just your line of sight as the light source, you see no shadows since they are hidden from your view, behind the object.

Now move the light source *behind* the cube, opposite your line of sight (something like watching an eclipse). You are in the cube's shadow, out of direct view of the light source.

Let's take shadowing one step further. Imagine watching the cube from sunup to sundown. The shadows change in size, direction and intensity as the sun moves in the sky throughout the day.

2.2.3 Reflection

An object reflects some light rays and absorbs others, depending on the color and reflectivity of the object. The reflected rays enter your eye, giving you a mental image of the object's shape, color and texture.

Let's try to picture this using the computer's visual rays. If the visual rays encounter a reflecting surface, they convey the reflection's color, brightness and degree of reflection. Then the visual rays travel onto an object that lies in the direction of the reflection. From that the object's color, brightness and reflection are established.

This process repeats until the visual rays encounter a non-reflecting surface, a dull surface, or no surface at all. Then the visual rays create a single color, brightness and reflectivity and display this data on the screen. The programming examples shown later explain the relationship between individual values and the final value.

2.2.4 Transparency

Transparency means that light or visual rays pass through the surface instead of reflecting. If your visual rays strike a transparent surface, they continue through this surface in the direction they were going before encountering this surface (Figure 2.2). Light rays divide (reflect and pass through) when a surface is transparent and reflective. However, a computer's visual rays cannot pass through a surface and be reflected at the same time, so a recursive algorithm must divide the visual rays.

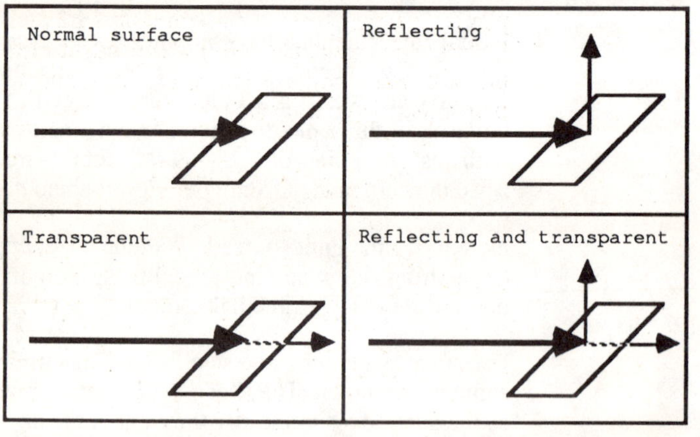

Figure 2.2

2.2.5 Limitations

The algorithms developed here can be modified to simulate colors, shadows and reflections. There are limitations, however. First, since you are working with visual rays instead of true light rays, you cannot simulate the light source actually reflecting in a mirror image. Also, graphics created by the algorithms have none of the effects caused by ambient, indirect or refracted light.

Another limitation: Real light rays comprise all of the colors of the visible spectrum, and not just a single color. An object reflects some of this spectrum and absorbs the rest. Computer simulations require a light source of predetermined color, not the entire spectrum.

2.3 Presentation in the Computer

A computer must have the outside world described to it mathematically before it can generate 3D graphics. Fairly simple three dimensional geometrical formulas let you define lines, planes and circles (see Chapter 7 for brief descriptions of the math used).

Planes

The plane is the basic geometric object, described by the following equation:

```
r + r1 + u*r2 = v*r3
```

r, r1, r2 and r3 are vectors and u and v are scalars (representing one dimension, magnitude without direction). r1 is any point that lies on a plane. The plane passes through points r2 and r3. r2 and r3 must be linearly (one dimensionally) independent of one another. This allows the insertion of all possible values for u and v, supplying all allowable points that lie on the plane:

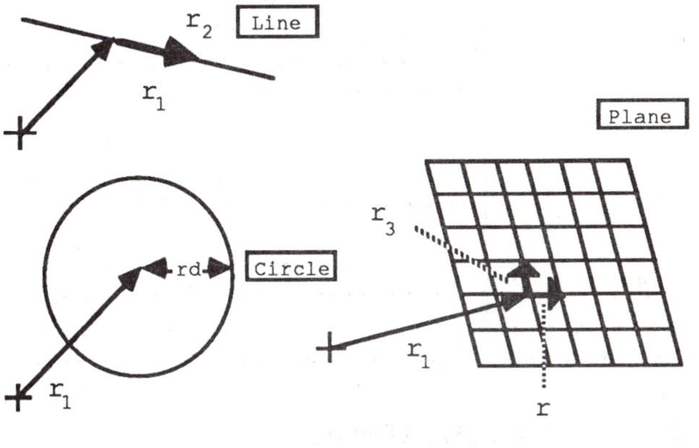

Figure 2.3

The plane has one disadvantage: It is infinite. This is fine for making a background, but you can't define a cube based on planes. Limit the definable area for u and v (e.g., [0,1], making u and v greater than zero and less than 1). This keeps the size within a specific range.

Parallelograms

If you allow all values of the limited u and v, the points create a parallelogram (Figure 2.4). A rectangle results if r2 and r3 are perpendicular to each other. Making r2 to r3 perpendicular and equal in length creates a square. And joining six squares of equal size together creates a cube:

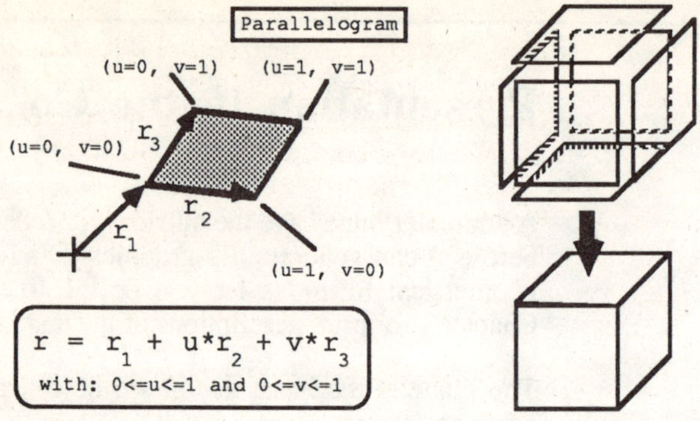

Figure 2.4

Our algorithm divides any body into triangles, so we need triangles in the basic figures. This requires a coordinate system and the equation:

```
y = -x + 1
```

The surface resulting from intersecting the base line and both axes looks very similar to a triangle. If you rearrange the formula, you get `x + y =1`. But where do `x` and `y` come from?

The coordinate system's axes look like vectors at the end (see Chapter 7 for a description of vectors). Let the `x` axis be vector `r2` and the the `y` axis be vector `r3`. Now replace `x` in the formula with `u`, and `y` with `v`. Because you want a triangular surface and not only an outline, replace the equal sign with a "<=". The result:

```
u + v <= 1
```

When `u` and `v` are both positive values, an infinite surface occurs. You make these a limitation for your plane. Insert all allowed values for `u` and `v` in the plane equation and all of the points lie inside of the triangle, which has `r2` and `r3` as two of the sides.

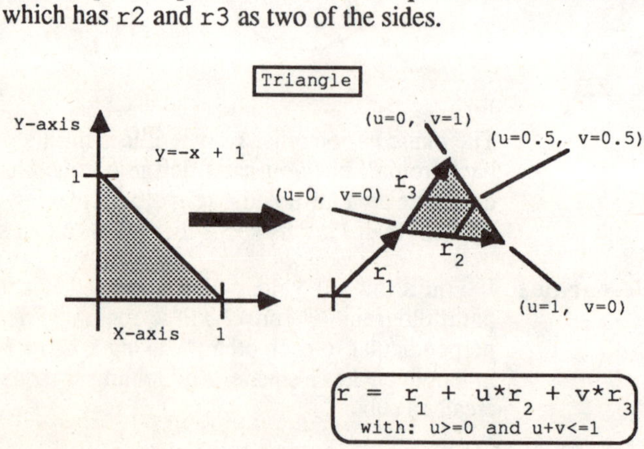

Figure 2.5

You can now display any number of rectangular objects using triangles and parallelograms. If you create an object from many smaller triangles, you have all the basic objects that you might ever need. Some disadvantages: Complicated objects require an enormous number of triangles, which take up a great deal of memory. Computer memory can expand only so far, so we must make some compromises about defining basic objects.

Circles

To describe the definition of a circle, we need to talk a bit more about how a circle appears in a plane. Remember the general circle formula:

```
x2 + y2 = rd2
```

`rd` equals the radius. The formula is simpler for the unit circle: `x2 + y2 = 1`. This is because the unit circle has a radius of 1. The same thing is true of our triangle: `r2` is the unit vector of the `x` axis, `r3` is the unit vector of the `y` axis, `u` is `x` and `v` is `y` (never substitute `x` for `u` instead). The formula now becomes:

```
u2 + v2 <= 1
```

This time you cannot assume that `u` and `v` are positive, even though the parallelogram equation required it. Insert all allowable values for `u` and `v`, and you get a circular object:

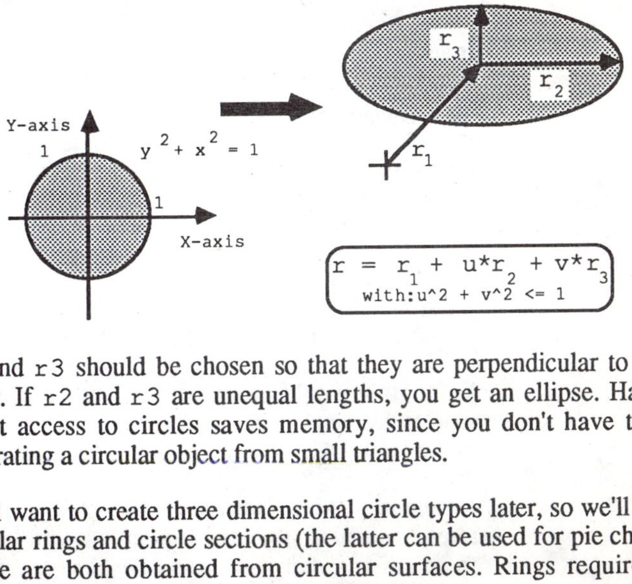

Figure 2.6

`r2` and `r3` should be chosen so that they are perpendicular to each other. If `r2` and `r3` are unequal lengths, you get an ellipse. Having direct access to circles saves memory, since you don't have to try generating a circular object from small triangles.

We'll want to create three dimensional circle types later, so we'll need circular rings and circle sections (the latter can be used for pie charts). These are both obtained from circular surfaces. Rings require the lengths of the vectors (u,v) from the circle ring:

```
l = u2 + v2
```

This means that `l` must lie in correct intervals between two values. This interval value controls the thickness of the circle ring.

You must do a bit more for the circle section. For the length `l` you must also compute the angle `w` that lies between (u,v) and the `r2` axis.

This requires figuring out the polar coordinates. Polar coordinates correspond in the 3D computer model to rotation in the real world. Compute the polar coordinates from (u,v). You must limit `w`, just as you had to limit `l` for the circle ring.

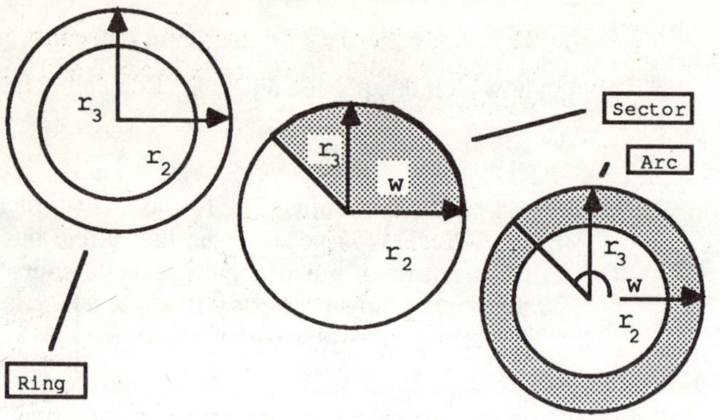

Figure 2.7

To conclude, you also limit `w` and `l`. The resulting figure is a circular arc.

Spheres

Now we have enough of the basic math to create a sphere. You need to know whether or not all possible objects can be broken down into triangles. The answer is yes. To create a plain circle out of triangles so small that the triangles can no longer be seen as triangles, you need about 50 to 100 triangles. You'd need approximately 5000 to 20000 triangles to create a sphere. A true sphere always has a completely round surface, and no corners and edges are visible. The general equation for spheres is as follows:

```
(r - r1)2 = rd2
```

`r1` is the midpoint of the sphere and `rd` is the radius. We will leave this discussion at the sphere and not try to master any new objects.

Wait. How would you define cylinders, cones and ellipsoids? These objects are more difficult to create than the basic objects, but they are created *using* the basic objects described above.

Until now you have formed additional objects by placing restrictions on already existing objects. This is impossible with the sphere because there are no other parameters besides the midpoint and radius. Now we'll define a three dimensional space for two dimensional objects:

```
r = r1 + u*r2 + v*r3 + w*r4
```

`r`, `r1`, `r2`, `r3`, and `r4` are vectors and `u`,`v` and `w` are scalars. In addition, `r2`, `r3` and `r4` should be perpendicular to each other. `r2`, `r3` and `r4` may not be co-planar, otherwise they would only form one plane. Keep `u`, `v` and `w` unrestricted so that every point in your computer universe is a point in your room.

Now let's try to create a cylinder. Place the ground surface of the body on the plane that runs through `r2` and `r3`. Because the ground surface of a cylinder is a circle, you can give it the limitation:

```
u2 + v2 = 1
```

This time there is no inequality because you don't want a filled cylinder. Limit w to values between 0 and 1 to keep your cylinder at a definite length:

```
u2 + v2 = 1 and 0<=w<=1
```

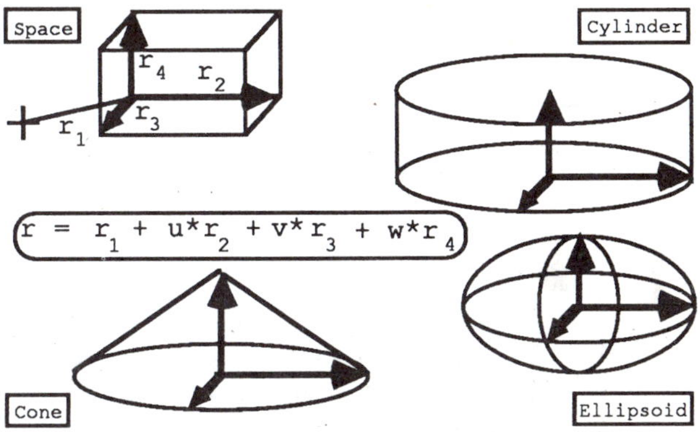

Figure 2.8

The cylinder is complete. You can give it a further limitation as you did to the circular surfaces: Assign an angle interval so that you get a cylinder section. Because the procedure is identical to the circular surface, specify additional limitations and it becomes a cone.

The bottom surface of the cone is a circle, so you already know some of the restrictions. How do you show that the sides of a cone run together to a point? A cone split vertically down the middle reminds us of a triangle. The limitation for a triangle is `x+y=1`. y equals w in this case and is also the parameter of the vector that rises to the point of the cone. x is the vector that points to a point at the base of the cone:

```
x+SQR(u2 + v2)
```

While you didn't need the square sign up until now (because the radius was one and `SQR(1)=1`), you must take it use it here to get a result similar to a cone. So you get:

```
SQR(u2 + v2) + w = 1
```

Here you can create a cone section as you did for the circle and cylinder by establishing an angle interval or a truncated cone as you restrict w.

Ellipsoid

The last basic object is the ellipsoid. You may wonder why you need an ellipsoid if you already have a sphere. Unlike the sphere, the ellipsoid can have any ellipse form, not just circular. The base surface is a circle, but so is the vertical cross-section. The limitations are similar to those for the cone, but this time a different equation is needed:

```
u2 + v2 + w2 = 1.
```

Make `r2`, `r3` and `r4` the same size to get a sphere. Now the second advantage of an ellipsoid: You can add limitations to create an ellipsoid section. This can look like an apple or melon slice. It is possible to limit the parameters to an interval; you can think about the results of this on your own. Cone and ellipsoid sections do not appear in the routines developed later in this chapter—you'll have to work these out on your own.

2.3.1 Data Structure

We must establish a data structure for the parameters of the objects to be displayed by our program. Because we defined the algorithm in BASIC, we used a multidimensional array named `K()` (see the Appendices for the complete program listings). We need four vectors for each element of `K`. These vectors contain information about the object type, the material constants and the restrictions. We came up with `K(MaxNumber,5,2)`. `MaxNumber` is the maximum number of objects that can be placed in the computer's environment. The elements of `K` are assigned the following parameters:

`K(n,0,0)`: `n` = Type of object. This element checks if the `n` object is handled as a plane, a sphere or other object. The following values correspond to the following basic objects:

0: Plane, infinite
1: Triangle
2: Parallelogram
3: Circle surface
4: Circle section
5: Circle arc

10: Sphere

20: Cylinder
21: Cylinder section
22: Cone
24: Ellipsoid

As you can see, not all of the above restrictions are built into the data structure. While `K(n,0,1)` is reserved for future use, `K(n,0,2)` contains the index of the materials used to create the object. Instead of placing all material constants into array K, the elements are placed in their own array called Mat. The array K(n,0,2) specifies the number of elements in Mat, which contains the material constant for the nth object. This means you can now assign the same material constant to multiple objects.

Note: Some later references to the K() array include periods in parentheses. These periods represent allowed values. For example, K(n,1,.) also refers to K(n,1,0), K(n,1,1), K(n,1,2), etc.

K(n,1,.) always contains the vector r1. K(n,1,0) is the x component, K(n,1,1) is the y component, and K(n,1,2) is the z component of the vector, which also works in conjunction with other vectors. K(n,2,.) through K(n,4,.) contain the vectors needed for their respective objects (vectors r2 through r4). For example, K(n,2,0) contains the radius of the sphere.

The restrictions overlap with vector r4, but that restriction does not apply to cylinders, cones and ellipsoids. K(n,4,0) is the lower limit and K(n,4,1) is the upper limit of the circle arc in the equation SQR(u2 + v2). The values must be between zero and one. K(n,5,1) contains the start angle for circle sections, circle arcs and cylinder sections. K(n,5,1) specifies the end angle in degrees. When they are placed all together they look like this:

```
K(n,0,0)  = type
K(n,0,1)  = reserved
K(n,0,2)  = index for material constants

K(n,1,.)  = r1

K(n,2,0)  = radius for sphere or
K(n,2,.)  = r2

K(n,3,.)  = r3

K(n,4,.)  = r4 or if circle arc
K(n,4,0)  = lower limit (inner radius)
K(n,4,1)  = upper limit (outer radius)
```

For circle section, circle arc or cylinder segment:

```
K(n,5,0)  = start angle
K(n,5,1)  = end angle
```

The data structure for the material constants is very easy. The field is dimensioned with Mat(Numbermat,6). The color of the material is established first: Mat(n,0) contains the red section, Mat(n,1) the green section and Mat(n,2) the blue section. No ambient light exists in our computer world, and this would make all shadows almost solid black. To alleviate this, we define a shade brightness for every material which defines the brightness of the material in the shadows. Assign this material a small value—a larger value makes it difficult to differentiate between shadows and where light actually falls.

`Mat(n,4)` contains the reflection factor. When this equals zero, the surface of the material is dull. When `Mat(n,4)` equals one, the surface appears as a highly polished mirror. `Mat(n,5)` contains the transparency factor, but our program doesn't use it, and `Mat(n,6)` is reserved for additions to the program. The data structure for `Mat` is as follows:

```
' Initial material brightness¶
' mat(n,0) = Red material brightness¶
' mat(n,1) = Green material brightness¶
' mat(n,2) = Blue material brightness¶
' mat(n,3) = Factor for unlit/shadow¶
' mat(n,4) = Factor for mirroring¶
' mat(n,5) = Factor for transparency (not implemented)¶
' mat(n,6) = reserved¶
```

All values must be between zero and one.

Here's an example. When you want to know the reflection factor of object number 47, get the material index:

```
PRINT K(47,0,2)
```

Imagine that you get the value 12. Now you can specify the reflection factor with:

```
PRINT Mat(12,4)
```

The abbreviated entry for this data is as follows:

```
PRINT Mat(K(47,0,2),4)
```

This syntax is the form used by the routines presented in the program.

2.4 Simulating Perception

The data structure assembles an artificial reality in our computer, and now we must bring it to the screen. First we must determine the point of view from which we want to see the graphic.

In your simulation model you sent out visual rays from every point on the screen in the direction of the lens. We will proceed with this method in our algorithm. We send visual rays from the projection point P in the direction of the screen, and assign one visual ray to each screen pixel. We must now determine the position of the screen. The main point H performs this task. H lies in the exact center of the screen. The vector P-H is the normal vector on your screen; it lies perpendicular from the projection point to the middle of the screen. The distance between P and H is called DPH.

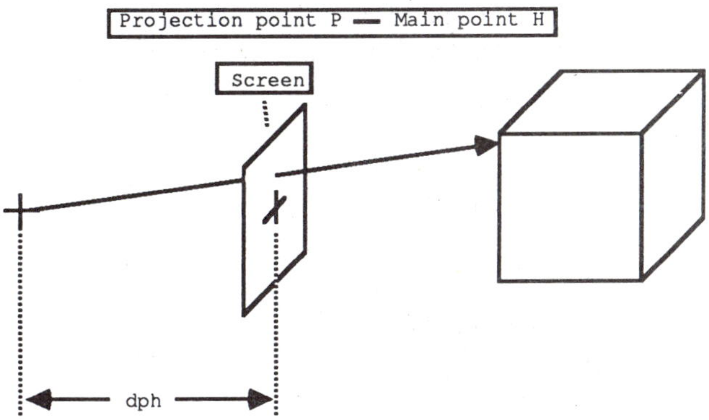

Figure 2.9

Because you must compute the picture using points (pixels), the algorithm is simple: Provide the three dimensional coordinate for every pixel you have to compute. Then send a visual ray from the projection point in the direction of this pixel and determine whether you see something. Our routine determines what we see and don't see, especially the color of the point. Once the program decides, the point is displayed on the screen. The entire procedure is in the following subroutine taken from the tracer program listed in the appendices.

Note: The example programs that follow contain some BASIC lines that must be entered on one line in AmigaBASIC even though they appear on two lines in this book. Fitting some formatted program listings in this book has caused some long BASIC lines to be split into two lines. End of paragraph characters (¶) in these program texts show the actual end of a line of BASIC code. These characters indicate when the <Return> key should be pressed in the BASIC editor.

```
Shadows:¶
'  Initialization¶
  Status$ = " Status: Shadows"+CHR$(0)¶
  CALL SetWindowTitles&(NWBase&,SADD(Status$),0)¶
¶
  GOSUB DeleteMenu¶
  ¶
  Status$ = " Status: Init"+CHR$(0)¶
  CALL SetWindowTitles&(NWBase&,SADD(Status$),0)¶
  GOSUB InitShadows¶
¶
  Status$ = " Status: InitMinMax"+CHR$(0)¶
  CALL SetWindowTitles&(NWBase&,SADD(Status$),0)¶
  GOSUB InitMinMax¶
¶
  Status$ = " Status: InitMinMaxLq"+CHR$(0)¶
  CALL SetWindowTitles&(NWBase&,SADD(Status$),0)¶
  GOSUB InitMinmaxLq¶
¶
  CALL Scron¶
¶
  Status$ = " Status: Shadows"+CHR$(0)¶
  CALL SetWindowTitles&(NWBase&,SADD(Status$),0)¶
¶
  XAOff = (BoxW% AND 1)*.5¶
  YAOff = (BoxH% AND 1)*.5¶
¶
    ' Offsets to guarantee correct point size¶
  IF XAOff = .5 THEN¶
    XBOff = .5¶
  ELSE¶
    XBOff = 1¶
  END IF¶
  IF YAOff = .5 THEN¶
    YBOff = .5¶
  ELSE¶
    YBOff = 1¶
  END IF¶
  ¶
  Body%=0¶
¶
  FOR yb%=YStart%+BoxH%/2 TO Yend%+BoxH%/2 STEP BoxH%¶
    FOR xb%=XStart%+BoxW%/2 TO XEnd%+BoxW%/2 STEP BoxW%¶
      CALL ReProjection(Rx,Ry,Rz,0!,FN Xresc(xb%),FN
Yresc(yb%))¶
¶
      Rx = Rx-Px¶
      Ry = Ry-Py¶
      Rz = Rz-Pz¶
¶
      StackPtr% =-1¶
¶
      Px1 = Px¶
      Py1 = Py¶
      Pz1 = Pz¶
      ¶
      Original! = True¶
      GOSUB Computepoint¶
```

```
    ¶
      Px = Px1¶
      Py = Py1¶
      Pz = Pz1¶
      ¶
      IF Stack(0,0)>=0 THEN  'If no Intersect point => -1¶
        Bright.r=Stack(0,0)*Qh.r¶
        Bright.g=Stack(0,1)*Qh.g¶
        Bright.b=Stack(0,2)*Qh.b¶
        CALL OSSetPoint&(CLNG(xb%-BoxW%/2+XAOff),
                         CLNG(yb%-BoxH%/2+YAOff),
                         CLNG(xb%+BoxW%/2-XBOff),
                         CLNG(yb%+BoxH%/2-YBOff),
                         CLNG(1024*Bright.r),
                         CLNG(1024*Bright.g),
                         CLNG(1024*Bright.b))¶
      END IF¶
    NEXT xb%¶
¶
    IF INKEY$ <> "" THEN¶
      IF yb% < Yend%+BoxH%/2 THEN¶
      ¶
        CALL Scroff¶
        a$="Next line:"+STR$(yb%+BoxH%)¶
        CALL PrintIt(a$,130,False)¶
        CALL DialogBox("Continue",0,True,x1a%,y1a%,x2a%,
y2a%,False)¶
        CALL DialogBox("Stop",2,False,x1b%,y1b%,x2b%,
y2b%,False)¶
¶
        CALL DoDialog(n%,0,x1a%,y1a%,x2a%,y2a%,-1,-1,-1,-
1,x1b%,y1b%,x2b%,y2b%)¶
¶
        CLS¶
        IF n% = 0 THEN¶
      ¶
          CALL Scron¶
         ELSE¶
          GOTO ShadowEnde¶
        END IF¶
      END IF  ¶
    END IF¶
  NEXT yb%¶
¶
  ShadowEnde:¶
 ¶
  CALL Scroff¶
  CLS¶
  GOSUB MakeMenu  ¶
RETURN¶
```

The above routine starts by initializing an open window, shadowing and the area to be shadowed. The important section begins with the two `FOR-TO` loops which check all of the screen points. `BoxW%` and `BoxH%` specify the width and height of the screen points in pixels (usually a value of 1). The loop calculates the three dimensional coordinates from the two dimensional screen coordinates.

`Reprojection` works like a return function to `Projection`, which projects three dimensional coordinates on the screen. The functions `Xresc` and `Yresc` help configure later enlargements of the screen area. Next, the vector runnig from `P` in the direction of the screen points is computed (`Rx,Ry,Rz`). Then `P` is saved and the `ComputePoint` function is called, which computes the color of the screen points. The result of the computation is stored in the zero element of `Stack()`. The red element of the color passes `Stack(0,0)`, the green element to `Stack(0,1)`, and the blue element to `Stack(0,2)`. The stack is there mainly for reflections.

When `Stack(0,0)` is negative, this screen point contains nothing, and we leave the background as it was. Otherwise the program considers the color of the light source (`Qh.r` = red element, `Qh.g` = green element, `Qh.b` = blue element) and displays the point with the `OSSetPoint&` routine. This presents a problem. This routine displays a rectangle on the screen and tries to arrive at a color as close as possible to the desired color.

After a line is computed, the routine checks to see if the user has pressed the spacebar. If so, the program asks if the user wants to stop the calculation. The `Scron/Scroff` calls only bring the graphic screen to the foreground or place it in the background (the `DialogBox` function is listed later in this book).

2.4.1 What Do You See?

Let's take a closer look at what happens on the screen.

We defined the basic objects using mathematical equations to make it easy to calculate points of intersection with a line. The line described here is the visual ray. This visual ray begins at projection point `P` and runs through the actual screen point. A line equation can also be written in point—direction form:

```
r = r1 + l*r2
```

`r`, `r1`, and `r2` are vectors and `l` is a scalar (see Figure 2.3). The point `r1` that runs through the line, is the equivalent of your projection point. `r2` specifies the direction of the line which is equivalent to your vector `R` (`Rx,Ry,Rz`) calculated above. To provide an intersection with the plane, you set the line and plane equations equal to each other so that you can figure out parameters `l`, `u` and `v`. You can obtain the intersection point by inserting `l` in the equation and calculating this. The following `SUB` program contains the intersection point calculation:

```
SUB IntersectpointPlane(n%,Px,Py,Pz,Rx,Ry,Rz,l) STATIC¶
SHARED Help(),K()                              ¶
  ' => l = exact parameter¶
  D=Ry*Help(n%,4)-Rx*Help(n%,3)-Rz*Help(n%,5)¶
```

```
  IF D<>0 THEN¶
    l=((Px-K(n%,1,0))*Help(n%,3)-(Py-K(n%,1,1))*Help(n%,4)+(Pz-
K(n%,1,2))*Help(n%,5))/D¶
  ELSE¶
    l=-1¶
  END IF¶
END SUB¶
```

You assign the end point of the line (Px,Py,Pz) and the direction vector (Rx,Ry,Rz). In addition, n% establishes which plane should be used to calculate the intersection point. The line parameter l is returned from the subroutine. When no intersection point exists, l = -1 is returned. l can be negative. This places the intersection point behind you (i.e., you can't see the intersection point). You should only be interested for now in the things that you can see.

You can read how to solve the equation system in the mathematical basics chapter (Chapter 7). You must first calculate the denominator determinant. This looks like the following:

$$\text{Line}: r = r_P + l*r_R, \quad \text{Plane}: r = r_1 + u*r_2 + v*r_3$$

$$\text{Intersect point}: l*r_R - u*r_2 - v*r_3 = (r_1 - r_P)$$

$$D = \begin{vmatrix} Rx & (K(n,2,0) & K(n,3,0) \\ Ry & (K(n,2,1) & K(n,3,1) \\ Rz & (K(n,2,2) & K(n,3,2) \end{vmatrix} \quad \text{Naming determinant}$$

$$D_L = \begin{vmatrix} K(n,1,0)-Px & K(n,2,0) & K(n,3,0) \\ K(n,1,1)-Py & K(n,2,1) & K(n,3,1) \\ K(n,1,2)-Pz & K(n,2,2) & K(n,3,2) \end{vmatrix} \qquad l = \frac{D_l}{D}$$

$$D_U = \begin{vmatrix} Rx & K(n,1,0)-Px & K(n,3,0) \\ Ry & K(n,1,1)-Py & K(n,3,1) \\ Rz & K(n,1,2)-Pz & K(n,3,2) \end{vmatrix} \qquad u = \frac{D_u}{D}$$

$$D_V = \begin{vmatrix} Rx & K(n,2,0)-Px & K(n,1,0)-Px \\ Ry & K(n,2,1)-Py & K(n,1,1)-Py \\ Rz & K(n,2,2)-Pz & K(n,1,2)-Pz \end{vmatrix} \qquad v = \frac{D_v}{D}$$

Figure 2.10

Only one line is unknown in this determinant—the direction of the line. You must solve the determinant for this line. The 2x2 sub-determinant contains all of the values that do not change. Here you calculate these values and store them in the array Help(). It looks like this:

```
Help(n%,3) = K(n%,2,1)*K(n%,3,2)-K(n%,3,1)*K(n%,2,2)
Help(n%,4) = K(n%,2,0)*K(n%,3,2)-K(n%,3,0)*K(n%,2,2)
Help(n%,5) = K(n%,2,0)*K(n%,3,1)-K(n%,3,0)*K(n%,2,1)
```

No intersection point exists if the denominator is zero. This means that the plane and the line are parallel. Instead, l is directly calculated and returned to the called program.

Before you calculate the intersection point for other basic objects, a few words about general procedure: For every object in your computer world, test for the intersection point with the visual ray. This way we find how many objects are next to it; we also search for an object with a minimal `l`. When we find this, we also get the number of objects that can be seen in the current screen.

Now on to the intersection points of other basic objects. The preceding subprogram is identical to that of the triangle except that the additional parameters `u` and `v` must be computed and then tested to see if the restrictions for the triangle are enough:

```
SUB IntersectpointTriangle(n%,Px,Py,Pz,Rx,Ry,Rz,l,a,b) STATIC¶
SHARED Help(),K()¶
  ' => l = exact parameter, a,b = area parameter¶
  D=Ry*Help(n%,4)-Rx*Help(n%,3)-Rz*Help(n%,5)¶
  IF D<>0 THEN¶
    l=((Px-K(n%,1,0))*Help(n%,3)-(Py-K(n%,1,1))*Help(n%,4)+(Pz-
K(n%,1,2))*Help(n%,5))/D¶
    IF l>0 THEN¶
      a=FN Det(Px-K(n%,1,0),K(n%,3,0),-Rx,Py-
K(n%,1,1),K(n%,3,1),-Ry,Pz-K(n%,1,2),K(n%,3,2),-Rz)/D¶
      b=FN Det(K(n%,2,0),Px-K(n%,1,0),-Rx,K(n%,2,1),Py-
K(n%,1,1),-Ry,K(n%,2,2),Pz-K(n%,1,2),-Rz)/D¶
      IF a<0 OR b<0 OR a>1 OR b>1 OR a+b>1 THEN¶
        l=-1¶
      END IF¶
    END IF¶
  ELSE¶
    l=-1¶
  END IF¶
END SUB¶
```

The `Det` function calculates only the value of a determinant. The intersection point calculation for the parallelogram, circle, circle section, and circle arc are similar—the only difference being the restrictions. The name of the `SUB` program appears in parentheses (see the complete listing in the appendices):

```
Parallelogram (IntersectpointRectangle):
IF a<0 OR b<0 OR a>1 OR b>1 THEN
  l = -1
END IF

CircleSurface (IntersectpointCircle:
IF a*a+b*b>1 THEN
  l = -1
END IF

CircleSection (IntersectpointCircleSector):
IF a*a+b*b< = 1 THEN
  CALL AngelInterval(l,n%,a,b)
ELSE
  l = -1
END IF

Circlearc (IntersectpointCircleRing):
d = SQR(a*a+b*b)
IF (d> = K(n%,4,0)) AND (d< = K(n%,4,1)) THEN
  CALL AngleInterval(l,n%,a,b)
ELSE
  l = -1
```

```
END IF
```

`AngleInterval` tests to see if the intersection point lies inside of the defined angle interval:

```
SUB AngleIntervall(l,n%,a,b) STATIC¶
SHARED Pi,Pm2,Pd2,K()¶
  IF a=0 THEN¶
    D=Pd2*SGN(b)¶
  ELSE¶
    D=ATN(b/a)¶
    IF a<0 THEN¶
      D = D+Pi¶
    END IF¶
  END IF¶
  IF D<0 THEN¶
    D = D+Pm2¶
  END IF¶
```

And now check if this lies in the defined interval:

```
  IF D<K(n%,5,0) OR D>K(n%,5,1) THEN¶
    l=-1¶
  END IF¶
END SUB¶
```

`Pi` is the circle value 3.141592, `Pm2` = `2*Pi` and `Pd2` = `Pi/2`. Here we see in detail how you can calculate the angle.

For the sphere, insert the line equation in the sphere equation and calculate this. We get a quadratic equation system that can be solved using the standard procedure. A problem: We can only compute a maximum of two intersection points. We must compute the parameter `l` for both. Then we choose where the next one lies.

```
SUB IntersectpointSphere(n%,Px,Py,Pz,Rx,Ry,Rz,l) STATIC¶
SHARED Help(),K(),Threshold¶
  ' => l = exact parameter¶
  D=Rx*Rx+Ry*Ry+Rz*Rz¶
  p=(Rx*(Px-K(n%,1,0))+Ry*(Py-K(n%,1,1))+Rz*(Pz-K(n%,1,2)))/D¶
  q=((Px-K(n%,1,0))^2+(Py-K(n%,1,1))^2+(Pz-K(n%,1,2))^2-
K(n%,2,0)*K(n%,2,0))/D¶
  D=p*p-q¶
  IF D>=0 THEN¶
    l=-p+SQR(D)¶
    L1=-p-SQR(D)¶
    IF (L1<l) AND (L1>Threshold) THEN¶
      SWAP l,L1¶
    END IF¶
  ELSE¶
    l=-1¶
  END IF¶
END SUB¶
```

This time we test to see if `L1` is greater than `Threshold` (set at 0.0001), instead of whether it is greater than zero. This `Threshold` is used for shades and reflection. Because they work with the same routine, the test must already exist.

Until now the routine to calculate the intersection point was straightforward, to a certain extent. Now we come to the cylinder and its uses.

There are three unknowns in the cylinder equation and one in the line equation, so setting them equal will not solve anything. To solve this we would have to solve a 4x4 determinant. Let's try something else.

A coordinate system is set up by the three direction vectors. When we convert the coordinates from P and R into this coordinate system (basis transformation), we can calculate the intersection point of the line with the cylinder. The cylinder equation is reduced to:

```
u^2 + v^2 = 1 and 0< = w< = 1
```

(u,v,w) should be the intersection point with the line. The line equation, split into three coordinate equations, reads:

```
u = Pxt + l*xt
v = Pyt + l*yt
w = Pzt + l*zt
```

(Pxt,Pyt,Pzt) is the transformed projection point and (xt,yt, zt) is the transformed direction vector. When we insert these in the cylinder equation, we get:

```
(Pxt + l*xt)^2 + (Pyt + l*yt)^2 =1
0 < = (pzt + l*zt) < = 1
```

Now there is only one unknown and this can be calculated after some rearranging:

```
l^2*(xt^2+yt^2) + l*(2*Pxt*xt+2*Pyt*yt) + (Pxt^2+Pyt^2-1) = 0
```

The further calculating of this equation is taken care of by the following SUB program:

```
SUB IntersectpointCylinder(n%,Px,Py,Pz,Rx,Ry,Rz,l,a,b,c,O
riginal!) STATIC¶
SHARED Threshold¶
  ' => l=exact parameter, a,b,c = transform Intersect point
coordinates¶
  CALL
Basistrans(n%,Pxt,Pyt,Pzt,Xt,Yt,Zt,Px,Py,Pz,Rx,Ry,Rz,Original!)¶
  D=Xt*Xt+Yt*Yt¶
  IF D<>0 THEN¶
    p=(Pxt*Xt+Pyt*Yt)/D¶
    q=(Pxt*Pxt+Pyt*Pyt-1)/D¶
    D=p*p-q¶
    IF D>=0 THEN¶
      l=-p+SQR(D)¶
      L1=-p-SQR(D)¶
      c=Pzt+l*Zt¶
      D=Pzt+L1*Zt¶
      'two solutions : l,c and L1,d. Which is right?
      IF L1<l AND L1>Threshold AND D>=0 AND D<=1 THEN¶
        SWAP l,L1¶
```

```
        SWAP c,D¶
      END IF¶

      'l and c contain the correct solution parameter:
      IF c<0 OR c>1 THEN¶
        l=-1¶
      ELSE¶
        a=Pxt+l*Xt¶
        b=Pyt+l*Yt¶
      END IF¶
    ELSE¶
      l=-1¶
    END IF¶
  ELSE¶
    l=-1¶
  END IF¶
END SUB¶
```

Here, like the sphere, two solutions are possible, and they both must be calculated. From these the intersection point is chosen. c and d satisfy both solutions for w and must be between zero and one. When an intersection point exists, a and b (the solutions for u and v) are computed.

This time an additional parameter comes in the parameter assignment: `Original!` This is needed for `BasisTrans`. `BasisTrans` converts the vectors P and R in the coordinate system of the cylinder:

```
SUB Basistrans(n%,Pxt,Pyt,Pzt,Xt,Yt,Zt,Px,Py,Pz,Rx,Ry,Rz,
Original!) STATIC¶
SHARED Help(),K()¶
  ' Transform (px,py,zy) => (pxt,pyt,pzt), (rx,ry,rz) =>
(xt,yt,zt)¶
¶
  IF Original! = True THEN¶
    Pxt=Help(n%,10)¶
    Pyt=Help(n%,11)¶
    Pzt=Help(n%,12)¶
  ELSE¶
    Pxt=(Px-K(n%,1,0))*Help(n%,13)-(Py-
K(n%,1,1))*Help(n%,14)+(Pz-K(n%,1,2))*Help(n%,15)¶
    Pyt=(Px-K(n%,1,0))*Help(n%,16)-(Py-
K(n%,1,1))*Help(n%,17)+(Pz-K(n%,1,2))*Help(n%,18)¶
    Pzt=(Px-K(n%,1,0))*Help(n%,19)-(Py-
K(n%,1,1))*Help(n%,20)+(Pz-K(n%,1,2))*Help(n%,21)¶
  END IF¶
  Xt=(Px+Rx-K(n%,1,0))*Help(n%,13)-(Py+Ry-
K(n%,1,1))*Help(n%,14)+(Pz+Rz-K(n%,1,2))*Help(n%,15)-Pxt¶
  Yt=(Px+Rx-K(n%,1,0))*Help(n%,16)-(Py+Ry-
K(n%,1,1))*Help(n%,17)+(Pz+Rz-K(n%,1,2))*Help(n%,18)-Pyt¶
  Zt=(Px+Rx-K(n%,1,0))*Help(n%,19)-(Py+Ry-
K(n%,1,1))*Help(n%,20)+(Pz+Rz-K(n%,1,2))*Help(n%,21)-Pzt¶
END SUB¶
```

The beauty is that the transformed coordinates of the projection point do not change during the entire calculation. We can calculate these beforehand and save them in our `Help` array. Because the intersection point routine is also used for reflection and shade calculation another point is inserted instead of the projection point (Px,Py,Pz). This is why we must write an IF-THEN-ELSE construct. When Original! is true, (Px,Py,Pz) contains the coordinates of the original projection point.

The basis transformation is the solution of an equation system with three unknowns. The transformed point is simply inserted in the body equation, which looks like the following for P:

```
P = r1 + u*r2 + v*r3 + w*r4
```

or solved in the coordinate equations:

```
Px = r1x + u*r2x + v*r3x + w*r4x
Py = r1y + u*r2y + v*r3y + w*r4y
Pz = r1z + u*r2z + v*r3z + w*r4z
```

The equations must now be solved and the parameters u, v and w must be computed. Since the denominator determinant is one, this time we don't have to do extra calculating. When computing the determinant we can use the fact that only one column is unknown while the two others are constant. We can calculate these beforehand and store them in Help.

With this, the intersection point of a line with a cylinder can be calculated. We must create a check of the angle interval of parameters a and b for a cylinder section:

```
(IntersectpointCylinderSegm)
l= -p+SQR(D)
L1 = -p-SQR(D)
c = Pzt+l*Zt
C1 = Pzt+L1*Zt

'Test for solution c,l angle interval

IF c> = 0 AND c< = 1 THEN
  CALL AngleInterval(l,n%,Pxt+l*Xt,Pyt+l*Yt)
ELSE
  l = -1
END IF

'Now for the second solution

IF C1> = 0 and C1<= 1 THEN
  CALL AngleInterval(l1,n%,Pxt+L1*Xt,Pyt+l1*yt)
ELSE
  L1 = -1
END IF

'If the second solution is better: Exchange

IF (l<-.5) OR (L1<l AND L1>Threshold) THEN
  SWAP l,l1
  SWAP c,C1
END IF

'Correct solution in c,l
```

```
a = Pxt+l*Xt
b = Pyt+l*Yt
```

The subprograms for cones and ellipsoids don't have any special differences from the one for the cylinder. The procedure is identical. The equations look a little different because the restrictions have a different form:

```
Cone (IntersectpointCone):
d = Xt*Xt+Yt*Yt-Zt*Zt
IF d<>0 THEN
  p = (Pxt*Xt+Pyt*Yt+Zt*(1-Pzt))/d
  q = (Pxt*Pxt+Pyt*Pyt-(1-Pzt)^2)/d
  d = p*p-q

  ...

END IF

Ellipsoid (IntersectpointEllipsoid):
d = Xt*Xt+Yt*Yt+Zt*Zt
IF d<>0 THEN
  p = (Pxt*Xt+Pyt*Yt+Pzt*Zt)/d
  q = (Pxt*Pxt+Pyt*Pyt+Pzt*Pzt-1)/d
  d = p*p-q

  ...

END IF
```

These two program sections are found in the SUB programs following the BasisTrans call in the complete tracer program (see the appendices for the listing).

We can now determine which objects we see in the picture at point bx,by. This is done by converting (bx,by) to three dimensional coordinates and testing for the line that goes through P at point R. Then we calculate all of the intersection points of this line and all bodies and find which is next to us. The equivalent SUB program is called WhichBody, because it establishes which body the line intersects:

```
SUB WhichBody (Kp%,Px,Py,Pz,Rx,Ry,Rz,Original!,Shadown!) STATIC¶
SHARED True,False,minmax%(),NumberK,minmaxlq(),
Help(),K(),xb%,yb%,Sx,Sy,Sz,Body%,Ac,Bc,Cc,la,Threshold¶
  ' => Body% = Nr the body under coordinates xb%,yb%,
S(sx,sy,sz)=Intersect point, la=intersection line¶
  ' => if Typ>=20: (ac,bc,cc) = transform Intersect point
coordinates¶
  la=-1¶
  Body%=0¶
¶
  FOR n%=1 TO NumberK¶
   ¶
    IF K(n%,0,0)=0 THEN¶
      CALL IntersectpointPlane(n%,Px,Py,Pz,Rx,Ry,Rz,1)¶
      GOTO Wkok¶
```

```
      END IF¶
      IF K(n%,0,0)=1 THEN¶
        CALL IntersectpointTriangle(n%,Px,Py,Pz,Rx,Ry,Rz,l,a,b)¶
        GOTO Wkok¶
      END IF¶
      IF K(n%,0,0)=2 THEN¶
        CALL IntersectpointRectangle(n%,Px,Py,Pz,Rx,Ry,Rz,l,a,b)¶
        GOTO Wkok¶
      END IF¶
      IF K(n%,0,0)=3 THEN¶
        CALL IntersectpointCircle(n%,Px,Py,Pz,Rx,Ry,Rz,l,a,b)¶
        GOTO Wkok¶
      END IF¶
      IF K(n%,0,0)=4 THEN¶
        CALL IntersectpointCircleSector(n%,Px,Py,Pz,Rx,Ry,Rz,l
,a,b)¶
        GOTO Wkok¶
      END IF¶
      IF K(n%,0,0)=5 THEN¶
        CALL IntersectpointCircleRing(n%,Px,Py,Pz,Rx,Ry,Rz,l,
a,b)¶
        GOTO Wkok¶
      END IF¶
      IF K(n%,0,0)=10 THEN¶
        CALL IntersectpointSphere(n%,Px,Py,Pz,Rx,Ry,Rz,l)¶
        GOTO Wkok¶
      END IF¶
      IF K(n%,0,0)=20 THEN¶
        CALL IntersectpointCylinder(n%,Px,Py,Pz,Rx,Ry,Rz,l,a,b,c,
Original!)¶
        GOTO Wkok¶
      END IF¶
      IF K(n%,0,0)=21 THEN¶
        CALL IntersectpointCylinderSegm(n%,Px,Py,Pz,Rx,Ry,Rz,l,a,
b,c, Original!)¶
        GOTO Wkok¶
      END IF¶
      IF K(n%,0,0)=22 THEN¶
        CALL IntersectpointCone(n%,Px,Py,Pz,Rx,Ry,Rz,l,a,b,c,
Original!)¶
        GOTO Wkok¶
      END IF¶
      IF K(n%,0,0)=24 THEN¶
        CALL IntersectpointEllipsoid(n%,Px,Py,Pz,Rx,Ry,Rz,l,a,b,c,
Original!)¶
      END IF¶
      Wkok:¶
      ' Work OK!¶
¶
      IF (l>Threshold) AND (la<=0 OR l<la) AND (n%<>Kp% OR
K(n%,0,0)>=10) THEN¶
        la=l¶
        Body%=n%¶
        IF K(n%,0,0)>=20 AND Kp%=0 THEN¶
          Ac=a¶
          Bc=b¶
          Cc=c¶
        END IF¶
      END IF¶
      Nxtk:¶
      ' Next body¶
    NEXT n%¶
```

```
  ¶
  IF Body%>0 AND Kp%=0 THEN¶
    Sx=Px+la*Rx¶
    Sy=Py+la*Ry¶
    Sz=Pz+la*Rz¶
  END IF  ¶
END SUB¶
```

`Original!` is set to true when it is established which object is visible at the current screen position. It is false when reflection is in effect. `Shadown!` becomes false when the shadow is calculated.

The endpoint of the (visual ray) line is assigned in (`Px`,`Py`,`Pz`) and the direction vector in (`Rx`,`Ry`,`Rz`). As a result you get the number of the body where (`Px`,`Py`,`Pz`) lies next in `Body%`. `Kp%` is needed for the shadow and is explained in that routine.

2.4.2 What You Should See

It's not enough simply to bring the color of the body to the screen. That would give us the outline of the body and nothing else. We need to see the brightness of the body's surface.

We already know that a surface shines brighter when light rays strike perpendicular to the surface. All we have to do is test for the angle that lies between the normal vector on the intersection point and the line from the intersection point to the light source. The brightness is at a maximum when this angle is zero, and when this angle is greater than 90 degrees, the point is dark because the light shines on it from "below."

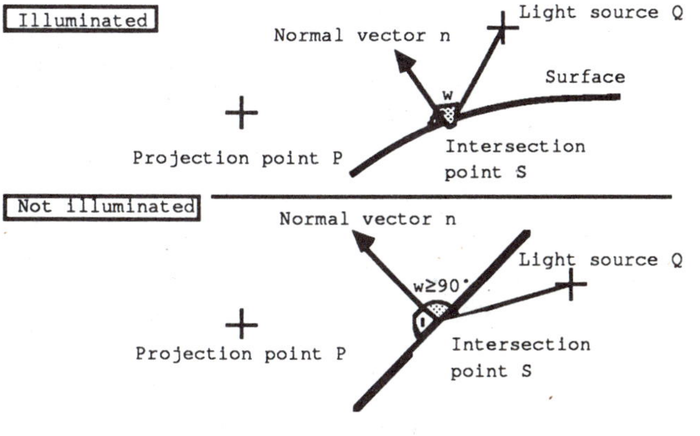

Figure 2.11

We have one simple way of determining whether a point of a surface is in the path of the light source. As a measurement for the brightness of the surface we take the cosine of the angle. This is convenient, because the cosine for perpendicular light rays (0 degrees) is one and for extremely flat light rays (90 degrees) is zero. We just have to multiply these by the three color intensities of the surface (red, green, blue) to get the correct color tone. The cosine for angles over 90 degrees is negative, so a simple test for a negative leading character sees if the point lies in the path of the light source.

In nature, there is no universal function to calculate the brightness of a surface. Different material can have different brightness under the same light. Because we cannot cover them all here, we use the cosine because the cosine of the angle between two vectors can be calculated very easily.

Now we need to find the normal vector. For planes, triangles, parallelograms, etc., this remains the same during calculation, so that we can compute it before the calculation and store it in `Help`. The normal vector is the product of vectors `r2` and `r3`, which cross the plane. The normal vector is easier to compute for the sphere. The normal vector is the same as the vector from the midpoint of the sphere to the intersection point.

It is more difficult for cylinders, cones, and ellipsoids. It's not enough to compute the normal vector in (`r2`,`r3`,`r4`) and then change it back. There are other options.

The normal vector is parallel to the base surface of the cylinder, so we need only consider vectors `r2` and `r3`. The base surface of the cylinder is (in the general case) an ellipse, and an equation for this already exists:

```
(x^2 / a^2) + (y^2 / b^2) = 1
```

Solution for `y`:

```
y = b * SQR(1-(x^2 / a^2))
y = b/a * SQR(a^2 - x^2)
```

This equation solves `y` and gives the slope of the `ellipse:`

```
y' = -b/a * x/SQR(a^2 - x^2)
```

When we regard `y'` as the slope of a line, it is perpendicular to our desired normal vector. We obtain the perpendicular by taking the negative return value of the slope. The slope of the perpendicular is equivalent to `ny/nx`, also the slope of the normal vector:

```
ny/nx = a/b * SQR(a^2 - x^2)/x
```

We split these into an equation for `nx` and for `ny` so that `ny/nx` does not change:

```
ny = (a*b)*SQR(a^2 - x^2)
```

```
nx = (b^2)*x
```

This seems rather arbitrary, but it solves the equation to our advantage. Now we insert the original ellipse equation in the formula for ny to solve the base, and for ny we get:

```
ny = (a*b)*(y*a/b) = >
ny = (a^2)*y
```

Now we have two equations for nx and ny. But the disadvantage is that in our cylinder equation we don't have a, b, x, or y. We must now determine which parameters each represents. a is the main axis of the ellipse which corresponds to the length of vector r2, or |r2|. b is the other axis and corresponds to the length of r3, or |r3|. x and y are coordinates of a point which we call u*r2 and v*r3, where u and v are intersection point parameters. Because our parameter vectors have different directions, we can add the equation for nx and ny. The result is the normal vector for the cylinder:

```
n = |r3|^2 * u*r2 + |r2|^2 * v*r3
```

Because the quadratic of the length of r2 and r3 does not change, we place these in our Help array, which saves us a lot of time.

Things look very similar for the cone, except that the normal vector arcs in the direction of the cone point. We first create the normal vector from the base ellipse. Then we change the length of the normal vector so it is exactly athe length of u*r2 + v*r3. Now we retain the length from r4 to the length of the normal vector, which is exactly the slope of the cone surface when we consider a longitudinal section of the cone. We get the calculation of the perpendicular from the normal vector on this point of the cone surface. n2 is the normal vector on the base surface as it was already written above for the cylinder. So:

```
n1 = n2/|n2| * |u*r2 + v*r3|
```

is the normal vector on the base surface with a length of u*r2+v*r3. The direction remains the same. The normal vector on the cone surface is given by:

```
n = |n1|/|r4| * r4 + |r4|/|n1| * n1
```

The derivation of the normal vector for the ellipsoid will not be discussed here because of page limitations. However, we can supply the equation which provides the solution:

```
n = (|r3|^2 + |r4|^2) * u*r2
  + (|r2|^2 + |r4|^2) * v*r3
  + (|r2|^2 + |r3|^2) * w*r4
```

Now we can test for the brightness of every point of the basic object surfaces, once we establish the location of the light source. It would be best if we could see the reflection of light on the surface of our object.

We calculate the reflected light rays; the angle between them and the visual rays; and the vector from intersection point to projection point. When this angle is zero, we are looking directly into the light source, and the reflected light is very dark. The larger the angle, the greater the reflection of light.

To obtain the reflected light rays we first compute the distance of light source `Q` from the plane that runs tangential to the surface through intersection point `S`. Now multiply the normal vector `n` by a factor that makes the length the same as the distance from `Q` to the tangent plane. After that test the reflected vector `SP` is as follows:

```
SP = (S-Q) + 2*n
```

Figure 2.12

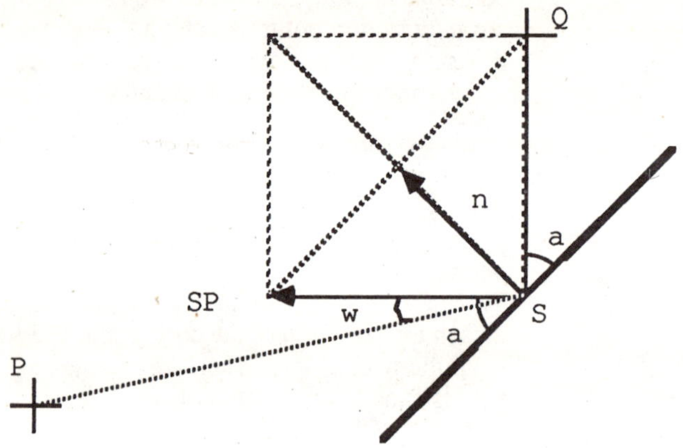

Instead of the angle, we use the cosine and store it in the variable `Mirror`. So the reflected light level stays low, we increase the result by a relatively high power so that the value of `Mirror` is close to zero for small angles.

Now we can finally put all of the calculations together to get the brightness of a point on a surface. We've put them into a `SUB` program named `SetBrightness`. The brightness is stored in the variable `Bright` and the reflection of the light source is stored in `Mirror`. This `SUB` program has nothing to do with the color of the body. This comes later.

```
SUB SetBrightness(n%,Px,Py,Pz,Mirror,Original!) STATIC¶
SHARED
Help(),K(),Mat(),Qx,Qy,Qz,Ac,Bc,Cc,Sx,Sy,Sz,Nx,Ny,Nz,Nl,Spx,Spy,
Spz,Bright ¶
  ' => Bright=Brightness, SP=Mirror Vector, Mirror=Intensity of
LQ-Mirrorung¶
¶
  IF K(n%,0,0)<=9 THEN¶
     ' Determine Mirror Vektor SP¶
    Nx=Help(n%,0)¶
    Ny=Help(n%,1)¶
    Nz=Help(n%,2)¶
```

```
    IF Original!<>True THEN¶
      IF FN CosinAngle(Nx,Ny,Nz,Px-Sx,Py-Sy,Pz-Sz)<0 THEN¶
        'Normal vector must point to projection point!¶
        Nx=-Nx¶
        Ny=-Ny¶
        Nz=-Nz¶
      END IF¶
    END IF¶
    Dqe=Nx*(Qx-Sx)+Ny*(Qy-Sy)+Nz*(Qz-Sz)¶
¶
    Spx=Sx-Qx+2*Dqe*Nx¶
    Spy=Sy-Qy+2*Dqe*Ny¶
    Spz=Sz-Qz+2*Dqe*Nz¶
¶
    Mirror=FN CosinAngle(Spx,Spy,Spz,Px-Sx,Py-Sy,Pz-Sz)¶
¶
    IF Mirror<0 THEN¶
      Mirror=0¶
    END IF¶
¶
    Bright=FN CosinAngle(Nx,Ny,Nz,Qx-Sx,Qy-Sy,Qz-Sz)¶
  ELSE¶
      ' Determine mirror vector SP¶
    IF K(n%,0,0)=10 THEN¶
      Nx=Sx-K(n%,1,0)¶
      Ny=Sy-K(n%,1,1)¶
      Nz=Sz-K(n%,1,2)¶
    END IF¶
¶
    IF K(n%,0,0)>=20 AND K(n%,0,0)<24 THEN¶
      Nx=Help(n%,4)*Ac+Help(n%,1)*Bc¶
      Ny=Help(n%,5)*Ac+Help(n%,2)*Bc¶
      Nz=Help(n%,6)*Ac+Help(n%,3)*Bc¶
¶
      IF K(n%,0,0)>=22 THEN¶
        Nl=SQR(Nx*Nx+Ny*Ny+Nz*Nz)¶
        IF Nl<>0 THEN¶
          a=(Ac*K(n%,2,0)+Bc*K(n%,3,0))^2¶
          a=a+(Ac*K(n%,2,1)+Bc*K(n%,3,1))^2¶
          a=(SQR(a+(Ac*K(n%,2,2)+Bc*K(n%,3,2))^2))/Nl¶
          Nx = Nx*a¶
          Ny = Ny*a¶
          Nz = Nz*a¶
          b=SQR(Nx*Nx+Ny*Ny+Nz*Nz)/Help(n%,7)¶
          Nx=K(n%,4,0)*b+Nx/b¶
          Ny=K(n%,4,1)*b+Ny/b¶
          Nz=K(n%,4,2)*b+Nz/b¶
        ELSE¶
          ' If a cone angle:¶
          Nx=K(n%,4,0)¶
          Ny=K(n%,4,1)¶
          Nz=K(n%,4,2)¶
        END IF¶
      END IF¶
    END IF¶
¶
    IF K(n%,0,0)>=24 THEN¶
      Nx=Ac*Help(n%,1)+Bc*Help(n%,4)+Cc*Help(n%,7)¶
      Ny=Ac*Help(n%,2)+Bc*Help(n%,5)+Cc*Help(n%,8)¶
      Nz=Ac*Help(n%,3)+Bc*Help(n%,6)+Cc*Help(n%,9)¶
    END IF¶
¶
```

```
    IF FN CosinAngle(Nx,Ny,Nz,Px-Sx,Py-Sy,Pz-Sz)<0 THEN¶
      ' => Normal vector points to projection point¶
     Nx=-Nx¶
     Ny=-Ny¶
     Nz=-Nz¶
    END IF¶
    Nl=SQR(Nx*Nx+Ny*Ny+Nz*Nz)¶
    Nx = Nx/Nl¶
    Ny = Ny/Nl¶
    Nz = Nz/Nl¶
¶
    Dqe=Nx*(Qx-Sx)+Ny*(Qy-Sy)+Nz*(Qz-Sz)¶
¶
    Spx=Sx-Qx+2*Dqe*Nx¶
    Spy=Sy-Qy+2*Dqe*Ny¶
    Spz=Sz-Qz+2*Dqe*Nz¶
¶
    Mirror=FN CosinAngle(Spx,Spy,Spz,Px-Sx,Py-Sy,Pz-Sz)¶
¶
    IF Mirror<0 THEN¶
     Mirror=0¶
    END IF¶
¶
    Bright=FN CosinAngle(Nx,Ny,Nz,Qx-Sx,Qy-Sy,Qz-Sz)¶
  END IF¶
¶
  IF Mat(K(n%,0,2),4)>0 THEN¶
    Mirror=1.5*Mirror^(30*Mat(K(n%,0,2),4))¶
  END IF¶
END SUB¶
```

The variables Ac, Bc, and Cc contain the intersection point parameters for u, v, and w in case it is an object like a cylinder, cone, or ellipsoid. The normal vector is regulated and has a length of one. This is important for later calculations. Dqe represents the distance from the light source to the tangent plane. The formula for calculating Mirror, located at the end of the SUB program, has been arbitrarily defined and can be experimented with. When we have defined a dull surface, and Mat(n,4) is relatively small, the reflected light from the light source is equally small.

2.4.3 The Dark Side of the World

Now that we have defined the formulas to our satisfaction, we can get to other things. We have the intersection point S of the visual ray with an object and the position of the light source Q. All we have to do is check whether the line from S to Q intersects with any object, and if this intersection point lies between S and Q.

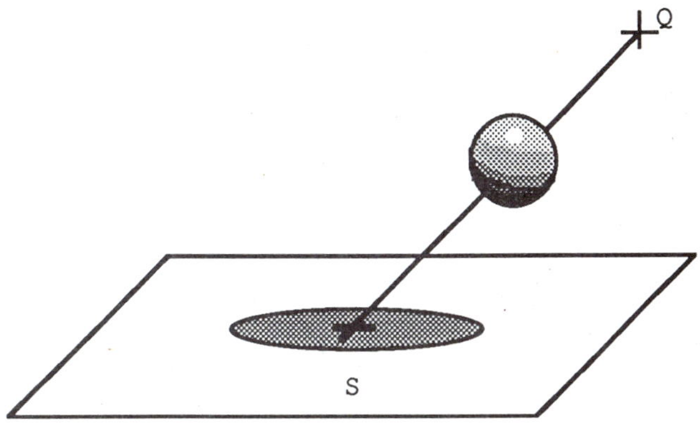

Figure 2.13

The line Q-S acts as the direction vector. Because of the inaccuracy of the operation using real numbers, we check the intersection point calculation to see if parameter l of the line is greater than a threshold, which is dependent on the numerical presentation of the inaccuracy (we talked about this earlier). Because we didn't pay attention to this, the same object that lies on the intersection point is calculated as the object throwing the shadow only, because the calculation of the inequality came out 0.00005 instead of 0.

Because there is no stray light in our computer world, the shadows are naturally solid black. Since this is undesirable, we assign every object a shadow brightness number between zero and one.

The check in our program is very simple because we already have a SUB program that calculates the intersection point between a line and all objects. We must call this SUB program again, but this time the line runs from the intersection point to the light source. When we get an intersection point as a result, the point lies in the shadows; otherwise we can assign it a normal color. The program section could look like the following:

```
 ' =>Compute Brightness of the point => stack¶
 CALL WhichBody(0,Px,Py,Pz,Rx,Ry,Rz,Original!,False)¶
¶
 IF Body% > 0 THEN¶

   CALL SetBrightness(Body%,Px,Py,Pz,Mirror,Original!) ¶
```

```
RestLght(StackPtr%)=Mat(K(Body%,0,2),4)¶
¶
IF Bright<=0 THEN¶
  ' unlit:      ¶
  Bright.r=Mat(K(Body%,0,2),0)*Mat(K(Body%,0,2),3)¶
  Bright.g=Mat(K(Body%,0,2),1)*Mat(K(Body%,0,2),3)¶
  Bright.b=Mat(K(Body%,0,2),2)*Mat(K(Body%,0,2),3)¶
ELSE¶

  Kp%=Body%¶
   'Shadow ?¶
  CALL WhichBody(Kp%,Sx,Sy,Sz,Qx-Sx,Qy-Sy,Qz-Sz,False,True)¶
  SWAP Body%,Kp%¶


  IF Kp%>0 AND la<1 THEN¶
      ' in shadow:¶
    Bright.r=Mat(K(Body%,0,2),0)*Mat(K(Body%,0,2),3)¶
    Bright.g=Mat(K(Body%,0,2),1)*Mat(K(Body%,0,2),3)¶
    Bright.b=Mat(K(Body%,0,2),2)*Mat(K(Body%,0,2),3)¶
  ELSE¶

     ' Mirror light source on interface:¶
    Bright=Bright*(1-RestLght(StackPtr%))¶

    IF Bright<Mat(K(Body%,0,2),3) THEN¶
      Bright=Mat(K(Body%,0,2),3)¶
    END IF¶

    Bright.r=Bright*Mat(K(Body%,0,2),0)+Mirror*
RestLght(StackPtr%)¶
    Bright.g=Bright*Mat(K(Body%,0,2),1)+Mirror*
RestLght(StackPtr%)¶
    Bright.b=Bright*Mat(K(Body%,0,2),2)+Mirror*
RestLght(StackPtr%)¶
  END IF¶
END IF¶
```

Now we must color in the point on the screen with the equivalent of the value from `Bright.r` (red), `Bright.g` (green), and `Bright.b` (blue). But we want to go a step further. We hope that you are not tired from all of these steps, because now it gets really interesting.

2.4.4 Reflection

As the last feature we should take a look at reflection. We can compute the reflected visual rays and their intersection point with an object. The problem remains of combining the different colors of the different surfaces.

The duller a surface is, the harder it is to see the reflection of this object. In nature, reflections also lose some intensity, constantly changing the original color information.

We will proceed as follows: First we'll compute all of the intersection points and their color as in the above program section. We place this color on the stack. After the last reflection we take the color and combine it with the last color. We combine the result with the color before last, and so on, until we return to the first color.

```
Computepoint:  ¶
  ' =>Compute Brightness of the point => stack¶
  StackPtr% = StackPtr% + 1¶
  CALL WhichBody(0,Px,Py,Pz,Rx,Ry,Rz,Original!,False)¶
¶
  IF Body% > 0 THEN¶
    CALL SetBrightness(Body%,Px,Py,Pz,Mirror,Original!) ¶
    RestLght(StackPtr%)=Mat(K(Body%,0,2),4)¶
    ¶
    IF Bright<=0 THEN¶
        ' unlit:    ¶
      Bright.r=Mat(K(Body%,0,2),0)*Mat(K(Body%,0,2),3)¶
      Bright.g=Mat(K(Body%,0,2),1)*Mat(K(Body%,0,2),3)¶
      Bright.b=Mat(K(Body%,0,2),2)*Mat(K(Body%,0,2),3)¶
    ELSE¶
      Kp%=Body%¶
        'Shadow ?¶
      CALL WhichBody(Kp%,Sx,Sy,Sz,Qx-Sx,Qy-Sy,Qz-Sz,False,True)¶
      SWAP Body%,Kp%¶
      IF Kp%>0 AND la<1 THEN¶
          ' in shadow:¶
        Bright.r=Mat(K(Body%,0,2),0)*Mat(K(Body%,0,2),3)¶
        Bright.g=Mat(K(Body%,0,2),1)*Mat(K(Body%,0,2),3)¶
        Bright.b=Mat(K(Body%,0,2),2)*Mat(K(Body%,0,2),3)¶
      ELSE¶
          ' Mirror light source on interface:¶
        Bright=Bright*(1-RestLght(StackPtr%))¶
        IF Bright<Mat(K(Body%,0,2),3) THEN¶
          Bright=Mat(K(Body%,0,2),3)¶
        END IF¶
        Bright.r=Bright*Mat(K(Body%,0,2),0)+Mirror*
RestLght(StackPtr%)¶
        Bright.g=Bright*Mat(K(Body%,0,2),1)+Mirror*
RestLght(StackPtr%)¶
        Bright.b=Bright*Mat(K(Body%,0,2),2)+Mirror*
RestLght(StackPtr%)¶
      END IF¶
    END IF¶
¶
    IF (RestLght(StackPtr%)>0) AND (StackPtr%<MaxStack%) THEN¶
        ' Determine Mirror interface¶
        ' Determine mirror vector to P-S:¶
      Dqe=Nx*(Px-Sx)+Ny*(Py-Sy)+Nz*(Pz-Sz)¶
      Rx=Sx-Px+2*Dqe*Nx¶
      Ry=Sy-Py+2*Dqe*Ny¶
      Rz=Sz-Pz+2*Dqe*Nz¶
¶
      Stack(StackPtr%,0)=Bright.r¶
      Stack(StackPtr%,1)=Bright.g¶
      Stack(StackPtr%,2)=Bright.b¶
¶
      Px = Sx¶
      Py = Sy¶
      Pz = Sz¶
      Original! = False¶
```

```
        GOSUB Computepoint          ' Recursion !!!!¶
        ¶
        Bright.r=Stack(StackPtr%,0)+Stack(StackPtr%+1,0)*
RestLght(StackPtr%)¶
        Bright.g=Stack(StackPtr%,1)+Stack(StackPtr%+1,1)*
RestLght(StackPtr%)¶
        Bright.b=Stack(StackPtr%,2)+Stack(StackPtr%+1,2)*
RestLght(StackPtr%)¶
      END IF¶
    ELSE¶
      IF StackPtr% = 0 THEN¶
        Bright.r=-1¶
        Bright.g=-1¶
        Bright.b=-1¶
      ELSE¶
        Bright.r=0¶
        Bright.g=0¶
        Bright.b=0¶
      END IF¶
    END IF¶
    Stack(StackPtr%,0)=Bright.r¶
    Stack(StackPtr%,1)=Bright.g¶
    Stack(StackPtr%,2)=Bright.b¶
    RestLght(StackPtr%)=0¶
    StackPtr% = StackPtr%-1¶
RETURN¶
```

This routine also contains the program section that was mentioned in the section describing shadows. The variables used were already discussed, so here we'll just introduce `StackPtr%`. In the main program, from which the calculated point is called, `StackPtr%` is set to -1. This increments by 1 for every reflection until there are no more reflections, or until the maximum stack depth (20) is reached.

2.4.5 Bringing Color to the Screen

The results of our calculations up until now have been three values that stand for the red, green, and blue hues of the color. Now we must somehow bring these colors onto the screen. Because we don't have many colors to insert, we must now figure out how to combine these colors until we get desired color.

You may be thinking, "Hold it. HAM mode gives us 4096 colors to use, and that's more than enough." That's correct, but any one pixel can only take on one of 64 colors: 16 basic colors plus 16 colors by changing the red intensity, 16 colors by changing the green intensity, and 16 colors by changing the blue intensity. This gives us a total of 64 colors.

We aren't done combining colors. We base the displayed color combination on the pattern defined. The pattern itself is two-color: One color is established using the foreground color, and the other is established using the background color. To get different color combinations, we define different patterns, some with more pixels from one color, and some with fewer pixels on one color. The pattern automatically used by the operating system gives you a rectangle when you set a pointer to it in the `RastPort` structure.

Now we have another problem that we cannot ignore: which two colors do we combine to get the desired color combination? It's not easy. When you want to display a picture in monochrome (gray scales), all you need are two shades of gray.

Problems occur when you switch to color display. Put the color in three dimensions: A red axis, a green axis, and a blue axis. The result is a cube that has one corner on the origin. To make the problem easier to visualize, here is an example:

A study of the color green appears below. Because we must economize on memory space, our screen has only four colors: black, red, green, and yellow. We need red and green because the picture contains red and green objects. When we display the colors in a coordinate system (which can be two dimensional in this case), we get the following picture:

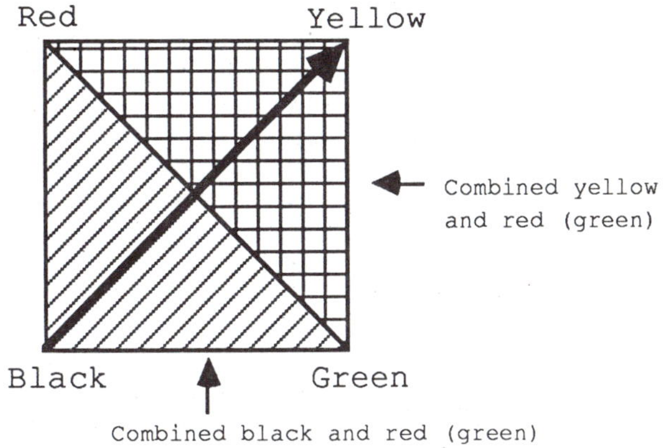

Figure 2.14

When the yellow intensity is less than 0.5, the color black seems to work best. The second best color is either red or green, because these colors are closer to yellow than black is to yellow. This provides an intermediate color between black and yellow. When the yellow intensity is greater than 0.5, yellow works best. Red or green are the next best colors. When red or green is chosen, in which case they are equal, both colors are the same distance from the desired color. The result can only be changed by increasing the number of the color.

It would be unacceptable if the algorithm went through all of the possibilities and took the best one. The routine in assembly language requires five seconds per pixel for 64 colors and 25 patterns. That means that one 320x200 picture would require more than three days to execute. And the time needed for an equivalent program in BASIC...well, let's just say it'll take more time.

Here's an alternative: Try the two colors whose hues are similar to the one you are searching for. The direction of the color vector must be tested for as well as its polar coordinates. Disadvantage: The calculation of the desired color in polar coordinates takes time. In addition, the result does not completely solve the problem. For example, to get a gray tone, you'd combine white and black instead of two shades of gray. Here a lot depends on the pattern itself, namely, the ratio in which the colors are mixed.

We must admit that we haven't found the ideal algorithm. We've used the first (combining the two closest colors). When the basic colors are well distributed you get good results, especially in HAM mode.

Because BASIC is not the fastest language, we programmed the algorithm in assembly language. It would be better if the entire tracer program was written in assembly language, but assembly language programs are harder for the average person to read and understand than BASIC programs. The program length also makes reading hard.

The assembly routine is written with ***AssemPro***. See the appendices for the source code (`SetPoint.ASM`) and a BASIC loader for those of you who do not have an assembler. If you want to implement this yourself, you must create PC-relative code with ***AssemPro***. You must also write out the addresses of the three subprograms and the variables `RastPort`, `Mode`, `MaxColors`, `Colors`, `RasterW`, and `RasterH`, and these must be added to the BASIC subprogram `InitSetPoint`. The created code must be saved as `SetPoint.B`. and the the routine can be loaded with `InitSetPoint`. The variables `RasterInit` and `ColorPalette` will be changed. The routine is called with:

```
CALL OSSetPoint&(x1,y1,x2,y2,red*1024,green*1024,blue*1024)
```

where (`x1`,`y1`) is the upper left corner and (`x2`,`y2`) is the lower right corner of the rectangle. The values for red, green, and blue must be between 0 and 1024. These values should generally be given as integer values.

The assumption for the `OSSpoint` routine is that the red, green, and blue values of the basic colors are stored in the array `OSColor`. This field is found directly behind the assembler routine and the values must be poked. Each element contains four values (16 bits): Number of the corresponding color register, red intensity*1024, green intensity*1024, and blue intensity*1024. The number of the basic color must be in `OSMaxColors`. `OSRastPort` contains a pointer for the `RastPort` of the window or screen, `OSMode` contains the presentation mode, for example, $800 for HAM mode. `OSRasterW` and `OSRasterH` contain the height and width of the window/screen because `OSSetPoint` takes its own clipping.

To get a good color palette, you should put in the optimal color palette for each picture. Allow the picture to go through a long calculation and note how the colors come out. Then alter the color palette so that for each color there is the widest range of color shades. It would be best to use the HAM (Hold and Modify) mode.

2.5 Optimization

The algorithm we have been formulating so far works. We should add some improvements. This algorithm has a built-in feature for computing printout parameters that remain unchanged during calculation. The `SUB` program that executes this for us is called `InitShadows`. The computed values are stored in the `Help` array, the elements in this array have different meanings for different objects. `Help` contains the normal vector for planes, and the denominator determinate for the basis transformation for cylinders, cones, and ellipsoids.

The next step encountered is the intersection point calculation. Examine the following diagram and imagine the objects are displayed on your screen:

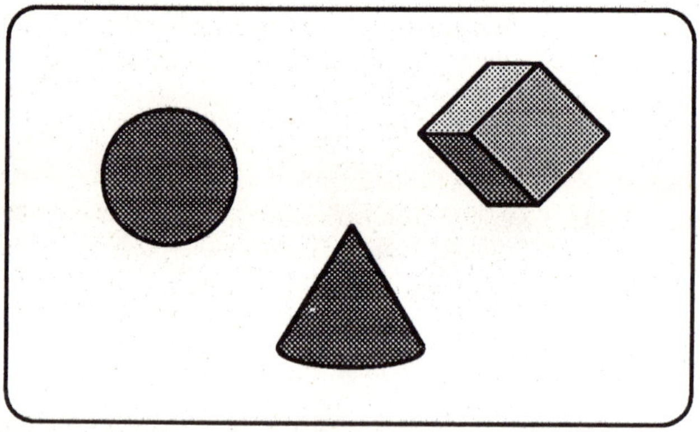

Figure 2.15

The objects take up a fairly large section of the screen. We can first establish a minimal rectangle in which all of the objects lie. Then our program needs to send out a visual ray for every point that lies inside of this rectangle.

Next we draw a minimal rectangle for each object, so that the object lies completely within it. In our `SUB` program `WhichBody` we check if the actual visual ray passes through this rectangle. If it does, we calculate the intersection point. This check for the current point within the rectangle goes much faster than the intersection point calculation, it must execute more determinate calculations (cylinder, cone, ellipsoid).

The rectangles for our above graphic can look like this example:

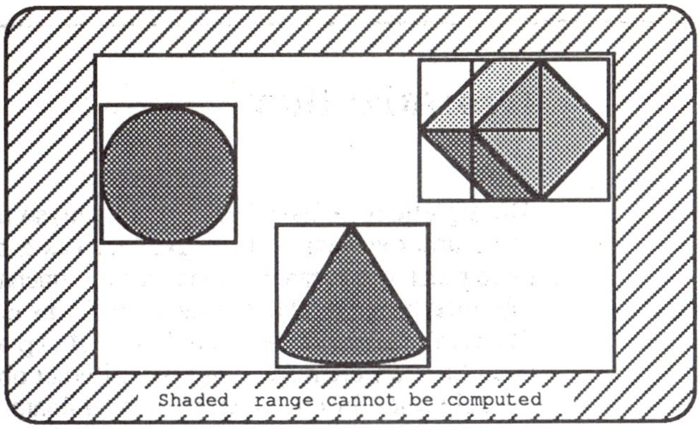

Figure 2.16

The rectangles for the individual objects are narrow and the rectangle for the screen section is wide. Notice that the cube is assembled from six parallelograms (sides), but only the visible three are shown here, because otherwise it would make the diagram hard to follow.

We can store the rectangle borders in an array, say `MinMax`. Each element of `MinMax` contains the following values:

```
MinMax(n,0)  = minimum x coordinate for object n
MinMax(n,1)  = minimum y coordinate for object n
MinMax(n,2)  = maximum x coordinate for object n
MinMax(n,3)  = maximum y coordinate for object n
```

The subroutine which calculates these rectangles is `InitMinMax`. For "round" objects (circular surfaces, cylinders, spheres, etc.), a rectangle or square is put around the object, and those corner points create the basis for the rectangle computation. Here you can put an octagon around an object and the rectangle calculations occur naturally.

This optimization only helps us when we send out visible rays for testing. It doesn't help for reflected visual rays or shadow calculation. We can't take any optics for the reflected visual rays because neither the starting point of the reflected visual ray nor its direction is confirmed.

But what about the shadows? The light source stays in the same position. The surface that lies in the shadows can be above everything, but it also cannot be confined to a plane, like the projection surface. When we calculate all objects relative to the light source instead of the rectangles, and establish minimums and maximums for both angles, we are dealing with shadows. `True` is tested to see if the polar coordinates of the intersection point lie inside the intervals set for each object.

Do you understand what is going on? Instead of the cartesian coordinates (x,y,z), we can also give a point in polar coordinates as (a,b,d). `a` and `b` are angles and `d` is the distance from the coordinate origin. We can give an `Amin` and an `Amax` for each object so that for each point of the object the angle a lies between Amin and Amax. The same thing can be done for b by setting a Bmin and Bmax.

When we determine in WhichBody whether an object casts a shadow on a point, you first compute the polar coordinates of the point (pa,pb,pd). Before you work through the intersection point calculation, test to see if pa lies between Amin and Amax and if pb lies between for Bmax and Bmin for this object. If this is not the case, this object cannot cast a shadow on the point and you can skip the intersection point calculation.

We can also limit the minimum distance of an object from the light source. We can then test if the distance of the object from the light source is greater than the distance of the point from the light source. This would also mean that we can skip the intersection point calculations.

The problem comes from the angles location, which can usually lie between -Pi and +Pi. When an object lies on the boundary between +Pi and -Pi, you get an incorrect angle interval. In this case we must add an angle interval so that the angle lies between 0 and 2*Pi. This increment must be kept for every object and must be considered during the test. The field that contains all of these values is called MinMaxLq, and its elements have the following meaning:

```
MinMaxLq(n,0): increment for angle a
MinMaxLq(n,1): minimum for angle a
MinMaxLq(n,2): maximum for angle a
MinMaxLq(n,3): increment for angle b
MinMaxLq(n,4): minimum for angle b
MinMaxLq(n,5): maximum for angle b
MinMaxLq(n,6): minimum distance of object n from q
```

This field is initialized in the subroutine InitMinMaxLq. The test for MinMax and MinMaxLq in WhichBody is:

```
SUB WhichBody (Kp%,Px,Py,Pz,Rx,Ry,Rz,Original!,Shadown!) STATIC¶
SHARED True,False,minmax%(),NumberK,minmaxlq(),Help(),K(),
xb%,yb%,Sx,Sy,Sz,Body%,Ac,Bc,Cc,la,Threshold¶
  ' => Body% = Nr the body under coordinates xb%,yb%,
S(sx,sy,sz)=Intersect point, la=intersection line¶
  ' => falls Typ>=20:
  '(ac,bc,cc) = transform Intersect points coordinates¶
  la=-1¶
  Body%=0¶
¶
  IF Shadown! = True THEN                    ¶
    CALL Calcablq(Anglea,Angleb,0!,0!,Px,Py,Pz)¶
    Dist=SQR(Rx*Rx+Ry*Ry+Rz*Rz)¶
  END IF¶
¶
  FOR n%=1 TO NumberK¶
    IF Original! = True THEN¶
      IF minmax%(n%,0)>xb% THEN¶
        GOTO Nxtk¶
```

```
    END IF¶
    IF minmax%(n%,1)>yb% THEN¶
      GOTO Nxtk¶
    END IF¶
    IF minmax%(n%,2)<xb% THEN¶
      GOTO Nxtk¶
    END IF¶
    IF minmax%(n%,3)<yb% THEN¶
      GOTO Nxtk¶
    END IF¶
  END IF¶
  ¶
  IF Shadown! = True THEN¶
    CALL NormalAngle(Wa,Anglea+minmaxlq(n%,0))¶
    CALL NormalAngle(Wb,Angleb+minmaxlq(n%,3))¶
    IF Wa<minmaxlq(n%,1) THEN¶
      GOTO Nxtk¶
    END IF¶
    IF Wa>minmaxlq(n%,2) THEN¶
      GOTO Nxtk¶
    END IF¶
    IF Wb<minmaxlq(n%,4) THEN¶
      GOTO Nxtk¶
    END IF¶
    IF Wb>minmaxlq(n%,5) THEN¶
      GOTO Nxtk¶
    END IF¶
    IF Dist<minmaxlq(n%,6) THEN¶
      GOTO Nxtk¶
    END IF¶
  END IF¶
  ¶
  IF K(n%,0,0)=0 THEN¶
    CALL IntersectpointPlane(n%,Px,Py,Pz,Rx,Ry,Rz,l)¶
    GOTO Wkok¶
  END IF¶
  IF K(n%,0,0)=1 THEN¶
    CALL IntersectpointTriangle(n%,Px,Py,Pz,Rx,Ry,Rz,l,a,b)¶
    GOTO Wkok¶
  END IF¶
  IF K(n%,0,0)=2 THEN¶
    CALL IntersectpointRectangle(n%,Px,Py,Pz,Rx,Ry,Rz,l,a,b)¶
    GOTO Wkok¶
  END IF¶
  IF K(n%,0,0)=3 THEN¶
    CALL IntersectpointCircle(n%,Px,Py,Pz,Rx,Ry,Rz,l,a,b)¶
    GOTO Wkok¶
  END IF¶
  IF K(n%,0,0)=4 THEN¶
    CALL IntersectpointCircleSector(n%,Px,Py,Pz,Rx,Ry,Rz,
l,a,b)¶
    GOTO Wkok¶
  END IF¶
  IF K(n%,0,0)=5 THEN¶
    CALL IntersectpointCircleRing(n%,Px,Py,Pz,Rx,Ry,Rz,l,a,b)¶
    GOTO Wkok¶
  END IF¶
  IF K(n%,0,0)=10 THEN¶
    CALL IntersectpointSphere(n%,Px,Py,Pz,Rx,Ry,Rz,l)¶
    GOTO Wkok¶
  END IF¶
  IF K(n%,0,0)=20 THEN¶
```

```
      CALL IntersectpointCylinder(n%,Px,Py,Pz,Rx,Ry,Rz,l,a,b,c,
Original!)¶
      GOTO Wkok¶
    END IF¶
    IF K(n%,0,0)=21 THEN¶
      CALL
IntersectpointCylinderSegm(n%,Px,Py,Pz,Rx,Ry,Rz,l,a,b,c,
Original!)¶
      GOTO Wkok¶
    END IF¶
    IF K(n%,0,0)=22 THEN¶
      CALL IntersectpointCone(n%,Px,Py,Pz,Rx,Ry,Rz,l,a,b,c,
Original!)¶
      GOTO Wkok¶
    END IF¶
    IF K(n%,0,0)=24 THEN¶
      CALL IntersectpointEllipsoid(n%,Px,Py,Pz,Rx,Ry,Rz,l,a,b,c,
Original!)¶
    END IF¶
    Wkok:¶
    ' Work OK!¶
¶
    IF (l>Threshold) AND (la<=0 OR l<la) AND (n%<>Kp% OR
K(n%,0,0)>=10) THEN¶
      la=l¶
      Body%=n%¶
      IF K(n%,0,0)>=20 AND Kp%=0 THEN¶
        Ac=a¶
        Bc=b¶
        Cc=c¶
      END IF¶
    END IF¶
    Nxtk:¶
    ' Next body¶
  NEXT n%¶
  ¶
  IF Body%>0 AND Kp%=0 THEN¶
    Sx=Px+la*Rx¶
    Sy=Py+la*Ry¶
    Sz=Pz+la*Rz¶
  END IF  ¶
END SUB¶
```

We leave you with a few words about calculation time. A super computer like a Cray needs a good twenty minutes to compute a picture. The tracer program is written in BASIC mainly because BASIC is an easy language to understand. BASIC is also a slow language. Picture calculation requires lots of time. Luckily the Amiga multitasks so that you aren't inhibited during calculation.

We recommend that you compile the tracer program or the one you create for this routine (see Chapter 8 for compiling instructions). That lowers the computation time for a 320x200 picture to under a day. When you have defined only a few unreflected objects, the computation time goes under a few hours. Rewriting this routine in assembly language will speed things up considerably.

3.
The Tracer Program

3. The Tracer Program

Now that we have discussed the basic algorithms required for three dimensional graphics, we'd like to show you our results. This chapter contains our realization of a ray tracing program. Before describing the routine we'd like to point out that the aim of this book is to teach you how to program three dimensional graphics. This book is not a programming tutor in itself. The routines are written in modular form so they can easily be adapted for use in your own programs. The optional disk contains the separate modules saved in ASCII format so they may be easily merged into your own program code.

3.1 Wire Models

Now that you've learned some of the theory of how ray tracing works, this section explains how to make three dimensional wire models.

3.1.1 From 3D to 2D

This wire model is used to display the objects on the screen before calculating the shadows. This saves a good deal of time and allows the objects to be placed on the screen in the best manner.

To display our objects, we must project all of the three dimensional points whose X, Y and Z coordinates were given onto the screen. Points that make up the room must also be put on the plane. The points projected on a plane can then be displayed on the screen.

It must be obvious from the screen display whether an object is placed in front of or behind another object. We must also create a perspective effect, so the computer gives the most realistic scene possible.

We first fix a stationary point inside the computer world. We do this by giving the coordinates of our stationary point with the variables `Px`, `Py`, and `Pz`. We named the given point `Projection point`.

Where do we see the scene from? With only a point in the room we cannot locate the direction of vision. We place a second point that is also appropriate for the vision direction. We call this point the `Main point`, whose coordinates are `Hx`, `Hy`, and `Hz`.

We place ourselves at the projection point and look in the direction of the main point.

The main point does more than determine the vision direction. This point is also a point of our projection plane—the plane on which our points are projected. Before the points are given on the screen, the projection plane must first be constructed.

But the projection point is not totally passive. The line through the projection point and the main point is perpendicular to the projection plane:

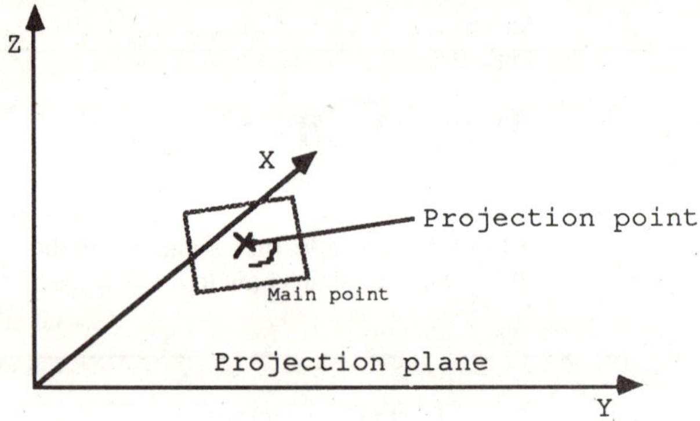

Figure 3.1

The line `PM` (projection point/main point) helps us determine the rotation angle around the coordinate axes, around which the projection plane must rotate so that it coincides with the `YZ` plane.

We first place the main point at the origin. We do this because the coordinates of all the points are taken from the coordinates of the main point.

The following diagram illustrates how we determine the rotation angle:

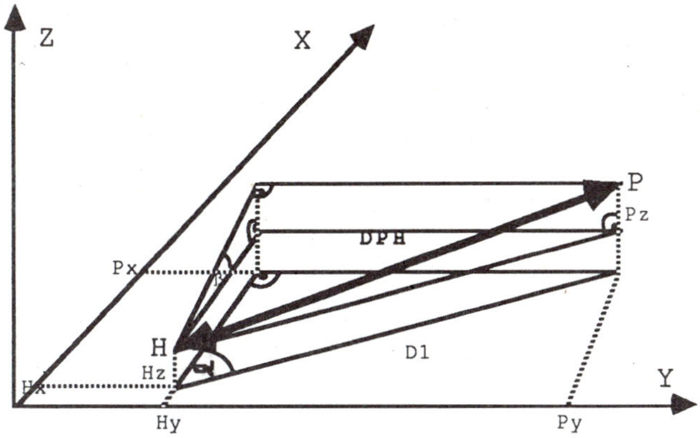

Figure 3.2

As you can see, the relationships for the angle `Alpha` (Z axis) and the angle `Beta` (Y axis) are:

```
Sin(alpha) = (Px-Hy)/D1
Cos(alpha) = (Px-Hx)/D1

Sin(beta) = (pz-Hz)/DPH  (DPH = Distance from projection
point to main point)
Cos(beta) = D1/DPH
```

The angle can be calculated using the ATN (arctangent) function of AmigaBASIC. This is possible because the tangent of an angle is also defined as the quotient of the sine and cosine of the angle:

```
Angle = ATN(Sin/Cos)
```

The angle from the X axis must be set very close to 0. As the diagram shows, when the projection plane lies in the `YZ` plane or the projection points lies on the X axis, the rotation angle does not need to be calculated any more.

The `InitialP` routine calculates the position of the main point and the projection point of the required rotation angle, as well as the distance from the main point to the projection point.

```
InitialP:¶
  D1=SQR((Px-Hx)^2+(Py-Hy)^2)¶
  DPH=SQR((Px-Hx)^2+(Py-Hy)^2+(Pz-Hz)^2)¶
¶
  IF D1=0 THEN¶
    Sina=0¶
    Cosa=1¶
  ELSE¶
    Sina=(Py-Hy)/D1¶
    Cosa=(Px-Hx)/D1¶
  END IF¶
¶
  IF DPH=0 THEN¶
    Sinb=0¶
    Cosb=1¶
```

```
    ELSE¶
      Sinb=(Pz-Hz)/DPH¶
      Cosb=D1/DPH¶
    END IF¶
    ¶
    Sinc=0                                ' Z-Axis angle not¶
    Cosc=1                                ' solely determined here¶
  ¶
    IF Cosa=0 THEN¶
      Alpha=Pd2¶
    ELSE¶
      Alpha=ATN(Sina/Cosa)                  ' compute cosinem and Sine¶
    END IF                                  ' angle¶
  ¶
    IF Cosa<0 THEN¶
      Alpha = Alpha+Pi¶
    END IF¶
  ¶
    IF Cosb=0 THEN¶
      Beta=Pd2¶
    ELSE¶
      Beta=ATN(Sinb/Cosb)¶
    END IF¶
  ¶
    IF Cosb<0 THEN¶
      Beta = Beta + Pi¶
    END IF¶
  ¶
    Gamma=0¶
  RETURN¶
```

When we calculate the rotation angle, we need to make sure that the point rotates around the coordinate axes. We must subject every point to the same rotation as the projection plane so that they lie on the YZ plane.

How do you rotate a point? Look at this illustration:

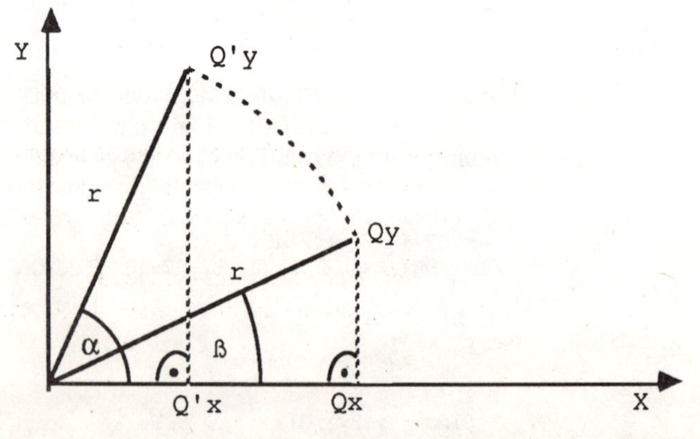

Figure 3.3

The point Q rotates around the angle alpha. Q' is the point rotated around the angle alpha. It is described by the following relationships:

$\sin(\beta) = Qy/r$ $\sin(\alpha-\beta) = Q'y/r$

```
Cos(β)  = Qx/r            Cos(α-β)  = Q'x/r
```

Insert this in the addition theorem and you get the formula for the rotation of a point around the angle `alpha`.

Addition theorem:

```
Cos(β-α)  = Cos(β)*Cos(α)+Sin(β)*Sin(α)
Sin(β-α)  = Sin(β)*Cos(α)-Cos(β)*Sin(α)
```

Substitution:

```
Q'x/r  = Cos(α)*Qx*r  +  Sin(α)*Qy*r
Q'y/r  = Cos(α)*Qy*r  -  Sin(α)*Qx*r

  Q'x  = Cos(α)*Qx  +  Sin(α)*Qy
  Q'y  = Cos(α)*Qy  -  Sin(α)*Qx
```

Now we need to rotate the points around all three coordinate axes according to the above formula. For example, we rotate a point around the Z axis, and the Z coordinate does not change. It is the same when rotating around the other two axes.

The rotations are shown in the following diagram:

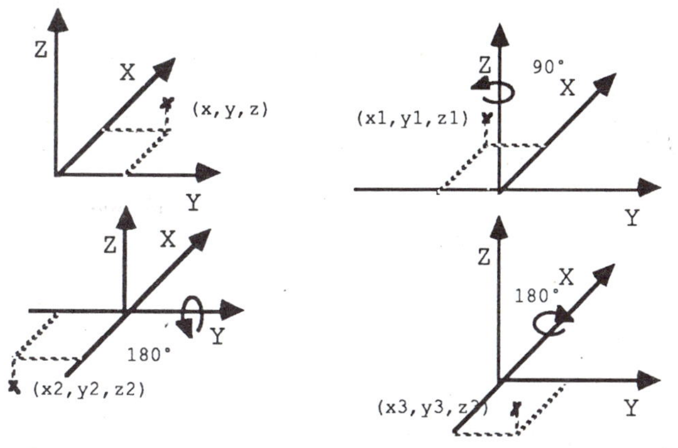

Figure 3.4

You should remember that for rotation around the Y axis the previously computed coordinates for the rotation around the Z axis are used. The results of the Y rotation are used for the rotation around the X axis.

Now we can concentrate on perspective. We examine the line through the projection point and the points that rotate around the coordinate axes:

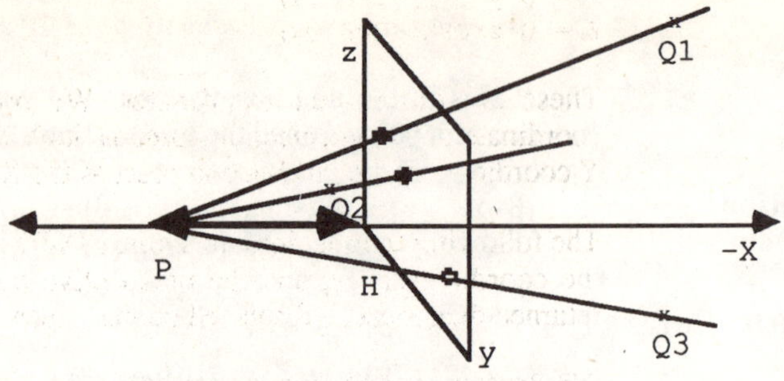

Figure 3.5

As you can see, the projection point now has the coordinates (DPH,0,0). We determine the rotation angle around the Z and Y axes from the projection-main point line so that the projection plane lies on the YZ plane. Because the line PH is perpendicular to this plane and the main point again lies on the coordinate origin, this means that the projection point lies in the range DPH on the X axis.

Now we look at the intersection points of the line with the plane. Each of these intersection points places a displayed point there. The coordinates of the individual intersection points can also be used for our screen output.

How do you determine these intersection points? We see the line equation of the line projection point—displayed point:

```
X   Qx         (Px-Qx)
Y = Qy + t *  (Py-Qy)
Z   Qz         (Pz-Qz)
```

We know that the intersection point must have the X coordinate 0 because the X coordinate of all points on the YZ plane is 0 (we determined through the rotations that the projection plane lies in the YZ plane).

Together with the coordinates of the projection points and the X coordinate of the intersection point we can set up the following relationships:

```
X   Qx         (DPH-Qx)
Y = Qy + t *  (0-Qy)
Z   Qz         (0-Qz)

X = Qx + t * (DPH-Qx)  = 0
                     t = -Qx/(DPH-Qx)
```

By inserting from t and converting the remaining equations you get the Y and Z coordinates of the intersection points (Q' is already rotated around all 3 axes):

```
Y = Q'y*DPH/(DPH-Qx)
Z = Q'z*DPH/(DPH-Qx)
```

These are our screen coordinates. We must now consider the Z coordinate of the intersection point as the Y screen coordinate, and the Y coordinate of the intersection point as the X coordinate of the screen.

The following routine does the entire 3D/2D conversion, the rotating of the coordinate axes, and the perspective transformation. The points returned then must be displayed on the screen.

```
SUB Projection(Px%,Py%,x,y,z) STATIC¶
SHARED Sina,Sinb,Sinc,Cosa,Cosb,Cosc,DPH,Hx,Hy,Hz¶
  ' 3D coordinates (x,y,z) to 2D (Px%,Py%) = Screen¶
¶
  x1=(x-Hx)*Cosa+(y-Hy)*Sina   ' Z-Axis rotation¶
  y1=(y-Hy)*Cosa-(x-Hx)*Sina¶
  x2=x1*Cosb+(z-Hz)*Sinb       ' Y-Axis rotation¶
  z2=(z-Hz)*Cosb-x1*Sinb¶
  y3=y1*Cosc+z2*Sinc           ' X-Axis rotation¶
  z3=z2*Cosc-y1*Sinc¶
¶
  IF DPH<>x3 THEN¶
    Px%=FN Xscale((y3*DPH)/(DPH-x2)) -4 ' Intersecting point
with projection point ¶
    Py%=FN Yscale((z3*DPH)/(DPH-x2)) -2 ' scaling¶
  ELSE¶
    Px% = FN Xscale(0) -4   ' Subtraction of 4 and 2 based on
drawing¶
    Py% = FN Yscale(0) -2   ' in a GIMMEZEROZERO-Window (BASIC-
Window)¶
  END IF¶
END SUB ¶
```

When examining this routine you will notice the following functions:

```
FN XSclae (x) = (x+PictureX) * Picturewidth   and
FN YScale (y) = (PictureY-y) * Pictureheight
```

They make sure that the intersection points with the YZ plane are shown with the correct enlargement. To understand what this user function does, we must first clarify the meaning of the variables:

`Picturewidth` and `Pictureheight` act as the enlargement (magnification) factors in the X and Y directions. `PictureX` and `PictureY` give the size of the window section whose contents should be enlarged:

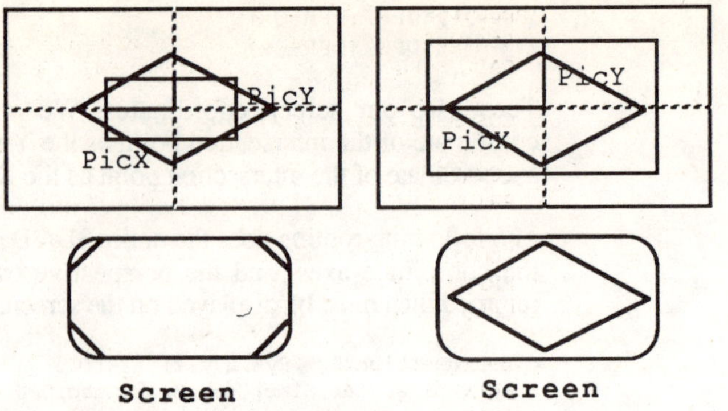

Figure 3.6

The larger PictureX and PictureY, the larger the area of points that must be presented on the screen. PictureX and PictureY are calculated as follows:

```
PictureX = RasterW2% / Picturewidth
PictureY = RasterH2% / Pictureheight
```

RasterW2% and RasterH2% are the screen coordinates of the mid point (For a 320x200 screen RasterW2% = 160 and RasterH2% = 100).

PictureX and PictureY get larger as Picturewidth and Pictureheight get smaller, and vice versa.

XScale and YScale ensure that the origin of the coordinate system (= transformed main point) transforms to the midpoint of the screen.

This occurred because the X coordinate of the intersection point is added to PictureX. Remove PictureY from the Y coordinate of the intersection point because the Y coordinates cross from top to bottom, not from bottom to top as in Cartesian coordinates.

Multiply the coordinates by the enlargement factors to make the points correct for the screen.

Until now we have always maintained that a main point and a projection point would be given. These two points are basically sufficient to develop a completely functioning 3D/2D routine.

These points can be changed in a program. First the program must be interrupted and one or more program lines changed, for example, to give new coordinates for the center point.

You can change the main point in the following routine, give a new projection point, change the rotation angle in degrees (not radians), and increase or decrease the distance DPH. A very small DPH distorts the three dimensional presentation on the screen, while a large DPH loses the central perspective effect (the picture is in parallel perspective).

```
InputH:¶
  Status$ = " Status: Main point"+CHR$(0)¶
  CALL SetWindowTitles&(NWBase&,SADD(Status$),0)¶
¶
  GOSUB DeleteMenu¶
¶
  LOCATE 10,1¶
  PRINT "        Main point: "¶
¶
  LOCATE 12,1¶
  PRINT "     Hx = ";¶
  CALL FormInput (Hx,30!,-1E+14,1E+14)¶
¶
  LOCATE 13,1¶
  PRINT "     Hy = ";¶
  CALL FormInput (Hy,30!,-1E+14,1E+14)¶
¶
  LOCATE 14,1¶
  PRINT "     Hz = ";¶
  CALL FormInput (Hz,30!,-1E+14,1E+14)¶
¶
  GOSUB Initial¶
  Newone! = True¶
  CLS¶
  GOSUB MakeMenu¶
RETURN¶
'¶
InputP:¶
  Status$ = " Status: Projection point"+CHR$(0)¶
  CALL SetWindowTitles&(NWBase&,SADD(Status$),0)¶
¶
  GOSUB DeleteMenu¶
¶
  LOCATE 10,1¶
  PRINT "        Projection point: "¶
  ¶
  LOCATE 12,1¶
  PRINT "        Px = ";¶
  CALL FormInput (Px,30!,-1E+14,1E+14)¶
¶
  LOCATE 13,1¶
  PRINT "        Py = ";¶
  CALL FormInput (Py,30!,-1E+14,1E+14)¶
¶
  LOCATE 14,1¶
  PRINT "        Pz = ";¶
  CALL FormInput (Pz,30!,-1E+14,1E+14)¶
  ¶
  GOSUB InitialP¶
  Newone! = True¶
  CLS¶
  GOSUB MakeMenu ¶
RETURN¶
'¶
InputDPH:¶
  Status$ = " Status: Spacing"+CHR$(0)¶
  CALL SetWindowTitles&(NWBase&,SADD(Status$),0)¶
  ¶
  GOSUB DeleteMenu¶
  ¶
  LOCATE 10,1¶
  PRINT "     Spacing of projection surface = ";¶
```

```
  CALL FormInput (DPH,30!,-1E+14,1E+14)¶
¶
  GOSUB Initial¶
  Newone! = True¶
  CLS¶
  GOSUB MakeMenu¶
RETURN¶
'¶
InputAngle:¶
  Status$ = " Status: Enter angle of rotation"+CHR$(0)¶
  CALL SetWindowTitles&(NWBase&,SADD(Status$),0)¶
  ¶
  GOSUB DeleteMenu¶
¶
  a=FN Deg(Alpha)¶
  b=FN Deg(Beta)¶
  c=FN Deg(Gamma)¶
  ¶
  LOCATE 10,1¶
  PRINT "     Angle of rotation (a,_,c): "¶
¶
  LOCATE 12,1¶
  PRINT "     Alpha (Z-Axis) = ";¶
  CALL FormInput (a,30!,0!,360!)¶
¶
  LOCATE 13,1¶
  PRINT "     Beta  (Y-Axis) = ";¶
  CALL FormInput (b,30!,0!,360!)¶
¶
  LOCATE 14,1¶
  PRINT "     Gamma (X-Axis) = ";¶
  CALL FormInput (c,30!,0!,360!)¶
¶
  Alpha=FN Rad(a)¶
  Beta=FN Rad(b)¶
  Gamma=FN Rad(c)¶
¶
  GOSUB Initial¶
  Newone! = True¶
  CLS¶
  GOSUB MakeMenu¶
RETURN¶
'End of Draw-Input.asc¶
```

When changing the main point, the distance `DPH` or the rotation angle, you should be careful because the position of the projection point is also changed. The main point is shown as the basis point now.

In `Initial`, the data of the new projection point is computed:

```
' ************************¶
' *   Input-Routine      *¶
' ************************¶
'¶
Initial:¶
  WHILE Alpha<0¶
     Alpha = Alpha + Pm2¶
  WEND¶
  WHILE Beta<0¶
     Beta = Beta + Pm2¶
  WEND¶
```

```
  WHILE Gamma<0¶
     Gamma = Gamma + Pm2¶
  WEND¶
  WHILE Alpha>Pm2¶
     Alpha = Alpha - Pm2¶
  WEND¶
  WHILE Beta>Pm2¶
     Beta = Beta - Pm2¶
  WEND¶
  WHILE Gamma>Pm2¶
     Gamma = Gamma - Pm2¶
  WEND¶
  Sina=SIN(Alpha)¶
  Cosa=COS(Alpha)¶
  Sinb=SIN(Beta)¶
  Cosb=COS(Beta)¶
  Sinc=SIN(Gamma)¶
  Cosc=COS(Gamma)¶
¶
  Px=Hx+DPH*Cosa*Cosb     ' Projection point basedon the ¶
  Py=Hy+DPH*Sina*Cosb     ' main point and the spacings¶
  Pz=Hz+DPH*Sinb          ' DPH and Alpha, Beta and Gamma¶
RETURN                           ¶
'¶
```

We can also move around the main point with the projection point, which gives our stationary point.

3.1.2 Objects and Surfaces

Now that we can display points from the space onto the screen, we want to present these points as objects and surfaces.

The principle here is very simple. From given information about the objects and surfaces you calculate specific pixels and project these pixels on the screen. To complete the particular object, the program draws lines from one pixel to the next ("connecting the dots" using these lines).

We get this information about the individual bodies and surfaces from the array `K()` which was dimensioned with `Dim K(NumberK,5,2)`. The following diagrams show you how the individual array elements must look or which values they must contain to present a certain body or surface:

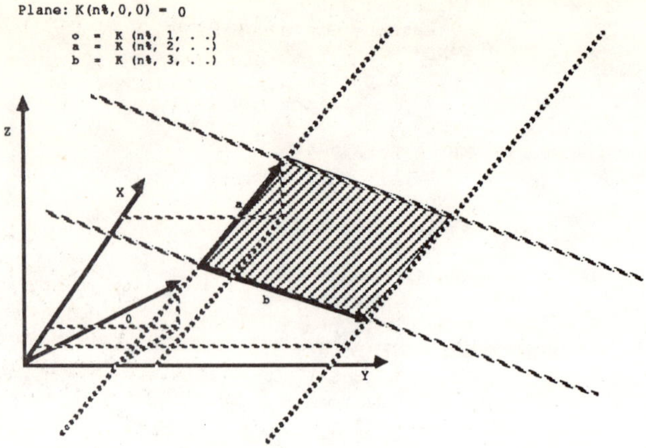

Figure 3.7

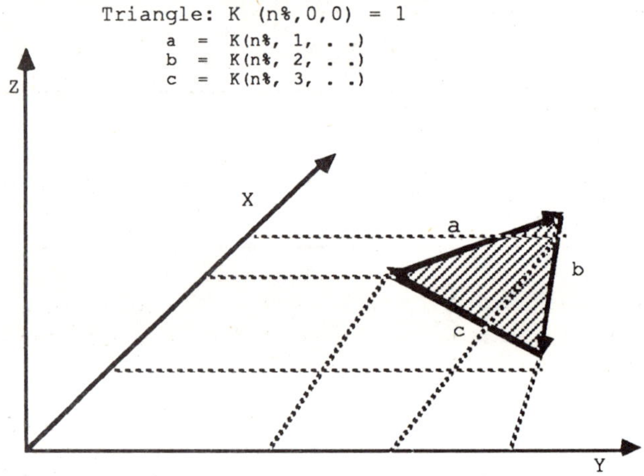

Figure 3.8

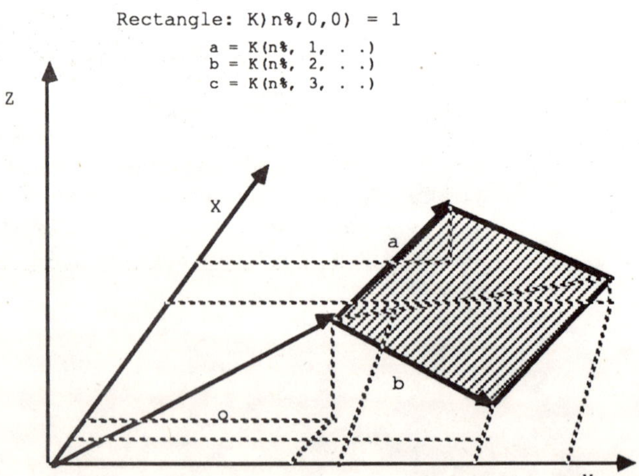

Figure 3.9

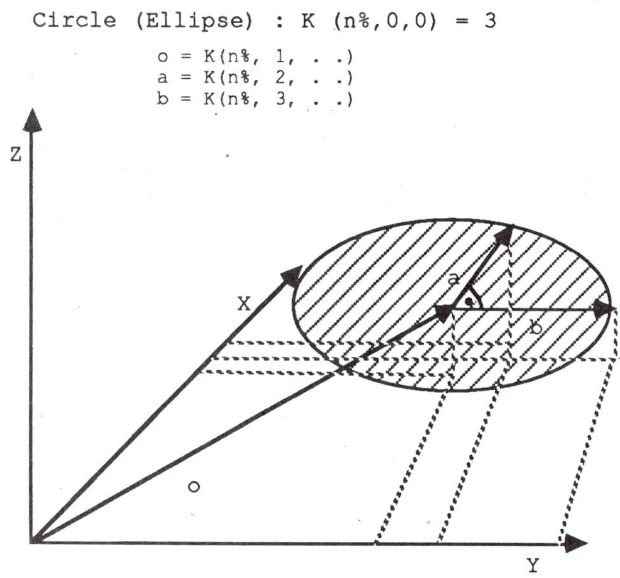

Figure 3.10

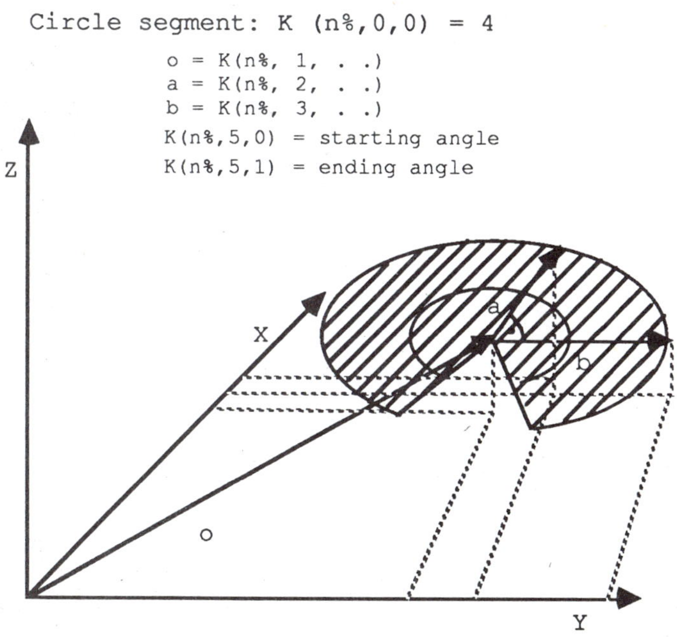

Figure 3.11

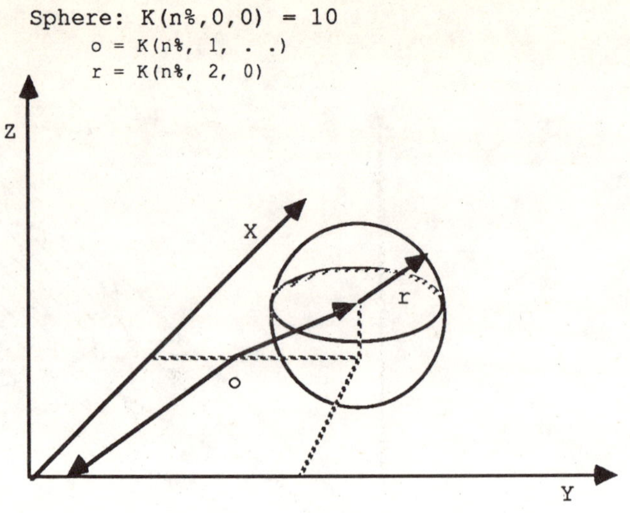

Figure 3.12

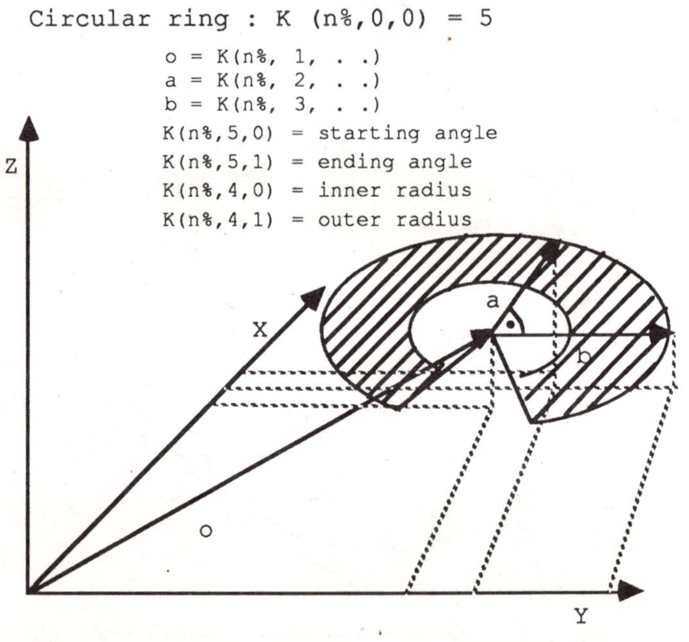

Figure 3.13

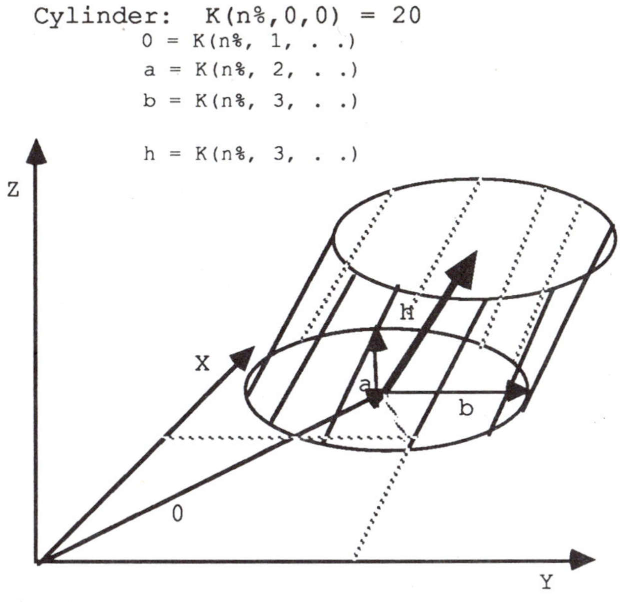

Figure 3.14

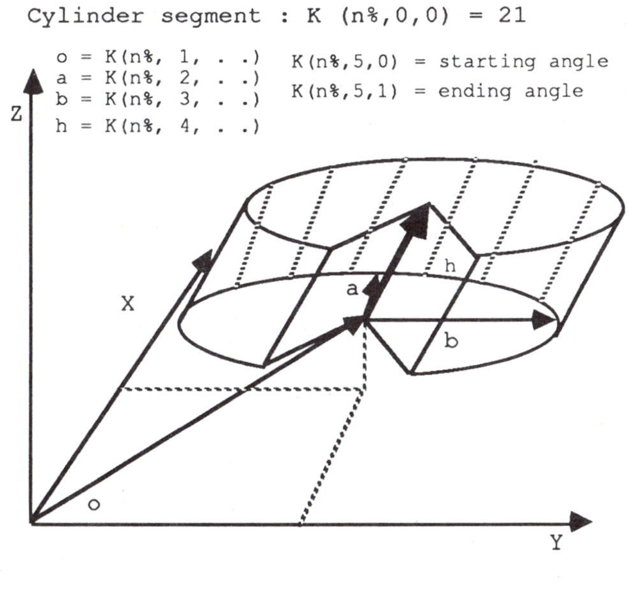

Figure 3.15

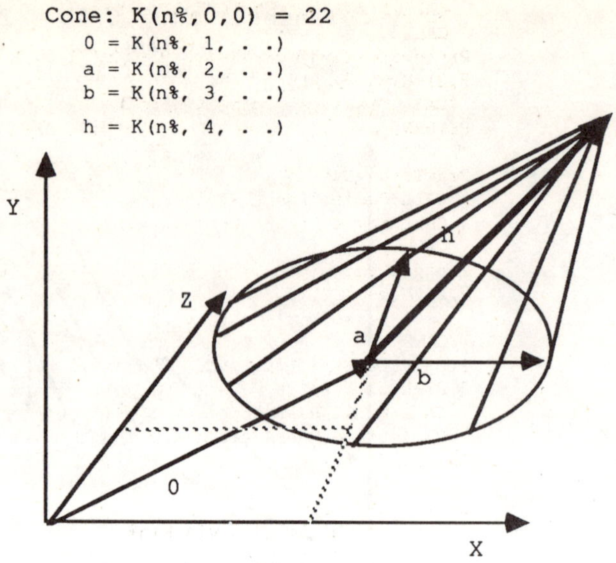

Figure 3.16

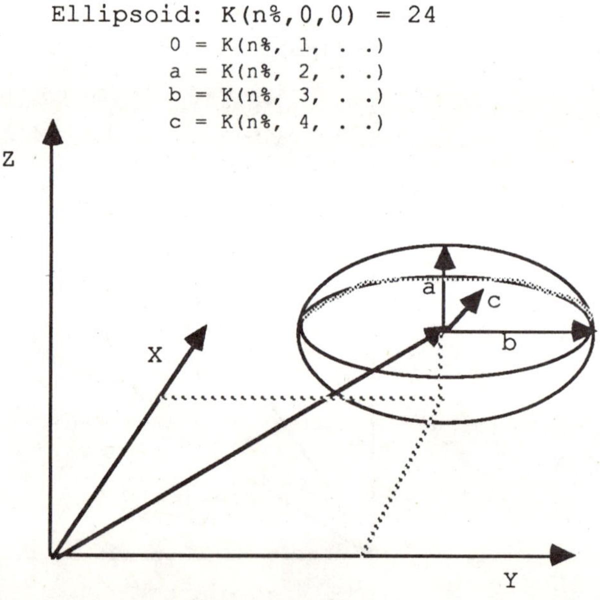

Figure 3.17

The following routines draw the characteristics of the individual objects and surfaces:

```
DrawPlane:¶
  CALL
Projection(Xp%,Yp%,K(n%,2,0)+K(n%,1,0),K(n%,2,1)+K(n%,1,1),K(n%,
2,2)+K(n%,1,2))¶
  CALL Move&(RastPort&,Xp%,Yp%)¶
  CALL Projection(Xp%,Yp%,K(n%,1,0),K(n%,1,1),K(n%,1,2))¶
```

```
  CALL Draw&(RastPort&,Xp%,Yp%)¶
  CALL
Projection(Xp%,Yp%,K(n%,3,0)+K(n%,1,0),K(n%,3,1)+K(n%,1,1),K(n%,
3,2)+K(n%,1,2))¶
  CALL Draw&(RastPort&,Xp%,Yp%)¶
RETURN¶
'¶
DrawTriangle:  ¶
  CALL Projection(x1%,y1%,K(n%,1,0),K(n%,1,1),K(n%,1,2))¶
  CALL Move&(RastPort&,x1%,y1%)¶
  CALL
Projection(Xp%,Yp%,K(n%,2,0)+K(n%,1,0),K(n%,2,1)+K(n%,1,1),K(n%,
2,2)+K(n%,1,2))¶
  CALL Draw&(RastPort&,Xp%,Yp%)¶
  CALL
Projection(Xp%,Yp%,K(n%,3,0)+K(n%,1,0),K(n%,3,1)+K(n%,1,1),K(n%,
3,2)+K(n%,1,2))¶
  CALL Draw&(RastPort&,Xp%,Yp%)¶
  CALL Draw&(RastPort&,x1%,y1%)¶
RETURN¶
'¶
DrawRectangle:¶
  CALL Projection(x1%,y1%,K(n%,1,0),K(n%,1,1),K(n%,1,2))¶
  CALL Move&(RastPort&,x1%,y1%)¶
  CALL
Projection(Xp%,Yp%,K(n%,2,0)+K(n%,1,0),K(n%,2,1)+K(n%,1,1),K(n%,
2,2)+K(n%,1,2))¶
  CALL Draw&(RastPort&,Xp%,Yp%)¶
  Dx=K(n%,2,0)+K(n%,3,0)+K(n%,1,0)¶
  Dy=K(n%,2,1)+K(n%,3,1)+K(n%,1,1)¶
  Dz=K(n%,2,2)+K(n%,3,2)+K(n%,1,2)¶
  CALL Projection(Xp%,Yp%,Dx,Dy,Dz)¶
  CALL Draw&(RastPort&,Xp%,Yp%)¶
  CALL
Projection(Xp%,Yp%,K(n%,3,0)+K(n%,1,0),K(n%,3,1)+K(n%,1,1),K(n%,
3,2)+K(n%,1,2))¶
  CALL Draw&(RastPort&,Xp%,Yp%)¶
  CALL Draw&(RastPort&,x1%,y1%)¶
RETURN¶
'¶
DrawCircle:¶
  CALL
Projection(Xp%,Yp%,K(n%,1,0)+K(n%,2,0),K(n%,1,1)+K(n%,2,1),K(n%,
1,2)+K(n%,2,2))¶
  ' SIN(0) = 0 and COS(0) = 1 goto K(n%,3,..), and K(n%,2,..)
takes over¶
  CALL Move&(RastPort&,Xp%,Yp%)¶
  w=Pm2/NumberSegments¶
  D=w¶
  Repeat1:¶
    Dx=K(n%,1,0)+K(n%,2,0)*COS(w)+K(n%,3,0)*SIN(w)¶
    Dy=K(n%,1,1)+K(n%,2,1)*COS(w)+K(n%,3,1)*SIN(w)¶
    Dz=K(n%,1,2)+K(n%,2,2)*COS(w)+K(n%,3,2)*SIN(w)¶
    CALL Projection(Xp%,Yp%,Dx,Dy,Dz)¶
    CALL Draw&(RastPort&,Xp%,Yp%)¶
    w = w+D¶
  IF (w<=Pm2+D/2) THEN GOTO Repeat1:¶
RETURN¶
'¶
DrawCircleSector:¶
  CALL Projection(x1%,y1%,K(n%,1,0),K(n%,1,1),K(n%,1,2))¶
  w=K(n%,5,0)¶
```

```
  Dx=K(n%,1,0)+K(n%,2,0)*COS(w)+K(n%,3,0)*SIN(w)¶
  Dy=K(n%,1,1)+K(n%,2,1)*COS(w)+K(n%,3,1)*SIN(w)¶
  Dz=K(n%,1,2)+K(n%,2,2)*COS(w)+K(n%,3,2)*SIN(w)¶
  CALL Projection(Xp%,Yp%,Dx,Dy,Dz)¶
  CALL Move&(RastPort&,x1%,y1%)¶
  CALL Draw&(RastPort&,Xp%,Yp%)¶
  D=Pm2/NumberSegments¶
  WHILE w<K(n%,5,1)¶
    w = w+D¶
    IF w>K(n%,5,1) THEN¶
      w=K(n%,5,1)¶
    END IF¶
    Dx=K(n%,1,0)+K(n%,2,0)*COS(w)+K(n%,3,0)*SIN(w)¶
    Dy=K(n%,1,1)+K(n%,2,1)*COS(w)+K(n%,3,1)*SIN(w)¶
    Dz=K(n%,1,2)+K(n%,2,2)*COS(w)+K(n%,3,2)*SIN(w)¶
    CALL Projection(Xp%,Yp%,Dx,Dy,Dz)¶
    CALL Draw&(RastPort&,Xp%,Yp%)¶
  WEND¶
  CALL Draw&(RastPort&,x1%,y1%)¶
RETURN¶
'¶
DrawCircleRing:¶
  w=K(n%,5,0)¶
  Dx=K(n%,1,0)+(K(n%,2,0)*COS(w)+K(n%,3,0)*SIN(w))*K(n%,4,0)¶
  Dy=K(n%,1,1)+(K(n%,2,1)*COS(w)+K(n%,3,1)*SIN(w))*K(n%,4,0)¶
  Dz=K(n%,1,2)+(K(n%,2,2)*COS(w)+K(n%,3,2)*SIN(w))*K(n%,4,0)¶
  CALL Projection(Xua%,Yua%,Dx,Dy,Dz)¶
  Dx=K(n%,1,0)+(K(n%,2,0)*COS(w)+K(n%,3,0)*SIN(w))*K(n%,4,1)¶
  Dy=K(n%,1,1)+(K(n%,2,1)*COS(w)+K(n%,3,1)*SIN(w))*K(n%,4,1)¶
  Dz=K(n%,1,2)+(K(n%,2,2)*COS(w)+K(n%,3,2)*SIN(w))*K(n%,4,1)¶
  CALL Projection(Xoa%,Yoa%,Dx,Dy,Dz)¶
  CALL Move&(RastPort&,Xua%,Yua%)¶
  CALL Draw&(RastPort&,Xoa%,Yoa%)¶
  D=Pm2/NumberSegments¶
  WHILE w<K(n%,5,1)¶
    w = w+D¶
    IF w>K(n%,5,1) THEN¶
      w=K(n%,5,1)¶
    END IF¶
    Dx=K(n%,1,0)+(K(n%,2,0)*COS(w)+K(n%,3,0)*SIN(w))*K(n%,4,0)¶
    Dy=K(n%,1,1)+(K(n%,2,1)*COS(w)+K(n%,3,1)*SIN(w))*K(n%,4,0)¶
    Dz=K(n%,1,2)+(K(n%,2,2)*COS(w)+K(n%,3,2)*SIN(w))*K(n%,4,0)¶
    CALL Projection(Xu%,Yu%,Dx,Dy,Dz)¶
    Dx=K(n%,1,0)+(K(n%,2,0)*COS(w)+K(n%,3,0)*SIN(w))*K(n%,4,1)¶
    Dy=K(n%,1,1)+(K(n%,2,1)*COS(w)+K(n%,3,1)*SIN(w))*K(n%,4,1)¶
    Dz=K(n%,1,2)+(K(n%,2,2)*COS(w)+K(n%,3,2)*SIN(w))*K(n%,4,1)¶
    CALL Projection(Xp%,Yp%,Dx,Dy,Dz)¶
    CALL Move&(RastPort&,Xua%,Yua%)¶
    CALL Draw&(RastPort&,Xu%,Yu%)¶
    CALL Move&(RastPort&,Xp%,Yp%)¶
    CALL Draw&(RastPort&,Xoa%,Yoa%)¶
    Xua%=Xu%¶
    Yua%=Yu%¶
    Xoa%=Xp%¶
    Yoa%=Yp%¶
  WEND¶
  CALL Move&(RastPort&,Xua%,Yua%)¶
  CALL Draw&(RastPort&,Xoa%,Yoa%)¶
RETURN¶
'¶
DrawSphere:¶
  D=Pm2/NumberSegments¶
```

```
    FOR w1=-Pd2+D TO Pd2-D/2 STEP D¶
      Dx=K(n%,1,0)¶
      Dy=K(n%,1,1)+K(n%,2,0)*COS(w1)¶
      Dz=K(n%,1,2)+K(n%,2,0)*SIN(w1)¶
      CALL Projection(Xp%,Yp%,Dx,Dy,Dz)¶
      CALL Move&(RastPort&,Xp%,Yp%)¶
      FOR w2=D TO Pm2+D/2 STEP D¶
        Dx=K(n%,1,0)+K(n%,2,0)*SIN(w2)*COS(w1)¶
        Dy=K(n%,1,1)+K(n%,2,0)*COS(w2)*COS(w1)¶
        Dz=K(n%,1,2)+K(n%,2,0)*SIN(w1)¶
        CALL Projection(Xp%,Yp%,Dx,Dy,Dz)¶
        CALL Draw&(RastPort&,Xp%,Yp%)¶
      NEXT w2¶
    NEXT w1¶
    FOR w1=-Pd2+D TO Pd2-D/2 STEP D¶
      Dy=K(n%,1,1)¶
      Dz=K(n%,1,2)+K(n%,2,0)*COS(w1)¶
      Dx=K(n%,1,0)+K(n%,2,0)*SIN(w1)¶
      CALL Projection(Xp%,Yp%,Dx,Dy,Dz)¶
      CALL Move&(RastPort&,Xp%,Yp%)¶
      FOR w2=D TO Pm2+D/2 STEP D¶
        Dy=K(n%,1,1)+K(n%,2,0)*SIN(w2)*COS(w1)¶
        Dz=K(n%,1,2)+K(n%,2,0)*COS(w2)*COS(w1)¶
        Dx=K(n%,1,0)+K(n%,2,0)*SIN(w1)¶
        CALL Projection(Xp%,Yp%,Dx,Dy,Dz)¶
        CALL Draw&(RastPort&,Xp%,Yp%)¶
      NEXT w2¶
    NEXT w1¶
  RETURN¶
  '¶
  DrawCylinder:¶
    Dx=K(n%,1,0)+K(n%,2,0)¶
    Dy=K(n%,1,1)+K(n%,2,1)¶
    Dz=K(n%,1,2)+K(n%,2,2)¶
    CALL Projection(Xua%,Yua%,Dx,Dy,Dz)¶
    Dx=K(n%,1,0)+K(n%,2,0)+K(n%,4,0)¶
    Dy=K(n%,1,1)+K(n%,2,1)+K(n%,4,1)¶
    Dz=K(n%,1,2)+K(n%,2,2)+K(n%,4,2)¶
    CALL Projection(Xoa%,Yoa%,Dx,Dy,Dz)¶
    D=Pm2/NumberSegments¶
    FOR w=D TO Pm2+D/2 STEP D¶
      Dx=K(n%,1,0)+K(n%,2,0)*COS(w)+K(n%,3,0)*SIN(w)¶
      Dy=K(n%,1,1)+K(n%,2,1)*COS(w)+K(n%,3,1)*SIN(w)¶
      Dz=K(n%,1,2)+K(n%,2,2)*COS(w)+K(n%,3,2)*SIN(w)¶
      CALL Projection(Xu%,Yu%,Dx,Dy,Dz)¶
      Dx=K(n%,1,0)+K(n%,2,0)*COS(w)+K(n%,3,0)*SIN(w)+K(n%,4,0)¶
      Dy=K(n%,1,1)+K(n%,2,1)*COS(w)+K(n%,3,1)*SIN(w)+K(n%,4,1)¶
      Dz=K(n%,1,2)+K(n%,2,2)*COS(w)+K(n%,3,2)*SIN(w)+K(n%,4,2)¶
      CALL Projection(Xp%,Yp%,Dx,Dy,Dz)¶
      CALL Move&(RastPort&,Xua%,Yua%)¶
      CALL Draw&(RastPort&,Xu%,Yu%)¶
      CALL Draw&(RastPort&,Xp%,Yp%)¶
      CALL Draw&(RastPort&,Xoa%,Yoa%)¶
      Xua%=Xu%¶
      Yua%=Yu%¶
      Xoa%=Xp%¶
      Yoa%=Yp%¶
    NEXT w¶
  RETURN¶
  '¶
  DrawCylinderSegm:¶
    w=K(n%,5,0)¶
```

```
    Dx=K(n%,1,0)+K(n%,2,0)*COS(w)+K(n%,3,0)*SIN(w)¶
    Dy=K(n%,1,1)+K(n%,2,1)*COS(w)+K(n%,3,1)*SIN(w)¶
    Dz=K(n%,1,2)+K(n%,2,2)*COS(w)+K(n%,3,2)*SIN(w)¶
    CALL Projection(Xua%,Yua%,Dx,Dy,Dz)¶
    Dx=K(n%,1,0)+K(n%,2,0)*COS(w)+K(n%,3,0)*SIN(w)+K(n%,4,0)¶
    Dy=K(n%,1,1)+K(n%,2,1)*COS(w)+K(n%,3,1)*SIN(w)+K(n%,4,1)¶
    Dz=K(n%,1,2)+K(n%,2,2)*COS(w)+K(n%,3,2)*SIN(w)+K(n%,4,2)¶
    CALL Projection(Xoa%,Yoa%,Dx,Dy,Dz)¶
    CALL Move&(RastPort&,Xua%,Yua%)¶
    CALL Draw&(RastPort&,Xoa%,Yoa%)¶
    D=Pm2/NumberSegments¶
    WHILE w<K(n%,5,1)¶
      w = w+D¶
      IF w>K(n%,5,1) THEN¶
        w=K(n%,5,1)¶
      END IF¶
      Dx=K(n%,1,0)+K(n%,2,0)*COS(w)+K(n%,3,0)*SIN(w)¶
      Dy=K(n%,1,1)+K(n%,2,1)*COS(w)+K(n%,3,1)*SIN(w)¶
      Dz=K(n%,1,2)+K(n%,2,2)*COS(w)+K(n%,3,2)*SIN(w)¶
      CALL Projection(Xu%,Yu%,Dx,Dy,Dz)¶
      Dx=K(n%,1,0)+K(n%,2,0)*COS(w)+K(n%,3,0)*SIN(w)+K(n%,4,0)¶
      Dy=K(n%,1,1)+K(n%,2,1)*COS(w)+K(n%,3,1)*SIN(w)+K(n%,4,1)¶
      Dz=K(n%,1,2)+K(n%,2,2)*COS(w)+K(n%,3,2)*SIN(w)+K(n%,4,2)¶
      CALL Projection(Xp%,Yp%,Dx,Dy,Dz)¶
      CALL Move&(RastPort&,Xua%,Yua%)¶
      CALL Draw&(RastPort&,Xu%,Yu%)¶
      CALL Draw&(RastPort&,Xp%,Yp%)¶
      CALL Draw&(RastPort&,Xoa%,Yoa%)¶
      Xua%=Xu%¶
      Yua%=Yu%¶
      Xoa%=Xp%¶
      Yoa%=Yp%¶
    WEND¶
  RETURN¶
  '¶
  DrawCone:¶
    CALL
Projection(x1%,y1%,K(n%,1,0)+K(n%,4,0),K(n%,1,1)+K(n%,4,1),K(n%,
1,2)+K(n%,4,2))¶
    CALL
Projection(Xp%,Yp%,K(n%,1,0)+K(n%,2,0),K(n%,1,1)+K(n%,2,1),K(n%,
1,2)+K(n%,2,2))¶
    CALL Move&(RastPort&,Xp%,Yp%)¶
    D=Pm2/NumberSegments¶
    FOR w=D TO Pm2+D/2 STEP D¶
      Dx=K(n%,1,0)+K(n%,2,0)*COS(w)+K(n%,3,0)*SIN(w)¶
      Dy=K(n%,1,1)+K(n%,2,1)*COS(w)+K(n%,3,1)*SIN(w)¶
      Dz=K(n%,1,2)+K(n%,2,2)*COS(w)+K(n%,3,2)*SIN(w)¶
      CALL Projection(Xp%,Yp%,Dx,Dy,Dz)¶
      CALL Draw&(RastPort&,Xp%,Yp%)¶
      CALL Move&(RastPort&,x1%,y1%)¶
      CALL Draw&(RastPort&,Xp%,Yp%)¶
    NEXT w¶
  RETURN¶
  '¶
  DrawEllipsoid:¶
    D=Pm2/NumberSegments¶
    FOR w1=-Pd2+D TO Pd2-D/2 STEP D¶
      Dx=K(n%,1,0)+K(n%,2,0)*COS(w1)+K(n%,4,0)*SIN(w1)¶
      Dy=K(n%,1,1)+K(n%,2,1)*COS(w1)+K(n%,4,1)*SIN(w1)¶
      Dz=K(n%,1,2)+K(n%,2,2)*COS(w1)+K(n%,4,2)*SIN(w1)¶
      CALL Projection(Xp%,Yp%,Dx,Dy,Dz)¶
```

```
    CALL Move&(RastPort&,Xp%,Yp%)¶
    FOR w2=D TO Pm2+D/2 STEP D¶

Dx=K(n%,1,0)+K(n%,2,0)*COS(w1)*COS(w2)+K(n%,3,0)*COS(w1)*SIN(w2)
+K(n%,4,0)*SIN(w1)¶

Dy=K(n%,1,1)+K(n%,2,1)*COS(w1)*COS(w2)+K(n%,3,1)*COS(w1)*SIN(w2)
+K(n%,4,1)*SIN(w1)¶

Dz=K(n%,1,2)+K(n%,2,2)*COS(w1)*COS(w2)+K(n%,3,2)*COS(w1)*SIN(w2)
+K(n%,4,2)*SIN(w1)¶
      CALL Projection(Xp%,Yp%,Dx,Dy,Dz)¶
      CALL Draw&(RastPort&,Xp%,Yp%)¶
    NEXT w2¶
  NEXT w1¶
  FOR w1=-Pd2+D TO Pd2-D/2 STEP D¶
    Dx=K(n%,1,0)+K(n%,2,0)*COS(w1)+K(n%,3,0)*SIN(w1)¶
    Dy=K(n%,1,1)+K(n%,2,1)*COS(w1)+K(n%,3,1)*SIN(w1)¶
    Dz=K(n%,1,2)+K(n%,2,2)*COS(w1)+K(n%,3,2)*SIN(w1)¶
    CALL Projection(Xp%,Yp%,Dx,Dy,Dz)¶
    CALL Move&(RastPort&,Xp%,Yp%)¶
    FOR w2=D TO Pm2+D/2 STEP D¶

Dx=K(n%,1,0)+K(n%,2,0)*COS(w1)*COS(w2)+K(n%,4,0)*COS(w1)*SIN(w2)
+K(n%,3,0)*SIN(w1)¶

Dy=K(n%,1,1)+K(n%,2,1)*COS(w1)*COS(w2)+K(n%,4,1)*COS(w1)*SIN(w2)
+K(n%,3,1)*SIN(w1)¶

Dz=K(n%,1,2)+K(n%,2,2)*COS(w1)*COS(w2)+K(n%,4,2)*COS(w1)*SIN(w2)
+K(n%,3,2)*SIN(w1)¶
      CALL Projection(Xp%,Yp%,Dx,Dy,Dz)¶
      CALL Draw&(RastPort&,Xp%,Yp%)¶
    NEXT w2¶
  NEXT w1¶
RETURN¶
'¶
'¶
```

Now for a word about circle presentation. The routines dealing with circles (almost everything except `DrawPlane`, `DrawRectangle`, and `DrawTriangle`) calculate the circle points in the same way: The segment points of the circle periphery are calculated depending on an angle. The more segment points, the rounder the circle.

The rounder the circle, the longer the computation time involved. We have limited the number of segment points of a circle to save time. When the shadow routines are called we will get completely round circles. The variable `NumberSegments` corresponds to the roundness of a circle:

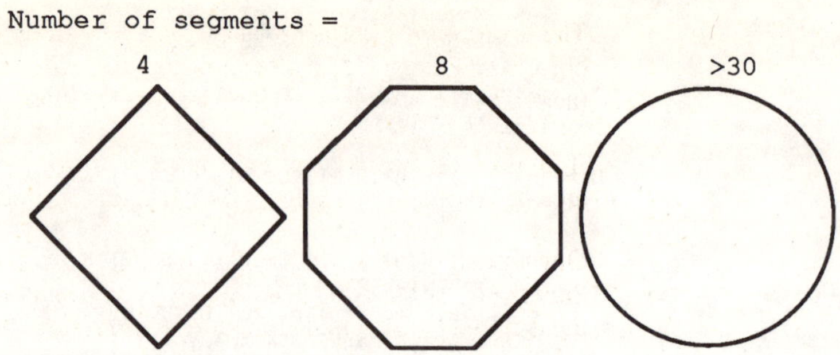

Figure 3.18

Back to object and surface presentation: The abovementioned Draw... routines are individul subroutines. What calls the individual routines? The following routine jumps to the corresponding Draw... routine with the help of K(n%,0,0):

```
DrawAll:¶
  ' Draw routine for calling each figure¶
  FOR n%=1 TO NumberK¶
    IF K(n%,0,0)=0 THEN¶
      GOSUB DrawPlane¶
    END IF¶
    IF K(n%,0,0)=1 THEN¶
      GOSUB DrawTriangle¶
    END IF¶
    IF K(n%,0,0)=2 THEN¶
      GOSUB DrawRectangle¶
    END IF¶
    IF K(n%,0,0)=3 THEN¶
      GOSUB DrawCircle¶
    END IF¶
    IF K(n%,0,0)=4 THEN¶
      GOSUB DrawCircleSector¶
    END IF¶
    IF K(n%,0,0)=5 THEN¶
      GOSUB DrawCircleRing¶
    END IF¶
    IF K(n%,0,0)=10 THEN¶
      GOSUB DrawSphere¶
    END IF¶
    IF K(n%,0,0)=20 THEN¶
      GOSUB DrawCylinder¶
    END IF¶
    IF K(n%,0,0)=21 THEN¶
      GOSUB DrawCylinderSegm¶
    END IF¶
    IF K(n%,0,0)=22 THEN¶
      GOSUB DrawCone¶
    END IF¶
    IF K(n%,0,0)=24 THEN¶
      GOSUB DrawEllipsoid¶
    END IF¶
  NEXT n%¶
RETURN¶
'¶
```

The DrawNew routine ensures that the screen is cleared before any objects are displayed, and takes all of the necessary steps before the call (activates the screen, waits for a key and returns to the user screen).

If none of the parameters (Projection point, Main point, etc.) are changed in the meantime, the picture is not refreshed.

Our tracer program allows you to choose backgrounds for your drawings. Should you choose a new background for the picture because the original background color is too distracting, DrawNew provides for this by clearing the background. The picture then appears over the selected background:

```
DrawNew:¶
  IF (Hg = False) AND (Newone! = True) THEN  ' no Background¶
    CALL SetRast&(RastPort&,0)              ' but new drawing¶
  END IF                                    ' => clear screen¶
  ¶
  CALL Scron  ¶
¶
  IF (Newone! = True) OR (Hg = True) THEN    ' Background and
New drawing¶
    GOSUB DeleteMenu¶
    RetRast& = RastPort&                  ' reserve RastPort ¶
    RastPort& = WINDOW(8)                 ' In Window-RastPort
(GIMMEZERO Window!)¶
    CALL SetAPen&(RastPort&,1)            ' the new Screens¶
    GOSUB DrawAll                       ' draw (because of Clipping)¶
    RastPort& = RetRast&¶
    BEEP¶
  END IF¶
  ¶
  IF WaitFlg! = True THEN                 ' wait for mouse or key
press¶
     GOSUB Pause                          ¶
     CALL Scroff¶
  END IF¶
¶
  IF (Newone! = True) OR (Hg = True) THEN¶
    Newone! = False                          ' Redraw picture ¶
    Hg = False                             ' and "paint over"¶
    GOSUB MakeMenu                         ' background ¶
  END IF¶
RETURN¶
'¶
```

3.2 The Editor

3.2.1 Why an Editor?

Our goal is to design a program that calculates any picture that is made up of simple objects and display it in 3D. The previous section described which objects and which data are needed to do this. It is also known that this data is stored in the arrays `K!` and `MAT!`. Now, how do we insert the data for our picture into this array? Many different methods are available.

One solution would be to manually calculate all of the data and enter it as program lines, then read the data with a corresponding routine. This is the easiest to implement, but the hardest to test. The advantage: you save a lot of time in program development. The disadvantage: the user must have the finished picture in mind and enter it by hand, and then he has no control over whether the data complies with his image.

It is also possibile to save the calculated numbers into a separate file with the help of a word processor. The program then reads these lines into memory. The disadvantage shown above applies to this case as well.

It would be better to enter the values into the computer and display these values graphically. This is done using a simple menu driven program which displays the data input as three pictures, and lets you make corrections. The next section shows how to do this in BASIC.

3.2.2 The Tasks Required of the Editor

Once the larger programming objective is established, all of the detail work is before us. All of the desired values and features of this editor must also be determined. For this we divide the editor into its individual, logical, and functional sections, called modules. The main task of the editor is to read in numerical data. We must add input and output procedures for this. Since we want this data presented both as numbers and as a wire model, the corresponding procedures must be developed. Some additional functions are used; they are not necessary, but make the program more user friendly. The individual modules are explained in the following sections.

The graphic output

The graphic presentation cannot be displayed as a finished three dimensonal graphic complete with light, shadows, hidden lines, or reflections. This would take far too much computation time. On the other hand, displaying the graphic as a wire model in perspective in the editor is possible but not to our advantage. The details would be barely recognizable and perspective would be distorted. We reserve both the wire model in perspective and the final shadowed graphic for our ray tracing program.

The method that shows the user input fastest and easiest is the projection of bodies from the three main views. The object appears in front, side, and top views, like a standard technical drawing. The front view is equivalent to the `xz` plane, the side view of the projection is equivalent to the `yz` plane, and the top view is equivalent to the projection of the `xy` plane. The illustration below shows perspective (1), top (2), side (3) and front (4) views of a simple 3D house:

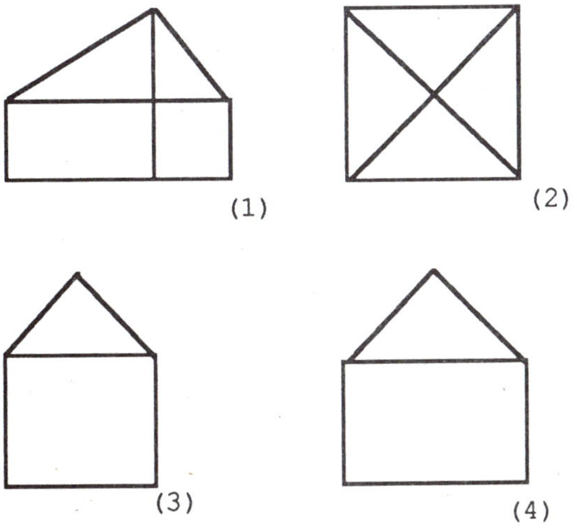

Figure 3.19

These three views are displayed in three windows at the same time. Because the screen doesn't divide very well into three sections, we divide it into quarters and have one section for data entry and text output. The windows are very small, but the user can enlarge and move them. It must also be possible to move and enlarge the section where the individual window is displayed so that large objects can be entered and that details can be recognized. The following example should make this clear.

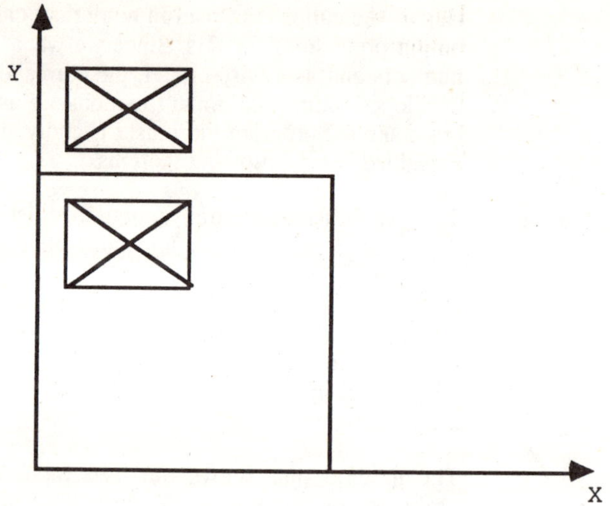

Figure 3.20

The rectangle surrounding the lower house represents the window; the lower house is visible, the house above remains hidden. By moving the border in the Y direction, the second house becomes visible:

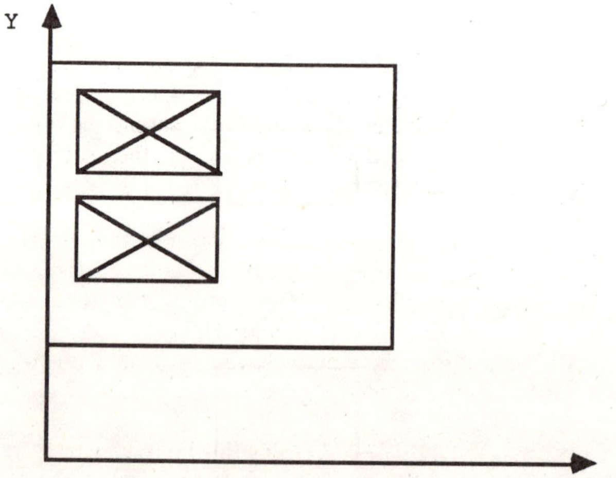

Figure 3.21

The section is made clear by examining the position of the upper left hand corner. In the first case this corner is (0,28,0) and in the second case it is (0,42,0).

Data input and output

A program should be designed so that the inexperienced user can easily use it, recognize incorrect input, and correct data already entered. The interface between the user and the program provides the use of menus on the Amiga.

Direct input of data is also required. In our editor program you can, for example, enter data at the following text:

```
Body  :1 Sphere
visible   :_    Material :_
M :__,__,__
r :__
```

This input could achieved using the `INPUT` statement. We don't advise this because you have no control over the entered characters. Writing your own routine that gives you control of the entered characters is a better solution. Besides correcting data, manipulating the entered data in our program would be very helpful. By manipulation we mean rotating, moving, enlarging and copying an object. Naturally old data sets must be either redisplayed or deleted. Adding the mouse as an input device eases the use of the editor. The mouse makes it possible to simply click on the necessary coordinates. You don't have to manually compute them and enter them in the computer through the keyboard.

Additional features

What most professional Amiga applications have in common is the ability to use gadgets (objects on the screen that can be selected with the mouse, such as sliders, text gadgets, etc.). Programming gadgets in AmigaBASIC can be complicated, but it makes the program easier for the average person to use.

One final point: The editor must make it easy to change a graphic made of many objects. If the user has a graphic made of 253 different objects, and object 253 is incorrect, should the user re-enter all 253 objects? No. We added a function that lets the user view each object, change it, and save it for later recall.

The abovementioned features have almost completely described our editor program; only the realization is missing. One possibility for programming such an editor is listed completely in the appendices. The following sections describes the most important routines of this editor. From these routines we can create a relatively simple and fast editor for creating 3D objects.

The optional disk for this book contains the sample editor program that is listed in the appendices. Section 4.1 of this book contains a brief usage guide for this editor. We recommend that you look at this program to get a feel of what is in store in the next pages. Before you put the book aside to get to work on your Amiga, we should offer you the following tip in case you have difficulties with the abovementioned projects. The optional disk has a data file named `House`. You must execute the following procedure to view this file from the optional disk:

```
1. Load AmigaBASIC
2. enter CLEAR,120000
3. enter LOAD "editor.bas"
4. start the program (with RUN)
5. wait a few seconds-be patient
6. select "Load List" from the "Disk" menu
7. type house and press RETURN
8. press CTRL-R
9. wait some more
10. look around (e.g., section)
```

3.2.3 Individual Components of the Editor

The following sections describe each module, refine them, and show them in BASIC program form. Then the long-range goals and associated problems are presented, and the simplest procedures solved. For example, the input module includes a procedure for reading the keyboard. This procedure comes from a normal string input routine, from which the input procedure for a real number is supported which is finally called from the procedure to read a vector. This principle of development allows the creation of more complex algorithms in the rest of the chapter.

3.2.3.1 The Input

When a number is entered in a program, an input error may occur if "onehundred23", "1a23" or something similar is entered. The input routine should make sure that the only active key is the one the user pressed. The <Delete>, <Backspace>, <Cursor left>, <Cursor right> and <Return> keys function as usual.

The INPUT routine of BASIC is unusable here. The procedure used instead of the INPUT routine is called `getstring`. It reads a variable length string from a certain place on the screen and places this string in a window. The character string can be scrolled left and right within this window.

To read a character string there must be a routine that sets the cursor on the screen, waits for a keypress, then erases the cursor. To display the cursor at a certain point on the screen, the character width and height must be known. This is dependent on the chosen character set. The important information for this is in the `RastPort` data structure. To explain what this has to do with the `RastPort` data structure and how it is constructed would be outside the realm of this book. It is important for our purposes that the character height and width can be found as follows:

```
rp&=WINDOW(8)     'take the pointer from RASTPORT
cw%=PEEKW(rp&+60)'character width
ch%=PEEKW(rp&+58)   'character height
```

Now to display the cursor so that the characters under the cursor remain readable, the screen section must be inverted. This is done simply with `SETDRMD`, a function that is found in the `graphics.library` and linked to our program with (our disk name is Tracer and the bmap files are located in the `libs` directory):

```
LIBRARY "Tracer:/graphics.library"
```

After this preparation the routine is simply:

```
SUB setcursor(z,s) STATIC¶
'TASK      :set cursor at specified position¶
'PARAMETER:=>z line¶
'             s column¶
  SHARED cw%,ch%¶
  CALL setdrmd&(WINDOW(8),2)¶
  LINE (s*cw%-cw%,z*ch%-ch%-1)-(s*cw%,z*ch%-1),3,bf¶
  CALL setdrmd&(WINDOW(8),1)¶
END SUB  ¶B
```

When `setcursor` is called twice with the same parameters, the cursor is erased again and the characters under it are presented normally:

```
SUB getkey(a$,z,s)STATIC¶
'TASK      :Read one character in¶
'PARAMETER:=>z line¶
'             s column¶
'           <=a$ pressed key¶
  CALL setcursor(z,s) ¶
  a$=""¶
  WHILE a$=""¶
    a$=INKEY$¶
  WEND¶
  CALL setcursor(z,s)¶
END SUB¶
¶
```

These two procedures are used in the procedure `getstring`. This routine requires the old contents of the string, the keypress, the allowable characters, window position, and window length. Passing the routine the old string contents allows changes to an existing character string without re-entering the string's contents.

```
SUB getstring(old$,a$,z$,z,s,inplen)STATIC¶
```

```
'TASK      :Reads two strings which can be edited from the input¶
'           line using cursor left/right,backspace and delete.¶
'           In addition the string scrolls when the input ¶
'           extends past the screen line ¶
'PARAMETER:=>old$ old value of string to be read¶
'             a$ key pressed ¶
'             z$ valid characters¶
'             z line¶
'             s column¶
'             inplen    Lenght of inout window¶
'           <=old$ specified  string¶
  IF inplen   =1 THEN 'if only one char entered? => no Return¶
    old$=a$¶
    WHILE INSTR(z$,old$)=0¶
      CALL getkey(old$,z,s)¶
    WEND¶
    LOCATE z,s¶
    PRINT old$¶
  ELSE¶
    i=1        'points to current string position¶
    position=1 'points to current screen position¶
    WHILE ASC(a$)><13¶
      IF INSTR(z$,a$)><0 THEN 'valid character?¶
        old$=LEFT$(old$,i-1)+a$+RIGHT$(old$,LEN(old$)-i+1)      ¶
        i=i+1¶
        position=position+1¶
        IF position>inplen    THEN¶
          position=inplen   ¶
        END IF  ¶
      ELSE ¶
        IF ASC(a$)=30 AND i<=LEN(old$) THEN  'Cursor right?¶
          i=i+1¶
          position=position+1¶
          IF position>inplen    THEN¶
            position=inplen   ¶
          END IF  ¶
        ELSE¶
          IF ASC(a$)=31 AND i>1 THEN 'Cursor left?¶
            i=i-1¶
            position=position-1¶
            IF position=0 THEN¶
              position=1¶
            END IF  ¶
          ELSE¶
            IF ASC(a$)=127 AND i<=LEN(old$) THEN  'delete ?¶
              old$=LEFT$(old$,i-1)+RIGHT$(old$,LEN(old$)-i)¶
            ELSE¶
              IF ASC(a$)=8 AND i>1 THEN  'Backspace ?¶
                i=i-1¶
                position=position-1¶
                IF position=0 THEN¶
                  position=1¶
                END IF¶
                old$=LEFT$(old$,i-1)+RIGHT$(old$,LEN(old$)-i)¶
              END IF¶
            END IF¶
          END IF¶
        END IF¶
      END IF¶
      LOCATE z,s¶
      PRINT MID$(old$+" ",i-position+1,inplen    )  'String
output¶
```

```
      CALL getkey(a$,z,s+position-1) 'get next key¶
    WEND ¶
  END IF¶
  IF i><position THEN¶
    CALL putstring(old$,z,s,inplen   )¶
  END IF  ¶
END SUB¶
¶
```

Next we examine if the length is equal to one or not. If so, it waits for a valid key and returns this, and in the other case the characters are read until the user presses the <Return> key. Each character is checked to see if one of the following five cases occurs:

1.) Valid characters (in `z$`), then INSTR(`z$,a$`) is unequal to zero and the characters are inserted in the corresponding place in `old$`. Then `i` and `position` must be increased to `ine`

2.) <Cursor right>, then `i` and `position` are increased by one

3.) <Cursor left>, `i` and `position` are lowered by one. I is important to make sure that these two varaibles do not take on an invalid value

4.) <Delete>, here the `i`th characters are removed from `old$`

5.) <Backspace>, a combination of <Cursor left> and <Delete>

The entire valid area of the string is displayed and the routine waits for the next key. When the user presses <Return>, the length of the characters is given. The `putstring` routine (described later in this section) is used.

The following routine simplifies the input of integers and real values:

```
SUB getreal(i!,a$,z,s,inplen   ,unt!,ob!) STATIC¶
'TASK      :Read in real value¶
'PARAMETER:=>i! old value¶
'             a$ pressed key¶
'             z line¶
'             s column¶
'             inplen    length of input line¶
'             unt! upper limit¶
'             ob! lower limit¶
'           <=i! specified value¶
  CALL conrealstr(i!,j$)¶
loop1:   ¶
  i$=j$¶
  CALL getstring(i$,a$,"1234567890-.",z,s,inplen   )¶
  j$=i$¶
  CALL constrreal(i$,i!)¶
  IF i$="" OR i!<unt! OR i!>ob! THEN¶
    a$=" "¶
    GOTO loop1¶
  END IF¶
END SUB¶
¶
```

The routine for reading an integer value is identical to the above routine, the only difference appearing in the call of `getstring` ("." is allowed in `getreal` but not in `getint`). The statement of the value range is necessary for the parameters already known, as well as the upper and lower limits of all valid numbers (`unt!,ob!`). Both procedures use two routines that have not been mentioned till now: the conversion routines `conrealstr` and `constrreal`:

```
SUB conrealstr(i!,i$)STATIC¶
'TASK      :convert real value into string¶
'           rounded to 3 decimal places¶
'PARAMETER:=>i! the real value¶
'           <=i$ the string¶
  i$=STR$(i!)¶
  j!=FIX(1000!*i!+.5*SGN(i!))/1000! 'round¶
  i$=STR$(j!)¶
  IF ABS(j!)>0 AND ABS(j!)<1 THEN  'if 0<j!<1 0 inserted¶
    i$=MID$(i$,1,1)+"0"+MID$(i$,2,LEN(i$))¶
  END IF¶
  IF j!>=0 THEN  'if 0<=j! truncate first place¶
    i$=RIGHT$(i$,LEN(i$)-1)¶
  END IF¶
END SUB¶
¶
SUB constrreal(i$,i!) STATIC¶
'TASK      :convert string into real value¶
'PARAMETER:=>i$ the string¶
'           <=i! the real value¶
'              i$ if conversion error i$=""¶
  i!=VAL(i$)¶
  IF i!>=0 THEN¶
    IF i!>0 AND i!<1 THEN¶
      i$=" "+RIGHT$(i$,LEN(i$)-1) 'insert space and cutoff 0¶
    ELSE  ¶
      i$=" "+i$  'insert space¶
    END IF¶
  END IF¶
  j!=i!-FIX(i!*1000!)/1000! 'round ¶
  IF i$><STR$(i!) OR j!><0 THEN 'Error ?¶
    i$=""¶
  END IF ¶
END SUB¶
¶
```

Notice that real values in both procedures have only three places after the decimal point, and the values whose sums lie between zero and one have a preceding zero. When the input does not satisfy these requirements, the `constrreal` routine makes the empty character string the output value for `i$`, as the result of incorrect input. The restriction to three places after the decimal point is necessary because exact input values change minutely when calculating the graphic later.

Besides character strings, integer and real numbers in our program need vectors as input. It is practical to write individual input procedures for these objects. A vector is presented by three real numbers separated by commas. We use the conversion routines (`con3realstr` and `constr3real`) in the input procedure, and for the first time the mouse position emerges, because mouse input is allowed. This only works when reading room coordinate vectors and not angle vectors. An additional parameter tells the procedure whether mouse input is allowed or not. The mouse position is stored in the global variables called `mox!`, `moy!` and `moz!`. To let the procedure know that the keyboard input doesn't count, we press <Return> and no other keys. And now the routine:

```
SUB get3real(i1!,i2!,i3!,a$,z,s,inplen    ,unt!,ob!,modus)
STATIC¶
'TASK      :read 3 Real values in¶
'PARAMETER:=>i1!,i2!,i3! old value¶
'             a$ key pressed¶
'             z line¶
'             s column¶
'             inplen    Lenght of input line¶
'             unt! lower limit¶
'             ob! upper limit¶
'             modus if=0  no mouse entry¶
'                   if=-1 mouse input  (position vector)¶
'                   if>0  mouse inout  (Difference vector)¶
'           <=i1!,i2!,i3! specified value¶
  SHARED mox!,moy!,moz!,k!()¶
  CALL con3realstr(i1!,i2!,i3!,j$)¶
  IF a$="" THEN¶
    CALL getkey(a$,z,s)¶
  END IF  ¶
  IF ASC(a$)=13 AND modus><0 THEN¶
    IF modus=-1 THEN¶
      i1!=mox!¶
      i2!=moy!¶
      i3!=moz!¶
    ELSE¶
      i1!=mox!-k!(modus,1,0)¶
      i2!=moy!-k!(modus,1,1)¶
      i3!=moz!-k!(modus,1,2)¶
    END IF¶
    CALL put3real(i1!,i2!,i3!,z,s,26)¶
  ELSE¶
loop2:¶
    i$=j$  ¶
    CALL getstring(i$,a$,"1234567890-.,",z,s,inplen   )¶
    j$=i$¶
    CALL constr3real(i$,i1!,i2!,i3!)¶
    IF i$="" OR i1!<unt! OR i2!<unt! OR i3!<unt! OR i1!>ob! OR
i2!>ob! OR i3!>ob! THEN¶
      a$=" "¶
      GOTO loop2¶
    END IF¶
  END IF¶
END SUB    ¶
¶
```

The single addition to this routine is the second `IF` check where the array `k!` emerges for the first time. First the program checks for an allowable mouse input. If so, the `modus` index selects from the mouse vector, or from the difference vector between the mouse vector and the reference vector of the object.

As before, we use the conversion routines (con3realstr and constr3real):

```
SUB constr3real(i$,i1!,i2!,i3!) STATIC¶
'TASK      :convert one string into 3 real values¶
'PARAMETER:=>i$ the string¶
'           <=i1!,i2!,i3! the real values¶
'             i$ if conversion error i$=""¶
  Problem=0¶
  i$=i$+","¶
  FOR i=1 TO 3¶
    comma=INSTR(i$,",") 'Mark comma position¶
    IF comma<=1 THEN     'Problem ?¶
      Problem=1¶
    ELSE¶
      a$=MID$(i$,1,comma-1) 'truncate string to be converted¶
      i$=RIGHT$(i$,LEN(i$)-comma) 'mark the rest¶
      CALL constrreal(a$,i!(i))    'convert¶
      IF a$="" THEN  'Problem ?¶
        Problem=1¶
      END IF  ¶
    END IF¶
  NEXT i¶
  IF Problem=1 THEN¶
    i$=""     ¶
  ELSE¶
    i$=" "¶
    i1!=i!(1)¶
    i2!=i!(2)¶
    i3!=i!(3)¶
  END IF¶
END SUB      ¶
    ¶
¶
SUB con3realstr(i1!,i2!,i3!,i$) STATIC¶
'TASK      :convert 3 real values into vector string¶
'PARAMETER:=>i1!,i2!,i3! the 3 Real values¶
'           <=i$ the string¶
  CALL conrealstr(i1!,i1$)¶
  CALL conrealstr(i2!,i2$)¶
  CALL conrealstr(i3!,i3$)¶
  i$=i1$+","+i2$+","+i3$¶
END SUB¶
¶
```

Both routines support the conversion procedures and operate in the same way. The constr3real procedure is a little complicated because the beginning position of the coordinates in the character string must be determined by using the INSTR function. After all this preparation, we want to program a menu for our editor. As an example, we use the menu for a circle section because it uses all of input procedures discussed so far. Next the location and length of the screen must be determined. These positions are arbitrary. To simplify the following program, these values are stored in an array (tabs).

A requirement for our menu was that a correction to entered data could be made at any time. This should be done with the <Cursor up> and <Cursor down> keys. <Cursor up> moves you to the previous cursor position and <Cursor down> moves you to the next position. So that the procedure knows which input follows, a number variable (nr) is used, which is in a certain range (0 <= nr <= number of input positions). Besides the object data, additional information is needed concerning whether the objects in the projection window should be visible or not. This boolean value is stored in k!(ptr,5,2) where ptr points to the given object and the type is entered in k!(ptr,0,0).

```
SUB getcrarc(ptr) STATIC¶
  SHARED k!(),tabs(),min!,max!,grad!,rad!¶
  tabs(0,0)=2¶
  tabs(1,0)=2¶
  tabs(2,0)=3¶
  tabs(3,0)=4¶
  tabs(4,0)=5¶
  tabs(5,0)=6¶
  tabs(6,0)=6¶
  tabs(7,0)=7¶
  tabs(8,0)=7¶
  tabs(0,1)=10¶
  tabs(1,1)=22¶
  tabs(2,1)=4¶
  tabs(3,1)=4¶
  tabs(4,1)=4¶
  tabs(5,1)=4¶
  tabs(6,1)=16¶
  tabs(7,1)=4¶
  tabs(8,1)=16¶
  nr=0¶
  WHILE nr<=8¶
    CALL getkey(a$,tabs(nr,0),tabs(nr,1))¶
    IF ASC(a$)=28 THEN¶
      IF nr>0 THEN¶
         nr=nr-1¶
      END IF   ¶
    ELSE ¶
      IF ASC(a$)=29 THEN¶
         nr=nr+1¶
      ELSE¶
        IF nr=0 THEN¶
          CALL getstring(b$,a$,"yn",tabs(nr,0),tabs(nr,1),1)¶
          IF b$="y"THEN¶
            k!(ptr,5,2)=1¶
          ELSE ¶
            k!(ptr,5,2)=0¶
          END IF¶
        END IF¶
        IF nr=1 THEN¶
          CALL
getint(k!(ptr,0,2),a$,tabs(nr,0),tabs(nr,1),5,1!,max!)¶
        END IF          ¶
        IF nr=2 THEN¶
          CALL
get3real(k!(ptr,1,0),k!(ptr,1,1),k!(ptr,1,2),a$,tabs(nr,0),tabs(
nr,1),26,min!,max!,-1)¶
        END IF¶
        IF nr=3 THEN¶
          CALL
get3real(k!(ptr,2,0),k!(ptr,2,1),k!(ptr,2,2),a$,tabs(nr,0),tabs(
nr,1),26,min!,max!,ptr)¶
```

```
        END IF¶
        IF nr=4 THEN¶
          CALL
get3real(k!(ptr,3,0),k!(ptr,3,1),k!(ptr,3,2),a$,tabs(nr,0),tabs(
nr,1),26,min0!,max!,ptr)¶
        END IF¶
        IF nr=5 THEN¶
          k!=grad!*k!(ptr,5,0)¶
          CALL getreal(k!,a$,tabs(nr,0),tabs(nr,1),8,min!,max!)¶
          k!(ptr,5,0)=rad!*k!¶
        END IF  ¶
        IF nr=6 THEN¶
          k!=grad!*k!(ptr,5,1)¶
          CALL getreal(k!,a$,tabs(nr,0),tabs(nr,1),8,min!,max!)¶
          k!(ptr,5,1)=rad!*k!¶
        END IF  ¶
        IF nr=7 THEN¶
          CALL
getreal(k!(ptr,4,0),a$,tabs(nr,0),tabs(nr,1),8,0!,1!)¶
        END IF  ¶
        IF nr=8 THEN¶
          CALL
getreal(k!(ptr,4,1),a$,tabs(nr,0),tabs(nr,1),8,0!,1!)¶
        END IF  ¶
        nr=nr+1¶
      END IF¶
    END IF¶
  WEND ¶
END SUB  ¶
¶
 ¶
```

As you see, implementation in BASIC is easy with this procedure. The read procedure for the rest of the objects uses similar programming, and should present no difficulty. If you have problems you should look at the finished editor in the appendices and on the optional disk.

3.2.3.2 The Output

The output routines display the value of a variable, with a certain length, on the screen. The simplest case is the output of a character string that uses the MID$ function to extract the correct section.

```
SUB putstring(s$,z,s,inplen   )STATIC¶
'TASK      :output of a string of a certain length¶
'PARAMETER:=>s$ the string¶
'            z line¶
'            s column¶
'            inplen    Lenght of output window¶
  LOCATE z,s            'clear specified range¶
  PRINT SPACE$(inplen    )¶
  LOCATE z,s            'display the string¶
  PRINT MID$(s$,1,inplen    )¶
END SUB¶
¶
```

As with the input procedures, the operations for real values and vectors can be simplified with this `putstring` routine. First the values must be converted into strings using the conversion functions, and then displayed with the `putstring` routine:

```
SUB putreal(i!,z,s,inplen    )STATIC¶
'TASK     :Display real value of predetermined length¶
'PARAMETER:=>i! the real value¶
'            z line¶
'            s column¶
'            inplen    Length of output window¶
  CALL conrealstr(i!,s$)¶
  CALL putstring(s$,z,s,inplen   )¶
END SUB¶
  ¶
SUB put3real(i1!,i2!,i3!,z,s,inplen    )STATIC¶
'TASK     :display  3 Real values of certain length¶
'PARAMETER:=>i1!,i2!,i3! the real values¶
'            z line¶
'            s column¶
'            inplen    Length of the output window¶
  CALL con3realstr(i1!,i2!,i3!,i$)¶
  CALL putstring(i$,z,s,inplen   )¶
END SUB¶
¶
```

Now all we need is the display procedure for object data. Unlike an input, where a separate routine must be constructed for each object, it can all be done in one output procedure:

```
SUB showelem(ptr) STATIC¶
'TASK     :data output of element ptr¶
'PARAMETER:=>ptr pointer to the specified element¶
  SHARED k!(),typ$(),empty$,grad!,rad!¶
  LOCATE 1,1¶
  FOR i=1 TO 7¶
    PRINT empty$¶
  NEXT i¶
  LOCATE 1,1¶
  PRINT "Body  :"¶
  CALL putreal(ptr*1!,1,8,5)¶
  typ=INT(k!(ptr,0,0))¶
  IF ptr><0 THEN¶
    LOCATE 1,14¶
    PRINT typ$(typ)¶
    LOCATE 2,1¶
    PRINT "visible :";¶
    IF k!(ptr,5,2)=0 THEN¶
      PRINT "n"¶
    ELSE ¶
      PRINT "y"¶
    END IF¶
    LOCATE 2,13¶
    PRINT "Material:"¶
    CALL putreal(k!(ptr,0,2),2,22,5)¶
    IF typ=10 THEN¶
      LOCATE 3,1¶
      PRINT "M :"¶
      PRINT "r :"¶
      CALL put3real(k!(ptr,1,0),k!(ptr,1,1),k!(ptr,1,2),3,4,26)¶
```

```
        CALL putreal(k!(ptr,2,0),4,4,8)¶
      ELSE¶
        LOCATE 3,1¶
        PRINT "M :"¶
        PRINT "A :"¶
        PRINT "B :"¶
        CALL put3real(k!(ptr,1,0),k!(ptr,1,1),k!(ptr,1,2),3,4,26)¶
        CALL put3real(k!(ptr,2,0),k!(ptr,2,1),k!(ptr,2,2),4,4,26)¶
        CALL put3real(k!(ptr,3,0),k!(ptr,3,1),k!(ptr,3,2),5,4,26)¶
        IF typ>=4 THEN¶
          IF typ>=20 THEN¶
            LOCATE 6,1¶
            PRINT "C :"¶
            CALL
put3real(k!(ptr,4,0),k!(ptr,4,1),k!(ptr,4,2),6,4,26)¶
            IF typ=21 THEN¶
              LOCATE 7,1¶
              PRINT "sw:"¶
              LOCATE 7,13¶
              PRINT "ew:"¶
              CALL putreal(grad!*k!(ptr,5,0),7,4,8)¶
              CALL putreal(grad!*k!(ptr,5,1),7,16,8)¶
            END IF¶
          ELSE¶
            LOCATE 6,1¶
            PRINT "sw:"¶
            LOCATE 6,13¶
            PRINT "ew:"¶
            CALL putreal(grad!*k!(ptr,5,0),6,4,8)¶
            CALL putreal(grad!*k!(ptr,5,1),6,16,8)¶
            IF typ=5 THEN¶
              LOCATE 7,1¶
              PRINT "ri:"¶
              LOCATE 7,13¶
              PRINT "ra:"¶
              CALL putreal(k!(ptr,4,0),7,4,8)¶
              CALL putreal(k!(ptr,4,1),7,16,8)¶
            END IF¶
          END IF¶
        END IF¶
      END IF¶
    END IF¶
END SUB¶
¶
```

This procedure is easy, but it must be remembered that the `CLS` statement, used for erasing the screen in BASIC, cannot be used in this program because a section of the screen must remain intact. To delete this section, every line is overwritten with a certain number of empty fields stored in `empty$`. Another critical point is the array `typ$` into which the object names for the individual type numbers are stored. The array `typ$` is installed as follows:

```
typ$(0)="Plane"           'arrange by type and name¶
typ$(1)="Triangle"¶
typ$(2)="Parallelogram"¶
typ$(3)="Circle"¶
typ$(4)="Circle segment"¶
typ$(5)="Arc"¶
```

```
typ$(10)="Sphere"¶
typ$(20)="Cylinder"¶
typ$(21)="Cylinder segment"¶
typ$(22)="Cone"¶
typ$(24)="Spheroid"  ¶
```

3.2.3.3 The Graphics

The graphic commands used in this program should consider that each object must be displayed in three different windows. To complicate the implementation of this routine, you must add the enlargement factor and the chosen section. This isn't easy, because pixel width is less than pixel height on the Amiga. This can be evened out by making a correction factor for the X coordinates. You may have seen this phenomenon for yourself, but if not, try to display a square with an edge length of 100. When you use the following command, you may see a rectangle on the screen instead of a square:

```
LINE (0,0)-(100,100),,b
```

To calculate the correction factor you must measure the height of the rectangle and divide it by its length. This value should change in the program to correspond to your screen (the variable is called `xcoorfac!` and is in the `init` `SUB` program).

The simplest graphic objects are points and lines. We use room coordinates in our program instead of screen coordinates. This means we must create our own procedures for these graphic objects. You'll need the coordinates of the point or line, the character color (`colour`), the statement of the section and the enlargement factor (`factor!`). The `WINDOW` function receives the data about the window display.

```
SUB setpoint(x!,y!)STATIC¶
'TASK      :set point in current output window¶
'PARAMETER:=>x!,y! Point coordinate¶
  SHARED mx!,my!,mz!,factor!,xcorrfac!,colour¶
  swindow=WINDOW(1)  ¶
  IF swindow=1 THEN¶
    LINE ((x!-mx!)*xcorrfac!*factor!,(my!-y!)*factor!)-((x!-
mx!)*xcorrfac!*factor!,(my!-y!)*factor!),colour¶
  ELSE¶
    IF swindow=2 THEN¶
      LINE ((x!-mx!)*xcorrfac!*factor!,(mz!-y!)*factor!)-((x!-
mx!)*xcorrfac!*factor!,(mz!-y!)*factor!),colour¶
    ELSE¶
      IF swindow=3 THEN¶
        LINE ((my!-x!)*xcorrfac!*factor!,(mz!-y!)*factor!)-
((my!-x!)*xcorrfac!*factor!,(mz!-y!)*factor!),colour¶
      END IF¶
    END IF¶
```

```
  END IF¶
END SUB¶
¶
SUB drawline(x!,y!)STATIC¶
'TASK     :draw line from last point to specified point¶
'PARAMETER:=>x!,y! Point coordinates¶
  SHARED mx!,my!,mz!,factor!,xcorrfac!,colour¶
  swindow=WINDOW(1)  ¶
  IF swindow=1 THEN¶
    LINE -((x!-mx!)*xcorrfac!*factor!,(my!-y!)*factor!),colour¶
  ELSE¶
    IF swindow=2 THEN¶
      LINE -((x!-mx!)*xcorrfac!*factor!,(mz!-
y!)*factor!),colour¶
    ELSE¶
      IF swindow=3 THEN¶
        LINE -((my!-x!)*xcorrfac!*factor!,(mz!-
y!)*factor!),colour¶
      END IF¶
    END IF¶
  END IF¶
END SUB¶
¶
```

Now comes the drawing routine for an ellipse. Let's think about how an ellipse can be constructed.

We have used a method that uses the midpoint of the ellipse and two more vectors which span the ellipse, clearly establishing the ellipse. The ellipse begins by rotating the two vectors around the midpoint. When a full rotation is executed, all of the points of the ellipse are set.

Because there are an infinite set of numbers between 0 and 360, it is impossible for every angle of the ellipse points to be calculated. For every circle or ellipse we approach a certain number of lines (`maxlines`). The larger the number, the more accurately the ellipse appears, but the more computation time needed. This number should be chosen later in the program so the user has some control over the drawing speed. Arcs (partial ellipses) can be calculated as well as complete ellipses—start and end angles act as additional parameters:

```
SUB drawellipse(ax!,ay!,bx!,by!,mx!,my!,sw!,ew!)STATIC¶
'TASK     :draw ellipse in current output window¶
'PARAMETER:=>ax!,ay!,bx!,by! span of ellipse¶
'           mx!,my! center point of ellipse¶
'           sw!,ew! the start angle and end angle¶
'                   to be used¶
  SHARED maxlines,pi2!¶
  alpha!=sw!¶
  numlines=ABS(sw!-ew!)*maxlines/pi2! 'Compute number of lines¶
  IF numlines=0 THEN¶
    numlines=maxlines  'if sw!=ew!, draw full ellipse¶
    beta!=pi2!/maxlines¶
  ELSE  ¶
    beta!=ABS(sw!-ew!)/numlines  'compute increment angle¶
  END IF¶
  x!=ax!*COS(alpha!)+bx!*SIN(alpha!)+mx! 'compute start point¶
  y!=ay!*COS(alpha!)+by!*SIN(alpha!)+my!¶
```

```
  CALL setpoint(x!,y!)  'Start point output¶
  FOR i=1 TO numlines¶
    alpha!=alpha!+beta!  'compute new angle¶
    x!=ax!*COS(alpha!)+bx!*SIN(alpha!)+mx!  'compute new point¶
    y!=ay!*COS(alpha!)+by!*SIN(alpha!)+my!¶
    CALL drawline(x!,y!)  'draw line from old point to new¶
  NEXT i¶
END SUB¶
```

The beginning of this routine calculates the number of lines. When a full ellipse is displayed, this number is the maximum; when only a half ellipse is desired, this number is halved, and so on. When this number is set, the step value, which increases the angle from the start value to the end value, can be found. The actual rotation of the vectors uses both the sine and cosine functions.

For an example of the above three routines, let's develop a display routine for a cone. This procedure should draw the cone in three windows then place the numeric output in the fourth window, which is used for text input and output. The base must be given first and then four lines drawn from this base to the cone peak. The beginning point of these lines runs through the base vectors:

```
SUB drawcone(ptr) STATIC¶
  SHARED k!(),pi2!¶
  mx!=k!(ptr,1,0)¶
  my!=k!(ptr,1,1)¶
  mz!=k!(ptr,1,2)¶
  ax!=k!(ptr,2,0)¶
  ay!=k!(ptr,2,1)¶
  az!=k!(ptr,2,2)¶
  bx!=k!(ptr,3,0)¶
  by!=k!(ptr,3,1)¶
  bz!=k!(ptr,3,2)¶
  cx!=k!(ptr,4,0)¶
  cy!=k!(ptr,4,1)¶
  cz!=k!(ptr,4,2)¶
  WINDOW OUTPUT 1¶
  CALL drawellipse(ax!,ay!,bx!,by!,mx!,my!,0!,pi2!)¶
  CALL setpoint(ax!+mx!,ay!+my!)¶
  CALL drawline(cx!+mx!,cy!+my!)¶
  CALL drawline(mx!-ax!,my!-ay!) ¶
  CALL setpoint(bx!+mx!,by!+my!)¶
  CALL drawline(cx!+mx!,cy!+my!)¶
  CALL drawline(mx!-bx!,my!-by!) ¶
  WINDOW OUTPUT 2¶
  CALL drawellipse(ax!,az!,bx!,bz!,mx!,mz!,0!,pi2!)¶
  CALL setpoint(ax!+mx!,az!+mz!)¶
  CALL drawline(cx!+mx!,cz!+mz!)¶
  CALL drawline(mx!-ax!,mz!-az!) ¶
  CALL setpoint(bx!+mx!,bz!+mz!)¶
  CALL drawline(cx!+mx!,cz!+mz!)¶
  CALL drawline(mx!-bx!,mz!-bz!) ¶
  WINDOW OUTPUT 3¶
  CALL drawellipse(ay!,az!,by!,bz!,my!,mz!,0!,pi2!)¶
  CALL setpoint(ay!+my!,az!+mz!)¶
  CALL drawline(cy!+my!,cz!+mz!)¶
  CALL drawline(my!-ay!,mz!-az!) ¶
  CALL setpoint(by!+my!,bz!+mz!)¶
```

```
  CALL drawline(cy!+my!,cz!+mz!)¶
  CALL drawline(my!-by!,mz!-bz!) ¶
  WINDOW OUTPUT 4¶
END SUB¶
¶
```

We are still missing the display routine for the other 10 objects, which are fairly easy to develop. You can explore these yourself. Check the complete editor listing in the appendices if you run into trouble.

3.2.3.4 Data Operations

Now you're familar with some of the tools that make up an editor, but there are still more. Suppose you entered some objects and want to work with the first object; or you want to recreate an object and you don't remember the data; or you notice that your last input makes no sense and you want to delete the object.

Let's begin with deleting elements in our array. We have several options. The first would be to move all objects that lie to the right of the one to be erased in array `k!` one position to the left. This method can take a large amount of time for very large arrays. Another method is to give each object a number which states whether it is active or deleted. Now we can mark the deleted elements as free. Then when the program is running the input routine can search for a free spot in array `k!` and the new element can be inserted in the free position. How can our program find the next free spot quickly?

There is a simple solution. You create a global variable (`kfree`) which points to a free position. When an object is deleted, the index of this object is stored in `kfree`. What if an element was erased previously? Then this information goes into this free position. You keep track of this pointer to build a list of free positions of `k!(kfree`,..,..), for example in `k!(kfree`,0,1). When more objects are erased while the program is running, a list of the free element is built. This is shown in the diagram below:

Figure 3.22

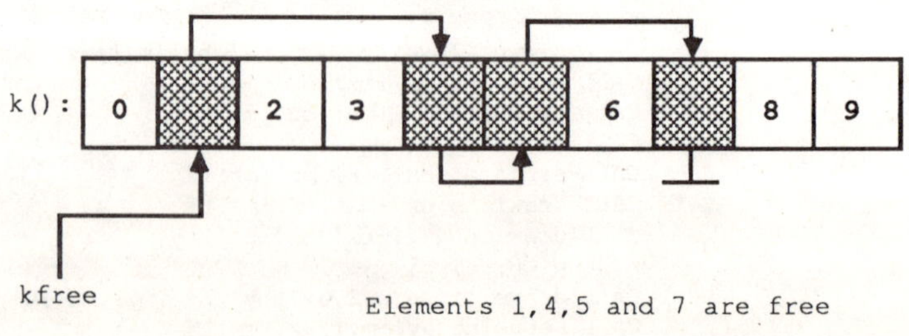

This task, building a list of the free elements, is taken on by the following procedure, which clears the non-zero elements because these have a special meaning as initializing elements:

```
SUB deleter(ptr) STATIC¶
'TASK      :delete one body¶
'PARAMETER:=>ptr points to the body¶
  SHARED k!(),kfree¶
  IF ptr><0 THEN 'not the starting element¶
    FOR i=0 TO 5 'Delete¶
      FOR j=0 TO 2¶
        k!(ptr,i,j)=0¶
      NEXT j¶
    NEXT i     ¶
    k!(ptr,0,0)=-1     'Add body to free list¶
    k!(ptr,0,1)=kfree¶
    kfree=ptr¶
    CALL lefts(ptr)¶
  END IF   ¶
END SUB¶
```

Now to request these as free memory, we add one procedure that marks the entire array `k!` as free at the start of the program and adds it to the free list:

```
SUB newelem(ptr) STATIC¶
'TASK      :get address of free place in list¶
'PARAMETER:<=ptr points to this area¶
  SHARED kfree,k!(),knum¶
  IF kfree<knum THEN¶
    ptr=kfree¶
    kfree=k!(ptr,0,1)¶
    k!(ptr,0,0)=0¶
    k!(ptr,0,1)=0¶
    k!(ptr,0,2)=1¶
  END IF   ¶
END SUB¶
¶
```

These are our own memory management routines, which work on the same principle as the Amiga's equivalent operating system procedures.

To copy an element in the array, we need a pointer to a free memory area, and then we write data from one element to another, value for value:

```
SUB copy(ptr) STATIC¶
'TASK      :copy one body¶
'PARAMETER:=>ptr points to the body¶
  SHARED k!()¶
  IF ptr><0 THEN  'not the starting element¶
    old=ptr        'save pointer¶
    CALL newelem(ptr)  'create new space¶
    FOR i=0 TO 5       'copy¶
      FOR j=0 TO 2¶
        k!(ptr,i,j)=k!(old,i,j)¶
      NEXT j¶
    NEXT i¶
  END IF¶
```

```
END SUB¶
¶
```

We need a procedure that can move objects around in the list. We want to move objects to the left in the list so the pointer can be lowered to element one, and we want to move objects to the right in the list so we can increase it past one. We must assume that until now the pointer was never negative, contained too large a value, or didn't point to an erased element:

```
SUB lefts(ptr) STATIC¶
'TASK      :get element to left of current elememt¶
'PARAMETER:=>ptr points to current body¶
  SHARED k!()¶
  IF ptr><0 THEN ¶
    ptr=ptr-1¶
  END IF¶
  WHILE k!(ptr,0,0)=-1¶
    ptr=ptr-1¶
  WEND¶
  CALL showelem(ptr)¶
END SUB         ¶
                    ¶
SUB rights(ptr) STATIC¶
'TASK      :get element to right of current element¶
'PARAMETER:=>ptr pointer to current body¶
  SHARED k!(),knum¶
  old=ptr¶
  IF ptr<knum THEN¶
    ptr=ptr+1¶
  END IF¶
  WHILE k!(ptr,0,0)=-1 AND ptr<knum¶
    ptr=ptr+1¶
  WEND¶
  IF k!(ptr,0,0)=-1 THEN¶
    ptr=old      ¶
  ELSE¶
    CALL showelem(ptr)¶
  END IF¶
END SUB¶
¶
```

Now we want to describe data manipulation and the enlarging, moving and rotation of a shape.

When the individual coordinates of a vector are multiplied by the same constant, the named vector is increased by this factor. When the coordinates are multiplied by different factors, the vector is unevenly stretched in the three basic directions, an effect that we shall add to our program.

To move our shape we must move its reference point. The new reference point can be entered either with the keyboard or the mouse.

It is more complicated with the rotation. The reference point stays in place and the difference vectors are changed. These vectors are rotated around three angles in the room according to the following formula:

`(x,y,z)`	is the original vector
`(alpha,beta,gamma)`	are the three angles around which the vector should be rotated
`(X,Y,Z)`	is the rotation vector given with the three help variables

```
a=x*cos(gamma)-y*sin(gamma)
b=x*sin(gamma)+y*cos(gamma)
c=a*sin(beta)-z*cos(beta)
```

from

```
X=a*cos(beta)+z*sin(beta)
Y=c*sin(alpha)+b*cos(beta)
Z=b*sin(alpha)-c*cos(alpha)
```

This formula must be taken for granted because the proof would fill a page. An object should be copied and then rotated, instead of just rotating it. It would help the user to be freed of this copy operation. Our rotation can can be defined by the following BASIC procedure :

```
SUB rotation(ptr) STATIC¶
'TASK      :rotate body by three angles¶
'PARAMETER:=>ptr points to the body¶
  SHARED k!(),grad!,rad!,min!,max!¶
  IF ptr><0 THEN¶
    WINDOW 5,"Rotation",(0,129)-(314,170),4,1¶
    vx!=grad!*vx!¶
    vy!=grad!*vy!¶
    vz!=grad!*vz!¶
    LOCATE 2,1¶
    PRINT"V :"¶
    PRINT"q<uit,d<o,c<opy&do :"¶
    CALL put3real(vx!,vy!,vz!,2,4,26)¶
    CALL get3real(vx!,vy!,vz!," ",2,4,26,min!,max!,0)¶
    CALL getstring(a$," ","qcd",3,21,1)¶
    vx!=rad!*vx!¶
    vy!=rad!*vy!¶
    vz!=rad!*vz!¶
    WINDOW CLOSE 5¶
    WINDOW OUTPUT 4¶
    IF a$><"q" THEN¶
      IF a$="c" THEN¶
        CALL copy(ptr)¶
      END IF¶
      IF k!(ptr,0,0)>=20 THEN ¶
        til=4¶
      ELSE¶
        til=3¶
      END IF¶
      FOR i=2 TO til¶
        a!=k!(ptr,i,0)*COS(vz!)-k!(ptr,i,1)*SIN(vz!)¶
        b!=k!(ptr,i,0)*SIN(vz!)+k!(ptr,i,1)*COS(vz!)¶
        c!=a!*SIN(vy!)-k!(ptr,i,2)*COS(vy!)  ¶
        k!(ptr,i,0)=a!*COS(vy!)+k!(ptr,i,2)*SIN(vy!)¶
        k!(ptr,i,1)=c!*SIN(vx!)+b!*COS(vx!)¶
```

```
        k!(ptr,i,2)=b!*SIN(vx!)-c!*COS(vx!)¶
      NEXT i¶
      CALL showelem(ptr)  ¶
      IF k!(ptr,5,2)=1 THEN¶
        CALL drawelem(ptr)¶
      END IF  ¶
    ELSE    ¶
      WINDOW CLOSE 5¶
    END IF¶
  END IF¶
END SUB¶
¶
```

With a few changes this procedure handles enlargement and movements:

1.) Eliminate the conversion from the different angle systems

2.) `get3real` is called in mode -1 for the movement, the check is made to see if `k!(ptr,0,0)>=20` and the `FOR` loops are set with:

```
k!(ptr,1,0)=vx!
k!(ptr,1,1)=vy!
k!(ptr,1,2)=vz!
```

3.) The instruction for the enlargement is set in the `FOR` loop:

```
k!(ptr,i,0)=vx!*(ptr,i,0)
k!(ptr,i,1)=vy!*(ptr,i,1)
k!(ptr,i,2)=vz!*k!(ptr,i,2)
```

Now two more routines editor are ready for adding to the editor.

3.2.3.5 Disk Operations

These operations are basically very simple. The contents of the array `k!()` are written to the disk, element by element. It should be possible to save only certain sections of the data, specified by the top and bottom limits of the indices. Before choosing this option in the progam, the elements that should be deleted should be marked so they are not written to the disk. The editor adds a file extension of `.list` to the filename to distinguish the file from any other file types on disk.

```
SUB savelist STATIC¶
'TASK   :See save routine for material list  ¶
  SHARED k!(),knum,legchar$,File$¶
  WINDOW 5,"Save List",(0,129)-(314,170),0,1¶
  PRINT "Name:"¶
  PRINT "from:1"¶
  PRINT "to   :"¶
  mfrom!=1¶
  mto!=knum¶
```

```
  CALL putreal(mto!,3,6,10)¶
  CALL getstring(File$," ",legchar$,1,6,10)¶
  CALL getint(mfrom!," ",2,6,10,1!,knum*1!)¶
  CALL getint(mto!," ",3,6,10,mfrom!,knum*1!)¶
  IF File$><"" THEN¶
    OPEN File$+".LIST" FOR OUTPUT AS 1¶
    quantity=0¶
    FOR i=mfrom! TO mto!     'determine number of elements to be
saved¶
      IF k!(i,0,0) ><-1 THEN¶
        quantity=quantity+1¶
      END IF¶
    NEXT i¶
    PRINT #1,quantity    ¶
    FOR ptr=mfrom! TO mto!¶
      IF k!(ptr,0,0)><-1 THEN  'forget blank elements¶
        FOR i=0 TO 5¶
          PRINT #1,k!(ptr,i,0);",";k!(ptr,i,1);",";k!(ptr,i,2)¶
        NEXT i¶
      END IF¶
    NEXT ptr¶
    CLOSE 1¶
    KILL File$+".LIST.info"¶
  END IF¶
  WINDOW CLOSE 5¶
  WINDOW OUTPUT 4¶
END SUB          ¶
¶

SUB loadlist STATIC¶
'TASK   :Load list  ¶
  SHARED k!(),knum,ptr,legchar$,File$¶
  WINDOW 5,"Load List",(0,129)-(314,150),0,1¶
  PRINT "Name:"¶
  CALL getstring(File$," ",legchar$,1,6,10)¶
  IF File$><"" THEN¶
    OPEN File$+".list" FOR INPUT AS 1¶
    INPUT #1,quantity¶
    WHILE NOT(EOF(1))¶
      CALL newelem(ptr)¶
      FOR i=0 TO 5¶
        INPUT #1,k!(ptr,i,0),k!(ptr,i,1),k!(ptr,i,2)¶
      NEXT i¶
    WEND  ¶
    CLOSE 1¶
  END IF¶
  WINDOW CLOSE 5¶
  WINDOW OUTPUT 4¶
  CALL showelem(ptr)¶
END SUB¶
¶
```

The procedure does not test for the existence of the file on disk. If the user enters a nonexistent name, the following error message appears:

```
FILE NOT FOUND
```

The program stops and the line with the OPEN instruction is displayed. You may wish to add error handling.

3.2.3.6 Mouse and Gadgets

Before we examine the gadgets that will be used in our program, we want to show you the mouse check routine we talked about earlier. Our mouse check routine executes by pressing the left mouse button and reading the coordinates of the mouse position. This should only happen when the chosen window is a projection window. It should not happen for our input and output window. In another case MOUSE(3) and MOUSE(4) check the X or Y coordinates of the mouse position. These coordinates represent the screen coordinates and not the room coordinates which interest us. You must also calculate if section, enlargement factor, and X correction factor should be considered. To mark the position clicked on, the program draws a small cross on the screen. Then the mouse coordinates are read:

```
'*******************¶
'** READ MOUSE    **¶
'*******************¶
¶
click:¶
  dummy=MOUSE(0)¶
  x!=MOUSE(3)/(factor!*xcorrfac!)   'Get mouse position and
compute¶
  y!=MOUSE(4)/factor!¶
  n=WINDOW(0)   'window clicked¶
  oldwindow=WINDOW(1) 'output window¶
  CALL activatewindow&(WINDOW(7))¶
   IF  n<4 THEN   'was projection windoiw clicked?¶
    WINDOW OUTPUT n¶
    LINE  (MOUSE(3)-1,MOUSE(4))-(MOUSE(3)+1,MOUSE(4)),3   'Draw
circle¶
    LINE  (MOUSE(3),MOUSE(4)-1)-(MOUSE(3),MOUSE(4)+1),3¶
    IF n=1 THEN     'compute spatial coordinates¶
      mox!=mx!+x!¶
      moy!=my!-y!¶
    ELSE¶
      IF n=2 THEN¶
        mox!=mx!+x!¶
        moz!=mz!-y!¶
      ELSE ¶
        IF n=3 THEN¶
          moy!=my!-x!¶
          moz!=mz!-y!¶
        END IF¶
      END IF¶
    END IF¶
    mox!=FIX(mox!+.5)  'round¶
    moy!=FIX(moy!+.5)¶
    moz!=FIX(moz!+.5)¶
    WINDOW OUTPUT 4¶
    mo$=STR$(mox!)+","+STR$(moy!)+","+STR$(moz!)¶
    LOCATE 10,8           'delete old mouse values and display new
ones¶
    PRINT SPACE$(26)¶
    LOCATE 10,8¶
```

```
    PRINT MID$(mo$,1,26) ¶
    WINDOW OUTPUT oldwindow¶
  ELSE¶
    CALL checkgadget  'was a gadget clicked?¶
  END IF¶
RETURN ¶
¶
```

This subroutine is incorporated into our program with `ON MOUSE GOSUB click`.

If you have carefully examined the subroutine, the call from `checkgadget` should attract your attention. This is where we implement the gadgets. We have chosen the following route:

The `initgadget` routine lets you establish where on the screen a certain gadget of a specific height and width should appear. All of this information goes into a special global array. When the user presses the left mouse button, the `checkgadget` routine is called. It checks for whether the mouse pointer lies inside of the gadget. If so, the following two possibilities exist:

1.) When the gadget is a slider, the old slider must be deleted and drawn at the new position. The position of the orginal slider is saved in the `gadget%` array in the fourth position.

2.) When the gadget is an icon, this icon whose picture information is in the array `gadgets%` is either inverted or is given a completely new icon graphic. This screen information is loaded at the start of the program with `GET` and is accessed by `PUT`. The additional gadget is stored temporarily in `gadget%`(4).

Another routine ensures that the gadgets which are no longer necessary are deleted from the screen:

```
SUB checkgadget STATIC¶
'TASK   :test whether a gadget has been clicked  ¶
  SHARED gadget%(),gadgets%()  ¶
  dummy=MOUSE(0)¶
  ax=MOUSE(3) 'Mouse position¶
  ay=MOUSE(4)¶
  i=0¶
  WHILE i<=10  'search entire array¶
    x%=gadget%(i,0)    'get values from array ¶
    y%=gadget%(i,1)¶
    h%=gadget%(i,2)¶
    l%=gadget%(i,3)¶
    valu%=gadget%(i,4)¶
    wind%=gadget%(i,5)¶
    yes%=gadget%(i,6)¶
    none%=gadget%(i,7)   'Mouse over gadget ?¶
    IF x%<ax AND x%+l%>ax AND y%<ay AND y%+h%>ay AND x%>=0 AND
WINDOW(0)=wind% THEN¶
      old=WINDOW(1) 'reserve output window¶
      WINDOW OUTPUT wind%   'delete old slider draw new one¶
      IF yes%=-1 THEN¶
        LINE (valu%+x%+1,y%+1)-(valu%+x%+1,y%+h%-1),0¶
```

```
          valu%=ax-x%-1¶
          LINE (valu%+x%+1,y%+1)-(valu%+x%+1,y%+h%-1),3¶
          gadget%(i,4)=valu%  'get new value¶
        ELSE¶
          IF none%=-1 THEN¶
            IF valu%=1 THEN  'first time, invert it¶
              gadget%(i,4)=0¶
              LINE (x%,y%)-(x%+l%,y%+h%),0,bf¶
              PUT (x%,y%),gadgets%(yes%),PRESET¶
            ELSE  ¶
              gadget%(i,4)=1  'else return ¶
              LINE (x%,y%)-(x%+l%,y%+h%),0,bf¶
              PUT (x%,y%),gadgets%(yes%)¶
            END IF¶
          ELSE    ¶
            IF valu%=1 THEN  'first time, display no output¶
              gadget%(i,4)=0¶
              LINE (x%,y%)-(x%+l%,y%+h%),0,bf¶
              PUT (x%,y%),gadgets%(none%)¶
            ELSE  ¶
              gadget%(i,4)=1 'else yes output¶
              LINE (x%,y%)-(x%+l%,y%+h%),0,bf¶
              PUT (x%,y%),gadgets%(yes%)¶
            END IF¶
          END IF¶
        END IF¶
        WINDOW OUTPUT old    'old output window active¶
        i=10    ¶
      END IF¶
      i=i+1¶
    WEND¶
END SUB      ¶
    ¶
¶
SUB initgadget(x%,y%,h%,l%,valu%,wind%,nr%,yes%,none%)STATIC¶
'TASK     :place a new gadget in the gadget array gadget%()¶
'PARAMETER:=>x%,y% Position of upper left corner¶
'           h%,l% border height and lenght¶
'           valu% Start value¶
'           wind% Output window¶
'           yes%,none% if yes%=-1,then slider¶
'                     if none%=-1,gadgets inverts when clicked¶
'                     else display another gadget¶
'                     yes% and none% supply the indices for
graphic information¶
'                     of the array gadgets ¶
'         <=nr% Position of the gadgets in array ¶
  SHARED gadget%(),gadgets%()¶
  IF x%>=0 AND y%>=0 AND h%>=2 AND l%>=3 AND valu%>=0 AND
valu%<l% AND wind%>0 THEN¶
    MOUSE OFF¶
    old=WINDOW(1)¶
    WINDOW OUTPUT wind%¶
    IF yes%=-1 THEN¶
      LINE  (x%,y%)-(x%,y%+h%)¶
      LINE -(x%+l%,y%+h%)¶
      LINE -(x%+l%,y%)¶
      LINE -(x%,y%)¶
      LINE (valu%+x%+1,y%+1)-(valu%+x%+1,y%+h%-1),3¶
    ELSE¶
      IF valu%=1 THEN¶
        PUT (x%,y%),gadgets%(yes%)¶
```

```
      ELSE¶
        PUT (x%,y%),gadgets%(none%)¶
      END IF¶
    END IF¶
    nr%=0¶
    WHILE gadget%(nr%,0)><-1 AND nr%<=9 ¶
      nr%=nr%+1¶
    WEND¶
    IF gadget%(nr%,0)=-1 THEN    ¶
      gadget%(nr%,0)=x%¶
      gadget%(nr%,1)=y%¶
      gadget%(nr%,2)=h%¶
      gadget%(nr%,3)=l%¶
      gadget%(nr%,4)=valu%¶
      gadget%(nr%,5)=wind%¶
      gadget%(nr%,6)=yes%¶
      gadget%(nr%,7)=none%¶
    END IF  ¶
    MOUSE ON¶
    WINDOW OUTPUT old¶
  END IF¶
END SUB¶
    ¶
SUB deletegadget(i) STATIC¶
'TASK     :delete a gadget¶
'PARAMETER:=>i Index of  gadgets in array  ¶
  SHARED gadget%()¶
  IF i>=0 AND i<=10 THEN¶
    gadget%(i,0)=-1¶
  END IF¶
END SUB   ¶
¶
¶
```

As an example for using this procedure we want to present two routines from the editor. Five real values must be read into this editor (a red value, green value and blue value, a value that tests for the brightness in the shadows and a reflection factor). All of these values must be between zero and one. Because a color should be established using the red, green, and blues values, it is very helpful if the user can see this color on the screen, which is built using the `PALETTE 2,..,..,..` instruction. The routine to indicate a material element is here also (the opposite of `showelem`):

```
SUB showmat(matptr) STATIC¶
'TASK    :See corresponding routine for the body list ¶
  SHARED mat!(),nr1%,nr2%,nr3%,nr4%,nr5%,nr6%¶
  CLS¶
  PRINT "Material:"¶
  CALL putreal(matptr*1!,1,10,10)¶
  IF matptr ><0 THEN¶
    LOCATE 1,20¶
    PRINT "R+G+B="¶
    PALETTE 2,mat!(matptr,0),mat!(matptr,1),mat!(matptr,2)¶
    LINE (250,0)-(260,7),2,bf¶
    PRINT "Red        :"¶
    PRINT ¶
    PRINT "Green      :"¶
    PRINT ¶
    PRINT "Blue       :"¶
```

```
        PRINT ¶
        PRINT "Shadow     :"¶
        PRINT ¶
        PRINT "Mirroring :"¶
        w1%=mat!(matptr,0)*101¶
        w2%=mat!(matptr,1)*101¶
        w3%=mat!(matptr,2)*101¶
        w4%=mat!(matptr,3)*101¶
        w5%=mat!(matptr,4)*101     ¶
        CALL initgadget(110,8,10,102,w1%,5,nr1%,-1,-1)¶
        CALL initgadget(110,24,10,102,w2%,5,nr2%,-1,-1)¶
        CALL initgadget(110,40,10,102,w3%,5,nr3%,-1,-1)¶
        CALL initgadget(110,56,10,102,w4%,5,nr4%,-1,-1)¶
        CALL initgadget(110,72,10,102,w5%,5,nr5%,-1,-1)      ¶
        CALL initgadget(110,88,15,30,1,5,nr6%,0,-1)¶
      END IF¶
    END SUB¶
    ¶
```

The zero in the last `initgadget` call is the address of the OK gadget which must be clicked to end data input.

The routine to read the material data is just as easy as the above procedure. It is called after `showmat`:

```
SUB getmat(matptr) STATIC¶
'TASK   :see corresponding routine for the body list ¶
  SHARED mat!(),gadget%(),nr1%,nr2%,nr3%,nr4%,nr5%,nr6%¶
  CALL showmat(matptr)¶
  WHILE gadget%(nr6%,4)><0¶
    PALETTE 2,gadget%(nr1%,4)/100,gadget%(nr2%,4)/100,
gadget%(nr3%,4)/100¶
  WEND ¶
  mat!(matptr,0)=gadget%(nr1%,4)/101¶
  mat!(matptr,1)=gadget%(nr2%,4)/101¶
  mat!(matptr,2)=gadget%(nr3%,4)/101¶
  mat!(matptr,3)=gadget%(nr4%,4)/101¶
  mat!(matptr,4)=gadget%(nr5%,4)/101¶
  CALL deletegadget(nr1%)¶
  CALL deletegadget(nr2%)¶
  CALL deletegadget(nr3%)¶
  CALL deletegadget(nr4%)¶
  CALL deletegadget(nr5%)¶
  CALL deletegadget(nr6%)¶
END SUB ¶
```

This was the last important routine for creating our ray tracer editor.

3.2.4 Tips on Writing an Editor

What we have presented so far is a collection of procedures. To get a complete program, additional functions must be inserted. One problem, for example, is how these functions should be accessed by the user.

Should there be individual commands that only run in the material editor, reconstruct the screen, or move the section? So that the user is spared a lot of unnecessary typing, it may be better to have all functions in a menu and combine this so some important functions can be activated by pressing a key. The important procedures for this are very easy and are basically a row of IF statements.

Next all of the global variables must be initialized and the global arrays dimensioned. A screen and four windows for the display and the text input and output be opened. The arrays `k!` and `mat!` should be linked at the beginning, declare all the elements as free, and put them in the free list.

It is useful to be able to change from the actual object element to any other. The `show` function displays the object in the projection windows (that means with another color). This is so you don't lose the overview of the picture with large data sections.

It is also important to be able to leave the program without having to execute a reset. A Quit procedure which checks if the user would actually like to quit the program is needed, perhaps using a requester.

Use the routines and ideas presented to create your own editor or see the complete listing in the appendices. The real fun of programming is in creating your own programs.

3.3 The Main Program

You probably noticed that we're aiming toward a specific goal. All of the routines listed up until now can be combined to make a complete program. The object editor is a self-sufficient module called from the main program. The tracer program has also been built using modules that can be combined to make a complete program or can be incorporated into your own programs.

The complete listing of the tracer program is in Appendix B. The example programs that follow contain some BASIC lines that must be entered on one line in AmigaBASIC, even though they appear on two lines in this book. Formatting the program listings to fit into this book has caused some long BASIC lines to be split into two lines. To show where a BASIC line is actually ended a ¶ will appear. This character only shows when the <Return> key should be pressed in the BASIC editor. For example, the following line is split into two lines in this book, but must be entered as one line in AmigaBASIC:

```
WinDef NWindow, 100, 50, 460, 150, 32+64+512&, 15&+4096&,
0&, Title$¶
```

The ¶ shows the actual end of the BASIC line.

3.3.1 The Remaining Tracer Routines

Now we come to the routines that are important to the completion to our main ray tracing program.

First we want to describe the `RasterInit` routine. The user and display screens are constructed in this routine. All input takes place on the user screen. The wire model and shadowed picture appear on the display screen. The tracer program functions in all screen modes, and works in either user mode (with 60/80 characters per line):

```
RasterInit:¶
  ' Select resolution and display mode  ¶
  WINDOW CLOSE 2 ' delete any windows and¶
  SCREEN CLOSE 1 ' screens ¶
¶
  WINDOW 1,"", (0,0)-(631,185),6  ' new window with Status-line¶
¶
  'PALETTE 0,0,0,0        ' Colour for user screen¶
  'PALETTE 1,1,1,1        ¶
  'PALETTE 2,.4,.4,1¶
```

```
¶
  NWBase& = WINDOW(7)¶
  NRastPort& = WINDOW(8)¶
  NWScreen& = PEEKL(NWBase&+46)¶
  ' Base address of Window-Structure¶
  ' from which the screen structure is taken¶
  ' RastPort belongs with the WINDOW() function¶
¶
  Status$ = " Status: Select resolution"+CHR$(0)     ' Status
line output¶
  dummy = SetWindowTitles(NWBase&,SADD(Status$),0)¶
¶
  DisplayM$(0)  =  " Normal          "¶
  DisplayM$(1)  =  " Hold and Modify"¶
  DisplayM$(2)  =  " Extra Halfbrite"¶
  ¶
  XResl$(0)  = " Normal"¶
  XResl$(1)  = " HIRES "¶
  ¶
  YResl$(0)  = " Normal    " ¶
  YResl$(1)  = " Interlaced"¶
  ¶
  x(0) = 0:x(1) = 0:x(2) = 0:x(3) = 4¶
  ' Which values or strings at which position ?¶
¶
  y = 0¶
  ' topmost line = Start line¶
¶
  Modulo(0) = 3¶
  Modulo(1) = 2¶
  Modulo(2) = 2¶
  Modulo(3) = 6¶
  ' How many values for each selection line ?¶
¶
  COLOR 1¶
¶
  Colours (0) = 1¶
  Colours (1) = 2¶
  Colours (2) = 2¶
  Colours (3) = 2¶
  ' First line  => white rest of the lines  => blue¶
  ¶
Outg:¶
  LOCATE 10,21¶
  COLOR Colours(0)¶
  PRINT  "Display mode : ";DisplayM$(x(0))¶
  LOCATE 12,21¶
  COLOR Colours(1)¶
  PRINT  "X-Resolution : ";XResl$(x(1))¶
  LOCATE 14,21¶
  COLOR Colours(2)¶
  PRINT  "Y-Resolution : ";YResl$(x(2))¶
  LOCATE 16,24¶
  COLOR Colours(3)¶
  PRINT  "BitPlanes : ";x(3)+1¶
   ¶
  Waiter: a$ = INKEY$¶
  IF a$ = "" THEN Waiter¶
  ¶
  IF a$ = CHR$(30) THEN x(y) = (x(y)+1) MOD Modulo(y)¶
  IF a$ = CHR$(31) THEN x(y) = x(y)-1 ¶
  ' CRSR Left/Right¶
```

```
¶
  IF x(y) < 0 THEN x(y) = Modulo(y)-1¶
  IF a$ = CHR$(28) THEN ¶
    Colours(y) = 2¶
    y = y-1¶
  END IF¶
  ' CRSR Up¶
¶
  IF a$ = CHR$(29) THEN¶
    Colours(y) = 2 ¶
    y = (y+1) MOD 4¶
  END IF¶
  ' CRSR Down¶
  ¶
  IF y<0 THEN y=3¶
¶
  Colours(y) = 1¶
¶
  IF (x(0) > 0) AND (y=0) THEN¶
    x(1) = 0                 ' Select HAM or Halfbrite ¶
    x(3) = 5                 ' 5+1 BitPlanes¶
    Modulo(3) = 6¶
  END IF¶
  ¶
  IF x(0)>0 THEN x(3) = 5 ' Number of BitPlanes unchanged by ¶
                          ' HAM or Halfbrite mode¶
¶
  IF (x(0) = 0) AND (x(1)<>1) THEN ¶
     Modulo(3) = 5¶
     IF x(3) > 4 THEN x(3) = 4  ' Maximum 4+1 BitPlanes¶
  END IF                        ' in Normal Mode¶
  ¶
  IF (x(1) = 1) AND (y = 1) THEN¶
    x(0) = 0                    ' HIRES and Normal¶
    IF x(3)>3 THEN x(3) = 3     ' Maximum 3+1 BitPlanes ¶
    Modulo(3) = 4¶
  END IF¶
¶
  IF a$<> CHR$(13) THEN GOTO Outg¶
¶
  COLOR 1¶
  ¶
  RasterW%=(x(1)+1)*320¶
  RasterH%=(x(2)+1)*200 'PAL-resolution = 256¶
¶
  IF x(0) = 1 THEN Modus% = &H800       'HAM¶
  IF x(0) = 2 THEN Modus% = &H80        'HalfBrite¶
  IF x(1) = 1 THEN Modus% = &H8000      'HIRES¶
    ' (HAM, Halfbrite) and HIRES close the same way ¶
¶
  IF x(2) = 1 THEN Modus% = Modus% OR 4 'LACE¶
   ¶
  CLS¶
  RasterT% = x(3)+1¶
  ¶
  IF RasterT% = 6 THEN RasterT% = 5¶
    ' If HAM, open a normalscreen ¶
    ' (max. 5 BitPlanes)¶
  ¶
  IF FRE(-1) < (RasterW%/8*RasterH%*RasterT%)+5000 THEN¶
    CLS¶
```

```
    CALL PrintIt ("Insufficent memory for bitmap
!!!",100,False)¶
    CALL PrintIt ("Please try a lower resoluiton or number of
bitmaps !!!",130,False)¶
    ¶
    CALL DialogBox("Ok",1,True,x1b%,y1b%,x2b%,y2b%,False)¶
    CALL DoDialog(n%,1,-1,-1,-1,-1,x1b%,y1b%,x2b%,y2b%,-1,-1,-
1,-1) ¶
    CLS¶
    GOTO Outg¶
  END IF¶
    ¶
  SCREEN 1,RasterW%,RasterH%,RasterT%,x(1)+(x(2)*2)+1¶
    '      Width  ,Height    ,Depth  ,Mode¶
  ¶
  WINDOW 2,"",(0,0)-(RasterW%-9,RasterH%-15),0,1¶
    ' Window layer¶
  ¶
  RasterT% = x(3)+1¶
    ' old RasterT value¶
  ¶
  WBase& = WINDOW(7)¶
  WScreen& = PEEKL(WBase&+46)¶
    ' Extract address of the new screen from window addrress¶
  ¶
  POKEL WBase&+24,&H100 OR &H800 OR 65536&¶
    ' Window Flags change: Borderless, RBMTrap, NoCareRefresh¶
¶
  Viewport& = PEEKL(WBase&+46)+44¶
  ColorMap& = PEEKL(Viewport&+4)¶
  RastPort& = Viewport&+40¶
  BitMap& = WScreen&+184¶
¶
  Adr = PEEKL(RastPort&+4)+8          ' BitPlanes for loading¶
  FOR i=0 TO RasterT%-1               ' and saving¶
    BitPlanes&(i) = PEEKL(Adr+4*i)¶
  NEXT i¶
¶
  BitPlane6& = BitMap&+28¶
    ' Where do you want the sixth bitplane address placed ?¶
  ¶
  Depth& = BitMap&+5¶
    ' Where do you want the new depth placed ?¶
  ¶
  CALL SetRast&(RastPort&,0)¶
  CALL SetRGB4&(Viewport&,1,15,15,15)¶
  CALL SetRGB4&(Viewport&,0,0,0,0)¶
    ' Clear new screen and set background ¶
 ¶
  IF RasterT% = 6 THEN¶
    Groesse& = RasterW%*(RasterH%\8)¶
    Flags& = 65536&+2                   ' MEMF_CHIP | MEMF_CLEAR¶
    Mem& = AllocMem&(Groesse&,Flags&)¶
    IF Mem& = 0 THEN¶
      CALL Scroff¶
      CALL PrintIt("Not enough memory for sixth BitPlane
!!!",100,False)¶
      CALL DialogBox("Sorry
!",1,True,x1a%,y1a%,x2a%,y2a%,False)¶
¶
      CALL DoDialog(n%,1,-1,-1,-1,-1,x1a%,y1a%,x2a%,y2a%,-1,-1,-
1,-1)¶
```

```
        GOSUB CloseIt¶
        RUN¶
      END IF¶
      ¶
      POKE Depth&,6¶
        ' New depth¶
      ¶
      POKEL BitPlane6&,Mem&¶
      BitPlanes&(5)=Mem&¶
        ' Poke address of the sixth BitPlane¶
      ¶
      POKEW Viewport&+32,Modus%¶
        ' Poke for display mode POKEN¶
      ¶
      dummy = RemakeDisplay(dummy&)¶
        ' compute new display ¶
    END IF  ¶
¶
    Status$ = " Status: Initializing"+CHR$(0)¶
    CALL SetWindowTitles&(NWBase&,SADD(Status$),0)¶
¶
    CALL Scroff¶
    CALL SetDrMd&(RastPort&,1)¶
      ¶
    RasterW1% = RasterW%-1  ' 319/639¶
    RasterH1% = RasterH%-1  ' 199/399¶
    RasterW2% = RasterW%/2  ' Screen middle¶
    RasterH2% = RasterH%/2¶
    ¶
    FactorX = (x(1)+1)/2¶
    FactorY = (x(2)+1)/2¶
¶
    POKEW OSModus&,Modus%¶
    POKEL OSRastPort&,RastPort&¶
    POKEW OSRasterW1&,RasterW1%¶
    POKEW OSRasterH1&,RasterH1%¶
¶
    MaxColour% = 2^RasterT%¶
    IF (RasterT% = 6) THEN¶
      IF (Modus% AND &H800) = &H800 THEN ¶
        MaxColour% = 16                 'HAM¶
      ELSE¶
        MaxColour% = 64                 'Halfbrite¶
      END IF¶
    END IF¶
¶
    POKEW OSMaxColour&,2^RasterT%  'If HAM: 64 Colour!¶
    DIM Colour(MaxColour%,3)¶
 ¶
    FOR m%=0 TO 3¶
      Colour(1,m%)=0        'Black¶
      Colour(2,m%)=1        'White¶
    NEXT m%¶
¶
    IF (Modus% AND &H80) = &H80 THEN  'HalfBrite¶
      MF%=MaxColour%/2¶
 ¶
      Colour(MF%+1,0)=MF%¶
      Colour(MF%+2,0)=MF%+1¶
      FOR m%=1 TO 3¶
        Colour(MF%+1,m%)=0¶
        Colour(MF%+2,m%)=.5¶
```

```
    NEXT m%¶
    RESTORE OptimaleHBColour¶
  ELSE¶
    MF%=MaxColour%¶
    RESTORE OptimaleColour¶
  END IF¶
¶
  FOR n% = 3 TO MF%¶
    READ r%,g%,b%¶
¶
    Colour(n%,0)=n%-1¶
    Colour(n%,1)=r%/15¶
    Colour(n%,2)=g%/15¶
    Colour(n%,3)=b%/15¶
    CALL SetRGB4&(Viewport&,n%-1,r%,g%,b%)¶
¶
    IF (Modus% AND &H80)<>0 THEN           'HalfBrite¶
      Colour(n%+MF%,0)=n%+MF%¶
      FOR m%=1 TO 3¶
        Colour(n%+MF%,m%)=(INT(Colour(n%,m%)*15)\2)/15¶
      NEXT m%¶
    END IF¶
¶
  NEXT n%¶
    ' => Colour(n,0)     = color index, ¶
    '    Colour(n,1..3)  = RGB brightness¶
¶
  ' Poke colors into assembler routines array:¶
¶
  FOR n%=0 TO MaxColour%-1¶
    POKEW OSColour&+n%*8,Colour(n%+1,0)¶
    FOR m%=1 TO 3¶
      POKEW OSColour&+n%*8+m%*2,Colour(n%+1,m%)*1024¶
    NEXT m%¶
  NEXT n%¶
  CLS¶
RETURN¶
```

The `RasterInit` routine also sets the colors for the user screen. If you are not happy with the default colors these may also be changed:

```
ColorPalette:¶
  Status$ = " Status: Color change"+CHR$(0)¶
  CALL SetWindowTitles&(NWBase&,SADD(Status$),0)¶
¶
  GOSUB DeleteMenu¶
¶
  CALL SetRast&(RastPort&,0)¶
  CALL Scron¶
  CALL PrintIt("Which color to change ?",100,True)¶
  ¶
  NumCol = MaxColour%¶
  IF NumCol = 64 THEN NumCol = 32 ' Halfbrite ?¶
  Widthe = (RasterW%-40)/NumCol¶
  LINE ((20+1),1)-(20+Widthe-1,RasterH%/10-1),1,b ¶
  FOR i=1 TO NumCol-1¶
      LINE ((20+i*Widthe+1),1)-((20+(i+1)*Widthe)-1,RasterH%/10-
1),i,BF¶
      IF MaxColour% = 64 THEN   'Halfbrite Colour output¶
        LINE ((20+i*Widthe+1),RasterH%/10)-((20+(i+1)*Widthe)-
1,RasterH%/5-1),i+32,BF¶
```

```
      END IF¶
    NEXT¶
    ¶
  LoopA:¶
    CALL EmptyBuffers¶
¶
    WHILE MOUSE(0) = 0¶
    WEND¶
    ¶
    x = MOUSE (1)¶
    y = MOUSE (2)¶
    ¶
    IF (x < 20) OR (x > RasterW%-20) THEN ¶
      GOTO LoopA:¶
    END IF ¶
    IF (y < 1) OR (y > RasterH%/10) THEN¶
      GOTO LoopA:¶
    END IF¶
¶
    Colr% = INT ((x-20)/Widthe)   ' which colors was clicked¶
    CALL Scroff¶
    red=INT(Colour(Colr%+1,1)*15.5)¶
    green=INT(Colour(Colr%+1,2)*15.5)¶
    blue=INT(Colour(Colr%+1,3)*15.5)¶
    ¶
    LOCATE 10,1¶
    PRINT " red-component   (0..15) : ";¶
    CALL FormInputInt (red,30!,0!,15!)¶
    ¶
    LOCATE 11,1¶
    PRINT " green-component (0..15) : ";¶
    CALL FormInputInt (green,30!,0!,15!)¶
    ¶
    LOCATE 12,1¶
    PRINT " blue-component  (0..15) : ";¶
    CALL FormInputInt (blue,30!,0!,15!)¶
    ¶
    Colour(Colr%+1,1)=red/15¶
    Colour(Colr%+1,2)=green/15¶
    Colour(Colr%+1,3)=blue/15¶
¶
    POKEW OSColour&+Colr%*8+2,red/15*1024¶
    POKEW OSColour&+Colr%*8+4,green/15*1024¶
    POKEW OSColour&+Colr%*8+6,blue/15*1024¶
¶
    IF MaxColour%=64 THEN                  'ExtraHalfBrite¶
      Colour(Colr%+33,1)=(red\2)/15¶
      Colour(Colr%+33,2)=(green\2)/15¶
      Colour(Colr%+33,3)=(blue\2)/15¶
¶
      POKEW OSColour&+Colr%*8+258,(red\2)/15*1024¶
      POKEW OSColour&+Colr%*8+260,(green\2)/15*1024¶
      POKEW OSColour&+Colr%*8+262,(blue\2)/15*1024¶
¶
    END IF¶
    ¶
    CALL
SetRGB4&(Viewport&,Colr%,CINT(red),CINT(green),CINT(blue))¶
¶
    CALL DialogBox ("End",0,True,x1a%,y1a%,x2a%,y2a%,False)¶
    CALL DialogBox ("Next
color",2,False,x1b%,y1b%,x2b%,y2b%,False)¶
```

```
¶
  CALL DoDialog (n%,0,x1a%,y1a%,x2a%,y2a%,-1,-1,-1,-
1,x1b%,y1b%,x2b%,y2b%)¶
  CLS¶
¶
  IF n% = 2 THEN ¶
    CALL Scron¶
    GOTO LoopA¶
  END IF¶
  Newone! = True¶
  Hg = False¶
  GOSUB MakeMenu¶
RETURN¶
'¶
```

The colors of the user screen can, if you want, be changed in the `RasterInit` routine by using the `PALETTE` statement.

We have provided for file access between computer and disk. You can build object definitions with the editor and then load existing definitions from disk into the tracer program. Or you can merge different object definitions and save all of the objects together on disk:

```
'  ********************************¶
'  *      'SERVICE' - Module      *¶
'  ********************************¶
'¶
Saver:  ¶
  ' Save array K() to disk¶
  GOSUB Directory¶
¶
  Status$ = " Status: Object Saver"+CHR$(0)¶
  CALL SetWindowTitles&(NWBase&,SADD(Status$),0)¶
  ¶
  LOCATE 3,1¶
  PRINT "  Under what name do you want the object saved?"¶
  PRINT    ¶
  PRINT "      Filename : ";¶
  dn$ = ""¶
  CALL FormInputString (dn$,30!)¶
¶
  CLS¶
  IF dn$<>"" THEN¶
    dn$ = dn$ + ".LIST"¶
    OPEN "O",#1,dn$,1024¶
    PRINT #1,NumberK¶
    FOR n%=1 TO NumberK¶
      FOR p%=0 TO 5¶
        PRINT #1,K(n%,p%,0),K(n%,p%,1),K(n%,p%,2)¶
      NEXT p%¶
    NEXT n%¶
    CLOSE #1¶
'The following will delete icons when included:¶
'    dn$ = dn$+".info"¶
'    KILL dn$¶
  END IF¶
  CLS¶
  GOSUB MakeMenu¶
RETURN¶
'¶
```

```
Loader:¶
  ' Load array K() from disk¶
  GOSUB Directory¶
¶
  Status$ = " Status: Object Loader"+CHR$(0)¶
  CALL SetWindowTitles&(NWBase&,SADD(Status$),0)¶
¶
  LOCATE 3,1¶
  PRINT "  Which object do you wish to load?"¶
  PRINT ¶
  PRINT "      Filename : ";¶
  dn$ = ""¶
  CALL FormInputString (dn$,30!)¶
¶
  CLS¶
  IF dn$ <> "" THEN¶
    dn$ = dn$+".LIST"¶
    OPEN "I",#1,dn$,1024¶
    INPUT #1,NumberK¶
    LOCATE 10,10¶
    PRINT "Total ";NumberK;" Object ("+dn$+")."¶
    PRINT¶
    PRINT "       Maximum number of objects? ";¶
    MaxNumber = NumberK¶
    CALL FormInputInt (MaxNumber,30!,1!,NumberK)¶
¶
    IF NumberK > MaxNumber THEN NumberK = MaxNumber¶
¶
    ERASE K¶
    DIM K(MaxNumber,5,2)¶
    ¶
    FOR n%=1 TO NumberK¶
      FOR p%=0 TO 5¶
        INPUT #1,K(n%,p%,0),K(n%,p%,1),K(n%,p%,2)¶
      NEXT p%¶
    NEXT n%¶
    CLOSE #1¶
    Newone! = True¶
    Start% = 1¶
  END IF¶
  CLS¶
  GOSUB MakeMenu¶
RETURN¶
'¶
Merger:¶
  ' Elements appended to available array K()¶
  IF (MaxNumber-NumberK) <= 0 THEN¶
    Status$ = " Status: Object Merger"+CHR$(0)¶
    CALL SetWindowTitles&(NWBase&,SADD(Status$),0)¶
¶
    a$ = "Insufficent memory for more objects!!!"¶
    CALL PrintIt (a$,100,False)¶
    a$ = "Please select New to create a cleared array K()!"¶
    CALL PrintIt (a$,130,False)¶
    CALL DialogBox("OK",1,True,x1a%,y1a%,x2a%,y2a%,False)¶
  ¶
    CALL DoDialog(n%,1,-1,-1,-1,-1,x1a%,y1a%,x2a%,y2a%,-1,-1,-
1,-1)¶
  ELSE ¶
    GOSUB Directory¶
¶
    Status$ = " Status: Object Merger"+CHR$(0)¶
```

```
    CALL SetWindowTitles&(NWBase&,SADD(Status$),0)¶
¶
    LOCATE 3,1¶
    PRINT " Which object would you like to merge?"¶
    PRINT¶
    dn$ = "" ¶
    PRINT "      Filename : ";¶
    CALL FormInputString (dn$,30!)¶
¶
    CLS¶
    IF dn$ <> "" THEN¶
      dn$ = dn$ + ".LIST"¶
      OPEN "I",#1,dn$,1024¶
      INPUT #1,x¶
    ¶
      LOCATE 6,1¶
      PRINT "        Total ";x;" Objects ("+dn$+")."¶
      PRINT ¶
      PRINT "        Sufficent memory for ";MaxNumber-NumberK;"
Objects."¶
      PRINT¶
      PRINT "    How many merges? ";¶
      num = x¶
      CALL FormInputInt (num,30!,1!,1000!)¶
¶
      IF x<num THEN num = x¶
      IF MaxNumber-NumberK<num THEN num = MaxNumber-NumberK¶
¶
      IF num>=1 THEN¶
        FOR n%=NumberK+1 TO NumberK+num¶
          FOR p%=0 TO 5¶
            INPUT #1,K(n%,p%,0),K(n%,p%,1),K(n%,p%,2)¶
          NEXT p%¶
        NEXT n%¶
        NumberK = NumberK+num¶
        Newone! = True¶
        Start% = 1¶
      END IF¶
      CLOSE #1¶
    END IF¶
  END IF¶
  CLS¶
  GOSUB MakeMenu¶
RETURN¶
'¶
```

When merging objects, array `K()`, where the objects are stored internally, must be large enough to accommodate these objects. The number of array elements is set in `ArrayInit`. Any object definitions stored previously here are lost:

```
ArrayInit:¶
  ' Create new array K()  ¶
  Status$ = " Status: New array creation"+CHR$(0)¶
  CALL SetWindowTitles&(NWBase&,SADD(Status$),0)¶
 ¶
  GOSUB DeleteMenu¶
  ¶
  LOCATE 10,1¶
  PRINT "        Maximum number of objects = ";¶
  a = MaxNumber¶
```

```
  CALL FormInputInt (a,30!,0!,1000!)¶
 ¶
  IF MaxNumber <> a THEN¶
    MaxNumber = a¶
    NumberK=0¶
    ERASE K¶
    DIM K(MaxNumber,5,2)¶
    Start% = 0¶
  END IF¶
¶
  CLS¶
  GOSUB MakeMenu¶
RETURN¶
'¶
'¶
```

In addition to object definitions, you can also load new material constants created in the editor from disk into the tracer:

```
LoadMat:¶
  GOSUB Directory¶
   ¶
  Status$ = " Status: Material constants loader"+CHR$(0)¶
  CALL SetWindowTitles&(NWBase&,SADD(Status$),0)¶
¶
  LOCATE 3,1¶
  PRINT "  Which material would you like to load?"¶
  PRINT  ¶
  PRINT "      Filename : ";¶
¶
  dn$ = ""¶
  CALL FormInputString (dn$,30!)¶
¶
  IF dn$<>"" THEN     ¶
    dn$=dn$+".MAT"¶
    OPEN "i",#1,dn$¶
    matptr = 1¶
    INPUT #1,NumberMat¶
    ERASE Mat¶
    DIM Mat(NumberMat,6)¶
    WHILE NOT(EOF(1))¶
      FOR i=0 TO 6¶
        INPUT #1,Mat(matptr,i)¶
      NEXT i¶
      matptr = matptr+1¶
    WEND¶
    CLOSE #1¶
  END IF¶
  CLS¶
  GOSUB MakeMenu¶
RETURN¶
```

We have added a routine for you that makes it possible to save the screens created by the tracer program as an IFF (Interchange File Format) file. A picture saved in this format can be used with any program that supports IFF (e.g., ***DeluxePaint***®):

```
ScreenSaver:¶
  GOSUB Directory¶
   ¶
```

```
  Status$ = " Status: Screen saver"+CHR$(0)¶
  CALL SetWindowTitles&(NWBase&,SADD(Status$),0)¶
¶
  LOCATE 3,1¶
  PRINT "  Under what name would you like the screen saved?"¶
  PRINT  ¶
  PRINT "      Filename : ";¶
  IFFFile$ = ""¶
  CALL FormInputString (IFFFile$,30!)¶
     ¶
  IF IFFFile$ <> "" THEN¶
    ¶
    Handle& = 0      ' File Handle¶
    Buffer& = 0      ' Buffer memory¶
    ' reserve buffer¶
    Flags& = 65537&     ' MEMF_PUBLIC | MEMF_CLEAR¶
    BufferSize& = 360¶
    Buffer& = AllocMem&(BufferSize&,Flags&)¶
    IF Buffer& = 0 THEN¶
      Dialog$ = "No more memory!!!"¶
      GOTO EndSave¶
    END IF¶
¶
    ColorBuffer& = Buffer&¶
¶
    Null& = 0¶
    PadByte%  = 0¶
    ¶
    IF RasterW% = 320 THEN¶
      IF RasterH% = 200 THEN¶
        Aspect% = &HA0B¶
      ELSE¶
        Aspect% = &H140B¶
      END IF¶
    ELSE¶
      IF RasterH% = 200 THEN¶
        Aspect% = &H50B¶
      ELSE¶
        Aspect% = &HA0B¶
      END IF¶
    END IF¶
¶
    IFFFile$ = IFFFile$ + CHR$(0)¶
    Handle& = xOpen&(SADD(IFFFile$),1006)¶
    IF Handle& = 0 THEN¶
      Dialog$ = "Can't open the file you wanted!!!"¶
      GOTO EndSave¶
    END IF¶
¶
¶
    ' How many bytes contain IFF-Chunks ?¶
    BMHDSize& = 20¶
    CMAPSize& = MaxColour%*3 + ((MaxColour%*3) AND 1)¶
    CAMGSize& = 4¶
    BODYSize& = (RasterW%/8)*RasterH%*RasterT%¶
    ' FORMsize& = Chunk-Length + 8 Bytes per Chunk-Header + 4
Bytes ("ILBM")¶
    FORMSize& = BMHDSize&+CMAPSize&+CAMGSize&+BODYSize&+36¶
¶
    ' FORM-Header ¶
    Chunk$ = "FORM"¶
    Length& = xWrite&(Handle&,SADD(Chunk$),4)¶
```

```
    Length& = xWrite&(Handle&,VARPTR(FORMSize&),4)¶
    ' + ILBM for BitMap-File¶
    Chunk$ = "ILBM"¶
    Length& = xWrite&(Handle&,SADD(Chunk$),4)¶
¶
    IF Length& <= 0 THEN¶
      Dialog$ = "Write error on FORM-Header !!!"¶
      GOTO EndSave¶
    END IF   ¶
¶
    ' BMHD-Chunk ¶
    Chunk$ = "BMHD"¶
    Length& = xWrite&(Handle&,SADD(Chunk$),4)¶
    Length& = xWrite&(Handle&,VARPTR(BMHDSize&),4)¶
    Length& = xWrite&(Handle&,VARPTR(RasterW%),2)¶
    Length& = xWrite&(Handle&,VARPTR(RasterH%),2)¶
    Length& = xWrite&(Handle&,VARPTR(Null&),4)¶
    Temp% = (256 * RasterT%) ' No MASKING¶
    Length& = xWrite&(Handle&,VARPTR(Temp%),2)¶
    Temp% = 0                ' No Packing¶
    Length& = xWrite&(Handle&,VARPTR(Temp%),2)¶
    Temp% = 0¶
    Length& = xWrite&(Handle&,VARPTR(Temp%),2)¶
    Length& = xWrite&(Handle&,VARPTR(Aspect%),2)¶
    Length& = xWrite&(Handle&,VARPTR(RasterW%),2)¶
    Length& = xWrite&(Handle&,VARPTR(RasterH%),2)¶
¶
    IF Length& <= 0 THEN¶
      Dialog$ = "Write error on BMHD-Chunk !!!"¶
      GOTO EndSave¶
    END IF   ¶
¶
    ' CMAP-Chunk ¶
    Chunk$ = "CMAP"¶
    Length& = xWrite&(Handle&,SADD(Chunk$),4)¶
    Length& = xWrite&(Handle&,VARPTR(CMAPSize&),4)¶
¶
    FOR i%=0 TO MaxColour%-1¶
      Colours% = GetRGB4%(ColorMap&,i%)¶
      blue = Colours% AND 15¶
      Colours% = Colours% - blue¶
      green = (Colours%/16) AND 15¶
      Colours% = Colours%-green*16¶
      red = (Colours%/256) AND 15¶
      POKE(ColorBuffer&+(i%*3)),red*16¶
      POKE(ColorBuffer&+(i%*3)+1),green*16 ¶
      POKE(ColorBuffer&+(i%*3)+2),blue*16¶
    NEXT¶
¶
    Length& = xWrite&(Handle&,ColorBuffer&,CMAPSize&)¶
¶
    IF Length& <= 0 THEN¶
      Dialog$ = "Write error on CMAP-Chunk !!!"¶
      GOTO EndSave¶
    END IF   ¶
¶
    ' CAMG-Chunk ¶
    Chunk$ = "CAMG"¶
    Length& = xWrite&(Handle&,SADD(Chunk$),4)¶
    Length& = xWrite&(Handle&,VARPTR(CAMGSize&),4)¶
    Modes& = PEEKW(Viewport& + 32)¶
    Length& = xWrite&(Handle&,VARPTR(Modes&),4)¶
```

```
¶
    IF Length& <= 0 THEN¶
      Dialog$ = "Write error on CAMG-Chunk !!!"¶
      GOTO EndSave¶
    END IF   ¶
    ¶
    ' BODY-Chunk (BitMaps)¶
    Chunk$ = "BODY"¶
    Length& = xWrite&(Handle&,SADD(Chunk$),4)¶
    Length& = xWrite&(Handle&,VARPTR(BODYSize&),4)¶
    BytesPerRow% = RasterW%/8¶
    FOR y1 = 0 TO RasterH%-1¶
      FOR b=0 TO RasterT%-1¶
        Adress& = BitPlanes&(b)+(y1*BytesPerRow%)¶
        Length& = xWrite&(Handle&,Adress&,BytesPerRow%)    ¶
        IF Length& <= 0 THEN¶
          Dialog$ = "Write error  on BODY-Chunk !!!"¶
          GOTO EndSave¶
        END IF      ¶
      NEXT¶
    NEXT¶
  ¶
    Dialog$ = "Saving OK"¶
¶
  EndSave:¶
    IF Handle& <> 0 THEN CALL xClose&(Handle&)¶
    IF Buffer& <> 0 THEN CALL FreeMem&(Buffer&,BufferSize&)¶
    CALL DialogBox(Dialog$,1,True,x1b%,y1b%,x2b%,y2b%,False)¶
    CALL DoDialog(n%,1,-1,-1,-1,-1,x1b%,y1b%,x2b%,y2b%,-1,-1,-
1,-1)  ¶
  END IF¶
  CLS ¶
  GOSUB MakeMenu¶
RETURN¶
'¶
```

Files created from this routine are not created in compressed form. More memory is required for saving an IFF file to disk, but IFF files save to disk 75% faster than normal files.

We also thought about printed output. The following hardcopy routine sends the graphic on a printer. It uses the printer driver that was chosen from Preferences:

```
HardCopy:¶
  Status$ = " Status: Screen hardcopy"+CHR$(0)¶
  CALL SetWindowTitles&(NWBase&,SADD(Status$),0)¶
¶
  GOSUB DeleteMenu¶
¶
  CALL DialogBox("No Printer",0,True,x1a%,y1a%,x2a%,y2a%,False)
¶
  CALL DialogBox("Printer
OK",2,False,x1c%,y1c%,x2c%,y2c%,False)¶
  CALL DoDialog(n%,0,x1a%,y1a%,x2a%,ya2%,-1,-1,-1,-
1,x1c%,y1c%,x2c%,y2c%)  ¶
  CLS¶
  IF n% <> 0 THEN¶
    Modes% = PEEKW(Viewport& + 32)¶
¶
```

```
    sigBit% =  AllocSignal%(-1)¶
    Flags& = 65537&                ' MEMF_PUBLIC | MEMF_CLEAR¶
    MsgPort& = AllocMem&(40,Flags&)¶
    IF MsgPort& = 0 THEN¶
      Dialog$ = "No 'MsgPort' !!!"¶
      GOTO EndPrinter4¶
    END IF¶
¶
    POKE(MsgPort& + 8), 4 ¶
    POKE(MsgPort& + 9), 0 ¶
    Nam$ = "PrtPort"+CHR$(0)¶
    POKEL(MsgPort& + 10), SADD(Nam$)¶
    POKE(MsgPort& + 14), 0 ¶
    POKE(MsgPort& + 15), sigBit%¶
    SigTask& = FindTask&(0)¶
    POKEL(MsgPort& + 16), SigTask&¶
¶
    CALL AddPort(MsgPort&)  'lsit Port¶
¶
    ioRequest& = AllocMem&(64,Flags&)¶
    IF ioRequest& = 0  THEN¶
      Dialog$ = "No ioRequest !!!"¶
      GOTO EndPrinter3¶
    END IF¶
¶
    POKE(ioRequest& + 8),5 ¶
    POKE(ioRequest& + 9),0 ¶
    POKEL(ioRequest& + 14), MsgPort&¶
¶
¶
    Nam$ = "printer.device"+CHR$(0)¶
    PrinterError& = OpenDevice&(SADD(Nam$),0,ioRequest&,0)¶
    IF PrinterError& <> 0  THEN¶
      Dialog$ = "No Printer ?!?"¶
      GOTO EndPrinter2¶
    END IF¶
¶
    POKEW(ioRequest& + 28), 11          ' DumpRastport to
Printer¶
    POKEL(ioRequest& + 32), RastPort&   ' Print entire screen ¶
    POKEL(ioRequest& + 36), ColorMap&¶
    POKEL(ioRequest& + 40), Modes%¶
    POKEW(ioRequest& + 44), 0¶
    POKEW(ioRequest& + 46), 0¶
    POKEW(ioRequest& + 48), RasterW%¶
    POKEW(ioRequest& + 50), RasterH%¶
    POKEL(ioRequest& + 52), 0&¶
    POKEL(ioRequest& + 56), 0&¶
    POKEW(ioRequest& + 60), &H84¶
¶
    CALL
DialogBox("Printing...",1,False,x1a%,y1a%,x2a%,y2a%,False)  ¶
  ¶
    PrinterError& = DoIO&(ioRequest&)¶
    IF PrinterError& <> 0 THEN¶
      Dialog$ = "DumpRPort Error ="+STR$(PrinterError&)+" !!!"¶
      GOTO EndPrinter¶
    END IF¶
¶
    CLS¶
    Dialog$ = "Hardcopy done"¶
  ¶
```

```
    EndPrinter:     ¶
      CALL CloseDevice(ioRequest&)¶
¶
    EndPrinter2:¶
      POKE(ioRequest& + 8), &HFF¶
      POKEL(ioRequest& + 20), -1¶
      POKEL(ioRequest& + 24), -1¶
      CALL FreeMem&(ioRequest&,64)¶
¶
    EndPrinter3:¶
      CALL RemPort(MsgPort&)¶
      POKE(MsgPort& + 8), &HFF  ¶
      POKEL(MsgPort& + 20), -1¶
      CALL FreeSignal(sigBit%)¶
      CALL FreeMem&(MsgPort&,40)¶
  ¶
    EndPrinter4:¶
      CALL DialogBox(Dialog$,1,True,x1b%,y1b%,x2b%,y2b%,False)¶
      CALL DoDialog(n%,1,-1,-1,-1,-1,x1b%,y1b%,x2b%,y2b%,-1,-1,-
1,-1)  ¶
  END IF¶
  CLS¶
  GOSUB MakeMenu  ¶
RETURN¶
'¶
```

We included a routine to create a new background for the picture created by the tracer routine. This can give more realism to the picture than the usual background color does. This is done using the routines `Background`, `Sky`, `Fhg` (floating colors) and `ScreenLoader`.

These routines allow you to choose between a simple pattern, a starry sky, a floating background that consists of a color and brightness change between colors, or an IFF picture that was created with a drawing program.

```
Background:¶
  ' Background Determine¶
  Status$ = " Status: Background selection"+CHR$(0)¶
  CALL SetWindowTitles&(NWBase&,SADD(Status$),0)¶
¶
  GOSUB DeleteMenu¶
  ¶
  CALL DialogBox("Pattern",0,True,x1a%,y1a%,x2a%,y2a%,False)¶
  CALL DialogBox("Load
screen",2,False,x1b%,y1b%,x2b%,y2b%,False)¶
  ¶
  CALL DoDialog(n%,0,x1a%,y1a%,x2a%,y2a%,-1,-1,-1,-
1,x1b%,y1b%,x2b%,y2b%)¶
  CLS  ¶
¶
  IF n%=2 THEN¶
    GOSUB ScreenLoader¶
    Hg = True¶
  ELSE¶
    CALL DialogBox("Pattern",0,True,x1a%,y1a%,x2a%,y2a%,False)¶
    CALL DialogBox("Sky",1,False,x1b%,y1b%,x2b%,y2b%,False)¶
    CALL
DialogBox("Floating",2,False,x1c%,y1c%,x2c%,y2c%,False)¶
¶
```

```
    CALL
DoDialog(n%,0,x1a%,y1a%,x2a%,y2a%,x1b%,y1b%,x2b%,y2b%,x1c%,y1c%,
x2c%,y2c%)    ¶
    CLS¶
¶
    IF n% = 0 THEN    ¶
    ¶
      CALL PrintIt("Background = Pattern",40,False)¶
      ¶
      LOCATE 10,1¶
      PRINT "       Number of the pattern (0..34) : ";¶
      a = 0¶
      CALL FormInputInt (Hx,30!,0!,34!)¶
      Xpattern% = a¶
¶
      LOCATE 11,1      ¶
      PRINT "       Foreground pen (APen) : ";¶
      a=APen%¶
      CALL FormInputInt (a,30!,0!,CSNG(MaxColour%-1))¶
      APen% = a¶
¶
      LOCATE 12,1      ¶
      PRINT "       Background pen (BPen) : ";¶
      a = BPen%¶
      CALL FormInputInt (a,30!,0!,CSNG(MaxColour%-1))¶
      BPen% = a¶
¶
      Xpattern% = Xpattern% MOD
(NumberPatternS%+NumberPatternX%*2+1)¶
¶
      IF Xpattern% > NumberPatternS% THEN¶
        CALL
ExtendedFill(0,0,RasterW1%,RasterH1%,PatternHX(Xpattern%-
NumberPatternS%),0!,1!,APen%,BPen%)¶
       ELSE¶
        CALL
StandardFill(0,0,RasterW1%,RasterH1%,PatternHS(NumberPatternS%-
Xpattern%),APen%,BPen%)   ¶
      END IF¶
      CLS¶
      Hg = True¶
    END IF¶
    ¶
    IF n% = 1 THEN¶
      LOCATE 3,1¶
      PRINT " Sky type:"¶
      PRINT "  0 = Stars (scattered)"¶
      PRINT "  1 = Stars (centered)"¶
      PRINT "  2 = Lines (scattered)"¶
      PRINT "  3 = Lines (centered)"¶
      PRINT "  4 = Lines (middle centered)" ¶
      ¶
      LOCATE 10,1¶
      PRINT " Type   : ";¶
      a = Art%¶
      CALL FormInputInt (a,30!,0!,4!)¶
      Art% = a¶
¶
      LOCATE 11,1¶
      PRINT " Color  : ";¶
      a = 1¶
      CALL FormInputInt (a,30!,0!,CSNG(MaxColour%-1))¶
```

```
        HColr% = a¶
              ¶
        LOCATE 12,1¶
        PRINT " Number : ";¶
        a = 100¶
        CALL FormInputInt (a,30!,0!,500!)¶
        num% = a¶
¶
        CLS¶
        CALL Sky (Art%,HColr%,num%)¶
        Hg = True¶
      END IF¶
      ¶
      IF n% = 2 THEN¶
        CLS¶
         ¶
        CALL PrintIt("Floating Background",40,False)¶
        ¶
        LOCATE 10,1¶
        PRINT "        from color: ";¶
        F1 = 0¶
        CALL FormInput (F1,30!,0!,CSNG(MaxColour%-1))¶
        Colours1%=F1¶
        LOCATE 12,1¶
        PRINT "        to color: ";¶
        F2 = 1¶
        CALL FormInput (F2,30!,0!,CSNG(MaxColour%-1))¶
        Colours2%=F2¶
   ¶
        CALL Fhg(Colours1%,Colours2%)¶
        Hg = True¶
      END IF¶
    END IF¶
    CLS  ¶
    GOSUB MakeMenu¶
RETURN¶



SUB Fhg(Colours1%,Colours2%) STATIC¶
SHARED RasterW1%,RasterH1%,Colour(),MaxColour%,WScreen&¶
SHARED NWBase&,RastPort&,OSSetPoint&,OSModus&,OSMaxColour&¶
    ' Produce floating passage between Colours1 and Colours2¶
    CALL Scron¶
      ¶
    red.s=Colour(Colours1%+1,1)¶
    green.s=Colour(Colours1%+1,2)¶
    blue.s=Colour(Colours1%+1,3)¶
    red.e=Colour(Colours2%+1,1)¶
    green.e=Colour(Colours2%+1,2)¶
    blue.e=Colour(Colours2%+1,3)¶
¶
    IF (PEEKW(OSModus&) AND &H800) = &H800 THEN  'HAM¶
¶
 'Background limited to 16 Colors, or else Objects disturbed.¶
¶
      POKEW OSMaxColour&,16¶
      FOR y%=0 TO RasterH1%¶
        red=red.s+(y%/RasterH1%)*(red.e-red.s)¶
        green=green.s+(y%/RasterH1%)*(green.e-green.s)¶
        blue=blue.s+(y%/RasterH1%)*(blue.e-blue.s)¶
'        CALL SetPoint(0,y%,RasterW1%,y%,red,green,blue)¶
```

```
        CALL
OSSetPoint&(0,y%,RasterW1%,y%,CLNG(1024*red),CLNG(1024*green),CL
NG(1024*blue))¶
      NEXT y%¶
      POKEW OSMaxColour&,64¶
    ELSE¶
      FOR y%=0 TO RasterH1%¶
        red=red.s+(y%/RasterH1%)*(red.e-red.s)¶
        green=green.s+(y%/RasterH1%)*(green.e-green.s)¶
        blue=blue.s+(y%/RasterH1%)*(blue.e-blue.s)¶
'        CALL SetPoint(0,y%,RasterW1%,y%,red,green,blue)¶
        CALL
OSSetPoint&(0,y%,RasterW1%,y%,CLNG(1024*red),CLNG(1024*green),CL
NG(1024*blue))¶
      NEXT y%¶
    END IF¶
    CALL Scroff¶
END SUB¶
'¶
SUB Sky(a%,Col%,num%) STATIC¶
SHARED WScreen&,NWBase&,RasterW%,RasterH%,RasterW1%¶
SHARED RasterH1%,RasterW2%,RasterH2%,RastPort&¶
    CALL Scron¶
      ¶
    CALL SetAPen&(RastPort&,Col%)¶
    CALL SetRast&(RastPort&,0)¶
    ¶
    FOR n%=1 TO num%¶
      RANDOMIZE TIMER¶
¶
      IF a%<4 THEN¶
        IF a% AND 1 THEN¶
          x%=RasterW2%+RasterW2%*RND*RND*SGN(RND-.5)¶
          y%=RasterH2%+RasterH2%*RND*RND*SGN(RND-.5)¶
        ELSE¶
          x%=RND*RasterW1%¶
          y%=RND*RasterH1%¶
        END IF¶
¶
        IF a% AND 2 THEN¶
          IF x%=RasterW2% AND y%=RasterH2% THEN¶
            dummy = WritePixel(RastPort&,x%,y%)¶
          ELSE¶
            x1%=(x%-RasterW2%)*.1+x%¶
            y1%=(y%-RasterH2%)*.1+y%¶
            IF x1%>=0 AND x1%<RasterW% AND y1%>=0 AND y1%<RasterH%
THEN¶
              CALL Move&(RastPort&,x%,y%)¶
              CALL Draw&(RastPort&,x1%,y1%)¶
            END IF¶
          END IF¶
        ELSE¶
¶
          IF RND<.9 THEN¶
            CALL WritePixel&(RastPort&,x%,y%)¶
          ELSE¶
            CALL Move&(RastPort&,x%-1,y%)¶
            CALL Draw&(RastPort&,x%+1,y%)¶
            CALL Draw&(RastPort&,x%,y%-1)¶
            CALL Draw&(RastPort&,x%,y%+1)¶
          END IF¶
        END IF¶
```

```
    ELSE¶
¶
      x%=RND*RasterW1%¶
      y%=RND*RasterH1%¶
      CALL Move&(RastPort&,RasterW2%,RasterH2%)¶
      CALL Draw&(RastPort&,x%,y%)¶
    END IF¶
  NEXT n%¶
¶
  CALL SetAPen&(RastPort&,1)¶
¶
  CALL Scroff  ¶
END SUB¶
'¶
¶
ScreenLoader:¶
  GOSUB Directory¶
   ¶
  Status$ = " Status: Screen Loader"+CHR$(0)¶
  CALL SetWindowTitles&(NWBase&,SADD(Status$),0)¶
¶
  LOCATE 3,1¶
    PRINT "  Which IFF-File would you like to load?"¶
  PRINT  ¶
  PRINT "      Filename : ";¶
  IFFFile$ = ""¶
  CALL FormInputString (IFFFile$,30!)¶
      ¶
  IF IFFFile$ <> "" THEN¶
¶
    BMHD = False¶
    CMAP = False¶
    CAMG = False¶
    Body = False¶
¶
    Handle& = 0¶
    Buffer& = 0¶
¶
    ' reserve buffer¶
    Flags& = 65537&       ' MEMF_PUBLIC | MEMF_CLEAR¶
    BufferSize& = 360¶
    Buffer& = AllocMem&(BufferSize&,Flags&)¶
    IF Buffer& = 0 THEN¶
      Dialog$ = "No more memory!!!"¶
      GOTO EndLoad¶
    END IF¶
¶
    InputBuffer& = Buffer&¶
    ColorBuffer& = Buffer& + 120¶
¶
¶
    IFFFile$ = IFFFile$ + CHR$(0)¶
    Handle& = xOpen&(SADD(IFFFile$),1005)¶
    IF Handle& = 0 THEN¶
      Dialog$ = "IFF-File can not be opened!!!"¶
      GOTO EndLoad¶
    END IF¶
¶
¶
    Length& = xRead&(Handle&,InputBuffer&,12)¶
    Chunk$ = ""¶
    FOR n% = 8 TO 11¶
```

```
      Chunk$ = Chunk$ + CHR$(PEEK(InputBuffer&+n%))¶
    NEXT¶
¶
    IF Chunk$ <> "ILBM" THEN ¶
      Dialog$ = "Not IFF-Format !!!"¶
      GOTO EndLoad¶
    END IF¶
¶
  ReadLoop:¶
    Length& = xRead&(Handle&,InputBuffer&,8)¶
    Chunkwinlen& = PEEKL(InputBuffer& + 4)¶
    Chunk$ = ""¶
    FOR n% = 0 TO 3¶
      Chunk$ = Chunk$ + CHR$(PEEK(InputBuffer&+n%))¶
    NEXT   ¶
    ¶
    IF Chunk$ = "BMHD" THEN         ' BitMap-Header ¶
      BMHD = True¶
      Length& = xRead&(Handle&,InputBuffer&,Chunkwinlen&)¶
      RDepth%        = PEEK(InputBuffer& + 8)  ¶
      Compression%   = PEEK(InputBuffer& + 10)¶
      RWidth%        = PEEKW(InputBuffer& + 16)¶
      RHeight%       = PEEKW(InputBuffer& + 18)¶
      BytesPerRow%   = RWidth%/8¶
      RMaxColors%    = 2^(RDepth%)¶
¶
      '  IFF-Picture adapted to Display-Screen ?¶
      IF (RWidth% <> RasterW%) OR (RHeight% <> RasterH%) THEN¶
        Dialog$ = "Format error: "+STR$(RWidth%)+"
x"+STR$(RHeight%)¶
        GOTO EndLoad¶
      END IF¶
¶
    ELSEIF Chunk$ = "CMAP" THEN  ' Color-Palette¶
      Length& = xRead&(Handle&,ColorBuffer&,Chunkwinlen&)¶
      CMAP = True¶
      ' Color-Palette set up¶
      FOR n% = 0 TO RMaxColors% - 1¶
        red%   = PEEK(ColorBuffer&+(n%*3))/16¶
        green% = PEEK(ColorBuffer&+(n%*3)+1)/16¶
        blue%  = PEEK(ColorBuffer&+(n%*3)+2)/16¶
        dummy = SetRGB4(Viewport&,n%,red%,green%,blue%)¶
                        ¶
        POKEW OSColour&+n%*8+2,red%/15*1024¶
        POKEW OSColour&+n%*8+4,green%/15*1024¶
        POKEW OSColour&+n%*8+6,blue%/15*1024¶
      NEXT¶
¶
    ELSEIF Chunk$ = "BODY" THEN  'BitMap Loader¶
      CALL Scron¶
      Body = True¶
      IF Compression% = 0 THEN  'No compression¶
        FOR y1 = 0 TO RHeight% -1¶
          FOR b = 0 TO RDepth% -1¶
            IF b<RasterT% THEN¶
              Adress& = BitPlanes&(b)+(y1*BytesPerRow%)¶
            ELSE¶
              Adress& = Buffer&¶
            END IF¶
            Length& = xRead&(Handle&,Adress&,BytesPerRow%)    ¶
          NEXT¶
        NEXT¶
```

```
¶
    ELSEIF Compression% = 1 THEN  'CmpByteRun1 compression¶
      FOR y1 = 0 TO RHeight% -1¶
        FOR b = 0 TO RDepth% -1¶
          IF b<RasterT% THEN¶
            Adress& = BitPlanes&(b)+(y1*BytesPerRow%)¶
          ELSE¶
            Adress& = Buffer&¶
          END IF¶
          NumBytes% = 0¶
            ¶
          WHILE (NumBytes% < BytesPerRow%)¶
            Length& = xRead&(Handle&,InputBuffer&,1)¶
            Code% = PEEK(InputBuffer&)¶
            IF Code% < 128 THEN         ' Code%-Bytes take over¶
              Length& = xRead&(Handle&,Adress& + NumBytes%,
Code%+1)¶
              NumBytes% = NumBytes% + Code% + 1¶
            ELSEIF Code% > 128 THEN     ' Byte replicates¶
              Length& = xRead&(Handle&,InputBuffer&,1)    ¶
              Byte% = PEEK(InputBuffer&)¶
              FOR n% = NumBytes% TO NumBytes% + 257 - Code%¶
                POKE(Adress&+n%),Byte%¶
              NEXT   ¶
              NumBytes% = NumBytes% + 257 - Code%¶
            END IF¶
          WEND¶
        NEXT¶
      NEXT¶
        ¶
      ELSE¶
        Dialog$ = "Unknown compression procedure!!!"¶
        GOTO EndLoad¶
      END IF¶
    CALL Scroff¶
    ELSE ¶
      ' "Unknown" Chunk-Typ¶
      FOR n = 1 TO Chunkwinlen&¶
        Length& = xRead&(Handle&,InputBuffer&,1)¶
      NEXT¶
      ' Chunks have even numnber of bytes¶
      IF (Chunkwinlen& AND 1) = 1 THEN ¶
        Length& = xRead&(Handle&,InputBuffer&,1)¶
      END IF¶
    END IF¶
¶
    ' All Chunks read?¶
    IF (BMHD = True) AND (CMAP = True) AND (Body = True) THEN¶
      GOTO LoadOK¶
    END IF¶
¶
    ' Read ok, get next Chunk¶
    IF Length& > 0 THEN GOTO ReadLoop¶
¶
    IF Length& < 0 THEN    ¶
      Dialog$ = "Read error!!!"¶
      GOTO EndLoad¶
    END IF   ¶
  ¶
    IF (BMHD=False) OR (CMAP=False) OR (Body=0) THEN¶
      Dialog$ = "Not all necessary ILBM-Chunks found!!!"¶
      GOTO EndLoad¶
```

```
    END IF¶
¶
    LoadOK:¶
      Dialog$ = "Loading OK"¶
¶
    EndLoad:¶
      IF Handle& <> 0 THEN CALL xClose&(Handle&)¶
      IF Buffer& <> 0 THEN CALL FreeMem&(Buffer&,BufferSize&)¶
      CALL DialogBox(Dialog$,1,True,x1b%,y1b%,x2b%,y2b%,False)¶
      CALL DoDialog(n%,1,-1,-1,-1,-1,x1b%,y1b%,x2b%,y2b%,-1,-1,-
1,-1) ¶
  END IF¶
  CLS¶
  GOSUB MakeMenu¶
RETURN¶
'¶
```

The next routine (`Info`) tells you how many free and used elements (object definitions) there are in array `K()`. The routine named `Help` displays information on how to control the program from the keyboard. The menus include information about which keyboard shortcut can be used for which command:

```
Info:¶
  ' Information about free elements of K()¶
  Status$ = " Status: Info"+CHR$(0)¶
  CALL SetWindowTitles&(NWBase&,SADD(Status$),0)¶
¶
  GOSUB DeleteMenu¶
¶
  CALL PrintIt("3D - CAD",60,False)¶
  CALL PrintIt("Original-Version: Peter Schulz (c)
1986",75,False)¶
  CALL PrintIt("Amiga-Version: Bruno Jennrich (c)
1987",90,False)¶
¶
  a$ = "Maximum number of objects : "+STR$(MaxNumber)¶
  CALL PrintIt(a$,105,False)¶
¶
  a$ = "Actual number of objects  : "+STR$(NumberK)¶
  CALL PrintIt(a$,120,False)¶
¶
  GOSUB Pause¶
¶
  CLS¶
  GOSUB MakeMenu¶
RETURN¶
'¶
Help:¶
  ' Which key press for which action¶
  Status$ = " Status: Help"+CHR$(0)¶
  CALL SetWindowTitles&(NWBase&,SADD(Status$),0)¶
¶
  GOSUB DeleteMenu¶
¶
  LOCATE 2,1¶
¶
  PRINT " P rojections point"¶
  PRINT " H Main point"¶
¶
  PRINT " W enter angle"¶
```

```
  PRINT " Cursor keys => rotate"¶
  PRINT " R otate (SHIFT,CONTROL)"¶
¶
  PRINT " D: spacing for main point"¶
  PRINT " +|-|*|/ Enlarge/reduce spacing (SHIFT+|-)"¶
¶
  PRINT " V Enlarge"¶
¶
  PRINT " L oad Object"¶
  PRINT " S ave Object"¶
  PRINT " M erge Object"¶
  PRINT " N ew, clear all objects"¶
  PRINT " B Screen saver"¶
  PRINT " Q => Program end (Quit)"  ¶
¶
  PRINT " F1  => Editor load"¶
¶
  PRINT " F9  => Shadows initialization"¶
  PRINT " F10 => Shadows"¶
  PRINT " <SPACE> => Show picture"¶
  PRINT " C lear screen";¶
¶
  GOSUB Pause¶
  CLS¶
  GOSUB MakeMenu¶
RETURN¶
'¶
```

Next is the routine used for enlargement or magnification of the screen image:

```
Enlargement:¶
  Status$ = " Status: Enlarge screen segment"+CHR$(0)¶
  CALL SetWindowTitles&(NWBase&,SADD(Status$),0)¶
  ¶
  GOSUB DeleteMenu¶
¶
  CALL
DialogBox("Proportional",0,True,x1a%,y1a%,x2a%,y2a%,False)¶
  CALL DialogBox("Distort",2,False,x1b%,y1b%,x2b%,y2b%,False)¶
¶
  CALL DoDialog(n%,0,x1a%,y1a%,x2a%,y2a%,x1b%,y1b%,x2b%,y2b%,-
1,-1,-1,-1)¶
  CLS¶
¶
  IF n%=0 THEN     ¶
    LOCATE 10,1¶
    PRINT " Enlargement Factor: ";¶
    a=1¶
    CALL FormInput (a,30!,.1,100!)¶
     ¶
    CLS  ¶
    Picturewidth=a*FactorX¶
    Pictureheight=a*FactorY¶
    Picturex=RasterW2%/Picturewidth¶
    Picturey=RasterH2%/Pictureheight¶
  ELSE¶
    WaitFlg! = False¶
    GOSUB DrawNew¶
    CALL Rubberbox (Sx%,Sy%,Widthe%,Heighte%,False)¶
    Picturewidth=RasterW%/Widthe% * FactorX¶
```

```
    Pictureheight=RasterH%/Heighte% * FactorY¶
    Picturex=(RasterW2%-Sx%)/FactorX¶
    Picturey=(RasterH2%-Sy%)/FactorY ¶
  END IF¶
  Newone! = True¶
  WaitFlg! = True¶
  GOSUB DrawNew¶
RETURN¶
```

PictureX and PictureY are recalculated for every enlargement (either proportional or distorted).

Menu control of programs is the norm for Amiga applications. Almost every program in existence uses menus, so ours will too. This routine constructs and reads menus:

```
MakeMenu:¶
  Status$ = " Status: Building menu"+CHR$(0)¶
  CALL SetWindowTitles&(NWBase&,SADD(Status$),0)¶
  ¶
  MENU 1,0,1, " Amiga"¶
    MENU 1,1,1," 3D-Cad-Info  I"¶
¶
  MENU 2,0,1,"File"¶
    MENU 2,1,1,         " Load              L"¶
    MENU 2,2,Start%,    " Save              S"¶
    MENU 2,3,1,         " Merge             M"¶
    MENU 2,4,1,         " New               N"¶
    MENU 2,5,0,         "------------------"¶
    MENU 2,6,1,         " Load material     "¶
    MENU 2,7,0,         "------------------"¶
    MENU 2,8,Start%,    " Background        "¶
    MENU 2,9,Start%,    " Save screen      P"¶
    MENU 2,10,Start%,   " Hardcopy          "¶
    MENU 2,11,0,        "------------------"¶
    MENU 2,12,Start%,   " Color palette    C"¶
    MENU 2,13,0,        "------------------"¶
    MENU 2,14,1,        " Program end     Q"¶
 ¶
  MENU 3,0,1,"Editor"¶
    MENU 3,1,1, " Load Editor          ^F1"¶
¶
  MENU 4,0,Start%,"Parameter"¶
    MENU 4,1,Start%, " Projection point  P"¶
    MENU 4,2,Start%, " Main point        H"¶
    MENU 4,3,Start%, " a, _, c           A"¶
    MENU 4,4,Start%, " Distance          D"¶
    MENU 4,5,0,      "---------------------"¶
    MENU 4,6,Start%, " Enlarge           V"¶
    MENU 4,7,Start%, " Number corner     E"¶
 ¶
  MENU 5,0,Start%,"Draw"¶
    MENU 5,1,Start%," Shadows          F10"¶
    MENU 5,2,Start%," Initialization   F9 "¶
    MENU 5,3,0,     "---------------------"¶
    MENU 5,4,Start%," Wire  model      < >"¶
    MENU 5,5,Start%," Clear screen     C  "¶
¶
  GOSUB NOOP¶
  CALL EmptyBuffers¶
RETURN¶
```

```
'¶
MessageEvent:¶
  MTitle = MENU(0)¶
  MPoint = MENU(1)¶
  ¶
  IF MTitle <> 0 THEN¶
  ¶
    IF MTitle = 1 THEN¶
      IF MPoint = 1 THEN GOSUB Info¶
      GOTO MessageEnde¶
    END IF¶
    ¶
    IF MTitle = 2 THEN¶
      IF MPoint = 1 THEN GOSUB Loader¶
      IF MPoint = 2 THEN GOSUB Saver¶
      IF MPoint = 3 THEN GOSUB Merger¶
      IF MPoint = 4 THEN GOSUB ArrayInit¶
      ' Mpoint = 5 : "---------"¶
      IF MPoint = 6 THEN GOSUB LoadMat¶
      ' MPoint = 7 : "---------"¶
      IF MPoint = 8 THEN GOSUB Background¶
      IF MPoint = 9 THEN GOSUB ScreenSaver¶
      IF MPoint = 10 THEN GOSUB HardCopy¶
      ' MPoint = 11 : "---------"¶
      IF MPoint = 12 THEN GOSUB ColorPalette¶
      ' MPoint = 13 : "---------"¶
      IF MPoint = 14 THEN GOSUB Quit¶
      GOTO MessageEnde¶
    END IF¶
    ¶
    IF MTitle = 3 THEN¶
      IF MPoint = 1 THEN GOSUB LoadEditor¶
      GOTO MessageEnde¶
    END IF¶
    ¶
    IF MTitle = 4 THEN¶
      IF MPoint = 1 THEN GOSUB InputP¶
      IF MPoint = 2 THEN GOSUB InputH¶
      IF MPoint = 3 THEN GOSUB InputAngle¶
      IF MPoint = 4 THEN GOSUB InputDPH¶
      ' MPoint =5: "-----------"¶
      IF MPoint = 6 THEN GOSUB Enlargement¶
      IF MPoint = 7 THEN GOSUB HowManyCorners¶
      GOTO MessageEnde¶
    END IF¶
  ¶
    IF MTitle = 5 THEN¶
      IF MPoint = 1 THEN GOSUB Shadows¶
      IF MPoint = 2 THEN GOSUB InitParameters¶
      IF MPoint = 4 THEN GOSUB DrawNew¶
      IF MPoint = 5 THEN GOSUB ClearScreen¶
    END IF¶
  END IF¶
  MessageEnde: ¶
RETURN¶
'¶
```

When you select a menu item, all other menu items should be deactivated, to avoid accidentally choosing another menu item at the same time. The menu items are listed internally and deacitivated one after another—no item is skipped. When we turn the menus off, the program ignores any accidental menu item selections:

```
DeleteMenu:¶
  MENU 1,0,0,"Amiga"¶
  MENU 2,0,0,"File"¶
  MENU 3,0,0,"Editor"¶
  MENU 4,0,0,"Parameter"¶
  MENU 5,0,0,"Draw"¶
RETURN¶
'¶
```

When we want to go back to the main loop where the menu items appear, we must reactivate the menus (call `MakeMenu`).

In addition to menu control, the program can accept keyboard shortcuts. Most menu items list these shortcuts in the right margin of the menu list. Because some functions can only be executed from the keyboard, we list the important shortcuts in the `Help` routine. You can access this routine by either pressing the <Help> key or the <?> key. Here is the routine which checks for a keypress:

```
KeyEvent:¶
  Key$=INKEY$¶
  IF Key$ <> "" THEN¶
  LOCATE 1,1¶
  ¶
   IF Start% = 1 THEN¶
     IF Key$ = " " THEN GOSUB DrawNew¶
     IF Key$ = "d" THEN GOSUB InputDPH¶
¶
     IF Key$ = "c" THEN GOSUB ColorPalette¶
¶
     IF Key$ = "*" OR Key$ = "/" OR Key$ = "+" OR Key$ = "-"
THEN¶
       IF Key$ = "+" THEN D = 10 ¶
       IF Key$ = "-" THEN D =-10¶
       IF Key$ = "*" THEN D = 100¶
       IF Key$ = "/" THEN D =-100¶
¶
       DPH = DPH + D¶
       GOSUB Initial¶
       Newone! = True¶
       WaitFlg! = True¶
       GOSUB DrawNew¶
     END IF¶
   ¶
     IF Key$ = "v" THEN GOSUB Enlargement¶
     IF Key$ = "p" THEN GOSUB InputP¶
     IF Key$ = "h" THEN GOSUB InputH¶
     IF Key$ = "a" THEN GOSUB InputAngle¶
     IF Key$ = "e" THEN GOSUB HowManyCorners¶
   ¶
     IF Key$ = "c" THEN GOSUB ClearScreen¶
  ¶
     IF Key$ = "s" THEN GOSUB Saver¶
     IF Key$ = "b" THEN GOSUB ScreenSaver¶
     IF Key$ = CHR$(137) THEN GOSUB InitParameters¶
     IF Key$ = CHR$(138) THEN GOSUB Shadows¶
```

```
  ¶
    IF (Key$ = CHR$(28)) OR (Key$ = CHR$(29)) OR (Key$ =
CHR$(30)) OR (Key$ = CHR$(31)) THEN¶
      IF Key$ = CHR$(28) THEN¶
        Beta = Beta + Pi/15¶
      END IF  ¶
      IF Key$ = CHR$(29) THEN¶
        Beta = Beta - Pi/15¶
      END IF  ¶
      IF Key$ = CHR$(30) THEN¶
        Alpha = Alpha + Pi/15¶
      END IF  ¶
      IF Key$ = CHR$(31) THEN¶
        Alpha = Alpha - Pi/15¶
      END IF¶
      GOSUB Initial¶
      Newone! = True¶
      WaitFlg! = True¶
      GOSUB DrawNew¶
    END IF¶
  ¶
    IF (Key$ = CHR$(18)) OR (Key$ = "R") THEN¶
      IF Key$ = CHR$(18) THEN    '^R¶
        Gamma = Gamma + Pi/15¶
      END IF ¶
      IF Key$ = "R" THEN¶
        Gamma = Gamma - Pi/15¶
      END IF¶
      GOSUB Initial¶
      Newone! = True¶
      WaitFlg! = True¶
      GOSUB DrawNew¶
    END IF     ¶
  END IF¶
  IF Key$ = "m" THEN GOSUB Merger¶
  IF Key$ = "n" THEN GOSUB ArrayInit  ¶
  IF Key$ = "l" THEN GOSUB Loader ¶
  IF Key$ = "?" OR Key$ = CHR$(139) THEN GOSUB Help¶
  IF Key$ = "q" THEN Quit¶
  IF Key$ = "i" THEN GOSUB Info¶
  ¶
  IF Key$ = CHR$(1) THEN GOSUB LoadEditor¶
 END IF  ¶
RETURN¶
'¶
```

No operations are performed when the program is waiting for user input, or when it isn't executing any shadow calculations. This is known as NOP (No Operation) status. This status appears in the top window line through the NOOP routine:

```
NOOP:  ¶
  Status$ = " Status: NOP"+CHR$(0)¶
  CALL SetWindowTitles&(NWBase&,SADD(Status$),0)¶
RETURN¶
'¶
```

The following routines allow the creation and control of requesters. These are contained in `DialogBox`, which draws the requester, and `DoDialog`, which waits for you to select a requester gadget:

```
SUB DialogBox(Dialog$,Position%,Ret,x1%,y1%,x2%,y2%,Scr) STATIC¶
SHARED RastPort&,NRastPort&,True,RasterW1%,RasterW2%¶
  ' Create your ownrequ requester¶
  ' Dialog$ = Text in Dialog Box¶
  ' Position% ¶
  '     0 = right¶
  '     1 = center¶
  '     2 = left¶
  ' Ret% = can you press <Return>?¶
  '     True  = Yes¶
  '     False = No¶
  ' x1%,y1%,x2%,y1% = Size of  'click'-Field (word returned)¶
  '     Scr = In which screen output ?¶
  '       True = Display-Screen¶
  '       False = User-Screen¶
¶
 IF Scr = True THEN¶
    rp& = RastPort&¶
    Middle& = RasterW2%¶
    SEnd& = RasterW1%¶
    ' Write to Display-Screen¶
  ELSE¶
    rp& = NRastPort&¶
    Middle& = 320¶
    SEnd& = 640¶
    ' RastPort des Basic Windows¶
  END IF¶
¶
  y1% = 150¶
  y2% = 150 + 6 + 10¶
¶
  Length& = TextLength&(rp&,SADD(Dialog$),LEN(Dialog$))¶
¶
  IF Position% = 0 THEN ¶
      x1% = 70¶
      x2% = x1% + Length& + 20¶
  END IF¶
¶
  IF Position% = 1 THEN¶
      x1% = Middle&-Length&/2-10¶
      x2% = Middle&+Length&/2+10¶
  END IF¶
¶
  IF Position% = 2 THEN ¶
      x1% = SEnd&-70-20-10-Length&¶
      x2% = SEnd&-70-10¶
  END IF¶
¶
  CALL Move&(rp&,x1%+10,y1%+10)¶
  CALL Text&(rp&,SADD(Dialog$),LEN(Dialog$)) ¶
¶
  IF Scr = True THEN¶
    CALL Box(rp&,x1%,y1%,x2%,y2%)¶
    CALL Box(rp&,x1%-4,y1%-2,x2%+4,y2%+2)¶
    IF Ret = True THEN CALL Box(rp&,x1%-2,y1%-1,x2%+2,y2%+1)¶
  ELSE¶
    LINE (x1%,y1%)-(x2%,y2%),,b¶
    LINE (x1%-2,y1%-2)-(x2%+2,y2%+2),,b¶
    IF Ret = True THEN LINE (x1%-1,y1%-1)-(x2%+1,y2%+1),,b¶
  END IF¶
END SUB¶
'¶
```

```
SUB DoDialog(n%,Ret%,x1a%,y1a%,x2a%,y2a%,x1b%,y1b%,x2b%,
y2b%,x1c%,y1c%,x2c%,y2c%) STATIC¶
  ' Dialog boxen read¶
  ' n%: which gadget clicked ?¶
  ' Ret%: which gadget specified by pressing <Return>?¶
  ' x1.,y1.,x2.,y2. coordinates ofthe box¶
  CALL EmptyBuffers¶
  n% = -1¶
  WHILE (n% = -1)¶
    IF MOUSE(0) <> 0 THEN¶
      x = MOUSE(1)¶
      y = MOUSE(2)¶
 ¶
      IF (x1a%<x) AND (x2a%>x) AND (y1a%<y) AND (y2a%>y) THEN n%
= 0¶
      IF (x1b%<x) AND (x2b%>x) AND (y1b%<y) AND (y2b%>y) THEN n%
= 1 ¶
      IF (x1c%<x) AND (x2c%>x) AND (y1c%<y) AND (y2c%>y) THEN n%
= 2¶
    END IF¶
    IF INKEY$ = CHR$(13) THEN n% = Ret%¶
  WEND¶
END SUB¶
'¶
```

The `PrintIt` routine displays centered text:

```
SUB PrintIt(Out$,y%,Scr) STATIC¶
SHARED RastPort&,NRastPort&,RasterW2%,True,Length&¶
  ' Centered text output on one of the two screens ¶
  ' Out$: Printed string¶
  ' y%: verticle Position ?¶
  ' Scr: User or Display Screen?¶
  IF Scr = True THEN¶
    rp& = RastPort&¶
    Middle& = RasterW2%¶
    ' write to new (Display) Screen¶
  ELSE¶
    rp& = NRastPort&¶
    Middle& = 320      ' User-Screen (NO OP Window)¶
  END IF¶
  Length& = TextLength&(rp&,SADD(Out$),LEN(Out$))¶
  Middle& = Middle& - Length&/2¶
  CALL Move& (rp&,Middle&,CLNG(y%))¶
  CALL Text& (rp&,SADD(Out$),LEN(Out$))¶
END SUB¶
'¶
```

The text is centered on the screen. This is especially useful for the information lines that appear inside requesters.

The `Box` routine draws a box around requesters, while the `RubberBox` routine keeps mouse movement within this requester:

```
SUB Box(RastPort&,x1%,y1%,x2%,y2%) STATIC¶
  ' rectangle in Display-Screen¶
  ' RastPort&: draw in which  RastPort ¶
  ' x1,y1,x2,y2 coordinaten ofthe rectangle¶
  CALL Move&(RastPort&,x1%,y1%)¶
  CALL Draw&(RastPort&,x2%,y1%)¶
  CALL Draw&(RastPort&,x2%,y2%)¶
```

```
  CALL Draw&(RastPort&,x1%,y2%)¶
  CALL Draw&(RastPort&,x1%,y1%+1)¶
END SUB¶
'¶
SUB Rubberbox( x%, y%, w%, h%, Back!) STATIC¶
SHARED RasterW1%,RasterH1%,WScreen&,NRastPort&,RastPort&,
NWScreen&,NWBase&,WBase&,Length&,True,False¶
  ' Make rectangle with mouse¶
  ' x%,y%: upper left corner¶
  ' w%,h%: Width, Height¶
  ' Back!: Return touser window ?¶
  CALL Scron¶
  CALL SetDrMd&(RastPort&,2)  'COMPLEMENT   ¶
  ¶
  CALL SetAPen&(RastPort&,1)¶
¶
 Repitition:¶
  Oldx% = 1¶
  OldY% = 1¶
  Flag! = 0¶
    ¶
  CALL EmptyBuffers¶
¶
   mouse1:    ¶
    x% = PEEKW(WScreen&+18)¶
    y% = PEEKW(WScreen&+16)¶
¶
      IF (x% <> Oldx%) OR (y%<>OldY%) THEN¶
        IF Flag! = 1 THEN ¶
          CALL Move&(RastPort&,Oldx%,0)¶
          CALL Draw&(RastPort&,Oldx%,RasterH1%)¶
          CALL Move&(RastPort&,0,OldY%)¶
          CALL Draw&(RastPort&,RasterW1%,OldY%)¶
        END IF¶
¶
        Flag! = 1¶
¶
        CALL Move&(RastPort&,x%,0)¶
        CALL Draw&(RastPort&,x%,RasterH1%)¶
        CALL Move&(RastPort&,0,y%)¶
        CALL Draw&(RastPort&,RasterW1%,y%)¶
        Oldx% = x%¶
        OldY% = y%¶
      END IF     ¶
¶
   IF MOUSE(0) = 0 GOTO mouse1¶
¶
   CALL Move&(RastPort&,x%,0)¶
   CALL Draw&(RastPort&,x%,RasterH1%)¶
   CALL Move&(RastPort&,0,y%)¶
   CALL Draw&(RastPort&,RasterW1%,y%)¶
     ¶
   Oldx% = -1¶
   OldY% = -1¶
   Flag! = 0¶
  ¶
   WHILE MOUSE(0) <> 0¶
    ¶
     w% = PEEKW(WScreen&+18)¶
     h% = PEEKW(WScreen&+16)¶
     IF (w% <> Oldx%) OR (h% <> OldY%) THEN¶
¶
```

```
        IF Flag! = 1 THEN CALL Box(RastPort&,x%,y%,Oldx%,OldY%)¶
        Flag! = 1¶
¶
          IF (w% < x%+6) THEN w% = x%+6¶
          IF (h% < y%+3) THEN h% = y%+3¶
        ¶
          IF (w% > x%) AND (h% > y%) THEN¶
            IF w%>RasterW1% THEN w% = RasterW1%¶
            IF h%>RasterH1% THEN h% = RasterH1%¶
            Oldx% = w%¶
            OldY% = h%¶
           ¶
            CALL Box(RastPort&,x%,y%,w%,h%)    ¶
          END IF                       ¶
        END IF¶
      WEND ¶
    ¶
      IF Flag = 1 THEN CALL Box(RastPort&,x%,y%,w%,h%)¶
       ¶
      CALL PrintIt("Section Ok ?",130,True)  ¶
¶
      Flag! = 0¶
      Oldx% = -1¶
      OldY% = -1¶
¶
      CALL DialogBox("OK",1,True,x1a%,y1a%,x2a%,y2a%,True)¶
  ¶
      CALL EmptyBuffers¶
  ¶
      a$ = ""¶
      WHILE (MOUSE(0) = 0) AND (a$ <> CHR$(13))    ¶
        a$ = INKEY$¶
      WEND¶
¶
      Mx% = PEEKW(WScreen&+18)¶
      My% = PEEKW(WScreen&+16)¶
¶
      TryAgain = True¶
      IF (Mx%>x1a%) AND (Mx%<x2a%) AND (My%>y1a%) AND (My%<y2a%)
THEN TryAgain = False¶
      IF a$ = CHR$(13) THEN TryAgain = False¶
      ¶
      CALL PrintIt("Section  Ok ?",130,True)  ¶
    ¶
      CALL DialogBox("OK",1,True,x1a%,y1a%,x2a%,y2a%,True)¶
 ¶
   IF TryAgain = True THEN GOTO Repitition       ¶
¶
   w% = w%-x%¶
   h% = h%-y%   ¶
¶
   CALL SetDrMd&(RastPort&,1)   'JAM2¶
   CALL SetDrMd&(NRastPort&,1)¶
   ¶
   IF Back! = True THEN CALL Scroff¶
END SUB¶
'¶
```

We have used our own `Box` routine instead of the `LINE` statement. This allows us to display requesters in both the display screen and the user screen. We can't use `LINE` in this case because we are accessing and changing the display screen using `Rastport`, which allows us to access the entire bitmap. We can also use the points that normally draw the border around a window or screen. This allows us to draw on the full screen.

The `Pause` routine waits for the user to press either a mouse button or a key.

We must make sure that the mouse and keyboard buffers are empty. So all the keypresses before the check are ignored and it can react to the new keypresses:

```
Pause: ¶
  ' Wait for (Mouse-) key press¶
  CALL EmptyBuffers                          ' clear buffer ¶
  WHILE (INKEY$ = "") AND (MOUSE (0) = 0)¶
  WEND¶
RETURN¶
'¶

SUB EmptyBuffers STATIC¶
  ' clear mouse and keyboard buffer ¶
  WHILE MOUSE(0) <> 0¶
  WEND¶
  WHILE (INKEY$<>"")¶
  WEND¶
END SUB¶
'¶
```

The following routines implement a completely different kind of input:

```
SUB FormInput (i,winlen,unt!,ob!) STATIC¶
'Enter indivudal real values¶
'i =>                number variables to be real (old value
displayed)¶
'winlen,unt!,ob! => see above.¶
  z=CSRLIN¶
  s=POS(0)¶
  a$ = " "¶
  CALL PutReal (i,z,s,winlen)¶
  CALL GetReal (i,a$,z,s,winlen,unt!,ob!)¶
END SUB¶
'¶
SUB FormInputInt (i,winlen,unt!,ob!) STATIC¶
'Enter an indivudal integer value¶
'i =>                number variavles to be read (old value
displayed)¶
'winlen,unt!,ob! => see above.¶
  z=CSRLIN¶
  s=POS(0)¶
  a$ = " "¶
  CALL PutReal (i,z,s,winlen)¶
  CALL GetInt (i,a$,z,s,winlen,unt!,ob!)¶
END SUB¶
'¶
SUB FormInputString (s$,winlen) STATIC¶
' String read (z.B. Filename)¶
  a$ = " "¶
  s = POS(0) ¶
```

```
  z = CSRLIN¶
  CALL PutString (s$,z,s,winlen)¶
  CALL GetString
(s$,a$,"abcdefghijklmnopqrstuvwxyzdv|_ABCDEFGHIJKLMNOPQRSTUVWXYZ
DV\1234567890.-_:/",z,s,winlen)¶
END SUB¶
'¶
```

These routines waits for the input of a real number, an integer value or a character string. The input routines of the editor are used for this.

Illegal characters (e.g., letters entered when numbers should be entered) are ignored. When we enter a value smaller than the given lower limit or larger than the upper limit, the screen flashes, to indicate an error.

All disk operations can either use the current subdirectory or change to a new one. The `Directory` routine makes this possible:

```
Directory:¶
  ' Directory read, or change drive¶
  Status$ = " Status: Directory"+CHR$(0)¶
  CALL SetWindowTitles&(NWBase&,SADD(Status$),0)¶
  ¶
  GOSUB DeleteMenu¶
  a$ = "Active Directory: "+ActDrive$¶
  CALL PrintIt(a$,50,False)¶
  CHDIR ActDrive$¶
  ¶
  RepeatD:¶
    CALL DialogBox("Files",0,False,x1a%,y1a%,x2a%,y2a%,False)¶
    CALL DialogBox("Load",1,True,x1b%,y1b%,x2b%,y2b%,False)¶
    CALL DialogBox("Chdir",2,False,x1c%,y1c%,x2c%,y2c%,False)¶
  ¶
    CALL
DoDialog(n%,1,x1a%,y1a%,x2a%,y2a%,x1b%,y1b%,x2b%,y2b%,x1c%,y1c%,
x2c%,y2c%)  ¶
¶
    CLS¶
    IF n% = 0 THEN¶
      FILES¶
      GOSUB Pause¶
      CLS¶
      GOTO RepeatD¶
    END IF¶
    IF n% = 2 THEN¶
      a$ = "Active Directory: "+ActDrive$¶
      CALL PrintIt(a$,50,False)¶
    ¶
      LOCATE 10,1¶
      PRINT "        New Directory: ";¶
      CALL FormInputString (ActDrive$,30!)¶
¶
      CHDIR ActDrive$¶
     ¶
      CLS¶
      GOTO RepeatD¶
    END IF  ¶
  CLS¶
 RETURN¶
```

Selecting a new disk directory makes it possible to use other disks. You may know the dilemma of suddenly having to make a disk swap (maybe because of a read error), but a `chdir` or `cd` can't be executed from the program. Sometimes data loss can occur. Not with our program: You can use a new disk by calling `Directory` without quitting the program.

When you want to leave the program, `Quit` is called. This routine asks you if you want to quit the program and gives you a chance to respond. If you exit the program, it releases all the memory it has occupied and closes all of the libraries and the newly opened display screen:

```
CloseIt:¶
  ' Close all and free memory¶
  GOSUB CloseGfx¶
  WINDOW CLOSE 2¶
  SCREEN CLOSE 1     ' automatic release of allocated 6th bitmap¶
  MENU RESET         ' ¶
¶
  IF SetPointAdr& <> 0 THEN CALL
FreeMem&(SetPointAdr&,SetPointNum&)¶
  IF PatternS& <> 0 THEN CALL
FreeMem&(PatternS&,(NumberPatternS%+1)*2*16)¶
  IF PatternX& <> 0 THEN CALL
FreeMem&(PatternX&,(NumberPatternX%*2+1)*2*16)¶
    'Save pattern and release ASSEM-Routine¶
  LIBRARY CLOSE¶
RETURN¶
'    ¶
¶
Quit:¶
  CALL Scroff¶
  Status$ = " Program end ?"+CHR$(0)¶
  CALL SetWindowTitles&(NWBase&,SADD(Status$),0)¶
  ¶
  GOSUB DeleteMenu¶
  ¶
  CALL PrintIt("Do you really wish to exit the
program?",100,False)¶
  ¶
  CALL DialogBox("No",0,True,x1a%,y1a%,x2a%,y2a%,False)¶
  CALL DialogBox("New start",1,False,x1b%,y1b%,x2b%,y2b%,False)¶
  CALL DialogBox("Yes",2,False,x1c%,y1c%,x2c%,y2c%,False)¶
  ¶
  CALL
DoDialog(n%,0,x1a%,y1a%,x2a%,y2a%,x1b%,y1b%,x2b%,y2b%,x1c%,y1c%,
x2c%,y2c%)  ¶
¶
  CLS¶
  IF n% > 0 THEN¶
    GOSUB CloseIt¶
    IF n% = 1 THEN¶
      RUN ¶
    ELSE¶
      END¶
    END IF¶
  END IF¶
  GOSUB MakeMenu¶
```

```
RETURN¶
'¶
```

This routine allows you to restart the program instead of ending the program.

The `Scron` and `Scroff` routines switch between the new display screen and the user screen. To erase the display screen (e.g., before redrawing a wire model) `ScreenErase` is called:

```
SUB Scroff STATIC¶
SHARED NWBase&,NWScreen&¶
  ' Display Screen off , User Screen on¶
  CALL ScreenToFront&(NWScreen&)¶
  WINDOW OUTPUT 1¶
  WINDOW 1¶
  CALL ActivateWindow&(NWBase&)¶
END SUB¶
'¶
SUB Scron STATIC¶
SHARED WScreen&,WBase&¶
  ' Display Screen on, User Screen off¶
  CALL ScreenToFront&(WScreen&)¶
  WINDOW OUTPUT 2¶
  WINDOW 2¶
  CALL ActivateWindow&(WBase&)¶
END SUB¶
'¶

ClearScreen:¶
  Status$ = " Status: Clear screen"+CHR$(0)¶
  CALL SetWindowTitles&(NWBase&,SADD(Status$),0)¶
  ¶
  CALL SetRast&(RastPort&,0)¶
  Hg = True¶
  ¶
  GOSUB NOOP¶
RETURN¶
'¶
```

You have the option of calling the object editor with `LoadEditor`:

```
LoadEditor:¶
  Status$ = " Status: Editor loading"+CHR$(0)¶
  CALL SetWindowTitles&(NWBase&,SADD(Status$),0)¶
¶
  GOSUB DeleteMenu¶
¶
  CALL DialogBox("not called",0,True,x1a%,y1a%,x2a%,y2a%,False)
¶
  CALL DialogBox("called",2,False,x1c%,y1c%,x2c%,y2c%,False)¶
  CALL DoDialog(n%,0,x1a%,y1a%,x2a%,ya2%,-1,-1,-1,-
1,x1c%,y1c%,x2c%,y2c%)  ¶
  CLS¶
  IF n% = 2 THEN¶
    CHDIR "Tracer:"  ¶
    GOSUB CloseIt¶
    CHAIN "Editor"¶
  END IF¶
  GOSUB MakeMenu  ¶
```

```
END¶
```

`ErrorHandling` keeps you informed of errors encountered. These can only be I/O (input/output) errors (e.g., a read/write error on the disk). If another error is encountered in your program, the editor displays the error number (e.g., 2 [Syntax error]). See Appendix B of your AmigaBASIC manual, or Appendix A of Abacus' ***AmigaBASIC Inside and Out*** for a list of error messages and numbers:

```
ErrorHandling:¶
  NumErr = ERR¶
  ¶
  Status$ = " Status: Next Big Error !!!"+CHR$(0)¶
  CALL SetWindowTitles&(NWBase&,SADD(Status$),0)¶
  ¶
  GOSUB DeleteMenu¶
  ¶
  Dialog$ = ""¶
  IF NumErr = 64 THEN          ' Bad File Mode¶
    Dialog$ = "Bad file name !!!"¶
  END IF¶
  ¶
  IF NumErr = 57 THEN          ' Device I/O Error¶
    Dialog$ = "Device I/O Error !!!"¶
  END IF¶
  ¶
  IF NumErr = 68 THEN          ' Device unable¶
    Dialog$ = "Device not found"¶
  END IF¶
  ¶
  IF NumErr = 61 THEN          ' Disk Full¶
    Dialog$ = "Diskette is full !!!"   ¶
  END IF¶
  ¶
  IF NumErr = 53 THEN          ' File not found¶
    Dialog$ = "File not found!!!"¶
  END IF¶
  ¶
  IF NumErr = 70 THEN          ' Permission denied¶
    Dialog$ = "Permission denied!!!"¶
  END IF¶
  ¶
  IF Dialog$ = "" THEN¶
    Dialog$ = "Error Number ="+STR$(NumErr)¶
  END IF¶
  ¶
  CALL DialogBox(Dialog$,1,True,x1a%,y1a%,x2a%,y2a%,False)¶
  ¶
  CALL DoDialog(n%,1,-1,-1,-1,-1,x1a%,y1a%,x2a%,y2a%,-1,-1,-1,-
1)¶
¶
  CLS¶
  GOSUB MakeMenu¶
  RESUME ok ¶
RETURN¶
'¶
```

3.3.2 Merging Tracer Modules into one Program

This explains all of the routines used in our tracer program. These routines are completely listed in the appendices and are contained on the optional disk in seven separate modules. This makes merging and adapting them to your own programs much easier.

Note: If you type in these modules yourself, here are a few ground rules which you must follow to complete the tracer program:

- Name the disk to which you are saving the files `tracer:` and create a directory called `modules`.
- Do not type the seven tracer modules in as one program. These seven modules must be entered separately and merged together as explained below. This method allows easy incorporation of these codes into other programs later on.
- Enter each module from AmigaBASIC and save each module in ASCII format under the exact name given in the appendices, in a directory named `modules`. For example, the first module must be saved as follows:

```
save "tracer:modules/init.asc",a
```

Now that you've seen all of the routines used in the tracer, we must combine the program modules (which are saved as ASCII files) into one program on disk.

Run AmigaBASIC and enter the following in the BASIC window:

```
clear ,140000
```

This reserves the necessary program memory (this command must be executed before each start of the tracer). This release only works on Amigas with at least 512K of RAM.

The optional disk (named `tracer`) has all of the modules in a directory called `modules`, so set the current directory to `tracer:modules` using the following AmigaBASIC command sequence:

```
chdir "tracer:modules"
```

Note: If you're using a backup copy of the optional disk, or you're using a disk that you named yourself, rename your disk to `tracer`.

Now we will combine the tracer modules found in the `modules` directory. Merge them using the following commands in direct mode (enter them in the BASIC window):

```
merge "Init.asc"
merge "System.asc"
merge "Wiremodel-draw.asc"
merge "Wiremodel-input.asc"
merge "Shadow-init.asc"
merge "Shadowing.asc"
merge "Service.asc"
```

Then the completed program should be saved as described below:

```
save "tracer:tracer"
```

You can save this program to the optional disk or to your own disk.

Note: Your own disk must have the name `tracer` for the tracer program to work correctly.

The tracer program, the editor program, and the machine language routine `SetPoint.B` must be available in the main directory of the disk. The `SetPoint.B` routine is described in Appendix D, which includes the source code and a BASIC loader.

You must ensure that the `.bmap files` are also on the disk, since the program uses `dos.bmap`, `exec.bmap`, `graphics.bmap`, and `intuition.bmap` libraries. These files are located in the `libs` directory of the optional disk. If you're using your own disk, you may have to create these libraries using the `FDConvert` program on your Extras disk.

The easiest procedure is to copy the entire disk with the `Diskcopy` command. After merging the individual modules you can erase these from the `modules` directory to get more room on the disk. Do this with the copy of the disk **only**, and not with the original disk! After saving the complete `tracer` the entire program is on the disk. You're ready to go into 3D mode.

4.
Using the Program

4. Using the Program

In our exploration of the program modules in Chapter Three, we didn't talk at all about operating the finished product. This chapter is a set of operating instructions for the tracer and editor programs.

4.1 Editor Documentation

4.1.1 Input—General Information

All input occurs in the windows. Input can be edited with the cursor keys, <Delete> and <Backspace> keys when input mode is active inside of the editor's main window. When input extends past the window, the window scrolls to the left and the characters at the beginning of the line scroll off the screen. The <Cursor left> and <Cursor right> keys let the visible section be accessible. It is important to note that only certain keys are accepted for certain prompts:

a) integer values: 0—9,-

b) real values: 0,1,..,9,-,.

c) vectors: 0,1,..,9,-,.,","

d) character strings: all characters

e) single characters:
for visible input: y,n
for enlargement, rotation, movement: q,c,d
for the Show function: d,m,f

Each input can be ended by pressing the <Return> key, regardless of the cursor location. You must press <Return> after characters because the program waits for the first valid key. For values greater than zero and less than one, a zero must precede the decimal point (e.g., 0.6 is acceptable, while .6 results in an error). If the user enters an input in an invalid form, or if the value entered lies outside the specified value range, the program ignores the input and returns the cursor to the beginning of the line for correction. Valid values are in the range [-10000..+10000], with the following four exceptions:

a) material type: 1..10000

b) inner or outer radius: 0..1

c) enlargement factor: 1/64..64

d) line view: 1..50

When a coordinate vector is required in an input position, which is always the case for us, you have two input options: conventional keyboard input or mouse input. When you use the mouse, the cursor must be at the beginning of the corresponding line—no valid keys can be pressed for this input. When using the mouse, the desired position in the window can be clicked on where the coordinates will be displayed in the input and output windows. When it is in the position you want, all you need to do is press <Return>. Then the mouse position in the input line takes charge, either directly or as the difference between the mouse vector and the direction vector.

There are some special cases to be aware of in menu input. For example, if you decide that there is an input error in the fifth input position, you don't need to start again. Instead you can return to the incorrect line. This is done with the <Cursor up> key. This is only active when no keys are pressed in the input line. You don't have to enter the entire line. Simply move the cursor to the error, correct it and press the <Return> key. Then move down to the old input line with the <Cursor down> key.

4.1.2 Entering Object Data

When the above program specifications for input are considered, entering object data is no longer a problem. You know which data is actually checked and how the input of a certain object is started. The information about the first point can be taken from the drawings below.

The last point is easy: All the predefined objects can be found under the `Body` menu item. When you want to enter a certain object from this list, you only need to choose it from the list. A new data set appears in the editor window and the cursor moves to the first position. The input can then begin. The object data is checked to see if the given object should be visible on the screen, and which material should be assigned to it. The materials can differ in color, shade intensity, and reflection factor, which are represented by numbers. The material belonging to this number is entered with the material editor, which is described in the next section. The following pictures show the simpler types of objects that can be entered.

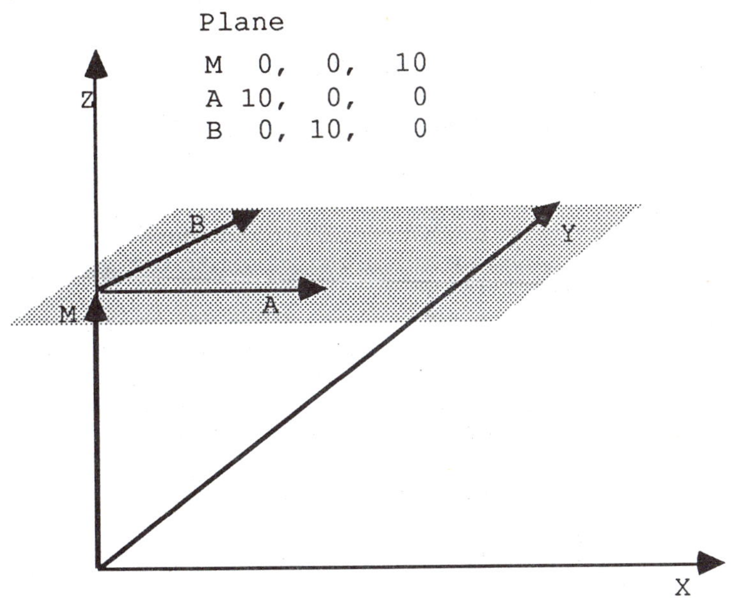
Plane
M 0, 0, 10
A 10, 0, 0
B 0, 10, 0
Z
B
Y
M
A
X

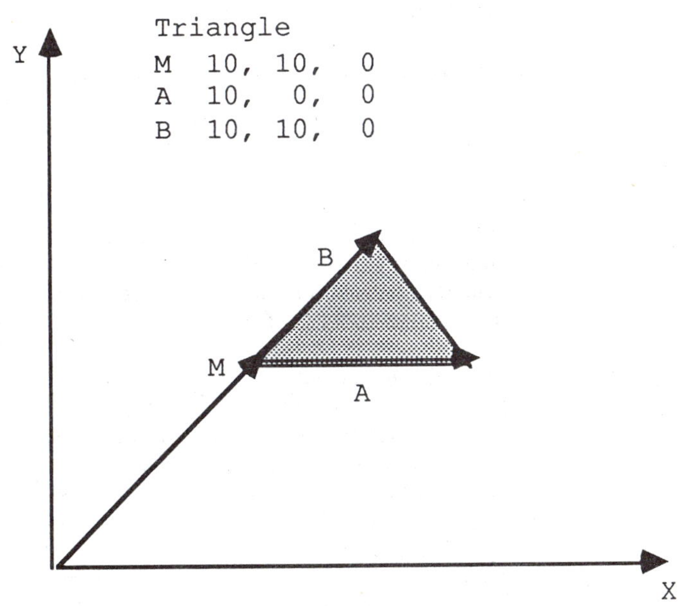
Triangle
M 10, 10, 0
A 10, 0, 0
B 10, 10, 0
Y
B
M
A
X

Figure 4.1

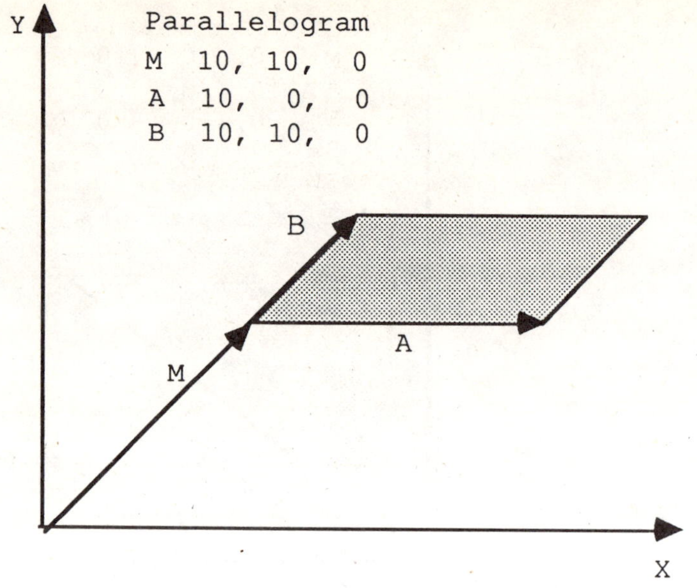
Parallelogram
M 10, 10, 0
A 10, 0, 0
B 10, 10, 0
Y
X
B
A
M

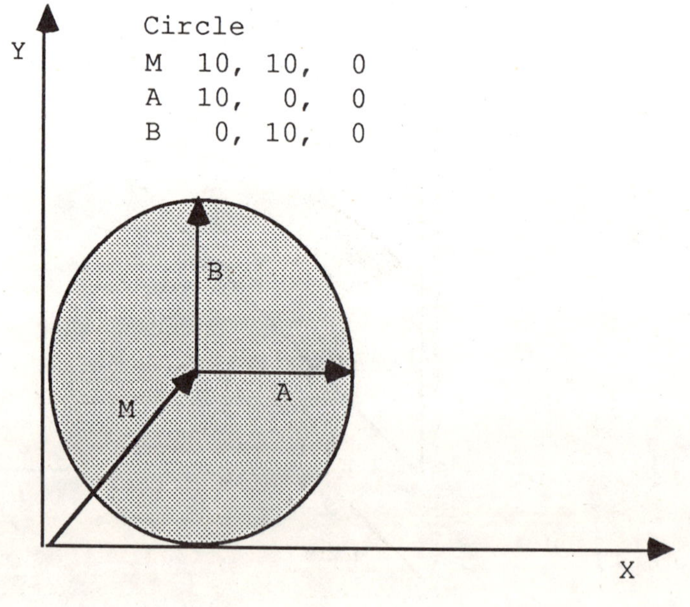
Circle
M 10, 10, 0
A 10, 0, 0
B 0, 10, 0
Y
X
B
A
M

Figure 4.2

```
Circular segment
M  10, 10,  0
A  10,  0,  0
B   0, 10,  0
SW  90°
EW  180°
```

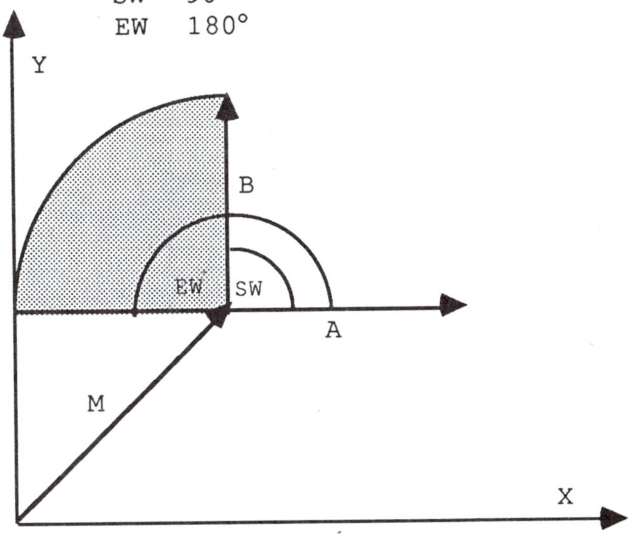


```
Arc
M  10, 10,  0
A  10,  0,  0
B   0, 10,  0
SW  90°
EW 180°
ri  0.6
ra  1
```

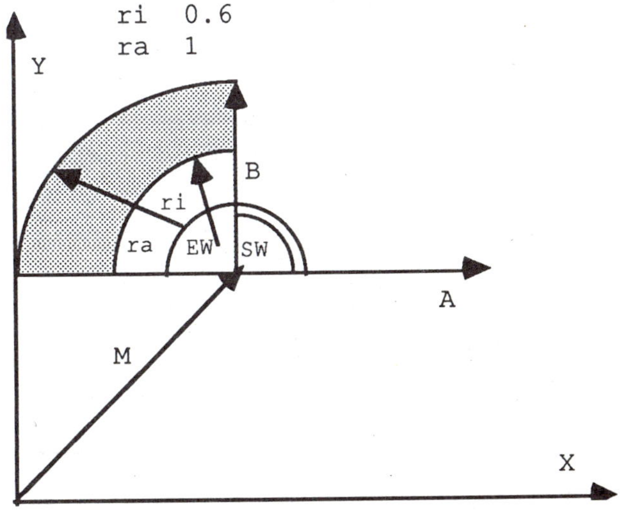

Figure 4.3

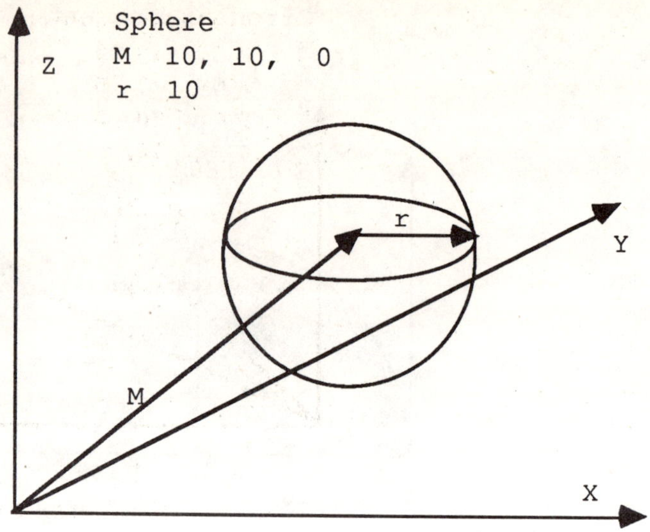
Sphere
M 10, 10, 0
r 10
Z
r
Y
M
X

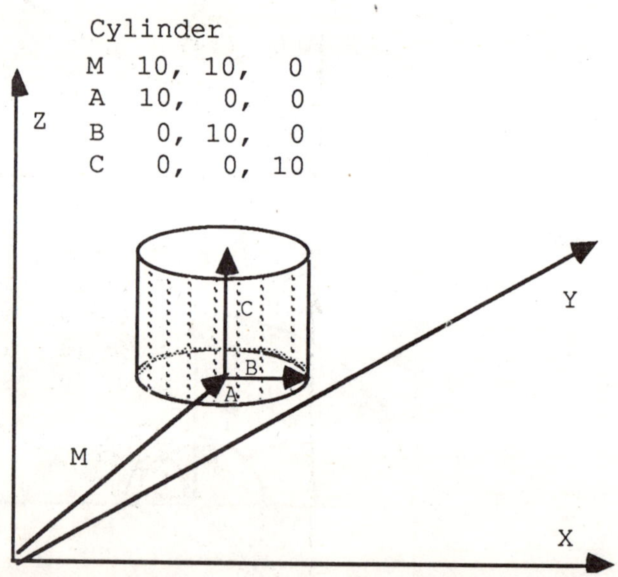
Cylinder
M 10, 10, 0
A 10, 0, 0
B 0, 10, 0
C 0, 0, 10
Z
C
B
A
Y
M
X

Figure 4.4

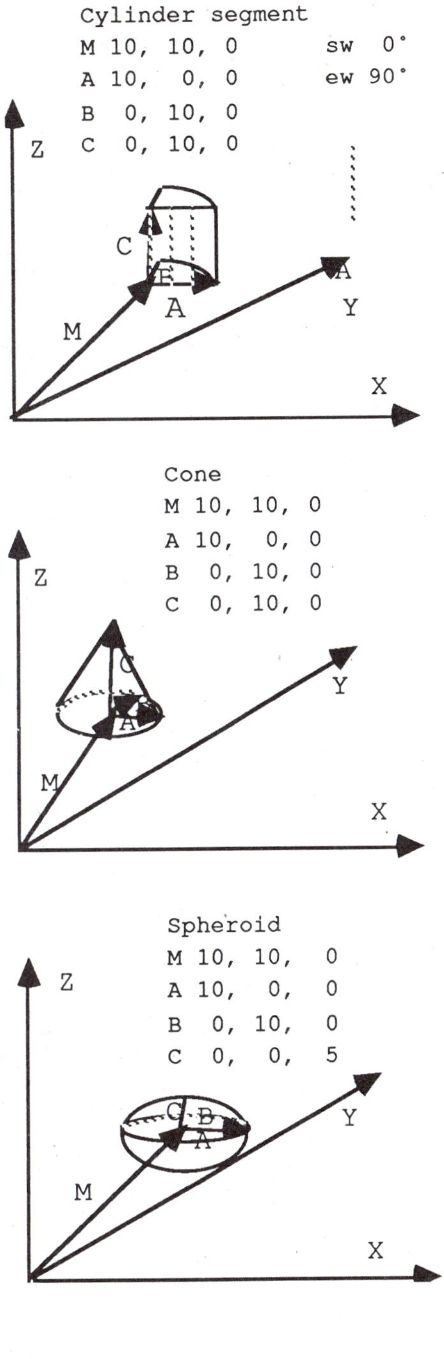
Cylinder segment
M 10, 10, 0 sw 0°
A 10, 0, 0 ew 90°
B 0, 10, 0
C 0, 10, 0
Z
C
A
M
Y
X
Cone
M 10, 10, 0
A 10, 0, 0
B 0, 10, 0
C 0, 10, 0
Z
Y
M
X
Spheroid
M 10, 10, 0
A 10, 0, 0
B 0, 10, 0
C 0, 0, 5
Z
Y
M
X

Figure 4.5

4.1.3 The Operations Menu

These functions make a number of operations available for working on object data. The most important ones can be called by pressing a key. With `Left` operations can be performed on the previous object. For example, when the data of the sixth object is visible, selecting the `Left` item displays the data for the fifth object. `Right` functions in the same manner, moving in the opposite direction. If no further objects exist, the current object is redisplayed.

By using `Segment` the visible section can be chosen in the graphic window (see the program description of the editor for detailed information on this). The next three menu items (`Factor`, `Factor*2` and `Factor/2`) change the enlargement factor. `Factor` increases or decreases the enlargement factor.`Factor*2` doubles the enlargement factor, while `Factor/2` halves the enlargement factor. The factor is doubled with the first, the second halves it, and the third can be chosen in intervals between [1/64..64]. The more the enlargement factor, the smaller the visible section, but the more recognizable the details. When the enlargement factor changes, the screen contents are unchanged because the display of large pictures takes too much time. A new drawing of the screen appears when you select the `Refresh` item.

The `Mat.editor` item enters the material editor section of the program (see Section 4.1.4 below for details). You have more control over the speed of the graphics with the `Lines` item. This procedure can test for the number of lines used in drawing a circle, and this value must be between 1 and 50. The `Show` item displays a certain body, either as data or in graphic form. Graphic display can appear either in the middle of each window or in red. You must enter which mode and which body are to be used. Pressing <d> displays the data; pressing <c> displays the graphic body in red. When you enter <m>, the body section moves to the center of the window in case you want to execute `Refresh`. The `Quit` item lets you end the program.

4.1.4 The Material Editor

When you have entered the entire object list, which contains the data of the picture to be calculated, you have to assign each object a material number as well as the necessary coordinates. Each of these numbers represents a specific material for which you have set a certain color, shade intensity, and reflection factor. The material input is done in the material editor. It assigns a number to each material so that you know each object has the color which you assigned to it.

All input in the material editor is done through mouse-controlled sliders. When you want to insert a value with these sliders, you must click the position inside of the corresponding slider, where the position on the left border means the value 0 and the position on the right border means the value 1. Here we cannot insert an exact value such as 0.765. A value like this means nothing to the materials. Besides, you wouldn't be able to see a visible difference between a reflection factor of 0.7 and 0.63.

The color can be adjusted with the first three sliders, which stand for red, green, and blue. Here you can judge the color in the rectangle that is found in the upper right corner. You can specify the brightness of a body with the shade intensity. A value near zero is a dark shade and a value near 1 is a light shade. Which value should be inserted cannot be determined because personal taste is important here. When you want a high, hard contrast, the value must be set at 0.1. This has the disadvantage that objects in the shadows are barely visible. You can experiment with this factor as well as the reflection factor.

Light that shines on the body should be reflected. When the body appears dull, the reflection factor should be increased. When it is placed at one, all of the light is reflected, and the body does not have its own color any more. When you also want to enter a material, select the `Material` item from the Mat. Editor menu, or just press the <m> key. After that input can begin. When all values are correctly entered, click on the **OK** gadget. You can move in the material list as usual using the `Left` and `Right` items. Should you want to erase a material, select the `Delete` menu item. To correct a material, select `Correction`. This reactivates the controller and the input of the desired material appears as usual. When all of the materials are entered, select `Quit` to return to the main program The material editor asks if you really want to exit. Click on the **Yes** or **No** gadget.

4.1.5 The Transform Menu

There are more possibilties here to change the entered object data. The simplest example is editing data. `Delete` deletes the object data set, while `Copy` copies the data. The following commands let you choose the current parameters of a certain mode. This mode is tested by pressing a key. When you press <q>, the program exits this section without doing anything else. Pressing <d> executes the operation on the current body, and <c> copies the body, then executes the transformation on this copy. The transitions are: rotation, enlargement, and translation.

The three angles of rotation must be given when the rotation is chosen. The midpoint remains unchanged throughout this. The new midpoint of the object must be entered with the translation, either through the keyboard or the mouse. The enlargement is just as easy. Three enlargement factors must be entered for the three main directions. The body is extended the same distance in all directions if these values stay the same. Otherwise the proportions of the body are distorted.

4.1.6 The Disk Menu

To save and reload the entered data of the object and the material list four items exist in the Disk menu: `Load list`, `Save list`, `Load mat`, and `Save mat`. When the user selects the `Load list` item from the Disk menu, the program asks for the names of the file to be read. The user just has to enter the filename in the string gadget and press the <Return> key. The program automatically adds the file extension `.list`.

Note: The program does not check to see if the given file is on the disk. If the user enters a filename that the program cannot find, the program displays an error message.

After the file loads correctly, the desired data set is found in memory and lists the last body entered.

When data is to be saved, select `Save list` from the Disk menu. Enter the filename without an extension, just as in loading data—the program automatically adds the file extension `.list`.

`Load mat` and `Save mat` handle the loading and saving of the materials lists from and to disk.

4.2 Tracer Documentation

You can edit and shade some objects if you have put all of the modules together and constructed a running program.

Editing and entering objects is made easier by the object editor. This section is limited to the `tracer` program (the main program).

4.2.1 After Starting

When you start the program and all the libraries open, you can specify the resolution and the appearance of the display screen. The display screen is the screen where the shaded picture and the wire model appear. The user screen is the screen used by AmigaBASIC. This is where all user input occurs.

The first screen that appears gives you the option of selecting resolution. The <Cursor up> and <Cursor down> keys let you scroll through the choices. You can view alternatives with <Cursor left> and <Cursor right>. So, for example, in the first line you can establish the display mode (normal, hold and modify, extra halfbrite), X resolution in the second line (normal and HIRES), and Y resolution in the third line (normal and interlace).

The last line in this screen specifies the number of bit planes. The program confirms that HAM and extra halfbrite run with 6 bit planes in the normal X resolution, and that the number of bit planes corresponds to the amount of memory available.

Having established the display mode and the resolution, you can press <Return> and go back to the main loop of the program. Not all of the menu items can be used at the beginning of the program. For example, it makes no sense to draw a wire model when there are no objects in the object memory. You can access ali of the menu items when the first object definition is loaded or merged.

4.2.2 Amiga Menu

The `3D-Cad-Info` menu item tells you the maximum number of objects in memory. The objects (surfaces and bodies) are saved in array `K()`. Furthermore, array `K()` shows how many objects already exist. The program variables `MaxNumber` and `NumberK` contain these values.

4.2.3 File Menu

The File menu contains items for controlling printer and disk access.

4.2.3.1 Loading and Saving Objects

Selecting the `Load` item lets you load object definitions into the computer. The current disk directory can be displayed using requesters before the object file is loaded. A requester displays three gadgets: **Files**, **Continue** and **Chdir**.

When you want to select another subdirectory from which the object file should be loaded, click on the **Chdir** gadget. Enter a new subdirectory or a new disk name. When using the optional disk for this book, click on the **Chdir** gadget. Move the cursor past the word `tracer:`. Enter the word `objects` and press <Return>.

A default gadget is a gadget surrounded by a bold rectangle. Either click on the default gadget or press <Return> to accept this gadget.

Click the **Continue** gadget or press <Return> to tell the program that you want to enter a filename for loading. Enter the filename without a file extension (`.list` for object definition lists and `.mat` for material lists). and press <Return>. The program automatically appends the `.list` file extension.

When the given file opens, the program asks how many objects should be loaded from this file. You can enter the number of objects currently in the file, a larger number or a smaller number. The default number is the number of objects currently in the file. In other words, this number is the number of elements in array `K()` actually containing objects. You should provide a large enough number here in case you want to load more objects later.

Then by selecting the `Merge` item you can add more objects to the ones that already exist. Here you should select the correct subdirectory as with all disk operations.

After you open the file, you are asked how many objects should be loaded. Please note that if you want to load more objects than are found in the object memory, memory fills up and the excess objects disappear.

You can avoid this by creating a large enough object memory using the `New` menu item. Objects are placed in the desired memory location. Memory set with `New` should be loaded with `Merge`. The object memory is reset when using `Load`.

You can also write objects from memory to disk. Only memory that contains objects is written to disk. Unused object memory (array elements of array `K()`) are not saved. If the user presses <Return> without entering a filename, the disk operation aborts and the program returns to the main loop.

4.2.3.2 Loading Materials

You can load materials that you created with the editor into the computer. You can also change the current subdirectory of the diskette. You only need enter the name of the new material's file. These are used instead of the default materials that are used for shadows. Do not include the file extension (`.mat` for material lists). The program automatically appends the `.mat` file extension to the file.

4.2.3.3 Background

By selecting the `Background` item you can brighten the background of the graphic to be shadowed. Usually when shadowing only the background color or a plane is presented. But you can change this: You are given the option of loading an IFF graphic from the disk or creating a pattern.

When you select `Load Screen`, a screen similar to the `Load object` screen appears. You can change directories, load an IFF graphic or view the files in the current directory. When you click on the **Continue** gadget the program asks for the name of the IFF file that contains the picture to be loaded. An IFF picture can be taken from any drawing program that supports Interchange File Format (IFF). Try this with pictures from ***Graphicraft®*** or ***DeluxePaint®***.

Now back to the background. When you decide on a pattern for the background, you can choose from three alternatives:

Pattern

Click on the **Pattern** gadget to fill the display screen with a fill pattern. Enter the first number of the desired pattern, which must be between 0 and 35. This gives you a set of 36 different fill patterns (standard and extended). Then you need only select the foreground and background pen colors. The display screen fills with the pattern in the given color.

Sky

Let's produce a starry sky. We won't go into forming individual stars here because the alternatives are automatically shown from the program.

After entering the star color and you enter the number of stars to be drawn, this background appears on the screen.

Floating background

Here you can display the changes from one color to another. Simply specify the number of the color register between whose colors the color path should be calculated.

For example, if you want the color bright green in color register 1 and the color dark green in color register 3, you simply enter 1 and 3 for a color cycle from light green to dark green.

Generally you should only create a background when you are sure that the next step will be shadowing. For example, if you are not sure if the position of an object is correct, you should try to determine this first. Loading a similar IFF file can be an easy test.

4.2.3.4 Saving Graphics

You can save graphics in IFF format on disk for later recall. Besides storing the picture, this lets you edit the picture later with a drawing program. Select the `Save Screen` item from the menu and enter the name of the file that should be written to disk.

4.2.3.5 Printing Graphics

You can also print your graphics on paper using the tracer program. `Hardcopy` creates a hard copy on the printer selected from Preferences. You will also need Preferences 1.3 if you want the picture printed sideways or in gray scales.

Select the `Hardcopy` item from the File menu. A requester asks whether a printer is connected. Click on the **Printer OK** gadget if so. Clicking the **No Printer** gadget returns you to the main menu.

4.2.3.6 Setting New Colors

Selecting the `Color palette` item displays all of the available colors on the display screen. Move the mouse pointer on the color to be changed and press the left mouse button to select the color. You can then set the new red, green, and blue components of the foreground and background colors. After that you can either leave the color palette screen or change the next color.

Note: Selecting `Color palette` deletes the current graphic from the display screen, replacing the graphic with the palette screen. Save graphics often.

4.2.3.7 Leaving the Program

When you want to leave the program select the `Program end` item. You will be asked if you really want to leave. Click on the **Yes** gadget to leave the program. Click on the **No** gadget to return to the main loop of the program.

By clicking on the **New start** gadget the entire program starts over as if you had just begun working. This option deletes any work that was in memory, so use with caution.

4.2.4 The Editor Menu

This item invokes the editor. Before the editor is called, confirm your choice. You can save a picture that was not previously saved by clicking on the **Cancel** gadget and saving the graphic.

4.2.5 The Parameter Menu

This menu contains routines which change the parameters for the three dimensional display.

You can reset the coordinates of the projection point with the `Projection point` item. The `Main point` item lets you control the coordinates of the main point. The rotation angle around the coordinate axes can be changed in α, β, χ. The distance from the projection to the main point can be reset from the `Distance` item.

As you know, the body of an object appears as a wire model. This is an alternative to the very slow shadow process. When you enlarge the wire model, the object also appears larger when it is shadowed. You have two options of enlargement:

Proportional Here you enter an enlargement factor. The picture is then enlarged in the X and Y directions by the same measurements.

Distorted A section of the screen must be selected with the mouse for a distorted enlargement. Press the left mouse button so the pointer position determines the upper left corner of the rectangle. Move the mouse while holding down the button and you can see how the mouse movement reduces and enlarges the rubberbanded rectangle.

When you have set the correct rectangle, release the left mouse button. You are then asked whether the chosen section is OK. Click on the **OK** gadget if it is. If you would prefer to enlarge another section, click anywhere outside of the **OK** gadget.

When the section is OK, the contents of the specified rectangle are enlarged.

The default proportional enlargement factor is one, which returns you to the original screen. In some cases you may see anything on the display screen after the enlargement. This can be remedied by choosing `Enlarge` again and this time entering a proportional factor of 1 to restore the original picture. Then select the `Enlarge` item and click on the **Distort** gadget to enlarge the appropriate section.

`Number of lines` should also be explained. Remember: the number here (`numbersegments`) gives the number of lines used to draw a circle in the wire model. Only numbers are given in the above menu items and no requesters are used.

4.2.6 The Draw Menu

This menu lists items for controlling the shadowing as well as drawing wire models.

4.2.6.1 Shadows

Select the `Shadows` item to start the shadowing process.

You must first determine the parameters used by the shadowing process first (Shadow window, etc.).

This is done by choosing `Initialization`. First you are asked about the actual shadow window. Click on the **All** gadget to shade the entire screen. **Section** gives you the option of choosing a particular screen section.

YA-YE gives you the option of specifying a vertical area (a stripe) to shade. This stripe covers the whole width of the screen; you can set its position and height. First move the mouse to the beginning position of the stripe to be shaded. A line drawn at the current mouse position helps with the positioning. When you have found the correct position, press and hold the left mouse button while moving the pointer to the desired end position. Release the mouse button to select the stripe.

You can decide the end first and then the start positions of the stripe. The sequence is the same. The program ensures that the sizes of the Y coordinate of the end and the smaller Y coordinate of the start position are correct.

We now come to more parameters for the shading. You must enter the coordinates of the light source. Simply enter the X, Y, and Z coordinates of the light source in `Qx`, `Qy`, and `Qz`. Be aware that the light source rotates around the coordinate axes.

You can also set the color of the light source. Enter the red, blue, and green components of the light source in values between 0 and 1. Three ones give a white light source.

For values between 0 and 1, be sure that you include a zero preceding the decimal point. For example, the program accepts the notation 0.5 in these cases, but will ignore an input of .5—remember the zero before the decimal point.

Because the shading can take many days or weeks on complicated pictures, the pixel sizes can be changed. This has the advantage that you can calculate a large picture within a few hours. All of the points of the shade window can be shaded by setting the pixel width and pixel height at 1. When an unpleasant result occurs, this can be changed by resetting some of the parameters.

Choosing a pixel width and pixel height larger than 1 makes every second, third, fourth, etc., point available for color calculation. The picture is also shaded in a `point width * point height` grid. The midpoint of such a grid rectangle is the color of the entire rectangle.

After all of these parameters are entered, you can then choose the `Shadows` menu item to start the shadow calculation process.

You can control the default values for shading by changing the values in the program. The picture on the cover of this book was produced by shading the entire screen with the light source is set at the coordinate (0,0,50) with the color (1,1,1,) = white. `Pixel width` and `Pixel height` are both 1. The projection point was 270,10,255 and the main point was 0,0,25. The object and material were loaded from the optional disk from the `Spheres.list` and `Spheres.mat` files. The enlargement factor was 4.

You shouldn't try to use the keyboard during shading. When you press any key during the shading operation, after the current line is shaded, the program asks if the shading should be continued or stopped.

You can, for example, let the computer shade overnight and save the picture in the morning. Naturally you could object that the Amiga is a multitasking machine. Therefore AmigaBASIC could be started from the `CLI` to allow other work in the AmigaDOS window. This is not recommended since too many interruptions of the shading task can cause a Guru Meditation.

4.2.6.2 The Wire Model

When you select the `Wire Model` item, the wire model of the object is redrawn on the display screen, or if it has already been drawn, the display screen is redisplayed.

This happens if no parameters (projection point, main point, distance to projection surface, rotation angle) have changed since the last selection of the `Wire model` item. When one of these parameters is changed, or the display screen is erased using the `Clear screen` item, or a background is chosen, the picture is redrawn.

After choosing a background for the display screen the new drawing is not erased. The wire model is drawn over the background. When the wire model finishes drawing, the screen flashes briefly. The wire model stays on the screen until you press a key. Then the program returns to the main loop.

4.2.7 Keyboard Program Control

We included keyboard shortcuts for some menu items to make the program easier to use. For example, pressing <Space> creates a wire model.

The menu items that can be addressed from the keyboard show the key to the right of the item name. There are also functions that can be called using the keyboard instead of the menu.

One of these is Help. By pressing the <Help> key a list of keyboard codes and their actions appears on the screen.

You know, for example, that the rotation angle can be increased and decreased using the cursor keys, the <R> key and <Ctrl><R>. The distance to the projection surface (DPH) can be changed using + - * /.

That's it for keyboard and menu control of the program. Going deeper into this subject is unnecessary, because you can only be a tracer expert through practice.

5.
Program Enhancements

5. Program Enhancements

The algorithms and routines in this book are not as complete as they could be. Improvements of all kinds could be made here and there throughout the program. We'll look in this chapter at some of the improvements that can be made to the programs you've read about so far. Perhaps you've already thought of your own enhancements to the tracer and editor programs, or perhaps this chapter will help you think of some improvements.

Extended objects

Let's start with the basic objects. We can give the objects more restrictions than already exist in the tracer and editor. For example, with a little reprogramming we could add cone segments, truncated cones, ellipsoid segments, etc., to our list of basic objects. Because these restrictions are not that different from the complete objects, they can be created from the existing subroutines and added to the editor's menu set as needed.

It's even possible to create new basic objects which have little basis in the original object routines. For example, imagine what might happen if you change the restrictions of an ellipsoid to u^10+v^10+w^10=1. What would you get? A cube with rounded corners? Change the restrictions of the other basic objects, perhaps by calculating a cube instead of a square, or something similar.

Triangles and extended objects

Another option for creating new forms consists of assembling multiple triangles. You can make almost any figure if you have enough triangles available for creating it. Unfortunately, it's rather time consuming to enter each individual triangle.

B-splines

Try both methods of creating a surface that has separate passages, but no corners or edges. This is done with B-splines that run through the points of the surface. The problem with this is that a surface must be divided into many triangles so that they function very smoothly.

The big advantage to B-splines lies in that you can get wonderful shapes with little programming hassle. You can define a wine glass for the computer to calculate with a few dozen points. By using Bezier or B-splines a few thousand triangles are created which then create a nearly perfect illusion.

Smooth shading

In addition to Bezier or B-spline, you can use smooth shading. Smooth shading erases the edges from surfaces by calculating the normal vectors of the two surfaces in such a way that they are continually changing. You must define which surface is being pushed against for each edge of the surface you are working with.

The calculation of these surfaces is fairly easy. You must find the normal vectors of the other surfaces and join them together independently of the distance of the intersection point from the shifted edge. When the intersection point is very far from the shifted edge, take the original normal vector, which is directly on the intersection point, and add the normal vectors of both surfaces in the ratio of 50 to 50.

You don't need to work out as many triangles with smooth shading because the borders are smooth. The program coding involved requires more memory, and the computation time increases as well. The disadvantage of smooth shading is that only the normal vectors are smoothed. The outline of the surface remains unchanged. If you change the surface of a cube into that of a circle, the border will keep the appearance of a cube.

Object rotation

Object rotations present another simplification of the input of objects. These can be done with cylinders, cones, and circle surfaces. You must write an editor that lets you enter the profile of a rotation body. From that profile the data of the object can be generated and saved to disk. You can create a section from a rotation body, but the cone section must also be implemented.

As you see, the basic objects have room for improvement. You can have more options for creating shapes by changing the surface structure of the objects.

Until now all of the objects have been the same in that they were smooth. We can define different material constants which affect only the color and reflection coefficient of the surface. Wouldn't it be nice if we could define any relief for a surface? Calculation solves this problem. In relationship to a function, which tests for the method of the relief, the normal vectors are bent. This happens in relationship to the position and is repeated periodically, and produces a very ordinary relief. A small disadvantage of the relief is that it is only related to the normal vectors; the surface itself remains smooth. You should always use small reliefs because they do not draw attention to themselves.

We define the relief function in relation to both parameters of the direction vectors `u` and `v` for planes. For spheres and ellipsoids we take the angle of the polar coordinates of the intersection point, and for cones we take the polar coordinate angle, which is responsible for the rotation around the `r4` axis, and the `w` parameter for the `r4` axis. We leave writing the relief function up to you and your imagination.

A pattern affects more changes in the surface. It's up to you to decide whether the pattern will be a chessboard pattern, stripes or small hearts.

Patterns do not change the normal vectors of a surface, but change colors or the entire material constant. The pattern should be defined periodically, in relation to the parameters or the polar coordinates. It is best if the pattern is defined in the `Mat` array. For example, take

`Mat(n,6)`, which is unoccupied. When this element is zero, this is valuable for the other elements we have defined. Otherwise `Mat(n,6)` gives the number of the pattern. For example:

1: Chessboard

2: Dotted

3: Lined

4: ...

`Mat(n,0)` through `Mat(n,5)` contain the material numbers for the different materials of the pattern. We can assign different materials for the black fields and the white fields of the chessboard pattern. The hearts could be multicolored, or you could define a red-and-blue Commodore symbol. We can define the pattern using parameters and polar coordinates like the relief. We could also use different methods, for example in relation to the Z coordinate so that you get high lines.

IFF

So far we've learned how to project a graphic on a surface and how to improve the data structure. Now we must build the ability to load an IFF graphic into the program. We must specify where the graphic should be on the surface and if it should lie next to it, like our pattern.

Instead of the color that is defined in the `Mat` array for the surface, we take the color that is used in the graphic. The X and Y coordinates of the graphic are calculated in the approved method from the parameters/polar coordinates. The other material attributes, like reflection, etc., can stay the same. Put a bottle, which was defined with Bezier, smoothed with smooth shading, and distorted with some good taste, into a BASIC program. We are operating our Amiga to the limits of its capabilities, both in computing time and in resolution and color.

Transparency

Now we want to turn to other things to make our graphic more realistic, such as transparency. We have already described how to simulate transparency. It's not enough to construct a `CalculatePoint` call in the respective subroutine. We must also consider that a transparent object allows light to pass through, so there is light beneath the object instead of a shadow, but light whose color is not quite the same as the original color.

We can build transparency for the place we have already prepared in our material data structure. We have constructed another call for this routine in `CalculatePoint`, before the recursive call from `CalculatePoint` for the reflection. The direction vector of the visual ray `(rx,ry,rz)` is unchanged. We must be careful that all variables that are needed for the `CalculatePoint` call are not changed. The object is searched first, the shadows thrown from the point in question, and the light source is next. Then the color of the light rays change according to the material structure of the object. After that the object must be searched, then the light source, and so on, until all of the objects that throw shadows on the point in question are known. The calculation of `Bright.r`, `Bright.g`, and `Bright.b` for the color must be considered. The consideration of the color of the light source must then be preferred and may not be executed twice in the case of shadows.

Calculating transparency is not quite as easy as reflection, and both things together make it even more complicated. For the definition of the materials the sum of the reflection and transparency coefficients should not exceed one because the brightness of the surface can eventually be greater than one, which would produce a realistic impression.

As a last feature we make it possible to define multiple light sources. We must execute all calculations for each light source and the colors we get. The addition of the brightnesses of all of the light sources should not give a value over one, because our graphic could get too bright. To be able to use the optimization, a `MinMaxLq` array must be calculated for each light source, or we enlarge the `MinMaxLq` array around one dimension which gives the number of the light source:

```
DIM MinMaxLq(NumberLq,Numberlk,6)
```

Maybe you like more optimizations, if only for more light sources. Or you have an idea for more shapes. This chapter only shows a starting point, which should give you an idea of the possibilities that are possible in ray tracing. These possibilities are left up to you to use and find. Computer graphics are a fascinating subject; make the best of it.

6.
3D Tricks and Tips

6. 3D Tricks and Tips

Now that you have read through most of this book, we'd like to give you some practical hints. These tricks and tips will help you design graphics for your current 3D system more easily, and help eliminate most errors.

Graphic planning

First the design. One of the most difficult problems is thinking about the scenery that the computer should calculate. At first, try it with just a few simple objects. Too many objects clutter the picture and confuse the viewer. Don't go into too much detail—limit yourself to the important items. This book lists some examples. Or load some objects from the optional disk if you don't want to type them in yourself.

When you have some idea of the body you want drawn, sit down and sketch it out on graph paper. Graph paper allows for easier measurement. Draw three views of your object, the way the editor will draw the object. You should also lay out the material constants for each object material and include these in the working sketch, where each material is assigned a number.

Handy tools

One of the best items you can have available for keeping track of your 3D parameters is a small notebook and pencil. Keep these next to the computer when using the tracer program. Write down original coordinates of graphics, experimental coordinates, colors, etc. (you may also want to write down whether these experiments worked or not).

Colors

When choosing color, try to keep the graphic from appearing too bold or too dull. Select colors that complement each other well, instead of using every color available. Assign these colors to individual objects where they will look best.

Shading and reflection

The shade brightness should be set at roughly the same value for all objects (0 to 0.25). The reflection value can be somewhat higher. Add reflective properties to single objects, instead of the entire scene. Have the appearances of the objects set in your mind to help add these properties to the actual graphic.

When the mental picture meets your satisfaction, start the editor and enter the individual objects. Later, when you have given more thought to the scene, you can divide it up into sections and enter the data directly into the editor.

Keeping it simple

To keep your graphic from becoming too complicated, you should set `visible` to `y` (yes) for all objects in the editor, so you can see exactly what you have entered. After entering each object and editing it to your satisfaction, save the object. Load the materials editor and add the material constants. Save the entire collection of data, then start the tracer.

Resolution

Now you must decide in which resolution you want the picture calculated. The HAM mode offers the most colors, but a HAM screen consumes quite a bit of memory. When you have enough memory, you can choose a HAM screen at the start because the color palette doesn't need to be selected so carefully.

Point of view

After you have loaded your objects and materials, you must consider at which angle the scene should be observed. Examine your sketch and consider the point of view from which you want to the scene to appear. Experiment with changing the main point first (the default when loading objects for the first time is usually 0,0,0). Try some negative and positive settings.

Next experiment with your distance between the projection point and the main point (`DPH`—see Section 2.4). Be careful not to make this figure too small, since this can greatly distort perspective of the graphic.

Projection point

Now enter your projection point. Enter the coordinates (-1000,-1000,1000) if you have no other position specifically in mind. Press <Space> to see the wire model. It is probably relatively small on the screen. Press <v> to enlarge the picture and select either the **Proportional** or **Distort** gadget. The object should almost fill the screen, without going past the edges. When you define reflecting objects, select a larger section so the reflections appear on the screen.

Experiment with each point until the display pleases you. Write down all of the values that you have entered, including the main point, enlargement factor, and either the projection point or angle and distance. This will help if you want to reproduce these conditions later.

Light source

Now specify the position of the light source. A recommended value is a position "to one side" of the observer, so the shadows are most distinct. Try the projection point at (-1000,-1000,1000), and the light source at (-1000,1000,1000) if you want the shadows to fall to the right. If you want short shadows, increase the Z coordinate of the light source's position. Decrease the Z value for longer shadows.

Write down the position of the light source in the notebook. Press <F9> to initialize shadowing parameters. Select the entire screen or a section, and enter the position of the light source. Enter (1,1,1) for the light source color, which provides a white light.

Big pixels for draft calculation

For the pixel height and width, enter 16 and 10 (1/20 of the screen height and width). This computes the shadowing in a blurred form. These pudgy pixels are enough for a draft display, since calculation time is 1/400 the time normally needed.

Press <F10> to calculate the picture. Clock the time between the setting of the first and last pixels. After the picture is complete, you can approximate the amount of time the computer needs to calculate the picture with normal single pixels. Use the following equation:

```
calculation_time * pixel_width * pixel_height
```

The result of this multiplication gives you a rough idea of the calculation time.

If you're nearsighted, take your glasses off and back away from the screen until the draft graphic looks close to a normal close-up view (people with normal vision can just back away). This gives you an idea of what the finished product will look like.

Colors

Now you can see if the colors came out as you had thought. It is very important that you set the color palette at the optimal setting, even for HAM pictures. Set the color palette so that many different shades of brightness are available for each color. The more colors you have to use, the more degrees of brightness you can set.

Set the color palette for HAM mode so each sudden transition from one color to another requires no more than two colors in the palette. Transitions from black to red, black to green, or black to blue are no problem, while a transition from black to gray cannot be done directly because this gray tone is not in the palette.

Once you have set the colors properly, the picture can be calculated. If you select a smaller pixel size (e.g., height and width of 2), you can recognize more features. When you are satisfied with the result, you can consider whether you want to stay with this display mode, or change modes. If you want to change, you should write down the color palette configuration for later reference.

Before you calculate the picture in normal pixel size, you should figure out how long the computer will take to compute the graphic (see calculation described above). It's not a bad idea to plan to let the Amiga calculate overnight.

Calculating in sections

If the computer needs days to compute, which happens in more elaborate graphics, you can calculate the picture in sections and save the screen. You can then calculate further by loading the graphic, setting the necessary parameters and selecting the sections not yet shadowed.

7. Mathematical Basics

7. Mathematical Basics

Some people suffer from math anxiety. This book was designed for the non-math person in mind, but we should list a few of the equations involved. We would like to show you some of the basics of three dimensional math in this chapter.

Before we go any further, let's remind you of a word you've seen repeated throughout this book. We first defined it in Chapter One, but it can't hurt to describe it again:

Algorithms

An algorithm is a step-by-step plan for problem solving, usually through computer programming. Often a computer book explains the algorithm needed for the particular task, then lists the program used to perform that task. We chose to do it the other way around. This book views algorithms as working programs instead of as formal "statements of intent." Therefore, we showed a segment of a program listing first, then we discussed the algorithms used by the program. In short, you saw the program code itself, then the reasoning behind the way the program code works. The programs were written as modules so you could incorporate the routines in your own programs. The completed program listings for the tracer and editor are listed in the appendices.

7.1 Vectors

First we should look at vectors. A vector acts as a connection between geometry and standard arithmetic. Vectors are graphically represented as arrows. Each vector arrow has a starting point and an end point; the arrow's "head" lies at the end point. Vectors with the same length and direction are *equal*, regardless of their location. The following illustration shows a set of equal vectors and a set of different vectors:

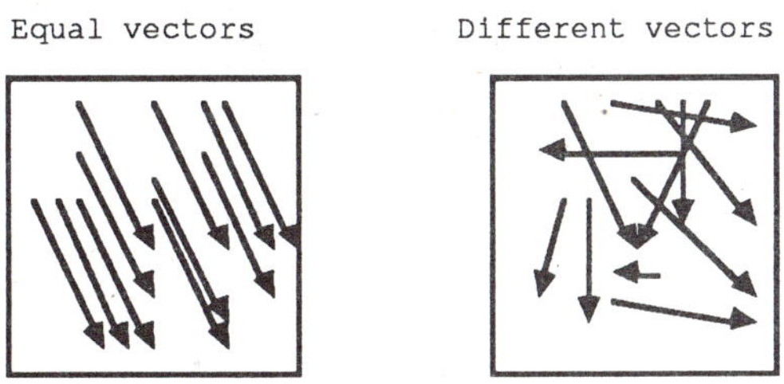

Figure 7.1

In geometry there are two ways to differentiate vectors:

1. position or equal vectors and
2. direction or difference vectors

Position vectors begin at the origin of the coordinate system (0,0,0). Position vectors require that you only give the end point–the beginning point is already set at 0,0,0. Parts of the space can also be assigned as position vectors.

Direction or difference vectors start at locations other than the origin and are usually the difference between two position vectors. The starting point of a direction vector is usually the end point of a position vector.

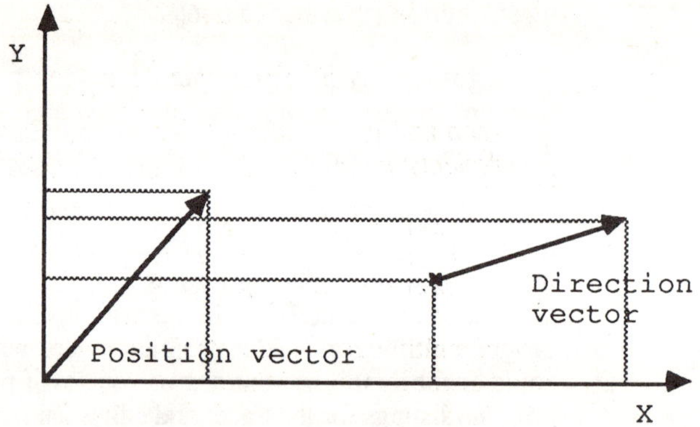

Figure 7.2

The difference vectors bring up an important subject: Computing with vectors. You can add and subtract vectors:

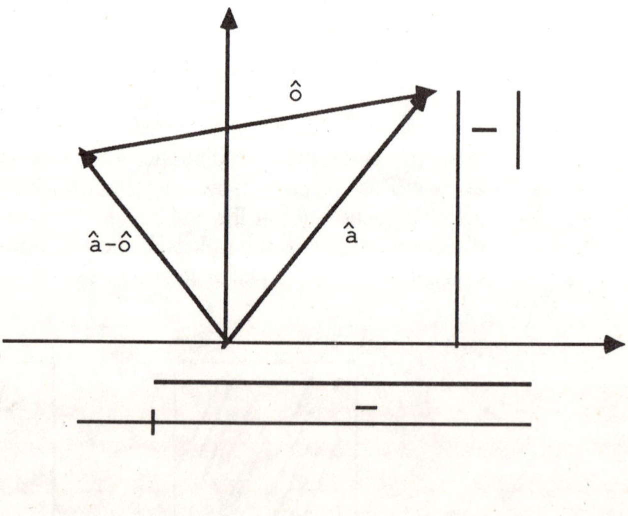

Figure 7.3

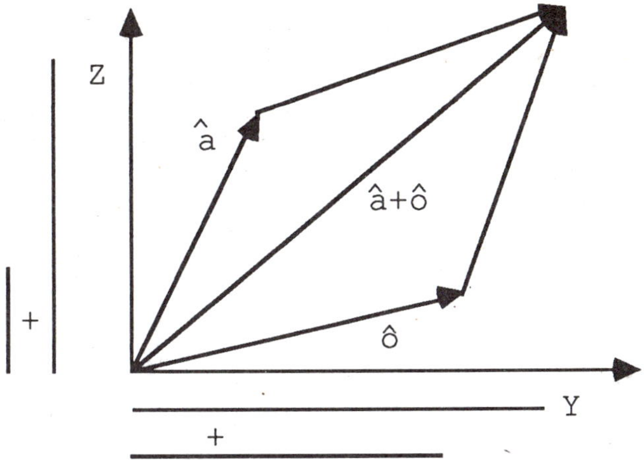

Figure 7.4

You can add or subtract the vector components (vectors have X,Y,Z *components*; points have X,Y,Z *coordinates*):

$$\hat{a}\pm\hat{o} = \begin{pmatrix} ax \\ ay \\ az \end{pmatrix} \pm \begin{pmatrix} ox \\ oy \\ oz \end{pmatrix} = \begin{pmatrix} ax\pm ox \\ ay\pm oy \\ az\pm oz \end{pmatrix} = \hat{u}$$

When multiplying a vector with a scalar (a real number), multiply each component by this number:

$$t * \hat{a} = t * \begin{matrix} ax \\ ay \\ az \end{matrix} = \begin{pmatrix} t*ax \\ t*ay \\ t*az \end{pmatrix} = \hat{u}$$

$$t * \hat{a} - t * \begin{matrix} ax \\ ay \\ az \end{matrix} - \begin{pmatrix} t*ax \\ t*ay \\ t*az \end{pmatrix} - \hat{u}$$

Figure 7.5

7.2 Using Vectors

You can describe all sorts of three dimensional bodies and surfaces with vectors; these are the connection between math and geometry—and computer graphics.

Lines are also represented by using vectors. You take a position vector that fixes a point on a line, and a direction vector that lies on a position vector. The following equation can describe a line:

```
x       ox          rx
y   =   oy + l *    ry
z       oz          rz
```

The above equation looks like the following in graphic form:

Figure 7.6

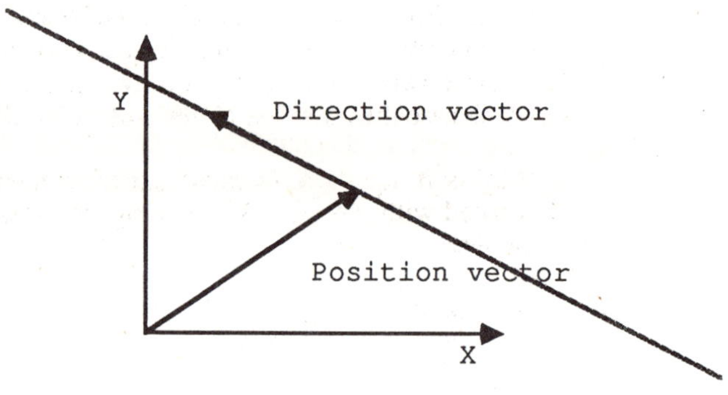

The direction vector extends like a telescope arm to the length stated in `l` and encompasses all of the points of the line.

Planes

Planes are presented in a similar way. Two linearly independent vectors are needed here. Linearly independent means that one vector is not a factor of the other. The plane equation looks like this:

```
x       ox   r1x      r2x
y   =   oy + a*r1y  + b* r2y
z       oz   r1z      r2z
```

Spheres

The equation used to prepare spheres may be a little more intimidating. The equation itself appears below:

```
(x      Mx)^2
(y -    My)^2
(z      Mz)^2
```

This diagram makes it somewhat clearer:

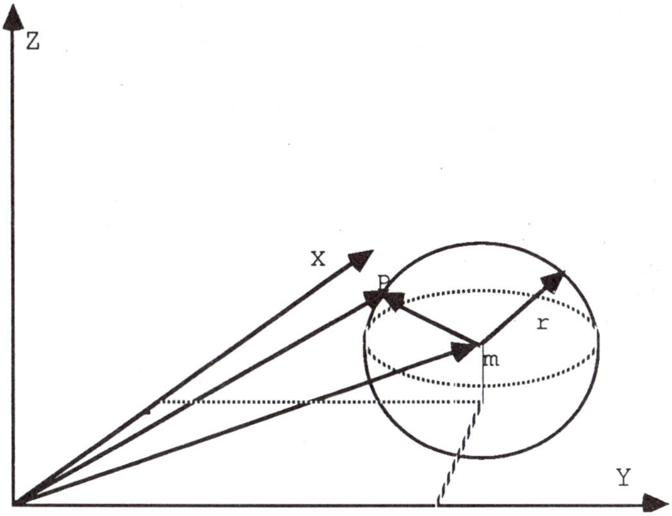

Figure 7.7

In the sphere equation notice that a point on the surface of the sphere is created from other vectors, instead of being based directly on the point of origin of the sphere. And the vector squaring is new. The difference of these two vectors (point on the sphere–midpoint) is the radius, in which case the point lies on the surface of the sphere.

Why is it squared? Because squaring must occur when a vector is equated with a scalar. By squaring, the scalar product becomes a real number:

```
x^2
y^2  =  x*x+y*y+z*z  =  a
z^2
```

When this number is equal to the square of the radius, you know:

	x	
The point (position vector)	y	lies on the sphere
	z	

This is also true for the basic objects and surfaces that can be created with vectors.

7.3 Angles Between Two Vectors

You can also test for the angle enclosed by two vectors. Let's move outside of the space in the plane and look at two perpendicular vectors:

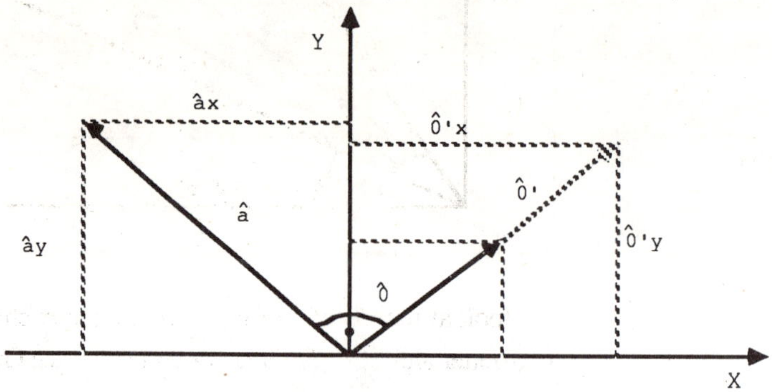

Figure 7.8

One of the vectors (ô) can be extended by S-multiplication until it is exactly as long as the other vector (â). Examine the coordinates or components of the vectors, then note that the following apply:

```
ax = -o'y    ay = o'x
```

Because ô' is a factor of vector ô, you can write k*ô for ô':

```
ax = -k*oy       ay = k*ox
```

By solving k and inserting and transforming the equation, you get:

```
ax*ox+ay*oy = 0
```

This is also a form of the scalar product placed between two vectors.

Consider two non-perpendicular vectors:

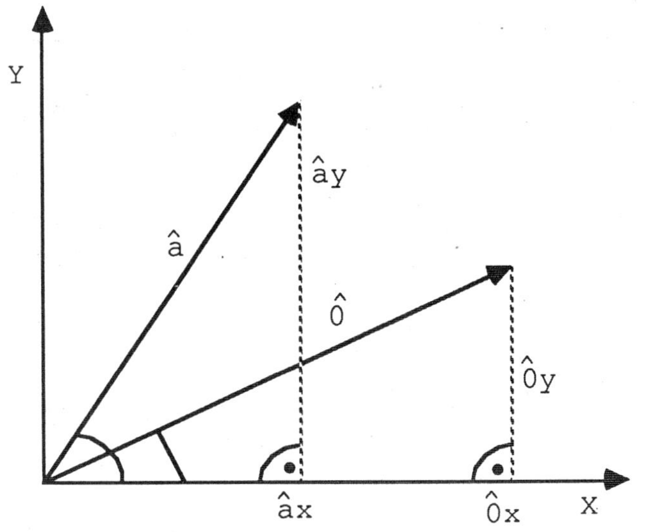

Figure 7.9

Now look at the equation for this (note: the α character represents the Greek letter alpha; the β character represents the Greek letter beta):

```
ax = Cos(α)  * |â|   ox = Cos(β)  * |ô|
ay = Sin(α)  * |â|   oy = Sin(β)  * |ô|
```

If you place these in the equation of the scalar product:

```
  Cos(α)  * |â| * Cos(β)  * |ô|
- Sin(α)  * |â| * Sin(β)  * |ô| = ax*ox +ay*oy

<=> (Cos(α)*Cos(β) - Sin(α)*Sin(β)) * |a| * |o| =
ax*ox+ay*oy
```

The expression with the many sine and cosine functions can be simplified by using the addition theorem of cosines :

```
(Cos (β-α) = Cos(α)*Cos(β)+Sin(α)*Sin(β))

                 ax*ox+ay*oy
Cos(β-α) =      -------------
                  |a| * |ô|
```

Where the angle β–α is enclosed by the vectors.

For the value of a vector (|â|) use the Pythagorean theorem:

```
|â| = Sqr (dax²+day²+daz²)
```

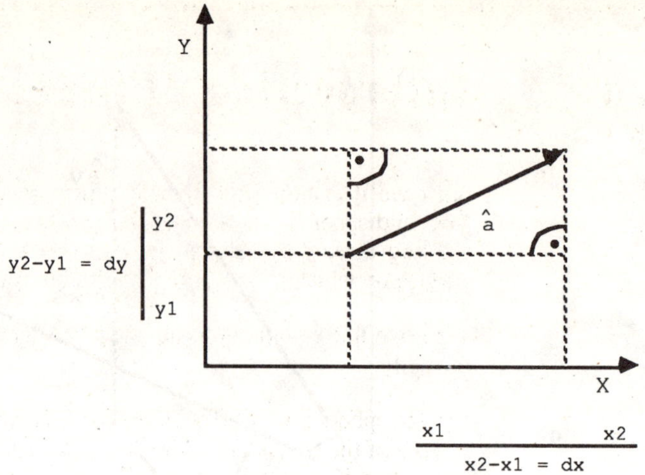

Figure 7.10

dax represents the difference of the X-end-component minus the X-starting-component of a vector. day and daz stand for the difference between the Y and Z components, respectively.

Insert the value of the vector in the formula for the cosine and examine the two vectors in the space, and you get two vectors for the formula of the cosine of the enclosed angle:

$$\mathrm{Cos}(\beta-\alpha) = \frac{ax*ox+ay*oy+az*oz}{\mathrm{Sqr}((dax^2+day^2+daz^2)*(dox^2+doy^2+doz^2))}$$

7.4 Intersecting Lines and Planes

Now we'll examine the intersection points of lines and planes, and lines and spheres. These intersection points are especially important in shading three dimensional bodies. You must test for the point of a surface on which a visual ray (light), represented by a line, falls.

We use a line equation for the visual ray, as well as a body equation for the body.

For the sphere you need to insert the line equation for the point on the surface of the sphere and view the individual components to understand the intersection point:

```
(ox        rx  Mx) 2
(oy +   l*ry  +My) 2
(oz        rz  Mz) 2
```

Take the x component, for example:

```
(l*rx + (ox+Mx)) 2 = r2
```

The `l`, for which the line and the sphere have an intersection point, can be tested with the help of the binomial formula and by solving the quadratic equation. The `l` is the *telescope factor* with which the direction vector of the line must be multiplied to meet on the sphere surface. When the quadratic equation is unsolvable, no intersection point exists.

Intersection point factors look more complicated still when considering a line and a plane. Here the line and the plane equations must be set to equality:

```
ôx       rx     âx       r1x      r2x
ôy + l*ry   = ây + a*r1y + b*r2y
ôz       rz     âz       r1z      r2z
```

Then you must create the equation for each component and ensure that all variable elements are on the left side of the equation, and constants are on the right side:

```
l*rx - a*r1x - b*r2x = âx-ôx
l*ry - a*r1y - b*r2y = ây-ôy
l*rz - a*r1z - b*r2z = âz-ôz
```

Now we have an equation system with three variables (`l`, `a` and `b`) and three equations. This 3x3 equation system can be solved using a determinant.

You must build a matrix from the equations. Take all of the coefficients of the variables and write these in a matrix:

```
rx -r1x -r2x | âx-ôx
ry -r1y -r2y | åy-ôy
rz -r1z -r2z | åz-ôz
```

The coefficients for the same variable must be beneath each other. The matrix also has the following form, where `a` stands for the coefficients and `b` stands for the constants:

```
a11 a12 a13 | b1
a21 a22 a23 | b2
a31 a32 a33 | b3
```

You can now begin constructing the determinant:

```
D = det A =     | a11 a12 a13|
                | a21 a22 a23|
                | a31 a32 a33|

          =    a11 a22 a33 + a12 a23 a31 + a13 a21 a32
             - a13 a22 a31 - a11 a23 a32 - a33 a12 a21
```

Besides this denominator determinant you must create three more number determinants:

```
                 |b1 a12 a13|
D1 = det A1 =    |b2 a22 a23|
                 |b3 a32 a33|

            =      b1 a22 a33 + a12 a23 b3 + a13 b2 a32
               - a13 a22 b3 - a23 a32 b1 - a33 a12 b2

                 |a11 b1 a13|
D2 = det A2 =    |a21 b2 a23|
                 |a31 b3 a33|

            =      a11 b2 a33 + b1 a23 a31 + a13 a21 b3
                 - a13 b2 a31 - a23 b3 a11 - a33 b1 a21

                 |a11 a12 b1|
D3 = det A1 =    |a21 a22 b2|
                 |a31 a32 b3|

            =      a11 a22 b3 + a12 b2 a31 + b1 a21 a32
                 - b1 a22 a31 - b2 a32 a11 - b3 a12 a21
```

Why these determinants are called *numerator determinants* and *denominator determinants* is something we'll discuss now. To solve the equation system you must get the quotient from a numerator and denominator determinant.

This depends on the positions of the variables in the equation system, which are used by the numerator determinant. In our example `l` stands in the first place. The quotient D1/D is made for this variable to test for the `l` of D.

The solution for `a` and `b` follows in the same way:

```
a=D2/D
b=D3/D
```

That functions only when the denominator determinant isn't equal to zero because division by zero is undefined. When `D=0` the equation system has no solution, or, in other words: the plane and line have no point in common.

We have addressed some basics of three dimensional math, and hope you have been able to understand them.

8.
The Optional Disk

8. The Optional Disk

The tracer program modules contained in this book are found on the optional disk in the `modules` subdirectory. The `screens` directory contains some ILBM format files generated with the tracer program that show the fantastic capabilities of this program.

You can see the sample graphics by booting the optional disk. Turn off your Amiga and eject any disks in the drives. Turn on your Amiga. When the Workbench disk hand icon appears, place the optional disk in drive df0:. A graphic appears on the screen. To end a graphic display click on the upper left corner of the screen. The next graphic then appears. Click the upper left corner to end the display and get to the `CLI` prompt (`1>`).

The C language routine that reads and displays IFF screens (`ShowILBM` in directory `c`) reads any IFF graphic once compiled. The routine's source listing appears in the `modules` directory.

We couldn't include more than two demonstration graphics on the disk due to memory restrictions. An executable tracer/editor disk requires the following files and directories:

- editor program (either `editor.bas` or `editor.run`)
- `libs` directory (contains the necessary `.bmap` files)
- complete tracer program (either your merged BASIC tracer or `tracer.run`)
- `SetPoint.B` program (see Appendix D)
- AmigaBASIC (if you're running uncompiled programs)
- `objects` directory (see description below)

Now we come to the last directory on the disk. Many object definitions are found in the `objects` directory. The results of three of these objects are found in the `screens` directory. The picture on the cover of this book was generated using the tracer program and the `Spheres.list` and `Spheres.mat` files. The point of projection was 270,10,25, the main point was 0,0,10 and the enlargement value was 4. Shadow initilization was ALL, light source was 0,0,50, light colour was 1,1,1 amd pixel width and height was 1,1. The picture took about two weeks to generate completely on the uncompiled tracer.

The optional disk also contains compiled versions of the editor and tracer programs, named `editor.run` and `tracer.run`. They were compiled using AC/BASIC V1.3. The programs required a few modifications to compile successfully. The next section explains these modifications in detail. We strongly recommend compiling these programs, since they run about 50 times faster than the original BASIC versions. For example, a graphic that the original BASIC version of the tracer needed three weeks to compute was finished in about six hours using the compiled tracer program.

8.1 Compiling the Programs

The fun of ray tracing wears thin very quickly once you find how much time the calculations require. The computations become even slower when the ray tracing program is written in a slow language. We decided to compile our programs to get the most speed out of them.

Please remember that the optional disk for this book already contains compiled versions of the editor and tracer. Do not try to compile these two pre-compiled programs. However, it may be worthwhile for you to try compiling the uncompiled versions of the programs after you read through this chapter.

Naturally you can use any compiler which is compatible with AmigaBASIC. At the time this book went to press, we only had one compiler available—the AC/BASIC Compiler from Absoft. The following description applies to Version 1.3 of this compiler, released April 10, 1988.

The first item of business is to make a backup copy of your disk. You'll use this backup disk for compiling: Remove any unnecessary files from the disk—keep only the uncompiled sources for the ray tracer and editor (do not copy the compiled versions of the tracer and editor).

Note: Never use an original disk for compiling. Always use a copy!

8.1.1 Compiling the Editor

First let's compile the editor. This is easy—load AmigaBASIC and enter the following in the BASIC window:

```
CLEAR ,140000
LOAD "Editor.bas"
```

Once the editor finishes loading, save it as an ASCII file using the following:

```
SAVE "Editor.cmp",a
```

The `",a` suffix saves the program in ASCII format. The compiler can only handle ASCII files—it can't compile straight AmigaBASIC programs. The `.cmp` extension saves the ASCII file without overwriting the original BASIC program. Quit AmigaBASIC.

Now load the editor source text into an editor (e.g., ED). You must do some adapting of commands, since the compiler cannot handle a few of the commands which appear in the source text. You could have made these changes using the AmigaBASIC editor, but since it has no search and replace facility, it will take longer. We recommend that you use a text editor or word processor.

Search for the `CHAIN` command. You'll find it in the `Ende` subroutine. Replace this command with END. The reason for doing this is that the compiled version will not recall the tracer properly. If you have a later version of the AC/BASIC Compiler (or another brand of compiler) which correctly accesses the `CHAIN` command, replace the `CHAIN` command with:

```
CHAIN "Tracer.run"
```

That's almost all you have to do to the source. Now for exiting the program. The compiler will not accept the `quit` variable. You could press <Ctrl><C> to exit, but that isn't very elegant. Look at the menu reading routine toward the beginning of the program for our key line:

```
IF chose=11 THEN
   CALL finish(quit)
END IF
```

Replace the `CALL finish(quit)` with the following:

```
GOTO Ende
```

Save the editor code and exit your text editor. Copy your editor source code to the RAM disk.

Make a backup copy of your AC/BASIC compiler disk. Discard all the unnecessary files from this backup to make room (e.g., drawers named `Chapter`, `bspread` and `examples`). All you should be able to see in this backup disk's window are the files `ac-basic` and `sortsubs`. Copy your editor source text from the RAM disk to the backup compiler disk.

If your `sortsubs` program is still straight BASIC code, compile it before you do anything else. Double-click the `sortsubs` icon. When `sortsubs` requests the filename, enter `editor.cmp` and press the

<Return> key. When `sortsubs` requests the location of temporary files, press the <Return> key (Yes). This program moves all the `SUB` programs to the end of the source text.

Once `sortsubs` ends, double-click the compiler icon. Select the following compiler options:

N: This ensures that the editor uses `ON MENU GOSUB` and `ON MOUSE GOSUB`

R: Link in the runtime library (the compiled editor won't do anything without looking for this first)

T: Keep temporary files on the RAM disk, which speeds up compilation (you can do this only if you have enough RAM—at least 1 megabyte)

Be sure enough memory exists on the disk (the editor requires 120K). Delete some graphics from the `screens` directory. The compiler overwrites any existing compiled versions of the program, so make sure you didn't have a copy of the original compiled version on the disk you're using for compiling. Start the compiler and wait a few minutes. If no errors occur, you're over the first hurdle. Rename the finished editor `editor.run`.

If you try out the compiled editor, you'll discover a big difference in speed from the uncompiled AmigaBASIC version.

8.1.2 Compiling the Tracer

We'll now walk you through the steps of compiling the tracer using the AC/BASIC Compiler. First make a backup of the disk containing the tracer modules (you may want to add AmigaBASIC to this disk temporarily). Name this backup disk `tracer` using the Workbench menu's `Rename` item.

Load AmigaBASIC. Enter the following in the BASIC window and press <Return> at the end of each line:

```
clear,140000
chdir "modules"
```

Enter the following commands in the BASIC window:

```
merge "Init.asc"
merge "System.asc"
merge "Wiremodel-draw.asc"
merge "Wiremodel-input.asc"
merge "Shadow-init.asc"
merge "Shadowing.asc"
```

```
merge "Service.asc"
```

Save the merged program to the main directory (NOT to the `modules` directory) using the command:

```
save "tracer:tracer.cmp",a
```

Notice the addition of the `.cmp` extension. This keeps you from accidentally overwriting the original code. Exit AmigaBASIC and start the `CLI`. Delete the modules from the backup disk's `modules` directory, and the backup's `modules` directory itself. Load the tracer source code into a text editor or word processor which has text search capabilities, since we have to change a few things in the code to get the tracer to compile properly.

Note: Some of the following changes require deleting lines of source code. We found that pressing the apostrophe (<'>) key to make lines into remarks is faster than deleting a line of text. So we recommend using the <'> key to mark the unnecessary lines as remarks.

Search for the `RasterInit:` routine. Delete or `REM` out the `Screen` and two `Window` commands if your want to be able to size the window for multitasking. Deletion of these commands is **optional.**

Search for the `CHAIN` command in the `LoadEditor:` routine and change it to `END`. Or change it to the following:

```
CHAIN "tracer:editor.run"
```

Next find the three occurrences of the `RUN` command and replace each occurrence with the following two lines:

```
CLEAR
GOTO StartUp
```

Many compilers have trouble compiling larger program code such as the tracer (129K of BASIC source code). The following directions apply to the AC/BASIC Compiler, Version 1.3. If you have a newer version of this compiler, test compile the original version of the merged program to see whether the original command sequences work.

Bypassing routines

You'll need to make lines in some of the source text's routines inactive. You have two ways of doing this: Either by making the problem lines comments by starting them with apostrophes, or by deleting the lines altogether. Search for the `SetPoint SUB` program, which isn't needed by the compiled program. It looks like this:

```
SUB SetPoint(x1%,y1%,x2%,y2%,Bright.r,Bright.g,Bright.b) STATIC
SHARED MaxColour%,Colour(),RasterH1%,RasterW1%,RastPort&
SHARED NumberPatternX%,PatternX&,PatternHX()
  IF x2%>RasterW1% THEN x2%=RasterW1%
'...more code follows...
```

```
  CALL RectFill&(RastPort&,x1%,y1%,x2%,y2%)
END SUB
```

Here are two ways of changing this routine—commenting and deleting:

```
' NOTE--all lines commented except label and END SUB
SUB SetPoint(x1%,y1%,x2%,y2%,Bright.r,Bright.g,Bright.b) STATIC
'SHARED MaxColour%,Colour(),RasterH1%,RasterW1%,RastPort&
'SHARED NumberPatternX%,PatternX&,PatternHX()
'  IF x2%>RasterW1% THEN x2%=RasterW1%
'...more code follows...
'  CALL RectFill&(RastPort&,x1%,y1%,x2%,y2%)
END SUB

' NOTE--lines deleted except label and END SUB
SUB SetPoint(x1%,y1%,x2%,y2%,Bright.r,Bright.g,Bright.b) STATIC
END SUB
```

The following routines must be deleted or commented out from the source text you intend to compile. If you try compiling the program without removing the contents of these routines, the program will probably crash.

Use your text editor's search function to find the label, then either delete the text between the label and `RETURN` or `END SUB`, or add an apostrophe to the beginning of each line after the label and before the `RETURN` or `END SUB`:

```
Hardcopy
InitPatternS
InitPatternX
StandardFill
ExtendedFill
```

Note: Users compiling with AC/BASIC Version 1.2 should remove the `ScreenLoader` subroutine as well as the routines listed above.

The program will now access the subroutine or `SUB` program label, ignore the deleted/commented text and return to the main program. Some of these routines can be replaced by others. For example, if you want to print a graphic, use a separate program available for printing IFF files. The `InitPatternS`, `InitPatternX`, `ExtendedFill` and `StandardFill` only come into play with patterned backgrounds. The speed increase from the compiled program is well worth the loss of a patterned background.

You will also need to change the `Background` routine, since the compiled version of the program deletes any background you might generate. Find the label—the code looks something like this:

```
Background:

  ' Background Determine
'   more code between here and RETURN...
RETURN
```

Comment out (or delete) the rest of the lines up to the RETURN. Add the two lines stated below so the routine looks something like this:

```
Background:
PRINT "Not implemented in compiled version"
FOR X=1 to 3000: NEXT X
CLS
  ' Background Determine
'   more code between here and RETURN...
RETURN
```

About backgrounds

The compiled tracer may not add any background to any objects you create and calculate. The ray tracing calculates properly (i.e., shading and colors), but without any background, the "leftovers" of the wire model may jut out from the edges of the finished graphic. You have a number of options for curing this problem:

- Save the graphic as an IFF file and load it into a program that will handle the number of bitplanes you used in computing the graphic. Then edit out the jagged edges left from the wire model.
- Configure the original BASIC program to add a default background of some sort of solid color, then compile it.

For AC/BASIC 1.2 users

Version 1.2 of the AC/BASIC compiler need the following changes. A bug occurs because of the Intuition function called TextLength, which crashes the 1.2-compiled version from time to time. Replace this TextLength function with the following if you are using AC/BASIC 1.2:

```
PEEKW(rp&+60)*LEN(.$)
```

rp& represents the RastPort passed as the first argument of the TextLength function. ".$" represents the string from which the length is calculated and passed on the to program as the string's address and length. Both commands work identically, provided you avoid proportional fonts.

Now we come to the most irritating error within AC/BASIC 1.2. The WINDOW n commands in Scron and Scroff don't work properly, and cause a Guru Meditation number 81000008. Search for the Scron and Scroff SUB programs. Delete WINDOW n from these routines.

One last problem with the 1.2 compiler. The program occasionally crashes when you exit it. Check the RAM disk for any data. This concludes the changes for AC/BASIC 1.2 users.

For all users

Save the tracer to the RAM disk and exit the editor to the Workbench.

Make a backup copy of your AC/BASIC compiler disk. Discard all the unnecessary files from this backup to make room (e.g., drawers named Chapter, bspread and examples). All you should be able to see in this backup disk's window are the files `ac-basic` and `sortsubs`. Copy your tracer source text from the RAM disk to the backup compiler disk. Make sure this disk has at least 230K available (click on the disk icon and select the `Info` item from the Workbench menu).

If the `sortsubs` program on the is still straight BASIC code, compile it before you do anything else. Double-click the `sortsubs` icon. When `sortsubs` requests the filename, enter `tracer.cmp` and press the <Return> key. When `sortsubs` requests the location of temporary files, press the <Return> key (Yes). This program moves all the `SUB` programs to the end of the source text.

Once `sortsubs` ends, double-click the compiler icon. Select the following compiler options:

A: Long addressing enabled

N: Tracer uses `ON MENU GOSUB` and `ON MOUSE GOSUB`

R: Link in the runtime library

T: Keep temporary files on the RAM disk (you can do this only if you have enough RAM—approximately 1 megabyte)

The tracer requires at least 50K of extra RAM to compile. Set your **WORK AREA** slider gadget (we chose 54K).

Click the **Compile** gadget. You shouldn't get any error messages. Exit the compiler and rename the compiled tracer `tracer.run`. Copy the compiled tracer to your copy of the optional disk.

If everything compiled according to plan, you can now try out the tracer. Amiga users with only 512K should open only one screen at a time. Now when you load objects and calculate them, the difference between compiled and uncompiled programs is like night and day.

The compiler manual offers some tips for speeding up your programs. For example, if you avoid `ON...GOSUB`s at all costs, this will speed things up considerably. Menu reading should be rewritten and `ON ERROR`s avoided. Furthermore, if you define all arrays as `STATIC`, this increases array access by a factor of 6. To do this, you must determine the sizes of all arrays, and not change them in the program. Also, all arrays must be defined in the main program. If you want to use this, you must delete all `ERASE` commands and put all array definitions in the program. For example, set a maximum size of 250 for `K()` (which is enough for all demo objects) and 50 for `Mat()`. Define all other arrays according to definition using numbers, or else the compiler will display errors. If you convert the tracer to use `STATIC` arrays, select the U option in the compiler. These methods can increase speed up to 70%.

Appendices

A. Modules of the Tracer

1. Initial Routines in `INIT.ASC`

```
DECLARE FUNCTIONs
InitMat
InitPatternS
InitPatternX
InitSetPoint
RasterInit
```

2. Trace system routines in `SYSTEM.ASC`

```
CloseIt
PrintIt
EmptyBuffers
Pause
Box
DialogBox
DoDialog
Rubberbox
NOOP
MakeMenu
DeleteMenu
MessageEvent
KeyEvent
ColorPalette
ErrorHandling
Quit
Scron
Scroff
GetString
GetReal
GetInit
GetKey
SetCursor see Editor
PutString
PutReal
conrealstr
constrreal

FormInput
FormInputInit
FormInputString
Directory
```

3. Wire model routines in `WIREMODEL-DRAW.ASC`

```
Projection

DrawPlane
DrawTriangle
DrawRectangle
DrawCircle
DrawCircleSector
DrawCircleRing
DrawSphere
DrawCylinder
DrawCylinderSegm
DrawCone
DrawEllipsoid

DrawAll
DrawNew

HowManyCorners
Enlargment
```

4. Input routines in `WIREMODEL-INPUT.ASC`

```
Initial
InitialP

InputP
InputH
InputDPH
InputAngle
```

5. Shadow initialization in `SHADOW-INIT.ASC`

```
InitParameters

Tranform
InitShadow

TransformMM
MinMaxtest
InitMinMax

NormAngle
DeltaSum3
DeltaSum4
Getxyzlq
Getxyzlqk
DistTest
ArcTan
```

```
Calcablq

MMlq3Test
MMlq4Test
MMlqKTest
MMlqkSphere
MMlqCylinder
MMlqCone
MMlqEllipsoid

InitMinMaxlq
```

6. Shadows in `SHADOWING.ASC`

```
IntersectionPointPlane
IntersectionPointTriangle
IntersectionPointRectangle
IntersectionPointCircle
AngleIntervall

IntersectionPointCircleSector
IntersectionPointCircleRing
IntersectionPointSphere
BasisTrans

IntersectionPointCylinder
IntersectionPointCylinderSegm
IntersectionPointCone
IntersectionPointEllipsoid

WhichBody
SetBrightness

StandardFill
ExtendedFill
SetPoint

Reprojection
ComputePoint

Shadows
```

7. Service module in `SERVICE.ASC`

```
Saver
Loader
Merger
ArrayInit
LoadMat
ScreenSaver
```

```
 ScreenLoader

 Hardcopy

LoadEditor
ClearScreen
 Info
 Help
 Sky
 Fhg
 Background
```

B. The Tracer Program

The complete tracer program is presented in this appendix as seven separate modules. These modules are on the optional diskette in the `modules` directory. If you type in the modules from this appendix, type them in one module at a time; you cannot enter the seven modules as one unit in AmigaBASIC. Save each module by the specified filename and in ASCII format. ASCII files can be easily merged to form the final BASIC tracer program, or as a single ASCII file for compiling. In addition, each module can be merged into your own program code.

When you're ready to merge the modules, see the merging instructions in Section 3.3.2 (page 141). Any changes you must make to the modules before compiling should be done from a text editor or word processor (see Chapter 8 for compiling suggestions).

The programs and modules in these appendices contain some BASIC lines that must be entered as one line in AmigaBASIC, even though they appear on two lines in this book. Formatting the program listings to fit into this book has caused some long BASIC lines to be split into two lines. To show where a BASIC line actually ends we'll insert an end of paragraph (¶) character. This marker is not to be entered by you: It simply shows when the <Return> key should be pressed in the BASIC editor when entering a line. For example, the following line is split into two lines in the paragraph below, but must be entered as one line in AmigaBASIC, as shown by the ¶ character:

```
WinDef NWindow, 100, 50, 460, 150, 32+64+512&, 15&+4096&,
0&, Title$¶
```

The ¶ shows the actual end of the BASIC line.

The following pages contain the listings of the seven modules used to make the completed tracer program.

The INIT.ASC module

```
'Init.asc start¶
' 3-D Graphics¶
'¶
' Peter Schulz, 1986¶
' AMIGA-Version Bruno Jennrich, 1987¶
'¶
' Mainpoint H (hx,hy,hz)¶
' Distance to projection point : DPH¶
' alpha, beta, gamma : three angle for all three axis¶
' => P(px,py,pz) : Projection point¶
'¶
' k(n,0,0)=Typ: 0=Plane, 1=Triangle, 2=Parallelogramm,¶
'             : 3=Circle, 4=Circle segment, 5=Circle arc¶
'             : 10=Sphere, 20=Cylinder, 22=Cone, 24=Ellipsoid¶
'             : 21=Cylinder segment¶
' k(n,0,1)=Reserved¶
' k(n,2,0)=Radius of the Sphere¶
' k(n,0,2)=Material number¶
' k(n,1,x)=Calculation point¶
' k(n,2,x)=Intersect vector (1,2) or distance vector (3)¶
' k(n,3,x)=Intersect vector (1,2) or distance vector (3)¶
' If Typ>=20: (k(n,2,x),k(n,3,x),k(n,4,x)) = Base¶
' If Circle segment/arc or cylinder segment:¶
'                  k(n,5,0)=Start angle, k(n,5,1)=End angle¶
' If Circle arc: k(n,4,0)=inner Radius [0..1], k(n,4,1)=outer Radius [0..1]¶
'¶
'demo:¶
'DATA 4¶
'DATA 10,0,8,0,0,0,50,0,0,0,0,0,0,0,0,0,0,0¶
'DATA 2,0,8,80,-30,30,0,60,0,-10,0,-60,0,0,0,0,0,0¶
'DATA 20,0,8,-30,-30,5,25,0,0,0,25,0,0,0,75,0,0,0¶
'DATA 10,0,5,30,-30,30,25,0,0,0,0,0,0,0,0,0,0,0¶
'¶
'  *************************************¶
'  *     Initial Routine and DATAs     *¶
'  *************************************¶
'¶
Material:¶
DATA 20¶
DATA 0,.9,0,0,0¶
DATA .6,.6,.6,0,.5¶
DATA .9,.9,.9,0,.8¶
DATA 1,1,1,.1,.9¶
DATA .7,0,.7,.2,0¶
DATA 1,1,1,0,.9¶
DATA 0,0,.5,0,0¶
DATA .8,0,0,.2,0¶
DATA 1,1,1,.2,.2¶
DATA 1,1,1,.2,.1¶
DATA .7,.7,0,0,0¶
DATA 1,1,1,0,1¶
DATA 0,.4,.4,.2,0¶
DATA 1,1,1,.2,.5¶
```

```
DATA 1,1,1,.1,.2¶
DATA 0,1,1,0,0¶
DATA 1,1,1,.05,0¶
DATA .3,.3,.3,.05,.5¶
DATA 1,0,0,.2,.3¶
DATA 0,0,1,.2,.3¶
'¶
PatternS:¶
' Number patterns -1¶
DATA 10  ¶
'¶
DATA 0       ¶
DATA &HFFFF¶
DATA &HFFFF¶
DATA &HFFFF    ¶
DATA &HFFFF¶
DATA &HFFFF¶
DATA &HFFFF¶
DATA &HFFFF¶
DATA &HFFFF¶
DATA &HFFFF¶
DATA &HFFFF¶
DATA &HFFFF¶
DATA &HFFFF¶
DATA &HFFFF¶
DATA &HFFFF¶
DATA &HFFFF¶
DATA &HFFFF¶
'¶
DATA 0.0234375¶
DATA &HFFFF¶
DATA &HFEFE¶
DATA &HFFFF¶
DATA &HFFFF¶
DATA &HFFFF¶
DATA &HFBFB¶
DATA &HFFFF¶
DATA &HFFFF¶
DATA &HFFFF¶
DATA &HEFEF¶
DATA &HFFFF¶
DATA &HFFFF¶
DATA &HFFFF¶
DATA &HBFBF¶
DATA &HFFFF¶
DATA &HFFFF¶
'¶
DATA 0.125¶
DATA &H5555¶
DATA &HFFFF¶
DATA &HAAAA¶
DATA &HFFFF¶
DATA &H5555¶
DATA &HFFFF¶
DATA &HAAAA¶
DATA &HFFFF¶
DATA &H5555¶
DATA &HFFFF¶
DATA &HAAAA¶
DATA &HFFFF¶
```

```
DATA &H5555¶
DATA &HFFFF¶
DATA &HAAAA¶
DATA &HFFFF¶
'¶
DATA 0.25¶
DATA &HFFFF¶
DATA &H5555¶
DATA &HFFFF¶
DATA &H5555¶
DATA &HFFFF¶
DATA &H5555¶
DATA &HFFFF¶
DATA &H5555¶
DATA &HFFFF¶
DATA &H5555¶
DATA &HFFFF¶
DATA &H5555¶
DATA &HFFFF¶
DATA &H5555¶
DATA &HFFFF¶
DATA &H5555¶
'¶
DATA 0.375¶
DATA &H5555¶
DATA &HBBBB¶
DATA &H5555¶
DATA &HBBBB¶
DATA &H5555¶
DATA &HBBBB¶
DATA &H5555¶
DATA &HBBBB¶
DATA &H5555¶
DATA &HBBBB¶
DATA &H5555¶
DATA &HBBBB¶
DATA &H5555¶
DATA &HBBBB¶
DATA &H5555¶
DATA &HBBBB¶
'¶
DATA 0.5¶
DATA &H5555¶
DATA &HAAAA¶
DATA &H5555¶
DATA &HAAAA¶
DATA &H5555¶
DATA &HAAAA¶
DATA &H5555¶
DATA &HAAAA¶
DATA &H5555¶
DATA &HAAAA¶
DATA &H5555¶
DATA &HAAAA¶
DATA &H5555¶
DATA &HAAAA¶
DATA &H5555¶
DATA &HAAAA¶
'¶
DATA 0.625¶
```

```
DATA &H1111¶
DATA &HAAAA¶
DATA &H4444¶
DATA &HAAAA¶
DATA &H1111¶
DATA &HAAAA¶
DATA &H4444¶
DATA &HAAAA¶
DATA &H1111¶
DATA &HAAAA¶
DATA &H4444¶
DATA &HAAAA¶
DATA &H1111¶
DATA &HAAAA¶
DATA &H4444¶
DATA &HAAAA¶
'¶
DATA 0.75¶
DATA &HAAAA¶
DATA &H0000¶
DATA &HAAAA¶
DATA &H0000¶
DATA &HAAAA¶
DATA &H0000¶
DATA &HAAAA¶
DATA &H0000¶
DATA &HAAAA¶
DATA &H0000¶
DATA &HAAAA¶
DATA &H0000¶
DATA &HAAAA¶
DATA &H0000¶
DATA &HAAAA¶
DATA &H0000¶
'¶
DATA 0.875¶
DATA &HAAAA¶
DATA &H0000 ¶
DATA &H5555¶
DATA &H0000¶
DATA &HAAAA¶
DATA &H0000 ¶
DATA &H5555¶
DATA &H0000¶
DATA &HAAAA¶
DATA &H0000 ¶
DATA &H5555¶
DATA &H0000¶
DATA &HAAAA¶
DATA &H0000 ¶
DATA &H5555¶
DATA &H0000¶
'¶
DATA 0.9765625¶
DATA &H0000¶
DATA &H0101¶
DATA &H0000¶
DATA &H0000¶
DATA &H0000¶
DATA &H0404¶
```

```
DATA &H0000¶
DATA &H0000¶
DATA &H0000¶
DATA &H1010¶
DATA &H0000¶
DATA &H0000¶
DATA &H0000¶
DATA &H4040¶
DATA &H0000¶
DATA &H0000¶
'¶
DATA 1¶
DATA &H0000¶
DATA &H0000¶
DATA &H0000¶
DATA &H0000¶
DATA &H0000¶
DATA &H0000¶
DATA &H0000¶
DATA &H0000¶
DATA &H0000¶
DATA &H0000¶
DATA &H0000¶
DATA &H0000¶
DATA &H0000¶
DATA &H0000¶
'¶
PatternX:¶
' Number Fill patterns - 1¶
DATA 12¶
'¶
DATA 0¶
DATA &H0000¶
DATA &H0000¶
DATA &H0000¶
DATA &H0000¶
DATA &H0000¶
DATA &H0000¶
DATA &H0000¶
DATA &H0000¶
DATA &H0000¶
DATA &H0000¶
DATA &H0000¶
DATA &H0000¶
DATA &H0000¶
DATA &H0000¶
DATA &H0000¶
DATA &H0000¶
'¶
DATA 0.00390625¶
DATA &H8000¶
DATA &H0000¶
DATA &H0000¶
DATA &H0000¶
DATA &H0000¶
DATA &H0000¶
DATA &H0000¶
DATA &H0000¶
DATA &H0000¶
DATA &H0000¶
```

```
DATA &H0000¶
DATA &H0000¶
DATA &H0000¶
DATA &H0000¶
DATA &H0000¶
DATA &H0000¶
'¶
DATA 0.0078125¶
DATA &H8000¶
DATA &H0000¶
DATA &H0000¶
DATA &H0000¶
DATA &H0000¶
DATA &H0000¶
DATA &H0000¶
DATA &H0000¶
DATA &H0080¶
DATA &H0000¶
DATA &H0000¶
DATA &H0000¶
DATA &H0000¶
DATA &H0000¶
DATA &H0000¶
DATA &H0000¶
'¶
DATA 0.015625¶
DATA &H8080¶
DATA &H0000¶
DATA &H0000¶
DATA &H0000¶
DATA &H0000¶
DATA &H0000¶
DATA &H0000¶
DATA &H0000¶
DATA &H8080¶
DATA &H0000¶
DATA &H0000¶
DATA &H0000¶
DATA &H0000¶
DATA &H0000¶
DATA &H0000¶
DATA &H0000¶
'¶
DATA 0.03125¶
DATA &H8080¶
DATA &H0000¶
DATA &H0000¶
DATA &H0000¶
DATA &H0808¶
DATA &H0000¶
DATA &H0000¶
DATA &H0000¶
DATA &H8080¶
DATA &H0000¶
DATA &H0000¶
DATA &H0000¶
DATA &H0808¶
DATA &H0000¶
DATA &H0000¶
DATA &H0000¶
```

```
'¶
DATA 0.0625¶
DATA &H8888¶
DATA &H0000¶
DATA &H0000¶
DATA &H0000¶
DATA &H8888¶
DATA &H0000¶
DATA &H0000¶
DATA &H0000¶
DATA &H8888¶
DATA &H0000¶
DATA &H0000¶
DATA &H0000¶
DATA &H8888¶
DATA &H0000¶
DATA &H0000¶
DATA &H0000¶
'       ¶
DATA 0.125¶
DATA &H8888¶
DATA &H0000¶
DATA &H2222¶
DATA &H0000¶
DATA &H8888¶
DATA &H0000¶
DATA &H2222¶
DATA &H0000¶
DATA &H8888¶
DATA &H0000¶
DATA &H2222¶
DATA &H0000¶
DATA &H8888¶
DATA &H0000¶
DATA &H2222¶
DATA &H0000¶
'¶
DATA 0.1875¶
DATA &H8888¶
DATA &H2222¶
DATA &H8888¶
DATA &H0000¶
DATA &H2222¶
DATA &H8888¶
DATA &H2222¶
DATA &H0000¶
DATA &H8888¶
DATA &H2222¶
DATA &H8888¶
DATA &H0000¶
DATA &H2222¶
DATA &H8888¶
DATA &H2222¶
DATA &H0000¶
'¶
DATA 0.25¶
DATA &HAAAA¶
DATA &H0000¶
DATA &HAAAA¶
DATA &H0000¶
```

```
DATA &HAAAA¶
DATA &H0000¶
DATA &HAAAA¶
DATA &H0000¶
DATA &HAAAA¶
DATA &H0000¶
DATA &HAAAA¶
DATA &H0000¶
DATA &HAAAA¶
DATA &H0000¶
DATA &HAAAA¶
DATA &H0000¶
'¶
DATA 0.3125¶
DATA &HAAAA¶
DATA &H1111¶
DATA &H4444¶
DATA &H1111¶
DATA &HAAAA¶
DATA &H1111¶
DATA &H4444¶
DATA &H1111¶
DATA &HAAAA¶
DATA &H1111¶
DATA &H4444¶
DATA &H1111¶
DATA &HAAAA¶
DATA &H1111¶
DATA &H4444¶
DATA &H1111¶
'¶
DATA 0.375¶
DATA &hAAAA¶
DATA &H1111¶
DATA &HAAAA¶
DATA &H4444¶
DATA &HAAAA¶
DATA &H1111¶
DATA &HAAAA¶
DATA &H4444¶
DATA &HAAAA¶
DATA &H1111¶
DATA &HAAAA¶
DATA &H4444¶
DATA &HAAAA¶
DATA &H1111¶
DATA &HAAAA¶
DATA &H4444¶
'¶
DATA 0.4375¶
DATA &HAAAA¶
DATA &H5555¶
DATA &HAAAA¶
DATA &H4444¶
DATA &HAAAA¶
DATA &H5555¶
DATA &HAAAA¶
DATA &H4444¶
DATA &HAAAA¶
DATA &H5555¶
```

```
DATA &HAAAA¶
DATA &H4444¶
DATA &HAAAA¶
DATA &H5555¶
DATA &HAAAA¶
DATA &H4444¶
'¶
DATA 0.5¶
DATA &HAAAA¶
DATA &H5555¶
DATA &HAAAA¶
DATA &H5555¶
DATA &HAAAA¶
DATA &H5555¶
DATA &HAAAA¶
DATA &H5555¶
DATA &HAAAA¶
DATA &H5555¶
DATA &HAAAA¶
DATA &H5555¶
DATA &HAAAA¶
DATA &H5555¶
DATA &HAAAA¶
DATA &H5555¶
'¶
StartUp:¶
  CHDIR "Tracer:libs"¶
¶
  DECLARE FUNCTION SetRast() LIBRARY¶
  DECLARE FUNCTION SetRGB4() LIBRARY¶
  DECLARE FUNCTION GetRGB4%() LIBRARY¶
  DECLARE FUNCTION SetDrMd() LIBRARY¶
  DECLARE FUNCTION SetAPen() LIBRARY¶
  DECLARE FUNCTION SetBPen() LIBRARY¶
  DECLARE FUNCTION Move() LIBRARY¶
  DECLARE FUNCTION Draw() LIBRARY¶
  DECLARE FUNCTION WritePixel() LIBRARY¶
  DECLARE FUNCTION RectFill() LIBRARY¶
  DECLARE FUNCTION Text() LIBRARY¶
  DECLARE FUNCTION TextLength&() LIBRARY¶
  LIBRARY "graphics.library"¶
                ¶
  DECLARE FUNCTION SetWindowTitles() LIBRARY¶
  DECLARE FUNCTION ScreenToFront()  LIBRARY¶
  DECLARE FUNCTION ScreenToBack()   LIBRARY¶
  DECLARE FUNCTION ActivateWindow() LIBRARY¶
  DECLARE FUNCTION RemakeDisplay() LIBRARY¶
  LIBRARY "intuition.library"¶
¶
  DECLARE FUNCTION AllocMem&() LIBRARY¶
  DECLARE FUNCTION FreeMem() LIBRARY¶
  DECLARE FUNCTION AllocSignal%() LIBRARY¶
  DECLARE FUNCTION FindTask&()    LIBRARY¶
  DECLARE FUNCTION DoIO&()        LIBRARY¶
  DECLARE FUNCTION OpenDevice&    LIBRARY¶
  LIBRARY "exec.library"¶
  ¶
  DECLARE FUNCTION xOpen& LIBRARY¶
  DECLARE FUNCTION xRead& LIBRARY¶
  DECLARE FUNCTION xWrite& LIBRARY¶
```

```
  LIBRARY "dos.library"¶
¶
  DEF FN Xscale(x)=(x+Picturex)*Picturewidth¶
  DEF FN Yscale(y)=(Picturey-y)*Pictureheight¶
  DEF FN Xresc(x)=x/Picturewidth-Picturex¶
  DEF FN Yresc(y)=Picturey-y/Pictureheight¶
¶
    ' Value of determinante with the vectors a,b and c:¶
  DEF FN Det(A1,B1,C1,A2,B2,C2,A3,B3,C3)=A1*(B2*C3-C2*B3)-B1*(A2*C3-
C2*A3)+C1*(A2*B3-B2*A3)¶
¶
    ' Cosine of the angle between vector a and Vector b:¶
  DEF FN
CosinAngle(ax,ay,az,bx,by,bz)=(ax*bx+ay*by+az*bz)/SQR((ax*ax+ay*ay+az*az)*(bx*bx+by
*by+bz*bz))¶
¶
    ' Radiant to Degree:¶
  DEF FN Deg(a)=a*180/Pi¶
  ¶
    ' Degree to Radiant:¶
  DEF FN Rad(a)=a*Pi/180¶
¶
  True = 1¶
  False = NOT(True)¶
¶
    ' Search depth for  calculation point¶
  MaxStack% = 19 ¶
  ¶
  Pi = 3.141592654#¶
  Pd2 = Pi/2¶
  Pm2 = 2*Pi¶
  ¶
  Threshold = .0001¶
    ¶
  Hx = 0¶
  Hy = 0¶
  Hz = 0 ¶
  ¶
  Px = 500¶
  Py = 0¶
  Pz = 0¶
    ¶
    ' Picture drawn after first call of new drawing¶
  Newone! = True¶
¶
    ' Wait in New Drawing mode for key or mouse¶
  WaitFlg! = True¶
¶
    ' All Menu points active?¶
  Start% = 0¶
  ¶
  DIM Stack(MaxStack%,2)¶
  DIM RestLght(MaxStack%)¶
¶
    ' Arrays for ERASE added to system¶
  DIM Help(0)¶
  DIM minmax%(0)¶
  DIM minmaxlq(0)¶
  DIM K(0)¶
  ¶
```

```
    ' Default-Object load:¶
  ¶
  'RESTORE demo¶
  'READ MaxNumber¶
  'NumberK=MaxNumber¶
  'FOR n%=1 TO NumberK¶
  '  FOR p%=0 TO 5¶
  '    FOR q%=0 TO 2¶
  '      READ K(n%,p%,q%)¶
  '    NEXT q%¶
  '  NEXT p%¶
  'NEXT n%¶
¶
    ' How many angles needed to compute in a circle ?¶
  NumberSegments = 4¶
  ¶
    ' Where is the light source ?¶
  Qx=1000&¶
  Qy=1000&¶
  Qz=1000&¶
¶
    ' Light source color: white¶
  Qh.r=1¶
  Qh.g=1¶
  Qh.b=1¶
  ¶
    ' Fill pattern = Standard¶
    ' Only need in case of SetPoint. OSSetPoint has its own pattern!¶
  PatternArt%=0¶
  ¶
    ' Point size for shadows¶
  BoxW%=1¶
  BoxH%=1  ¶
¶
    ' Actual Drive¶
  ActDrive$ = "tracer:"¶
  CHDIR ActDrive$¶
¶
  GOSUB InitSetPoint¶
  GOSUB OpenGfx¶
  GOSUB RasterInit¶
¶
    ' Shadow window (Default)¶
  XStart%=0¶
  YStart%=0¶
  XEnd%=RasterW1%¶
  Yend%=RasterH1%¶
¶
  Picturewidth=FactorX          ' for enlarging¶
  Pictureheight=FactorY¶
  Picturex=RasterW2% / Picturewidth¶
  Picturey=RasterH2% / Pictureheight¶
  ¶
  GOSUB InitMat¶
  GOSUB InitPatternS  ¶
  GOSUB InitPatternX¶
  GOSUB InitialP¶
    ¶
  GOSUB MakeMenu¶
REM remove after testing  ¶
```

```
REM  ON ERROR GOTO ErrorHandling¶
¶
ok:          ' Main loop¶
  MENU ON¶
  WHILE 1¶
    ON MENU GOSUB MessageEvent¶
    GOSUB KeyEvent¶
  WEND¶
'¶
InitMat:¶
  ' Initial material brightness¶
  ' mat(n,0) = Red material brightness¶
  ' mat(n,1) = Green material brightness¶
  ' mat(n,2) = Blue material brightness¶
  ' mat(n,3) = Factor for unlit/shadow¶
  ' mat(n,4) = Factor for mirroring¶
  ' mat(n,5) = Factor for Transparecy, not implemented¶
  ' mat(n,6) = reserved¶
  RESTORE Material¶
  READ NumberMat¶
  DIM Mat(NumberMat,6)¶
  FOR n%=1 TO NumberMat¶
    FOR m%=0 TO 4¶
      READ Mat(n%,m%)¶
    NEXT m%¶
  NEXT n%¶
RETURN¶
'¶
InitPatternS:¶
  ' Initialize fill pattern (Standard)¶
  RESTORE PatternS¶
  READ NumberPatternS% ¶
¶
  DIM PatternHS(NumberPatternS%)¶
  PatternS& = AllocMem&((NumberPatternS%+1)*2*16,65536&+2)¶
  IF PatternS& = 0 THEN¶
    CLS¶
    CALL DialogBox("No free Chip-Memory!!!",1,True,x1a%,y1a%,x2a%,y2a%,False)¶
    CALL DoDialog(n%,1,-1,-1,-1,-1,x1a%,y1a%,x2a%,y2a%,-1,-1,-1,-1)¶
    GOSUB CloseIt¶
    END¶
  END IF¶
   ¶
  FOR i%=0 TO NumberPatternS%¶
    READ PatternHS(i%)¶
    FOR j%=0 TO 15¶
      READ TempPattern%¶
      POKEW (PatternS&+i%*32+j%*2),TempPattern%¶
    NEXT j%¶
  NEXT i%¶
RETURN¶
'¶
InitPatternX:¶
  ' Initialize fill pattern (Extended)¶
  RESTORE PatternX¶
  READ NumberPatternX%¶
¶
  DIM PatternHX(NumberPatternX%*2)¶
  PatternX& = AllocMem&((NumberPatternX%*2+1)*2*16,65536&+2)¶
  IF PatternX& = 0 THEN¶
```

```
    CLS¶
    CALL DialogBox("No free Chip-Memory!!!",1,True,x1a%,y1a%,x2a%,y2a%,False)¶
    CALL DoDialog(n%,1,-1,-1,-1,-1,x1a%,y1a%,x2a%,y2a%,-1,-1,-1,-1)¶
    GOSUB CloseIt¶
    END¶
  END IF¶
  FOR i%=0 TO NumberPatternX%¶
    READ PatternHX(i%)¶
    PatternHX(NumberPatternX%*2-i%)= 1 - PatternHX(i%)¶
    FOR j%=0 TO 15¶
      READ TempPattern%¶
      POKEW (PatternX&+i%*32+j%*2),TempPattern%¶
      POKEW (PatternX&+NumberPatternX%*2*32-i%*32+j%*2),NOT(TempPattern%) ¶
    NEXT j%¶
  NEXT i%¶
RETURN¶
'¶
InitSetPoint:¶
  ' Read assembler routine for Point-drawing:¶
¶
  REM read binary data:¶
¶
  OPEN "I",#1,"Tracer:SetPoint.B"¶
  SetPointNum&=LOF(1)¶
  SetPointAdr& = AllocMem&(SetPointNum&,65536&+2)¶
¶
  IF SetPointAdr&=0 THEN¶
    CLOSE #1¶
    GOSUB CloseIt¶
    END¶
  END IF¶
¶
  FOR n%=0 TO SetPointNum&\2-1¶
    h%=CVI(INPUT$(2,#1))¶
    POKEW SetPointAdr&+2*n%,h%¶
  NEXT n%                    ¶
¶
  CLOSE #1¶
¶
  REM subroutine call addresses:¶
¶
  LET OSOpenGfx&=SetPointAdr&¶
  LET OSCloseGfx&=SetPointAdr&+&H1E¶
  LET OSSetPoint&=SetPointAdr&+&H38¶
¶
  REM Addresses of the variables:¶
¶
  LET OSColour&=SetPointAdr&+&H3F8¶
  LET OSMaxColour&=SetPointAdr&+&H27A¶
  LET OSModus&=SetPointAdr&+&H27C¶
  LET OSRastPort&=SetPointAdr&+&H276¶
  LET OSRasterW1&=SetPointAdr&+&H27E¶
  LET OSRasterH1&=SetPointAdr&+&H280¶
RETURN¶
'¶
OpenGfx:¶
  CALL OSOpenGfx&¶
RETURN¶
'¶
CloseGfx:¶
```

```
  CALL OSCloseGfx&¶
RETURN¶
'¶
RasterInit:¶
  ' Select resolution and display mode  ¶
  WINDOW CLOSE 2 ' delete any windows and¶
  SCREEN CLOSE 1 ' screens ¶
¶
  WINDOW 1,"", (0,0)-(631,185),6  ' new window with Status-line¶
¶
  'PALETTE 0,0,0,0       ' Colour for user screen¶
  'PALETTE 1,1,1,1       ¶
  'PALETTE 2,.4,.4,1¶
¶
  NWBase& = WINDOW(7)¶
  NRastPort& = WINDOW(8)¶
  NWScreen& = PEEKL(NWBase&+46)¶
  ' Base address of Window-Structure¶
  ' from which the screen structure is taken¶
  ' RastPort belongs with the WINDOW() function¶
¶
  Status$ = " Status: Select resolution"+CHR$(0)    ' Status line output¶
  dummy = SetWindowTitles(NWBase&,SADD(Status$),0)¶
¶
  DisplayM$(0) =  " Normal         "¶
  DisplayM$(1) =  " Hold and Modify"¶
  DisplayM$(2) =  " Extra Halfbrite"¶
  ¶
  XResl$(0) = " Normal"¶
  XResl$(1) = " HIRES "¶
  ¶
  YResl$(0) = " Normal    " ¶
  YResl$(1) = " Interlaced"¶
  ¶
  x(0) = 0:x(1) = 0:x(2) = 0:x(3) = 4¶
  ' Which values or strings at which position ?¶
¶
  y = 0¶
  ' topmost line = Start line¶
¶
  Modulo(0) = 3¶
  Modulo(1) = 2¶
  Modulo(2) = 2¶
  Modulo(3) = 6¶
  ' How many values for each selection line ?¶
¶
  COLOR 1¶
¶
  Colours (0) = 1¶
  Colours (1) = 2¶
  Colours (2) = 2¶
  Colours (3) = 2¶
  ' First line  => white rest of the lines  => blue¶
  ¶
Outg:¶
  LOCATE 10,21¶
  COLOR Colours(0)¶
  PRINT  "Display mode : ";DisplayM$(x(0))¶
  LOCATE 12,21¶
  COLOR Colours(1)¶
```

```
  PRINT  "X-Resolution : ";XResl$(x(1))¶
  LOCATE 14,21¶
  COLOR Colours(2)¶
  PRINT  "Y-Resolution : ";YResl$(x(2))¶
  LOCATE 16,24¶
  COLOR Colours(3)¶
  PRINT  "BitPlanes : ";x(3)+1¶
   ¶
  Waiter: a$ = INKEY$¶
  IF a$ = "" THEN Waiter¶
  ¶
  IF a$ = CHR$(30) THEN x(y) = (x(y)+1) MOD Modulo(y)¶
  IF a$ = CHR$(31) THEN x(y) = x(y)-1 ¶
  ' CRSR Left/Right¶
¶
  IF x(y) < 0 THEN x(y) = Modulo(y)-1¶
  IF a$ = CHR$(28) THEN ¶
    Colours(y) = 2¶
    y = y-1¶
  END IF¶
  ' CRSR Up¶
¶
  IF a$ = CHR$(29) THEN¶
    Colours(y) = 2 ¶
    y = (y+1) MOD 4¶
  END IF¶
  ' CRSR Down¶
  ¶
  IF y<0 THEN y=3¶
¶
  Colours(y) = 1¶
¶
  IF (x(0) > 0) AND (y=0) THEN¶
    x(1) = 0              ' Select HAM or Halfbrite ¶
    x(3) = 5              ' 5+1 BitPlanes¶
    Modulo(3) = 6¶
  END IF¶
  ¶
  IF x(0)>0 THEN x(3) = 5 ' Number of BitPlanes unchanged by HAM or¶
                          ' Halfbrite mode¶
 ¶
  IF (x(0) = 0) AND (x(1)<>1) THEN ¶
     Modulo(3) = 5¶
     IF x(3) > 4 THEN x(3) = 4  ' Maximum 4+1 BitPlanes¶
  END IF                        ' in Normal Mode¶
  ¶
  IF (x(1) = 1) AND (y = 1) THEN¶
    x(0) = 0                    ' HIRES and Normal¶
    IF x(3)>3 THEN x(3) = 3     ' Maximum 3+1 BitPlanes ¶
    Modulo(3) = 4¶
  END IF¶
¶
  IF a$<> CHR$(13) THEN GOTO Outg¶
¶
  COLOR 1¶
  ¶
  RasterW%=(x(1)+1)*320¶
  RasterH%=(x(2)+1)*200 '256 for PAL-resolution¶
¶
  IF x(0) = 1 THEN Modus% = &H800       'HAM¶
```

```
  IF x(0) = 2 THEN Modus% = &H80         'HalfBrite¶
  IF x(1) = 1 THEN Modus% = &H8000       'HIRES¶
    ' (HAM, Halfbrite) and HIRES close the same way ¶
¶
  IF x(2) = 1 THEN Modus% = Modus% OR 4 'LACE¶
   ¶
  CLS¶
  RasterT% = x(3)+1¶
  ¶
  IF RasterT% = 6 THEN RasterT% = 5¶
    ' If HAM, open a normal screen ¶
    ' (max. 5 BitPlanes)¶
  ¶
  IF FRE(-1) < (RasterW%/8*RasterH%*RasterT%)+5000 THEN¶
    CLS¶
    CALL PrintIt ("Insufficent memory for bitmap !!!",100,False)¶
    CALL PrintIt ("Please try a lower resolution or number of bitmaps
!!!",130,False)¶
    ¶
    CALL DialogBox("Ok",1,True,x1b%,y1b%,x2b%,y2b%,False)¶
    CALL DoDialog(n%,1,-1,-1,-1,-1,x1b%,y1b%,x2b%,y2b%,-1,-1,-1,-1)  ¶
    CLS¶
    GOTO Outg¶
  END IF¶
    ¶
  SCREEN 1,RasterW%,RasterH%,RasterT%,x(1)+(x(2)*2)+1¶
    '      Width  ,Height    ,Depth  ,Mode¶
  ¶
  WINDOW 2,"",(0,0)-(RasterW%-9,RasterH%-15),0,1¶
    ' Window layer¶
  ¶
  RasterT% = x(3)+1¶
    ' old RasterT value¶
  ¶
  WBase& = WINDOW(7)¶
  WScreen& = PEEKL(WBase&+46)¶
    ' Extract address of the new screen from window addrress¶
  ¶
  POKEL WBase&+24,&H100 OR &H800 OR 65536&¶
    ' Window Flags change: Borderless, RBMTrap, NoCareRefresh¶
¶
  Viewport& = PEEKL(WBase&+46)+44¶
  ColorMap& = PEEKL(Viewport&+4)¶
  RastPort& = Viewport&+40¶
  BitMap& = WScreen&+184¶
¶
  Adr = PEEKL(RastPort&+4)+8          ' BitPlanes for loading¶
  FOR i=0 TO RasterT%-1               ' and saving¶
    BitPlanes&(i) = PEEKL(Adr+4*i)¶
  NEXT i¶
¶
  BitPlane6& = BitMap&+28¶
    ' Where do you want the sixth bitplane address placed ?¶
  ¶
  Depth& = BitMap&+5¶
    ' Where do you want the new depth placed ?¶
  ¶
  CALL SetRast&(RastPort&,0)¶
  CALL SetRGB4&(Viewport&,1,15,15,15)¶
  CALL SetRGB4&(Viewport&,0,0,0,0)¶
```

```
    ' Clear new screen and set background ¶
 ¶
  IF RasterT% = 6 THEN¶
    RSize& = RasterW%*(RasterH%\8)¶
    Flags& = 65536&+2                    ' MEMF_CHIP | MEMF_CLEAR¶
    Mem& = AllocMem&(Rsize&,Flags&)¶
    IF Mem& = 0 THEN¶
      CALL Scroff¶
      CALL PrintIt("Not enough memory for sixth BitPlane !!!",100,False)¶
      CALL DialogBox("Sorry !",1,True,x1a%,y1a%,x2a%,y2a%,False)¶
¶
      CALL DoDialog(n%,1,-1,-1,-1,-1,x1a%,y1a%,x2a%,y2a%,-1,-1,-1,-1)¶
      GOSUB CloseIt¶
      RUN¶
    END IF¶
    ¶
    POKE Depth&,6¶
      ' New depth¶
    ¶
    POKEL BitPlane6&,Mem&¶
    BitPlanes&(5)=Mem&¶
      ' Poke address of the sixth BitPlane¶
    ¶
    POKEW Viewport&+32,Modus%¶
      ' Poke for display mode POKEN¶
    ¶
    dummy = RemakeDisplay(dummy&)¶
      ' compute new display ¶
  END IF  ¶
¶
  Status$ = " Status: Initializing"+CHR$(0)¶
  CALL SetWindowTitles&(NWBase&,SADD(Status$),0)¶
¶
  CALL Scroff¶
  CALL SetDrMd&(RastPort&,1)¶
    ¶
  RasterW1% = RasterW%-1  ' 319/639¶
  RasterH1% = RasterH%-1  ' 199/399¶
  RasterW2% = RasterW%/2  ' Screen middle¶
  RasterH2% = RasterH%/2¶
  ¶
  FactorX = (x(1)+1)/2¶
  FactorY = (x(2)+1)/2¶
¶
  POKEW OSModus&,Modus%¶
  POKEL OSRastPort&,RastPort&¶
  POKEW OSRasterW1&,RasterW1%¶
  POKEW OSRasterH1&,RasterH1%¶
¶
  MaxColour% = 2^RasterT%¶
  IF (RasterT% = 6) THEN¶
    IF (Modus% AND &H800) = &H800 THEN ¶
      MaxColour% = 16                 'HAM¶
    ELSE¶
      MaxColour% = 64                 'Halfbrite¶
    END IF¶
  END IF¶
¶
  POKEW OSMaxColour&,2^RasterT%  'If HAM: 64 Colour!¶
  DIM Colour(MaxColour%,3)¶
```

```
 ¶
  FOR m%=0 TO 3¶
    Colour(1,m%)=0          'Black¶
    Colour(2,m%)=1          'White¶
  NEXT m%¶
¶
  IF (Modus% AND &H80) = &H80 THEN  'HalfBrite¶
    MF%=MaxColour%/2¶
 ¶
    Colour(MF%+1,0)=MF%¶
    Colour(MF%+2,0)=MF%+1¶
    FOR m%=1 TO 3¶
      Colour(MF%+1,m%)=0¶
      Colour(MF%+2,m%)=.5¶
    NEXT m%¶
    RESTORE OptimaleHBColour¶
  ELSE¶
    MF%=MaxColour%¶
    RESTORE OptimaleColour¶
  END IF¶
¶
  FOR n% = 3 TO MF%¶
    READ r%,g%,b%¶
¶
    Colour(n%,0)=n%-1¶
    Colour(n%,1)=r%/15¶
    Colour(n%,2)=g%/15¶
    Colour(n%,3)=b%/15¶
    CALL SetRGB4&(Viewport&,n%-1,r%,g%,b%)¶
¶
    IF (Modus% AND &H80)<>0 THEN          'HalfBrite¶
      Colour(n%+MF%,0)=n%+MF%¶
      FOR m%=1 TO 3¶
        Colour(n%+MF%,m%)=(INT(Colour(n%,m%)*15)\2)/15¶
      NEXT m%¶
    END IF¶
¶
  NEXT n%¶
    ' => Colour(n,0)     = color index, ¶
    '    Colour(n,1..3)  = RGB brightness¶
¶
  ' Poke colors into assembler routines array:¶
¶
  FOR n%=0 TO MaxColour%-1¶
    POKEW OSColour&+n%*8,Colour(n%+1,0)¶
    FOR m%=1 TO 3¶
      POKEW OSColour&+n%*8+m%*2,Colour(n%+1,m%)*1024¶
    NEXT m%¶
  NEXT n%¶
  CLS¶
RETURN¶
¶
OptimaleHBColour:  'HalfBrite¶
DATA 10,0,0¶
DATA 0,10,0¶
DATA 0,0,10¶
DATA 10,10,0¶
DATA 10,0,10¶
DATA 0,10,10¶
DATA 10,10,10¶
```

```
DATA 15,10,0¶
DATA 15,0,10¶
DATA 15,10,10¶
DATA 10,15,0¶
DATA 0,15,10¶
DATA 10,15,10¶
DATA 0,10,15¶
DATA 10,0,15¶
DATA 10,10,15¶
DATA 15,15,10¶
DATA 15,10,15¶
DATA 10,15,15¶
DATA 13,13,13¶
DATA 8,8,8¶
DATA 8,0,0¶
DATA 0,8,0¶
DATA 0,0,8¶
¶
' and the next six Colours¶
¶
OptimaleColour:¶
DATA 15,0,0¶
DATA 0,15,0¶
DATA 0,0,15¶
DATA 15,15,0¶
DATA 15,0,15¶
DATA 0,15,15¶
DATA 7,0,0¶
DATA 0,7,0¶
DATA 0,0,7¶
DATA 7,7,0¶
DATA 7,0,7¶
DATA 0,7,7¶
DATA 7,7,7¶
DATA 15,7,0¶
DATA 15,0,7¶
DATA 15,7,7¶
DATA 7,15,0¶
DATA 0,15,7¶
DATA 7,15,7¶
DATA 0,7,15¶
DATA 7,0,15¶
DATA 7,7,15¶
DATA 15,15,7¶
DATA 15,7,15¶
DATA 7,15,15¶
DATA 3,3,3¶
DATA 10,10,10¶
DATA 10,0,0¶
DATA 0,10,0¶
DATA 0,0,10¶
'¶
'end of INIT.ASC¶
'¶
```

The SYSTEM.ASC module

```
'SYSTEM.ASC start ¶
'  ******************************************¶
'  *           Trace-System-Routines        *¶
'  ******************************************¶
'¶
CloseIt:¶
  ' Close all and free memory¶
  GOSUB CloseGfx¶
  WINDOW CLOSE 2¶
  SCREEN CLOSE 1     ' automatic release of allocated 6th bitmap¶
  MENU RESET         ' ¶
¶
  IF SetPointAdr& <> 0 THEN CALL FreeMem&(SetPointAdr&,SetPointNum&)¶
  IF PatternS& <> 0 THEN CALL FreeMem&(PatternS&,(NumberPatternS%+1)*2*16)¶
  IF PatternX& <> 0 THEN CALL FreeMem&(PatternX&,(NumberPatternX%*2+1)*2*16)¶
    'Save pattern and release ASSEM-Routine¶
  LIBRARY CLOSE¶
RETURN¶
'    ¶
SUB PrintIt(Out$,y%,Scr) STATIC¶
SHARED RastPort&,NRastPort&,RasterW2%,True,Length&¶
  ' Centered text output on one of the two screens ¶
  ' Out$: Printed string¶
  ' y%: verticle Position ?¶
  ' Scr: User or Display Screen?¶
  IF Scr = True THEN¶
    rp& = RastPort&¶
    Middle& = RasterW2%¶
    ' write to new (Display) Screen¶
  ELSE¶
    rp& = NRastPort&¶
    Middle& = 320     ' User-Screen (NO OP Window)¶
  END IF¶
  Length& = TextLength&(rp&,SADD(Out$),LEN(Out$))¶
  Middle& = Middle& - Length&/2¶
  CALL Move& (rp&,Middle&,CLNG(y%))¶
  CALL Text& (rp&,SADD(Out$),LEN(Out$))¶
END SUB¶
'¶
SUB EmptyBuffers STATIC¶
  ' clear mouse and keyboard buffer ¶
  WHILE MOUSE(0) <> 0¶
  WEND¶
  WHILE (INKEY$<>"")¶
  WEND¶
END SUB¶
'¶
Pause: ¶
  ' Wait for (Mouse-) key press¶
  CALL EmptyBuffers                    ' clear buffer ¶
  WHILE (INKEY$ = "") AND (MOUSE (0) = 0)¶
  WEND¶
RETURN¶
```

```
'¶
SUB Box(RastPort&,x1%,y1%,x2%,y2%) STATIC¶
  ' rectangle in Display-Screen¶
  ' RastPort&: draw in which  RastPort ¶
  ' x1,y1,x2,y2 coordinates of the rectangle¶
  CALL Move&(RastPort&,x1%,y1%)¶
  CALL Draw&(RastPort&,x2%,y1%)¶
  CALL Draw&(RastPort&,x2%,y2%)¶
  CALL Draw&(RastPort&,x1%,y2%)¶
  CALL Draw&(RastPort&,x1%,y1%+1)¶
END SUB¶
'¶
SUB DialogBox(Dialog$,Position%,Ret,x1%,y1%,x2%,y2%,Scr) STATIC¶
SHARED RastPort&,NRastPort&,True,RasterW1%,RasterW2%¶
  ' Create your own requester¶
  ' Dialog$ = Text in Dialog Box¶
  ' Position% ¶
  '    0 = right¶
  '    1 = center¶
  '    2 = left¶
  ' Ret% = can you press <Return>?¶
  '    True  = Yes¶
  '    False = No¶
  ' x1%,y1%,x2%,y1% = Size of  'click'-Field (word returned)¶
  '    Scr = In which screen output ?¶
  '      True = Display-Screen¶
  '      False = User-Screen¶
¶
 IF Scr = True THEN¶
    rp& = RastPort&¶
    Middle& = RasterW2%¶
    SEnd& = RasterW1%¶
    ' Write to Display-Screen¶
  ELSE¶
    rp& = NRastPort&¶
    Middle& = 320¶
    SEnd& = 640¶
    ' RastPort of Basic Windows¶
  END IF¶
¶
  y1% = 150¶
  y2% = 150 + 6 + 10¶
¶
  Length& = TextLength&(rp&,SADD(Dialog$),LEN(Dialog$))¶
¶
  IF Position% = 0 THEN ¶
      x1% = 70¶
      x2% = x1% + Length& + 20¶
  END IF¶
¶
  IF Position% = 1 THEN¶
      x1% = Middle&-Length&/2-10¶
      x2% = Middle&+Length&/2+10¶
  END IF¶
¶
  IF Position% = 2 THEN ¶
      x1% = SEnd&-70-20-10-Length&¶
      x2% = SEnd&-70-10¶
  END IF¶
¶
```

```
  CALL Move&(rp&,x1%+10,y1%+10)¶
  CALL Text&(rp&,SADD(Dialog$),LEN(Dialog$)) ¶
¶
  IF Scr = True THEN¶
    CALL Box(rp&,x1%,y1%,x2%,y2%)¶
    CALL Box(rp&,x1%-4,y1%-2,x2%+4,y2%+2)¶
    IF Ret = True THEN CALL Box(rp&,x1%-2,y1%-1,x2%+2,y2%+1)¶
  ELSE¶
    LINE (x1%,y1%)-(x2%,y2%),,b¶
    LINE (x1%-2,y1%-2)-(x2%+2,y2%+2),,b¶
    IF Ret = True THEN LINE (x1%-1,y1%-1)-(x2%+1,y2%+1),,b¶
  END IF¶
END SUB¶
'¶
SUB DoDialog(n%,Ret%,x1a%,y1a%,x2a%,y2a%,x1b%,y1b%,x2b%,y2b%,x1c%,y1c%,x2c%,y2c%)
STATIC¶
  ' Dialog box read¶
  ' n%: which gadget clicked ?¶
  ' Ret%: which gadget specified by pressing <Return>?¶
  ' x1.,y1.,x2.,y2. coordinates of the box¶
  CALL EmptyBuffers¶
  n% = -1¶
  WHILE (n% = -1)¶
    IF MOUSE(0) <> 0 THEN¶
      x = MOUSE(1)¶
      y = MOUSE(2)¶
 ¶
      IF (x1a%<x) AND (x2a%>x) AND (y1a%<y) AND (y2a%>y) THEN n% = 0¶
      IF (x1b%<x) AND (x2b%>x) AND (y1b%<y) AND (y2b%>y) THEN n% = 1 ¶
      IF (x1c%<x) AND (x2c%>x) AND (y1c%<y) AND (y2c%>y) THEN n% = 2¶
    END IF¶
    IF INKEY$ = CHR$(13) THEN n% = Ret%¶
  WEND¶
END SUB¶
'¶
SUB Rubberbox( x%, y%, w%, h%, Back!) STATIC¶
SHARED
RasterW1%,RasterH1%,WScreen&,NRastPort&,RastPort&,NWScreen&,NWBase&,WBase&,Length&,
True,False¶
  ' Make rectangle with mouse¶
  ' x%,y%: upper left corner¶
  ' w%,h%: Width, Height¶
  ' Back!: Return to user window ?¶
  CALL Scron¶
  CALL SetDrMd&(RastPort&,2)  'COMPLEMENT   ¶
  ¶
  CALL SetAPen&(RastPort&,1)¶
¶
 Repitition:¶
  Oldx% = 1¶
  OldY% = 1¶
  Flag! = 0¶
    ¶
  CALL EmptyBuffers¶
¶
   mouse1:   ¶
    x% = PEEKW(WScreen&+18)¶
    y% = PEEKW(WScreen&+16)¶
¶
      IF (x% <> Oldx%) OR (y%<>OldY%) THEN¶
```

```
        IF Flag! = 1 THEN ¶
          CALL Move&(RastPort&,Oldx%,0)¶
          CALL Draw&(RastPort&,Oldx%,RasterH1%)¶
          CALL Move&(RastPort&,0,OldY%)¶
          CALL Draw&(RastPort&,RasterW1%,OldY%)¶
        END IF¶
¶
        Flag! = 1¶
¶
        CALL Move&(RastPort&,x%,0)¶
        CALL Draw&(RastPort&,x%,RasterH1%)¶
        CALL Move&(RastPort&,0,y%)¶
        CALL Draw&(RastPort&,RasterW1%,y%)¶
        Oldx% = x%¶
        OldY% = y%¶
      END IF      ¶
¶
   IF MOUSE(0) = 0 GOTO mouse1¶
¶
   CALL Move&(RastPort&,x%,0)¶
   CALL Draw&(RastPort&,x%,RasterH1%)¶
   CALL Move&(RastPort&,0,y%)¶
   CALL Draw&(RastPort&,RasterW1%,y%)¶
     ¶
   Oldx% = -1¶
   OldY% = -1¶
   Flag! = 0¶
  ¶
   WHILE MOUSE(0) <> 0¶
    ¶
     w% = PEEKW(WScreen&+18)¶
     h% = PEEKW(WScreen&+16)¶
     IF (w% <> Oldx%) OR (h% <> OldY%) THEN¶
¶
       IF Flag! = 1 THEN CALL Box(RastPort&,x%,y%,Oldx%,OldY%)¶
       Flag! = 1¶
¶
         IF (w% < x%+6) THEN w% = x%+6¶
         IF (h% < y%+3) THEN h% = y%+3¶
       ¶
         IF (w% > x%) AND (h% > y%) THEN¶
           IF w%>RasterW1% THEN w% = RasterW1%¶
           IF h%>RasterH1% THEN h% = RasterH1%¶
           Oldx% = w%¶
           OldY% = h%¶
          ¶
           CALL Box(RastPort&,x%,y%,w%,h%)    ¶
         END IF                  ¶
       END IF¶
     WEND ¶
   ¶
     IF Flag = 1 THEN CALL Box(RastPort&,x%,y%,w%,h%)¶
      ¶
     CALL PrintIt("Section Ok ?",130,True)   ¶
¶
     Flag! = 0¶
     Oldx% = -1¶
     OldY% = -1¶
¶
     CALL DialogBox("OK",1,True,x1a%,y1a%,x2a%,y2a%,True)¶
```

```
  ¶
     CALL EmptyBuffers¶
  ¶
     a$ = ""¶
     WHILE (MOUSE(0) = 0) AND (a$ <> CHR$(13))    ¶
       a$ = INKEY$¶
     WEND¶
¶
     Mx% = PEEKW(WScreen&+18)¶
     My% = PEEKW(WScreen&+16)¶
¶
     TryAgain = True¶
     IF (Mx%>x1a%) AND (Mx%<x2a%) AND (My%>y1a%) AND (My%<y2a%) THEN TryAgain =
False¶
     IF a$ = CHR$(13) THEN TryAgain = False¶
     ¶
     CALL PrintIt("Section  Ok ?",130,True)  ¶
    ¶
     CALL DialogBox("OK",1,True,x1a%,y1a%,x2a%,y2a%,True)¶
 ¶
  IF TryAgain = True THEN GOTO Repitition        ¶
¶
  w% = w%-x%¶
  h% = h%-y%   ¶
¶
  CALL SetDrMd&(RastPort&,1)  'JAM2¶
  CALL SetDrMd&(NRastPort&,1)¶
  ¶
  IF Back! = True THEN CALL Scroff¶
END SUB¶
'¶
NOOP:  ¶
  Status$ = " Status: NOP"+CHR$(0)¶
  CALL SetWindowTitles&(NWBase&,SADD(Status$),0)¶
RETURN¶
'¶
MakeMenu:¶
  Status$ = " Status: Building menu"+CHR$(0)¶
  CALL SetWindowTitles&(NWBase&,SADD(Status$),0)¶
  ¶
  MENU 1,0,1, " Amiga"¶
    MENU 1,1,1," 3D-Cad-Info  I"¶
 ¶
  MENU 2,0,1,"File"¶
    MENU 2,1,1,        " Load           L"¶
    MENU 2,2,Start%,   " Save           S"¶
    MENU 2,3,1,        " Merge          M"¶
    MENU 2,4,1,        " New            N"¶
    MENU 2,5,0,        "-----------------"¶
    MENU 2,6,1,        " Load material   "¶
    MENU 2,7,0,        "-----------------"¶
    MENU 2,8,Start%,   " Background      "¶
    MENU 2,9,Start%,   " Save screen    P"¶
    MENU 2,10,Start%,  " Hardcopy        "¶
    MENU 2,11,0,       "-----------------"¶
    MENU 2,12,Start%,  " Color palette  C"¶
    MENU 2,13,0,       "-----------------"¶
    MENU 2,14,1,       " Program end    Q"¶
  ¶
  MENU 3,0,1,"Editor"¶
```

```
    MENU 3,1,1, " Load Editor          ^F1"¶
¶
  MENU 4,0,Start%,"Parameter"¶
    MENU 4,1,Start%, " Projection point  P"¶
    MENU 4,2,Start%, " Main point        H"¶
    MENU 4,3,Start%, " a, _, c           A"¶
    MENU 4,4,Start%, " Distance          D"¶
    MENU 4,5,0,      "-------------------"¶
    MENU 4,6,Start%, " Enlarge           V"¶
    MENU 4,7,Start%, " Number corner     E"¶
 ¶
  MENU 5,0,Start%,"Draw"¶
    MENU 5,1,Start%," Shadows          F10"¶
    MENU 5,2,Start%," Initialization   F9 "¶
    MENU 5,3,0,     "--------------------"¶
    MENU 5,4,Start%," Wire  model      < >"¶
    MENU 5,5,Start%," Clear screen     C  "¶
¶
  GOSUB NOOP¶
  CALL EmptyBuffers¶
RETURN¶
'¶
DeleteMenu:¶
  MENU 1,0,0,"Amiga"¶
  MENU 2,0,0,"File"¶
  MENU 3,0,0,"Editor"¶
  MENU 4,0,0,"Parameter"¶
  MENU 5,0,0,"Draw"¶
RETURN¶
'¶
MessageEvent:¶
  MTitle = MENU(0)¶
  MPoint = MENU(1)¶
  ¶
  IF MTitle <> 0 THEN¶
  ¶
    IF MTitle = 1 THEN¶
      IF MPoint = 1 THEN GOSUB Info¶
      GOTO MessageEnde¶
    END IF¶
    ¶
    IF MTitle = 2 THEN¶
      IF MPoint = 1 THEN GOSUB Loader¶
      IF MPoint = 2 THEN GOSUB Saver¶
      IF MPoint = 3 THEN GOSUB Merger¶
      IF MPoint = 4 THEN GOSUB ArrayInit¶
      ' Mpoint = 5 : "---------"¶
      IF MPoint = 6 THEN GOSUB LoadMat¶
      ' MPoint = 7 : "---------"¶
      IF MPoint = 8 THEN GOSUB Background¶
      IF MPoint = 9 THEN GOSUB ScreenSaver¶
      IF MPoint = 10 THEN GOSUB HardCopy¶
      ' MPoint = 11 : "---------"¶
      IF MPoint = 12 THEN GOSUB ColorPalette¶
      ' MPoint = 13 : "---------"¶
      IF MPoint = 14 THEN GOSUB Quit¶
      GOTO MessageEnde¶
    END IF¶
    ¶
    IF MTitle = 3 THEN¶
```

```
      IF MPoint = 1 THEN GOSUB LoadEditor¶
      GOTO MessageEnde¶
    END IF¶
    ¶
    IF MTitle = 4 THEN¶
      IF MPoint = 1 THEN GOSUB InputP¶
      IF MPoint = 2 THEN GOSUB InputH¶
      IF MPoint = 3 THEN GOSUB InputAngle¶
      IF MPoint = 4 THEN GOSUB InputDPH¶
      ' MPoint =5: "-----------"¶
      IF MPoint = 6 THEN GOSUB Enlargement¶
      IF MPoint = 7 THEN GOSUB HowManyCorners¶
      GOTO MessageEnde¶
    END IF¶
  ¶
    IF MTitle = 5 THEN¶
      IF MPoint = 1 THEN GOSUB Shadows¶
      IF MPoint = 2 THEN GOSUB InitParameters¶
      IF MPoint = 4 THEN GOSUB DrawNew¶
      IF MPoint = 5 THEN GOSUB ClearScreen¶
    END IF¶
  END IF¶
  MessageEnde: ¶
RETURN¶
'¶
KeyEvent:¶
  Key$=INKEY$¶
  IF Key$ <> "" THEN¶
  LOCATE 1,1¶
  ¶
   IF Start% = 1 THEN¶
     IF Key$ = " " THEN GOSUB DrawNew¶
     IF Key$ = "d" THEN GOSUB InputDPH¶
¶
     IF Key$ = "c" THEN GOSUB ColorPalette¶
¶
     IF Key$ = "*" OR Key$ = "/" OR Key$ = "+" OR Key$ = "-" THEN¶
       IF Key$ = "+" THEN D = 10 ¶
       IF Key$ = "-" THEN D =-10¶
       IF Key$ = "*" THEN D = 100¶
       IF Key$ = "/" THEN D =-100¶
¶
       DPH = DPH + D¶
       GOSUB Initial¶
       Newone! = True¶
       WaitFlg! = True¶
       GOSUB DrawNew¶
     END IF¶
   ¶
     IF Key$ = "v" THEN GOSUB Enlargement¶
     IF Key$ = "p" THEN GOSUB InputP¶
     IF Key$ = "h" THEN GOSUB InputH¶
     IF Key$ = "a" THEN GOSUB InputAngle¶
     IF Key$ = "e" THEN GOSUB HowManyCorners¶
   ¶
     IF Key$ = "c" THEN GOSUB ClearScreen¶
  ¶
     IF Key$ = "s" THEN GOSUB Saver¶
     IF Key$ = "b" THEN GOSUB ScreenSaver¶
     IF Key$ = CHR$(137) THEN GOSUB InitParameters¶
```

```
      IF Key$ = CHR$(138) THEN GOSUB Shadows¶
   ¶
      IF (Key$ = CHR$(28)) OR (Key$ = CHR$(29)) OR (Key$ = CHR$(30)) OR (Key$ =
CHR$(31)) THEN¶
        IF Key$ = CHR$(28) THEN¶
          Beta = Beta + Pi/15¶
        END IF  ¶
        IF Key$ = CHR$(29) THEN¶
          Beta = Beta - Pi/15¶
        END IF  ¶
        IF Key$ = CHR$(30) THEN¶
          Alpha = Alpha + Pi/15¶
        END IF  ¶
        IF Key$ = CHR$(31) THEN¶
          Alpha = Alpha - Pi/15¶
        END IF¶
        GOSUB Initial¶
        Newone! = True¶
        WaitFlg! = True¶
        GOSUB DrawNew¶
      END IF¶
   ¶
      IF (Key$ = CHR$(18)) OR (Key$ = "R") THEN¶
        IF Key$ = CHR$(18) THEN   '^R¶
          Gamma = Gamma + Pi/15¶
        END IF ¶
        IF Key$ = "R" THEN¶
          Gamma = Gamma - Pi/15¶
        END IF¶
        GOSUB Initial¶
        Newone! = True¶
        WaitFlg! = True¶
        GOSUB DrawNew¶
      END IF     ¶
    END IF¶
    IF Key$ = "m" THEN GOSUB Merger¶
    IF Key$ = "n" THEN GOSUB ArrayInit  ¶
    IF Key$ = "l" THEN GOSUB Loader ¶
    IF Key$ = "?" OR Key$ = CHR$(139) THEN GOSUB Help¶
    IF Key$ = "q" THEN Quit¶
    IF Key$ = "i" THEN GOSUB Info¶
   ¶
    IF Key$ = CHR$(1) THEN GOSUB LoadEditor¶
 END IF  ¶
RETURN¶
'¶
'¶
ColorPalette:¶
  Status$ = " Status: Color change"+CHR$(0)¶
  CALL SetWindowTitles&(NWBase&,SADD(Status$),0)¶
¶
  GOSUB DeleteMenu¶
¶
  CALL SetRast&(RastPort&,0)¶
  CALL Scron¶
  CALL PrintIt("Which color to change ?",100,True)¶
  ¶
  NumCol = MaxColour%¶
  IF NumCol = 64 THEN NumCol = 32 ' Halfbrite ?¶
  Widthe = (RasterW%-40)/NumCol¶
```

```
  LINE ((20+1),1)-(20+Widthe-1,RasterH%/10-1),1,b ¶
  FOR i=1 TO NumCol-1¶
      LINE ((20+i*Widthe+1),1)-((20+(i+1)*Widthe)-1,RasterH%/10-1),i,BF¶
      IF MaxColour% = 64 THEN   'Halfbrite Colour output¶
        LINE ((20+i*Widthe+1),RasterH%/10)-((20+(i+1)*Widthe)-1,RasterH%/5-
1),i+32,BF¶
      END IF¶
  NEXT¶
  ¶
 LoopA:¶
  CALL EmptyBuffers¶
¶
  WHILE MOUSE(0) = 0¶
  WEND¶
  ¶
  x = MOUSE (1)¶
  y = MOUSE (2)¶
  ¶
  IF (x < 20) OR (x > RasterW%-20) THEN ¶
    GOTO LoopA:¶
  END IF ¶
  IF (y < 1) OR (y > RasterH%/10) THEN¶
    GOTO LoopA:¶
  END IF¶
 ¶
  Colr% = INT ((x-20)/Widthe)  ' which color was clicked¶
  CALL Scroff¶
  red=INT(Colour(Colr%+1,1)*15.5)¶
  green=INT(Colour(Colr%+1,2)*15.5)¶
  blue=INT(Colour(Colr%+1,3)*15.5)¶
  ¶
  LOCATE 10,1¶
  PRINT " red-component   (0..15) : ";¶
  CALL FormInputInt (red,30!,0!,15!)¶
  ¶
  LOCATE 11,1¶
  PRINT " green-component (0..15) : ";¶
  CALL FormInputInt (green,30!,0!,15!)¶
  ¶
  LOCATE 12,1¶
  PRINT " blue-component  (0..15) : ";¶
  CALL FormInputInt (blue,30!,0!,15!)¶
  ¶
  Colour(Colr%+1,1)=red/15¶
  Colour(Colr%+1,2)=green/15¶
  Colour(Colr%+1,3)=blue/15¶
 ¶
  POKEW OSColour&+Colr%*8+2,red/15*1024¶
  POKEW OSColour&+Colr%*8+4,green/15*1024¶
  POKEW OSColour&+Colr%*8+6,blue/15*1024¶
 ¶
  IF MaxColour%=64 THEN                 'ExtraHalfBrite¶
    Colour(Colr%+33,1)=(red\2)/15¶
    Colour(Colr%+33,2)=(green\2)/15¶
    Colour(Colr%+33,3)=(blue\2)/15¶
 ¶
    POKEW OSColour&+Colr%*8+258, (red\2)/15*1024¶
    POKEW OSColour&+Colr%*8+260, (green\2)/15*1024¶
    POKEW OSColour&+Colr%*8+262, (blue\2)/15*1024¶
 ¶
```

```
  END IF¶
  ¶
  CALL SetRGB4&(Viewport&,Colr%,CINT(red),CINT(green),CINT(blue))¶
¶
  CALL DialogBox ("End",0,True,x1a%,y1a%,x2a%,y2a%,False)¶
  CALL DialogBox ("Next color",2,False,x1b%,y1b%,x2b%,y2b%,False)¶
¶
  CALL DoDialog (n%,0,x1a%,y1a%,x2a%,y2a%,-1,-1,-1,-1,x1b%,y1b%,x2b%,y2b%)¶
  CLS¶
¶
  IF n% = 2 THEN ¶
    CALL Scron¶
    GOTO LoopA¶
  END IF¶
  Newone! = True¶
  Hg = False¶
  GOSUB MakeMenu¶
RETURN¶
'¶
'¶
ErrorHandling:¶
  NumErr = ERR¶
  ¶
  Status$ = " Status: Next Big Error !!!"+CHR$(0)¶
  CALL SetWindowTitles&(NWBase&,SADD(Status$),0)¶
  ¶
  GOSUB DeleteMenu¶
  ¶
  Dialog$ = ""¶
  IF NumErr = 64 THEN         ' Bad File Mode¶
    Dialog$ = "Bad file name !!!"¶
  END IF¶
  ¶
  IF NumErr = 57 THEN         ' Device I/O Error¶
    Dialog$ = "Device I/O Error !!!"¶
  END IF¶
  ¶
  IF NumErr = 68 THEN         ' Device unable¶
    Dialog$ = "Device not found"¶
  END IF¶
  ¶
  IF NumErr = 61 THEN         ' Disk Full¶
    Dialog$ = "Diskette is full !!!"   ¶
  END IF¶
  ¶
  IF NumErr = 53 THEN         ' File not found¶
    Dialog$ = "File not found!!!"¶
  END IF¶
  ¶
  IF NumErr = 70 THEN         ' Permission denied¶
    Dialog$ = "Permission denied!!!"¶
  END IF¶
  ¶
  IF Dialog$ = "" THEN¶
    Dialog$ = "Error Number ="+STR$(NumErr)¶
  END IF¶
  ¶
  CALL DialogBox(Dialog$,1,True,x1a%,y1a%,x2a%,y2a%,False)¶
  ¶
  CALL DoDialog(n%,1,-1,-1,-1,-1,x1a%,y1a%,x2a%,y2a%,-1,-1,-1,-1)¶
```

```
¶
  CLS¶
  GOSUB MakeMenu¶
  RESUME ok ¶
RETURN¶
'¶
Quit:¶
  CALL Scroff¶
  Status$ = " Program end ?"+CHR$(0)¶
  CALL SetWindowTitles&(NWBase&,SADD(Status$),0)¶
  ¶
  GOSUB DeleteMenu¶
  ¶
  CALL PrintIt("Do you really wish to exit the program?",100,False)¶
  ¶
  CALL DialogBox("No",0,True,x1a%,y1a%,x2a%,y2a%,False)¶
  CALL DialogBox("New start",1,False,x1b%,y1b%,x2b%,y2b%,False)¶
  CALL DialogBox("Yes",2,False,x1c%,y1c%,x2c%,y2c%,False)¶
  ¶
  CALL DoDialog(n%,0,x1a%,y1a%,x2a%,y2a%,x1b%,y1b%,x2b%,y2b%,x1c%,y1c%,x2c%,y2c%)
¶
¶
  CLS¶
  IF n% > 0 THEN¶
    GOSUB CloseIt¶
    IF n% = 1 THEN¶
      RUN ¶
    ELSE¶
      END¶
    END IF¶
  END IF¶
  GOSUB MakeMenu¶
RETURN¶
'¶
SUB Scroff STATIC¶
SHARED NWBase&,NWScreen&¶
  ' Display Screen off , User Screen on¶
  CALL ScreenToFront&(NWScreen&)¶
  WINDOW OUTPUT 1¶
  WINDOW 1¶
  CALL ActivateWindow&(NWBase&)¶
END SUB¶
'¶
SUB Scron STATIC¶
SHARED WScreen&,WBase&¶
  ' Display Screen on, User Screen off¶
  CALL ScreenToFront&(WScreen&)¶
  WINDOW OUTPUT 2¶
  WINDOW 2¶
  CALL ActivateWindow&(WBase&)¶
END SUB¶
'¶
SUB GetString(old$,a$,z$,z,s,winlen)STATIC¶
'TASK      :Read a string while allowing the user to edit the string¶
'           i.e.:cursor left/right, backspace and delete functions.¶
'           In addition the string should be scrollable ¶
'           if the input is longer than the line¶
'PARAMETER:=>old$ old value of string to be read¶
'             a$ key pressed¶
'             z$ legal characters¶
```

```
'             z line¶
'             s column¶
'             winlen Length of input windpow¶
'           <=old$ of specified string¶
 IF winlen=1 THEN 'if only 1 character entered? => no <Return> needed¶
   old$=a$¶
   WHILE INSTR(z$,old$)=0¶
     CALL GetKey(old$,z,s)¶
   WEND¶
   LOCATE z,s¶
   PRINT old$¶
 ELSE¶
   i=1        'display current string position¶
   Position=1 'display the actual screen position          ¶
   WHILE a$><CHR$(13)¶
     IF INSTR(z$,a$)><0 THEN 'legal character?¶
       old$=LEFT$(old$,i-1)+a$+RIGHT$(old$,LEN(old$)-i+1)      ¶
       i=i+1¶
       Position=Position+1¶
       IF Position>winlen THEN¶
         Position=winlen¶
       END IF  ¶
     ELSE ¶
       IF a$ = CHR$(30) AND i<=LEN(old$) THEN  'Cursor right?¶
         i=i+1¶
         Position=Position+1¶
         IF Position>winlen THEN¶
           Position=winlen¶
         END IF  ¶
       ELSE¶
         IF a$ = CHR$(31) AND i>1 THEN 'Cursor left?¶
           i=i-1¶
           Position=Position-1¶
           IF Position=0 THEN¶
             Position=1¶
           END IF  ¶
         ELSE¶
           IF a$ = CHR$(127) AND i<=LEN(old$) THEN  'delete ?¶
             old$=LEFT$(old$,i-1)+RIGHT$(old$,LEN(old$)-i)¶
           ELSE¶
             IF a$=CHR$(8) AND i>1 THEN  'Backspace ?¶
               i=i-1¶
               Position=Position-1¶
               IF Position=0 THEN¶
                 Position=1¶
               END IF¶
               old$=LEFT$(old$,i-1)+RIGHT$(old$,LEN(old$)-i)¶
             END IF¶
           END IF¶
         END IF¶
       END IF¶
     END IF¶
     LOCATE z,s¶
     PRINT MID$(old$+" ",i-Position+1,winlen)  'String output¶
     CALL GetKey(a$,z,s+Position-1) 'get next key                    ¶
   WEND ¶
 END IF¶
 IF i><Position THEN¶
   CALL PutString(old$,z,s,winlen)¶
 END IF  ¶
```

```
END SUB¶
¶
SUB GetReal(i!,a$,z,s,winlen,unt!,ob!) STATIC¶
'TASK      :Read a real value¶
'PARAMETER:=>i! old value¶
'            a$ pressed key¶
'            z line¶
'            s column¶
'            winlen length of input line¶
'            unt! lower limit¶
'            ob! upper limit¶
'          <=i! given value¶
  CALL conrealstr(i!,j$)¶
loop1:   ¶
  i$=j$¶
  CALL GetString(i$,a$,"1234567890-.",z,s,winlen)¶
  j$=i$¶
  CALL constrreal(i$,i!)¶
  IF i$="" OR i!<unt! OR i!>ob! THEN¶
    a$=" "¶
    BEEP¶
    GOTO loop1¶
  END IF¶
END SUB¶
'¶
SUB GetInt(i!,a$,z,s,winlen,unt!,ob!) STATIC¶
'TASK      :Read a Integer value¶
'PARAMETER:=>i! old value¶
'            a$ key pressed¶
'            z line¶
'            s column¶
'            winlen Length of input line¶
'            unt! upper limit¶
'            ob! lower limit¶
'          <=i! given value¶
  CALL conrealstr(i!,j$)¶
loop3:   ¶
  i$=j$¶
  CALL GetString(i$,a$,"1234567890-",z,s,winlen)¶
  j$=i$¶
  CALL constrreal(i$,i!)¶
  IF i$="" OR i!<unt! OR i!>ob! THEN¶
    a$=" "¶
    BEEP¶
    GOTO loop3¶
  END IF¶
END SUB¶
'¶
SUB GetKey(a$,z,s)STATIC¶
'TASK      :Read a Character ¶
'PARAMETER:=>z line¶
'            s column¶
'          <=a$ key pressed¶
  CALL SetCursor(z,s) ¶
  a$=""¶
  WHILE a$=""¶
    a$=INKEY$¶
  WEND¶
  CALL SetCursor(z,s)¶
END SUB¶
```

```
'¶
SUB SetCursor(z,s) STATIC¶
'TASK      :set the cursor to the given position¶
'PARAMETER:=>z line¶
'             s column¶
  rp&=WINDOW(8)¶
  Cw%=PEEKW(rp&+60)¶
  Ch%=PEEKW(rp&+58)¶
  CALL SetDrMd&(rp&,2)¶
  LINE (s*Cw%-Cw%,z*Ch%-Ch%)-(s*Cw%,z*Ch%),3,BF¶
  CALL SetDrMd&(rp&,1)¶
END SUB  ¶
'¶
SUB PutString(s$,z,s,winlen)STATIC¶
'TASK      :Output a string of the specified length¶
'PARAMETER:=>s$ the string¶
'             z line¶
'             s column¶
'             winlen lenghtof the output string¶
  LOCATE z,s             'delete given range¶
  PRINT SPACE$(winlen)¶
  LOCATE z,s             'output the string¶
  PRINT MID$(s$,1,winlen)¶
END SUB¶
'       ¶
SUB PutReal(i!,z,s,winlen)STATIC¶
'TASK      :Output a real value of the specified length¶
'PARAMETER:=>i! the real value¶
'             z line¶
'             s column¶
'             winlen length of the output window¶
  CALL conrealstr(i!,s$)¶
  CALL PutString(s$,z,s,winlen)¶
END SUB¶
'  ¶
SUB conrealstr(i!,i$)STATIC¶
'TASK      :convert one real value to a string¶
'           rounding off value to three decimal places¶
'PARAMETER:=>i! the Real value¶
'           <=i$ the string¶
  i$=STR$(i!)¶
  j!=FIX(1000!*i!+.5*SGN(i!))/1000! 'round¶
  i$=STR$(j!)¶
  IF ABS(j!)>0 AND ABS(j!)<1 THEN  'Insert 0 if 0<j!<1 ¶
    i$=MID$(i$,1,1)+"0"+MID$(i$,2,LEN(i$))¶
  END IF¶
  IF j!>=0 THEN  'falls 0<=j! truncate first place¶
    i$=RIGHT$(i$,LEN(i$)-1)¶
  END IF¶
END SUB¶
'¶
SUB constrreal(i$,i!) STATIC¶
'TASK      :convert  string to real value¶
'PARAMETER:=>i$ the  string¶
'           <=i! the real value¶
'             i$ If  conversion error i$=""¶
  i!=VAL(i$)¶
  IF i!>=0 THEN¶
    IF i!>0 AND i!<1 THEN¶
      i$=" "+RIGHT$(i$,LEN(i$)-1) 'Insert space and remove 0¶
```

```
    ELSE  ¶
      i$=" "+i$  'insert space¶
    END IF¶
  END IF¶
  j!=i!-FIX(i!*1000!)/1000! 'round ¶
  IF i$><STR$(i!) OR j!><0 THEN 'error ?¶
    i$=""¶
  END IF ¶
END SUB¶
'¶
SUB FormInput (i,winlen,unt!,ob!) STATIC¶
'Enter indivudal real values¶
'i =>                number variables to be real (old value displayed)¶
'winlen,unt!,ob! => see above.¶
  z=CSRLIN¶
  s=POS(0)¶
  a$ = " "¶
  CALL PutReal (i,z,s,winlen)¶
  CALL GetReal (i,a$,z,s,winlen,unt!,ob!)¶
END SUB¶
'¶
SUB FormInputInt (i,winlen,unt!,ob!) STATIC¶
'Enter an indivudal integer value¶
'i =>                number variavles to be read (old value displayed)¶
'winlen,unt!,ob! => see above.¶
  z=CSRLIN¶
  s=POS(0)¶
  a$ = " "¶
  CALL PutReal (i,z,s,winlen)¶
  CALL GetInt (i,a$,z,s,winlen,unt!,ob!)¶
END SUB¶
'¶
SUB FormInputString (s$,winlen) STATIC¶
' String read (e.g. Filename)¶
  a$ = " "¶
  s = POS(0) ¶
  z = CSRLIN¶
  CALL PutString (s$,z,s,winlen)¶
  CALL GetString
(s$,a$,"abcdefghijklmnopqrstuvwxyzdv|_ABCDEFGHIJKLMNOPQRSTUVWXYZDV\1234567890.-
_:/",z,s,winlen)¶
END SUB¶
'¶
Directory:¶
  ' Directory read, or change drive¶
  Status$ = " Status: Directory"+CHR$(0)¶
  CALL SetWindowTitles&(NWBase&,SADD(Status$),0)¶
  ¶
  GOSUB DeleteMenu¶
  a$ = "Active Directory: "+ActDrive$¶
  CALL PrintIt(a$,50,False)¶
  CHDIR ActDrive$¶
  ¶
  RepeatD:¶
    CALL DialogBox("Files",0,False,x1a%,y1a%,x2a%,y2a%,False)¶
    CALL DialogBox("Continue",1,True,x1b%,y1b%,x2b%,y2b%,False)¶
    CALL DialogBox("Chdir",2,False,x1c%,y1c%,x2c%,y2c%,False)¶
  ¶
    CALL DoDialog(n%,1,x1a%,y1a%,x2a%,y2a%,x1b%,y1b%,x2b%,y2b%,x1c%,y1c%,x2c%,y2c%)
¶
```

```
¶
    CLS¶
    IF n% = 0 THEN¶
      FILES¶
      GOSUB Pause¶
      CLS¶
      GOTO RepeatD¶
    END IF¶
    IF n% = 2 THEN¶
      a$ = "Active Directory: "+ActDrive$¶
      CALL PrintIt(a$,50,False)¶
    ¶
      LOCATE 10,1¶
      PRINT "          New Directory: ";¶
      CALL FormInputString (ActDrive$,30!)¶
¶
      CHDIR ActDrive$¶
     ¶
      CLS¶
      GOTO RepeatD¶
    END IF  ¶
  CLS¶
RETURN    ¶
'End of SYSTEM.ASC¶
'¶
```

The WIREMODEL-DRAW.ASC module

```
'WIREMODEL-Draw.ASC¶
'¶
'¶
'  *************************¶
'  *      Wire model       *¶
'  *************************¶
'¶
'¶
SUB Projection(Px%,Py%,x,y,z) STATIC¶
SHARED Sina,Sinb,Sinc,Cosa,Cosb,Cosc,DPH,Hx,Hy,Hz¶
  ' 3D coordinates (x,y,z) to  2D (Px%,Py%) = Screen¶
¶
  x1=(x-Hx)*Cosa+(y-Hy)*Sina   ' Z-Axis rotation¶
  y1=(y-Hy)*Cosa-(x-Hx)*Sina¶
  x2=x1*Cosb+(z-Hz)*Sinb       ' Y-Axis rotation¶
  z2=(z-Hz)*Cosb-x1*Sinb¶
  y3=y1*Cosc+z2*Sinc           ' X-Axis rotation¶
  z3=z2*Cosc-y1*Sinc¶
¶
  IF DPH<>x3 THEN¶
    Px%=FN Xscale((y3*DPH)/(DPH-x2)) -4 ' Intersecting point with projection point
¶
    Py%=FN Yscale((z3*DPH)/(DPH-x2)) -2 ' scaling¶
  ELSE¶
    Px% = FN Xscale(0) -4    ' Subtraction of 4 and 2 based on drawing¶
    Py% = FN Yscale(0) -2    ' in a GIMMEZEROZERO-Window (BASIC-Window)¶
  END IF¶
END SUB ¶
'¶
'¶
DrawPlane:¶
  CALL
Projection(Xp%,Yp%,K(n%,2,0)+K(n%,1,0),K(n%,2,1)+K(n%,1,1),K(n%,2,2)+K(n%,1,2))¶
  CALL Move&(RastPort&,Xp%,Yp%)¶
  CALL Projection(Xp%,Yp%,K(n%,1,0),K(n%,1,1),K(n%,1,2))¶
  CALL Draw&(RastPort&,Xp%,Yp%)¶
  CALL
Projection(Xp%,Yp%,K(n%,3,0)+K(n%,1,0),K(n%,3,1)+K(n%,1,1),K(n%,3,2)+K(n%,1,2))¶
  CALL Draw&(RastPort&,Xp%,Yp%)¶
RETURN¶
'¶
DrawTriangle:  ¶
  CALL Projection(x1%,y1%,K(n%,1,0),K(n%,1,1),K(n%,1,2))¶
  CALL Move&(RastPort&,x1%,y1%)¶
  CALL
Projection(Xp%,Yp%,K(n%,2,0)+K(n%,1,0),K(n%,2,1)+K(n%,1,1),K(n%,2,2)+K(n%,1,2))¶
  CALL Draw&(RastPort&,Xp%,Yp%)¶
  CALL
Projection(Xp%,Yp%,K(n%,3,0)+K(n%,1,0),K(n%,3,1)+K(n%,1,1),K(n%,3,2)+K(n%,1,2))¶
  CALL Draw&(RastPort&,Xp%,Yp%)¶
  CALL Draw&(RastPort&,x1%,y1%)¶
RETURN¶
'¶
```

```
DrawRectangle:¶
  CALL Projection(x1%,y1%,K(n%,1,0),K(n%,1,1),K(n%,1,2))¶
  CALL Move&(RastPort&,x1%,y1%)¶
  CALL
Projection(Xp%,Yp%,K(n%,2,0)+K(n%,1,0),K(n%,2,1)+K(n%,1,1),K(n%,2,2)+K(n%,1,2))¶
  CALL Draw&(RastPort&,Xp%,Yp%)¶
  Dx=K(n%,2,0)+K(n%,3,0)+K(n%,1,0)¶
  Dy=K(n%,2,1)+K(n%,3,1)+K(n%,1,1)¶
  Dz=K(n%,2,2)+K(n%,3,2)+K(n%,1,2)¶
  CALL Projection(Xp%,Yp%,Dx,Dy,Dz)¶
  CALL Draw&(RastPort&,Xp%,Yp%)¶
  CALL
Projection(Xp%,Yp%,K(n%,3,0)+K(n%,1,0),K(n%,3,1)+K(n%,1,1),K(n%,3,2)+K(n%,1,2))¶
  CALL Draw&(RastPort&,Xp%,Yp%)¶
  CALL Draw&(RastPort&,x1%,y1%)¶
RETURN¶
'¶
DrawCircle:¶
  CALL
Projection(Xp%,Yp%,K(n%,1,0)+K(n%,2,0),K(n%,1,1)+K(n%,2,1),K(n%,1,2)+K(n%,2,2))¶
  ' SIN(0) = 0 and COS(0) = 1 goto K(n%,3,..), and K(n%,2,..) takes over¶
  CALL Move&(RastPort&,Xp%,Yp%)¶
  w=Pm2/NumberSegments¶
  D=w¶
  Repeat1:¶
    Dx=K(n%,1,0)+K(n%,2,0)*COS(w)+K(n%,3,0)*SIN(w)¶
    Dy=K(n%,1,1)+K(n%,2,1)*COS(w)+K(n%,3,1)*SIN(w)¶
    Dz=K(n%,1,2)+K(n%,2,2)*COS(w)+K(n%,3,2)*SIN(w)¶
    CALL Projection(Xp%,Yp%,Dx,Dy,Dz)¶
    CALL Draw&(RastPort&,Xp%,Yp%)¶
    w = w+D¶
  IF (w<=Pm2+D/2) THEN GOTO Repeat1:¶
RETURN¶
'¶
DrawCircleSector:¶
  CALL Projection(x1%,y1%,K(n%,1,0),K(n%,1,1),K(n%,1,2))¶
  w=K(n%,5,0)¶
  Dx=K(n%,1,0)+K(n%,2,0)*COS(w)+K(n%,3,0)*SIN(w)¶
  Dy=K(n%,1,1)+K(n%,2,1)*COS(w)+K(n%,3,1)*SIN(w)¶
  Dz=K(n%,1,2)+K(n%,2,2)*COS(w)+K(n%,3,2)*SIN(w)¶
  CALL Projection(Xp%,Yp%,Dx,Dy,Dz)¶
  CALL Move&(RastPort&,x1%,y1%)¶
  CALL Draw&(RastPort&,Xp%,Yp%)¶
  D=Pm2/NumberSegments¶
  WHILE w<K(n%,5,1)¶
    w = w+D¶
    IF w>K(n%,5,1) THEN¶
      w=K(n%,5,1)¶
    END IF¶
    Dx=K(n%,1,0)+K(n%,2,0)*COS(w)+K(n%,3,0)*SIN(w)¶
    Dy=K(n%,1,1)+K(n%,2,1)*COS(w)+K(n%,3,1)*SIN(w)¶
    Dz=K(n%,1,2)+K(n%,2,2)*COS(w)+K(n%,3,2)*SIN(w)¶
    CALL Projection(Xp%,Yp%,Dx,Dy,Dz)¶
    CALL Draw&(RastPort&,Xp%,Yp%)¶
  WEND¶
  CALL Draw&(RastPort&,x1%,y1%)¶
RETURN¶
'¶
DrawCircleRing:¶
  w=K(n%,5,0)¶
```

```
  Dx=K(n%,1,0)+(K(n%,2,0)*COS(w)+K(n%,3,0)*SIN(w))*K(n%,4,0)¶
  Dy=K(n%,1,1)+(K(n%,2,1)*COS(w)+K(n%,3,1)*SIN(w))*K(n%,4,0)¶
  Dz=K(n%,1,2)+(K(n%,2,2)*COS(w)+K(n%,3,2)*SIN(w))*K(n%,4,0)¶
  CALL Projection(Xua%,Yua%,Dx,Dy,Dz)¶
  Dx=K(n%,1,0)+(K(n%,2,0)*COS(w)+K(n%,3,0)*SIN(w))*K(n%,4,1)¶
  Dy=K(n%,1,1)+(K(n%,2,1)*COS(w)+K(n%,3,1)*SIN(w))*K(n%,4,1)¶
  Dz=K(n%,1,2)+(K(n%,2,2)*COS(w)+K(n%,3,2)*SIN(w))*K(n%,4,1)¶
  CALL Projection(Xoa%,Yoa%,Dx,Dy,Dz)¶
  CALL Move&(RastPort&,Xua%,Yua%)¶
  CALL Draw&(RastPort&,Xoa%,Yoa%)¶
  D=Pm2/NumberSegments¶
  WHILE w<K(n%,5,1)¶
    w = w+D¶
    IF w>K(n%,5,1) THEN¶
      w=K(n%,5,1)¶
    END IF¶
    Dx=K(n%,1,0)+(K(n%,2,0)*COS(w)+K(n%,3,0)*SIN(w))*K(n%,4,0)¶
    Dy=K(n%,1,1)+(K(n%,2,1)*COS(w)+K(n%,3,1)*SIN(w))*K(n%,4,0)¶
    Dz=K(n%,1,2)+(K(n%,2,2)*COS(w)+K(n%,3,2)*SIN(w))*K(n%,4,0)¶
    CALL Projection(Xu%,Yu%,Dx,Dy,Dz)¶
    Dx=K(n%,1,0)+(K(n%,2,0)*COS(w)+K(n%,3,0)*SIN(w))*K(n%,4,1)¶
    Dy=K(n%,1,1)+(K(n%,2,1)*COS(w)+K(n%,3,1)*SIN(w))*K(n%,4,1)¶
    Dz=K(n%,1,2)+(K(n%,2,2)*COS(w)+K(n%,3,2)*SIN(w))*K(n%,4,1)¶
    CALL Projection(Xp%,Yp%,Dx,Dy,Dz)¶
    CALL Move&(RastPort&,Xua%,Yua%)¶
    CALL Draw&(RastPort&,Xu%,Yu%)¶
    CALL Move&(RastPort&,Xp%,Yp%)¶
    CALL Draw&(RastPort&,Xoa%,Yoa%)¶
    Xua%=Xu%¶
    Yua%=Yu%¶
    Xoa%=Xp%¶
    Yoa%=Yp%¶
  WEND¶
  CALL Move&(RastPort&,Xua%,Yua%)¶
  CALL Draw&(RastPort&,Xoa%,Yoa%)¶
RETURN¶
'¶
DrawSphere:¶
  D=Pm2/NumberSegments¶
  FOR w1=-Pd2+D TO Pd2-D/2 STEP D¶
    Dx=K(n%,1,0)¶
    Dy=K(n%,1,1)+K(n%,2,0)*COS(w1)¶
    Dz=K(n%,1,2)+K(n%,2,0)*SIN(w1)¶
    CALL Projection(Xp%,Yp%,Dx,Dy,Dz)¶
    CALL Move&(RastPort&,Xp%,Yp%)¶
    FOR w2=D TO Pm2+D/2 STEP D¶
      Dx=K(n%,1,0)+K(n%,2,0)*SIN(w2)*COS(w1)¶
      Dy=K(n%,1,1)+K(n%,2,0)*COS(w2)*COS(w1)¶
      Dz=K(n%,1,2)+K(n%,2,0)*SIN(w1)¶
      CALL Projection(Xp%,Yp%,Dx,Dy,Dz)¶
      CALL Draw&(RastPort&,Xp%,Yp%)¶
    NEXT w2¶
  NEXT w1¶
  FOR w1=-Pd2+D TO Pd2-D/2 STEP D¶
    Dy=K(n%,1,1)¶
    Dz=K(n%,1,2)+K(n%,2,0)*COS(w1)¶
    Dx=K(n%,1,0)+K(n%,2,0)*SIN(w1)¶
    CALL Projection(Xp%,Yp%,Dx,Dy,Dz)¶
    CALL Move&(RastPort&,Xp%,Yp%)¶
    FOR w2=D TO Pm2+D/2 STEP D¶
```

```
      Dy=K(n%,1,1)+K(n%,2,0)*SIN(w2)*COS(w1)¶
      Dz=K(n%,1,2)+K(n%,2,0)*COS(w2)*COS(w1)¶
      Dx=K(n%,1,0)+K(n%,2,0)*SIN(w1)¶
      CALL Projection(Xp%,Yp%,Dx,Dy,Dz)¶
      CALL Draw&(RastPort&,Xp%,Yp%)¶
    NEXT w2¶
  NEXT w1¶
RETURN¶
'¶
DrawCylinder:¶
  Dx=K(n%,1,0)+K(n%,2,0)¶
  Dy=K(n%,1,1)+K(n%,2,1)¶
  Dz=K(n%,1,2)+K(n%,2,2)¶
  CALL Projection(Xua%,Yua%,Dx,Dy,Dz)¶
  Dx=K(n%,1,0)+K(n%,2,0)+K(n%,4,0)¶
  Dy=K(n%,1,1)+K(n%,2,1)+K(n%,4,1)¶
  Dz=K(n%,1,2)+K(n%,2,2)+K(n%,4,2)¶
  CALL Projection(Xoa%,Yoa%,Dx,Dy,Dz)¶
  D=Pm2/NumberSegments¶
  FOR w=D TO Pm2+D/2 STEP D¶
    Dx=K(n%,1,0)+K(n%,2,0)*COS(w)+K(n%,3,0)*SIN(w)¶
    Dy=K(n%,1,1)+K(n%,2,1)*COS(w)+K(n%,3,1)*SIN(w)¶
    Dz=K(n%,1,2)+K(n%,2,2)*COS(w)+K(n%,3,2)*SIN(w)¶
    CALL Projection(Xu%,Yu%,Dx,Dy,Dz)¶
    Dx=K(n%,1,0)+K(n%,2,0)*COS(w)+K(n%,3,0)*SIN(w)+K(n%,4,0)¶
    Dy=K(n%,1,1)+K(n%,2,1)*COS(w)+K(n%,3,1)*SIN(w)+K(n%,4,1)¶
    Dz=K(n%,1,2)+K(n%,2,2)*COS(w)+K(n%,3,2)*SIN(w)+K(n%,4,2)¶
    CALL Projection(Xp%,Yp%,Dx,Dy,Dz)¶
    CALL Move&(RastPort&,Xua%,Yua%)¶
    CALL Draw&(RastPort&,Xu%,Yu%)¶
    CALL Draw&(RastPort&,Xp%,Yp%)¶
    CALL Draw&(RastPort&,Xoa%,Yoa%)¶
    Xua%=Xu%¶
    Yua%=Yu%¶
    Xoa%=Xp%¶
    Yoa%=Yp%¶
  NEXT w¶
RETURN¶
'¶
DrawCylinderSegm:¶
  w=K(n%,5,0)¶
  Dx=K(n%,1,0)+K(n%,2,0)*COS(w)+K(n%,3,0)*SIN(w)¶
  Dy=K(n%,1,1)+K(n%,2,1)*COS(w)+K(n%,3,1)*SIN(w)¶
  Dz=K(n%,1,2)+K(n%,2,2)*COS(w)+K(n%,3,2)*SIN(w)¶
  CALL Projection(Xua%,Yua%,Dx,Dy,Dz)¶
  Dx=K(n%,1,0)+K(n%,2,0)*COS(w)+K(n%,3,0)*SIN(w)+K(n%,4,0)¶
  Dy=K(n%,1,1)+K(n%,2,1)*COS(w)+K(n%,3,1)*SIN(w)+K(n%,4,1)¶
  Dz=K(n%,1,2)+K(n%,2,2)*COS(w)+K(n%,3,2)*SIN(w)+K(n%,4,2)¶
  CALL Projection(Xoa%,Yoa%,Dx,Dy,Dz)¶
  CALL Move&(RastPort&,Xua%,Yua%)¶
  CALL Draw&(RastPort&,Xoa%,Yoa%)¶
  D=Pm2/NumberSegments¶
  WHILE w<K(n%,5,1)¶
    w = w+D¶
    IF w>K(n%,5,1) THEN¶
      w=K(n%,5,1)¶
    END IF¶
    Dx=K(n%,1,0)+K(n%,2,0)*COS(w)+K(n%,3,0)*SIN(w)¶
    Dy=K(n%,1,1)+K(n%,2,1)*COS(w)+K(n%,3,1)*SIN(w)¶
    Dz=K(n%,1,2)+K(n%,2,2)*COS(w)+K(n%,3,2)*SIN(w)¶
```

```
    CALL Projection(Xu%,Yu%,Dx,Dy,Dz)¶
    Dx=K(n%,1,0)+K(n%,2,0)*COS(w)+K(n%,3,0)*SIN(w)+K(n%,4,0)¶
    Dy=K(n%,1,1)+K(n%,2,1)*COS(w)+K(n%,3,1)*SIN(w)+K(n%,4,1)¶
    Dz=K(n%,1,2)+K(n%,2,2)*COS(w)+K(n%,3,2)*SIN(w)+K(n%,4,2)¶
    CALL Projection(Xp%,Yp%,Dx,Dy,Dz)¶
    CALL Move&(RastPort&,Xua%,Yua%)¶
    CALL Draw&(RastPort&,Xu%,Yu%)¶
    CALL Draw&(RastPort&,Xp%,Yp%)¶
    CALL Draw&(RastPort&,Xoa%,Yoa%)¶
    Xua%=Xu%¶
    Yua%=Yu%¶
    Xoa%=Xp%¶
    Yoa%=Yp%¶
  WEND¶
RETURN¶
'¶
DrawCone:¶
  CALL
Projection(x1%,y1%,K(n%,1,0)+K(n%,4,0),K(n%,1,1)+K(n%,4,1),K(n%,1,2)+K(n%,4,2))¶
  CALL
Projection(Xp%,Yp%,K(n%,1,0)+K(n%,2,0),K(n%,1,1)+K(n%,2,1),K(n%,1,2)+K(n%,2,2))¶
  CALL Move&(RastPort&,Xp%,Yp%)¶
  D=Pm2/NumberSegments¶
  FOR w=D TO Pm2+D/2 STEP D¶
    Dx=K(n%,1,0)+K(n%,2,0)*COS(w)+K(n%,3,0)*SIN(w)¶
    Dy=K(n%,1,1)+K(n%,2,1)*COS(w)+K(n%,3,1)*SIN(w)¶
    Dz=K(n%,1,2)+K(n%,2,2)*COS(w)+K(n%,3,2)*SIN(w)¶
    CALL Projection(Xp%,Yp%,Dx,Dy,Dz)¶
    CALL Draw&(RastPort&,Xp%,Yp%)¶
    CALL Move&(RastPort&,x1%,y1%)¶
    CALL Draw&(RastPort&,Xp%,Yp%)¶
  NEXT w¶
RETURN¶
'¶
DrawEllipsoid:¶
  D=Pm2/NumberSegments¶
  FOR w1=-Pd2+D TO Pd2-D/2 STEP D¶
    Dx=K(n%,1,0)+K(n%,2,0)*COS(w1)+K(n%,4,0)*SIN(w1)¶
    Dy=K(n%,1,1)+K(n%,2,1)*COS(w1)+K(n%,4,1)*SIN(w1)¶
    Dz=K(n%,1,2)+K(n%,2,2)*COS(w1)+K(n%,4,2)*SIN(w1)¶
    CALL Projection(Xp%,Yp%,Dx,Dy,Dz)¶
    CALL Move&(RastPort&,Xp%,Yp%)¶
    FOR w2=D TO Pm2+D/2 STEP D¶

Dx=K(n%,1,0)+K(n%,2,0)*COS(w1)*COS(w2)+K(n%,3,0)*COS(w1)*SIN(w2)+K(n%,4,0)*SIN(w1)¶

Dy=K(n%,1,1)+K(n%,2,1)*COS(w1)*COS(w2)+K(n%,3,1)*COS(w1)*SIN(w2)+K(n%,4,1)*SIN(w1)¶


Dz=K(n%,1,2)+K(n%,2,2)*COS(w1)*COS(w2)+K(n%,3,2)*COS(w1)*SIN(w2)+K(n%,4,2)*SIN(w1)¶
      CALL Projection(Xp%,Yp%,Dx,Dy,Dz)¶
      CALL Draw&(RastPort&,Xp%,Yp%)¶
    NEXT w2¶
  NEXT w1¶
  FOR w1=-Pd2+D TO Pd2-D/2 STEP D¶
    Dx=K(n%,1,0)+K(n%,2,0)*COS(w1)+K(n%,3,0)*SIN(w1)¶
    Dy=K(n%,1,1)+K(n%,2,1)*COS(w1)+K(n%,3,1)*SIN(w1)¶
    Dz=K(n%,1,2)+K(n%,2,2)*COS(w1)+K(n%,3,2)*SIN(w1)¶
    CALL Projection(Xp%,Yp%,Dx,Dy,Dz)¶
    CALL Move&(RastPort&,Xp%,Yp%)¶
```

```
    FOR w2=D TO Pm2+D/2 STEP D¶

Dx=K(n%,1,0)+K(n%,2,0)*COS(w1)*COS(w2)+K(n%,4,0)*COS(w1)*SIN(w2)+K(n%,3,0)*SIN(w1)¶

Dy=K(n%,1,1)+K(n%,2,1)*COS(w1)*COS(w2)+K(n%,4,1)*COS(w1)*SIN(w2)+K(n%,3,1)*SIN(w1)¶

Dz=K(n%,1,2)+K(n%,2,2)*COS(w1)*COS(w2)+K(n%,4,2)*COS(w1)*SIN(w2)+K(n%,3,2)*SIN(w1)¶
      CALL Projection(Xp%,Yp%,Dx,Dy,Dz)¶
      CALL Draw&(RastPort&,Xp%,Yp%)¶
    NEXT w2¶
  NEXT w1¶
RETURN¶
'¶
'¶
DrawAll:¶
  ' Draw routine for calling each figure¶
  FOR n%=1 TO NumberK¶
    IF K(n%,0,0)=0 THEN¶
      GOSUB DrawPlane¶
    END IF¶
    IF K(n%,0,0)=1 THEN¶
      GOSUB DrawTriangle¶
    END IF¶
    IF K(n%,0,0)=2 THEN¶
      GOSUB DrawRectangle¶
    END IF¶
    IF K(n%,0,0)=3 THEN¶
      GOSUB DrawCircle¶
    END IF¶
    IF K(n%,0,0)=4 THEN¶
      GOSUB DrawCircleSector¶
    END IF¶
    IF K(n%,0,0)=5 THEN¶
      GOSUB DrawCircleRing¶
    END IF¶
    IF K(n%,0,0)=10 THEN¶
      GOSUB DrawSphere¶
    END IF¶
    IF K(n%,0,0)=20 THEN¶
      GOSUB DrawCylinder¶
    END IF¶
    IF K(n%,0,0)=21 THEN¶
      GOSUB DrawCylinderSegm¶
    END IF¶
    IF K(n%,0,0)=22 THEN¶
      GOSUB DrawCone¶
    END IF¶
    IF K(n%,0,0)=24 THEN¶
      GOSUB DrawEllipsoid¶
    END IF¶
  NEXT n%¶
RETURN¶
'¶
DrawNew:¶
  IF (Hg = False) AND (Newone! = True) THEN  ' no Background¶
    CALL SetRast&(RastPort&,0)              ' but new drawing¶
  END IF                                    ' => clear screen¶
  ¶
  CALL Scron  ¶
```

```
¶
  IF (Newone! = True) OR (Hg = True) THEN    ' Background and New drawing¶
    GOSUB DeleteMenu¶
    RetRast& = RastPort&              ' reserve RastPort ¶
    RastPort& = WINDOW(8)             ' In Window-RastPort (GIMMEZERO Window!)¶
    CALL SetAPen&(RastPort&,1)        ' the new Screens¶
    GOSUB DrawAll                   ' draw (because of Clipping)¶
    RastPort& = RetRast&¶
    BEEP¶
  END IF¶
  ¶
  IF WaitFlg! = True THEN             ' wait for mouse or key press¶
     GOSUB Pause                      ¶
     CALL Scroff¶
  END IF¶
¶
  IF (Newone! = True) OR (Hg = True) THEN¶
    Newone! = False                       ' Redraw picture ¶
    Hg = False                         ' and "paint over"¶
    GOSUB MakeMenu                     ' background ¶
  END IF¶
RETURN¶
'¶
HowManyCorners:¶
  Status$ = " Status: Draw angles at n-corners"+CHR$(0)¶
  CALL SetWindowTitles&(NWBase&,SADD(Status$),0)¶
¶
  GOSUB DeleteMenu¶
¶
  LOCATE 10,1¶
  PRINT "     How many corners : ";¶
  CALL FormInputInt (NumberSegments,30!,0!,200!)¶
  Newone! = True¶
  CLS¶
  GOSUB MakeMenu¶
RETURN¶
'¶
Enlargement:¶
  Status$ = " Status: Enlarge screen segment"+CHR$(0)¶
  CALL SetWindowTitles&(NWBase&,SADD(Status$),0)¶
  ¶
  GOSUB DeleteMenu¶
¶
  CALL DialogBox("Proportional",0,True,x1a%,y1a%,x2a%,y2a%,False)¶
  CALL DialogBox("Distort",2,False,x1b%,y1b%,x2b%,y2b%,False)¶
¶
  CALL DoDialog(n%,0,x1a%,y1a%,x2a%,y2a%,x1b%,y1b%,x2b%,y2b%,-1,-1,-1,-1)¶
  CLS¶
¶
  IF n%=0 THEN      ¶
    LOCATE 10,1¶
    PRINT " Enlargement Factor: ";¶
    a=1¶
    CALL FormInput (a,30!,.1,100!)¶
     ¶
    CLS   ¶
    Picturewidth=a*FactorX¶
    Pictureheight=a*FactorY¶
    Picturex=RasterW2%/Picturewidth¶
    Picturey=RasterH2%/Pictureheight¶
```

```
  ELSE¶
    WaitFlg! = False¶
    GOSUB DrawNew¶
    CALL Rubberbox (Sx%,Sy%,Widthe%,Heighte%,False)¶
    Picturewidth=RasterW%/Widthe% * FactorX¶
    Pictureheight=RasterH%/Heighte% * FactorY¶
    Picturex=(RasterW2%-Sx%)/FactorX¶
    Picturey=(RasterH2%-Sy%)/FactorY ¶
  END IF¶
  Newone! = True¶
  WaitFlg! = True¶
  GOSUB DrawNew¶
RETURN¶
'END of Wire-model.asc¶
'¶
```

The WIREMODEL-INPUT.ASC module

```
'WIREMODEL-INPUT.ASC
'  ************************¶
'  *   Input-Routine      *¶
'  ************************¶
'¶
Initial:¶
  WHILE Alpha<0¶
     Alpha = Alpha + Pm2¶
  WEND¶
  WHILE Beta<0¶
     Beta = Beta + Pm2¶
  WEND¶
  WHILE Gamma<0¶
     Gamma = Gamma + Pm2¶
  WEND¶
  WHILE Alpha>Pm2¶
     Alpha = Alpha - Pm2¶
  WEND¶
  WHILE Beta>Pm2¶
     Beta = Beta - Pm2¶
  WEND¶
  WHILE Gamma>Pm2¶
     Gamma = Gamma - Pm2¶
  WEND¶
  Sina=SIN(Alpha)¶
  Cosa=COS(Alpha)¶
  Sinb=SIN(Beta)¶
  Cosb=COS(Beta)¶
  Sinc=SIN(Gamma)¶
  Cosc=COS(Gamma)¶
¶
  Px=Hx+DPH*Cosa*Cosb   ' Projection point based on the ¶
  Py=Hy+DPH*Sina*Cosb   ' main point and the spacings¶
  Pz=Hz+DPH*Sinb        ' DPH and Alpha, Beta and Gamma¶
RETURN                         ¶
'¶
InitialP:¶
  D1=SQR((Px-Hx)^2+(Py-Hy)^2)¶
  DPH=SQR((Px-Hx)^2+(Py-Hy)^2+(Pz-Hz)^2)        ¶
¶
  IF D1=0 THEN¶
    Sina=0¶
    Cosa=1¶
  ELSE¶
    Sina=(Py-Hy)/D1¶
    Cosa=(Px-Hx)/D1¶
  END IF¶
¶
  IF DPH=0 THEN¶
    Sinb=0¶
    Cosb=1¶
  ELSE¶
    Sinb=(Pz-Hz)/DPH¶
```

```
    Cosb=D1/DPH¶
  END IF¶
  ¶
  Sinc=0                              ' Z-Axis angle not¶
  Cosc=1                              ' solely determined here¶
¶
  IF Cosa=0 THEN¶
    Alpha=Pd2¶
  ELSE¶
    Alpha=ATN(Sina/Cosa)              ' compute cosinemand sine¶
  END IF                              ' angle¶
¶
  IF Cosa<0 THEN¶
    Alpha = Alpha+Pi¶
  END IF¶
¶
  IF Cosb=0 THEN¶
    Beta=Pd2¶
  ELSE¶
    Beta=ATN(Sinb/Cosb)¶
  END IF¶
¶
  IF Cosb<0 THEN¶
    Beta = Beta + Pi¶
  END IF¶
¶
  Gamma=0¶
RETURN¶
'¶
InputP:¶
  Status$ = " Status: Projection point"+CHR$(0)¶
  CALL SetWindowTitles&(NWBase&,SADD(Status$),0)¶
¶
  GOSUB DeleteMenu¶
¶
  LOCATE 10,1¶
  PRINT "        Projection point: "¶
  ¶
  LOCATE 12,1¶
  PRINT "        Px = ";¶
  CALL FormInput (Px,30!,-1E+14,1E+14)¶
¶
  LOCATE 13,1¶
  PRINT "        Py = ";¶
  CALL FormInput (Py,30!,-1E+14,1E+14)¶
¶
  LOCATE 14,1¶
  PRINT "        Pz = ";¶
  CALL FormInput (Pz,30!,-1E+14,1E+14)¶
  ¶
  GOSUB InitialP¶
  Newone! = True¶
  CLS¶
  GOSUB MakeMenu ¶
RETURN¶
'¶
'¶
InputH:¶
  Status$ = " Status: Main point"+CHR$(0)¶
  CALL SetWindowTitles&(NWBase&,SADD(Status$),0)¶
```

```
¶
  GOSUB DeleteMenu¶
¶
  LOCATE 10,1¶
  PRINT "        Main point: "¶
¶
  LOCATE 12,1¶
  PRINT "     Hx = ";¶
  CALL FormInput (Hx,30!,-1E+14,1E+14)¶
¶
  LOCATE 13,1¶
  PRINT "     Hy = ";¶
  CALL FormInput (Hy,30!,-1E+14,1E+14)¶
¶
  LOCATE 14,1¶
  PRINT "     Hz = ";¶
  CALL FormInput (Hz,30!,-1E+14,1E+14)¶
¶
  GOSUB Initial¶
  Newone! = True¶
  CLS¶
  GOSUB MakeMenu¶
RETURN¶
'¶
InputDPH:¶
  Status$ = " Status: Spacing"+CHR$(0)¶
  CALL SetWindowTitles&(NWBase&,SADD(Status$),0)¶
  ¶
  GOSUB DeleteMenu¶
  ¶
  LOCATE 10,1¶
  PRINT "     Spacing of projection surface = ";¶
  CALL FormInput (DPH,30!,-1E+14,1E+14)¶
¶
  GOSUB Initial¶
  Newone! = True¶
  CLS¶
  GOSUB MakeMenu¶
RETURN¶
'¶
InputAngle:¶
  Status$ = " Status: Enter angle of rotation"+CHR$(0)¶
  CALL SetWindowTitles&(NWBase&,SADD(Status$),0)¶
  ¶
  GOSUB DeleteMenu¶
¶
  a=FN Deg(Alpha)¶
  b=FN Deg(Beta)¶
  c=FN Deg(Gamma)¶
  ¶
  LOCATE 10,1¶
  PRINT "     Angle of rotation (a,_,c): "¶
¶
  LOCATE 12,1¶
  PRINT "     Alpha (Z-Axis) = ";¶
  CALL FormInput (a,30!,0!,360!)¶
¶
  LOCATE 13,1¶
  PRINT "     Beta  (Y-Axis) = ";¶
  CALL FormInput (b,30!,0!,360!)¶
```

```
¶
  LOCATE 14,1¶
  PRINT "     Gamma (X-Axis) = ";¶
  CALL FormInput (c,30!,0!,360!)¶
¶
  Alpha=FN Rad(a)¶
  Beta=FN Rad(b)¶
  Gamma=FN Rad(c)¶
¶
  GOSUB Initial¶
  Newone! = True¶
  CLS¶
  GOSUB MakeMenu¶
RETURN¶
'End of wiremodel-Input.asc¶
'¶
```

The SHADOW-INIT.ASC module

```
'SHADOW-INIT.ASC¶
'  *************************************¶
'  *      Shadows  initialization       *¶
'  *************************************¶
'¶
InitParameters:¶
  Status$ = " Status: Parameter initialization"+CHR$(0)¶
  CALL SetWindowTitles&(NWBase&,SADD(Status$),0)¶
 ¶
  GOSUB DeleteMenu¶
¶
  CALL PrintIt("Shadow window?",130,False)¶
  CALL DialogBox("All",0,True,x1a%,y1a%,x2a%,y2a%,False)¶
  CALL DialogBox("Section",1,False,x1b%,y1b%,x2b%,y2b%,False)¶
  CALL DialogBox("YA - YE",2,False,x1c%,y1c%,x2c%,y2c%,False)¶
        ¶
  CALL DoDialog(n%,0,x1a%,y1a%,x2a%,y2a%,x1b%,y1b%,x2b%,y2c%,x1c%,y1c%,x2c%,y2c%)¶
  CLS¶
  ¶
  IF n% = 0 THEN¶
    XStart% = 0¶
    YStart% = 0¶
    XEnd% = RasterW1%¶
    Yend% = RasterH1%¶
  END IF¶
¶
  IF n% = 1 THEN¶
    CALL Rubberbox(Sx%,Sy%,Widthe%,Heighte%,True)¶
      ¶
    XStart%=Sx%¶
    YStart%=Sy%¶
    XEnd%=Sx%+Widthe%¶
    Yend%=Sy%+Heighte%¶
  END IF¶
  ¶
  IF n% = 2 THEN¶
    CALL Scron¶
¶
    CALL SetDrMd&(RastPort&,2)     ¶
¶
    XStart% = 0¶
    XEnd% = RasterW1%¶
    ¶
    CALL EmptyBuffers¶
    OldY% = -1¶
    Flag = 0¶
    ¶
    WHILE (MOUSE(0) = 0)¶
      y% = PEEKW(NWScreen&+16)¶
      IF y% <> OldY% THEN¶
        CALL Move&(RastPort&,0,y%)¶
        CALL Draw&(RastPort&,RasterW1%,y%)¶
        IF Flag <> 0 THEN¶
```

```
          CALL Move&(RastPort&,0,OldY%)¶
          CALL Draw&(RastPort&,RasterW1%,OldY%)¶
        END IF¶
        Flag = 1¶
        OldY% = y%¶
      END IF¶
    WEND¶
    ¶
    YStart% = y%¶
¶
    OldY% = -1¶
    Flag = 0¶
    ¶
    WHILE (MOUSE(0) <> 0)¶
      y% = PEEKW(NWScreen&+16)¶
      IF y% <> OldY% THEN¶
        CALL Move&(RastPort&,0,y%)¶
        CALL Draw&(RastPort&,RasterW1%,y%)¶
        IF Flag <> 0 THEN¶
          CALL Move&(RastPort&,0,OldY%)¶
          CALL Draw&(RastPort&,RasterW1%,OldY%)¶
        END IF¶
        Flag = 1¶
        OldY% = y%¶
      END IF¶
    WEND¶
¶
    Yend% = y%¶
    ¶
    IF YStart% > Yend% THEN SWAP YStart%,Yend%¶
¶
    CALL Move&(RastPort&,0,YStart%)¶
    CALL Draw&(RastPort&,RasterW1%,YStart%)¶
¶
    CALL Move&(RastPort&,0,Yend%)¶
    CALL Draw&(RastPort&,RasterW1%,Yend%)¶
    ¶
    CALL SetDrMd&(RastPort&,1)      ¶
¶
    CALL Scroff¶
  END IF¶
  ¶
  LOCATE 2,1¶
  PRINT "     Xstart = ";XStart%;", Xend = ";XEnd%¶
  PRINT "     Ystart = ";YStart%;", Yend = ";Yend%¶
¶
  LOCATE 6,1¶
  PRINT "    Position of light source :"¶
  ¶
  LOCATE 8,1¶
  PRINT "     Qx = ";¶
  CALL FormInput (Qx,30!,-1E+14,1E+14)¶
¶
  LOCATE 9,1¶
  PRINT "     Qy = ";¶
  CALL FormInput (Qy,30!,-1E+14,1E+14)¶
¶
  LOCATE 10,1¶
  PRINT "     Qz = ";¶
  CALL FormInput (Qz,30!,-1E+14,1E+14)¶
```

```
  ¶
  LOCATE 13,1¶
  PRINT "    Color of light source"¶
  ¶
  LOCATE 15,1¶
  PRINT "     red-intensity (0..1)  = ";¶
  CALL FormInput (Qh.r,30!,0!,1!)¶
  LOCATE 16,1¶
  PRINT "     green-intensity (0..1) = ";¶
  CALL FormInput (Qh.g,30!,0!,1!)¶
  LOCATE 17,1¶
  PRINT "     blue-intensity (0..1) = ";¶
  CALL FormInput (Qh.b,30!,0!,1!)¶
¶
  LOCATE 19,1¶
  PRINT "    Pixel width : ";¶
  a = BoxW%¶
  CALL FormInputInt (a,30!,1!,CSNG(RasterW1%))¶
  BoxW% = a¶
¶
  LOCATE 20,1¶
  PRINT "    pixel height  : ";¶
  a = BoxH%¶
  CALL FormInputInt (a,30!,1!,CSNG(RasterH1%))¶
  BoxH% = a¶
¶
' CALL PrintIt("Which pattern?",130,False)¶
' CALL DialogBox("Standard",0,True,x1a%,y1a%,x2a%,y2a%,False)¶
' CALL DialogBox("Extended",2,False,x1b%,y1b%,x2b%,y2b%,False)¶
'¶
' CALL EmptyBuffers¶
' CALL DoDialog(PatternArt%,0,x1a%,y1a%,x2a%,y2a%,-1,-1,-1,-
' PatternArt% = PatternArt% AND 1¶
  ¶
  CLS¶
  GOSUB MakeMenu¶
RETURN¶
'¶
'¶
SUB Transform(Xt,Yt,Zt,x,y,z,n%) STATIC¶
SHARED K(),Help()¶
  ' => (xt,yt,zt) = transformation vector  base k(n%)¶
¶
  Xt=FN Det(x-K(n%,1,0),K(n%,3,0),K(n%,4,0),y-K(n%,1,1),K(n%,3,1),K(n%,4,1),z-
K(n%,1,2),K(n%,3,2),K(n%,4,2))/Help(n%,0)¶
  Yt=FN Det(K(n%,2,0),x-K(n%,1,0),K(n%,4,0),K(n%,2,1),y-
K(n%,1,1),K(n%,4,1),K(n%,2,2),z-K(n%,1,2),K(n%,4,2))/Help(n%,0)¶
  Zt=FN Det(K(n%,2,0),K(n%,3,0),x-K(n%,1,0),K(n%,2,1),K(n%,3,1),y-
K(n%,1,1),K(n%,2,2),K(n%,3,2),z-K(n%,1,2))/Help(n%,0)¶
END SUB¶
'¶
InitShadows:¶
  ' Write as much as was computed previously into the help array¶
  ERASE Help¶
  DIM Help(NumberK,21)¶
  ¶
  FOR n%=1 TO NumberK¶
    IF K(n%,0,0)<=9 THEN¶
      ' Triangle, Rectangle or Circle => Help(n,0..2) = normal vector on surface¶
      ' Help(n,3..5) = 2*2-Determinante for x,y,z¶
```

```
      Nx=K(n%,2,1)*K(n%,3,2)-K(n%,2,2)*K(n%,3,1)¶
      Ny=K(n%,2,2)*K(n%,3,0)-K(n%,2,0)*K(n%,3,2)¶
      Nz=K(n%,2,0)*K(n%,3,1)-K(n%,2,1)*K(n%,3,0)¶
      IF FN CosinAngle(Nx,Ny,Nz,Px-K(n%,1,0),Py-K(n%,1,1),Pz-K(n%,1,2))<0 THEN¶
        ' => Normal vector points to Projection point¶
        Nx=-Nx¶
        Ny=-Ny¶
        Nz=-Nz¶
      END IF¶
      Nl=SQR(Nx*Nx+Ny*Ny+Nz*Nz)¶
      Nx = Nx/Nl¶
      Ny = Ny/Nl¶
      Nz = Nz/Nl¶
¶
      Help(n%,0)=Nx¶
      Help(n%,1)=Ny¶
      Help(n%,2)=Nz¶
      Help(n%,3)=K(n%,2,1)*K(n%,3,2)-K(n%,3,1)*K(n%,2,2)¶
      Help(n%,4)=K(n%,2,0)*K(n%,3,2)-K(n%,3,0)*K(n%,2,2)¶
      Help(n%,5)=K(n%,2,0)*K(n%,3,1)-K(n%,3,0)*K(n%,2,1)¶
    END IF¶
    IF K(n%,0,0)>=20 THEN¶
      ' Help(n,0)=Names determinant, 1-6=for Normal vector cylinder, 7=length
(n,4,x)¶
      ' 10-12=transform Projection point¶
      ' 13-21=2*2-Determinantes for P/R-Transformation¶
      Help(n%,0)=FN
Det(K(n%,2,0),K(n%,3,0),K(n%,4,0),K(n%,2,1),K(n%,3,1),K(n%,4,1),K(n%,2,2),K(n%,3,2
),K(n%,4,2))¶
      IF Help(n%,0)=0 THEN¶
        a$="The basis of object "+STR$(n%)+" is no basis"¶
        CALL PrintIt(a$,130,False)¶
        CALL DialogBox("Pitch",1,True,x1a%,y1a%,x2a%,y2a%,False)¶
        ¶
        CALL DoDialog(n%,1,-1,-1,-1,-1,x1a%,y1a%,x2a%,y2a%,-1,-1,-1,-1)¶
        GOSUB CloseIt¶
        RUN ¶
      END IF¶
      a=K(n%,2,0)^2+K(n%,2,1)^2+K(n%,2,2)^2¶
      b=K(n%,3,0)^2+K(n%,3,1)^2+K(n%,3,2)^2¶
      IF K(n%,0,0)>=24 THEN¶
        c=K(n%,4,0)^2+K(n%,4,1)^2+K(n%,4,2)^2¶
        Help(n%,1)=b*c*K(n%,2,0)¶
        Help(n%,2)=b*c*K(n%,2,1)¶
        Help(n%,3)=b*c*K(n%,2,2)¶
        Help(n%,4)=a*c*K(n%,3,0)¶
        Help(n%,5)=a*c*K(n%,3,1)¶
        Help(n%,6)=a*c*K(n%,3,2)¶
        Help(n%,7)=a*b*K(n%,4,0)¶
        Help(n%,8)=a*b*K(n%,4,1)¶
        Help(n%,9)=a*b*K(n%,4,2)¶
      ELSE¶
        Help(n%,1)=a*K(n%,3,0)¶
        Help(n%,2)=a*K(n%,3,1)¶
        Help(n%,3)=a*K(n%,3,2)¶
        Help(n%,4)=b*K(n%,2,0)¶
        Help(n%,5)=b*K(n%,2,1)¶
        Help(n%,6)=b*K(n%,2,2)¶
        Help(n%,7)=SQR(K(n%,4,0)^2+K(n%,4,1)^2+K(n%,4,2)^2)¶
      END IF¶
```

```
      CALL Transform(Xt,Yt,Zt,Px,Py,Pz,n%)¶
      Help(n%,10)=Xt¶
      Help(n%,11)=Yt¶
      Help(n%,12)=Zt¶
      Help(n%,13)=(K(n%,3,1)*K(n%,4,2)-K(n%,4,1)*K(n%,3,2))/Help(n%,0)¶
      Help(n%,14)=(K(n%,3,0)*K(n%,4,2)-K(n%,4,0)*K(n%,3,2))/Help(n%,0)¶
      Help(n%,15)=(K(n%,3,0)*K(n%,4,1)-K(n%,4,0)*K(n%,3,1))/Help(n%,0)¶
      Help(n%,16)=(-K(n%,2,1)*K(n%,4,2)+K(n%,4,1)*K(n%,2,2))/Help(n%,0)¶
      Help(n%,17)=(-K(n%,2,0)*K(n%,4,2)+K(n%,4,0)*K(n%,2,2))/Help(n%,0)¶
      Help(n%,18)=(-K(n%,2,0)*K(n%,4,1)+K(n%,4,0)*K(n%,2,1))/Help(n%,0)¶
      Help(n%,19)=(K(n%,2,1)*K(n%,3,2)-K(n%,3,1)*K(n%,2,2))/Help(n%,0)¶
      Help(n%,20)=(K(n%,2,0)*K(n%,3,2)-K(n%,3,0)*K(n%,2,2))/Help(n%,0)¶
      Help(n%,21)=(K(n%,2,0)*K(n%,3,1)-K(n%,3,0)*K(n%,2,1))/Help(n%,0)¶
    END IF¶
  NEXT n%¶
RETURN¶
'¶
'¶
SUB Transformmm(x,y,z) STATIC¶
SHARED Sina,Sinb,Sinc,Cosa,Cosb,Cosc,RasterW1%,RasterH1%¶
SHARED DPH,Hx,Hy,Hz,Xt,Yt,Zt¶
  ' => xt,yt,zt for minmax¶
¶
  x1=(x-Hx)*Cosa+(y-Hy)*Sina  ' Rotation Z-Axis¶
  y1=(y-Hy)*Cosa-(x-Hx)*Sina¶
  Xt=x1*Cosb+(z-Hz)*Sinb      ' Rotation Y-Axis¶
  z2=(z-Hz)*Cosb-x1*Sinb¶
  y3=y1*Cosc+z2*Sinc          ' Rotation X-Axis¶
  z3=z2*Cosc-y1*Sinc¶
¶
  IF DPH<>Zt THEN¶
    Yt =FN Xscale((y3*DPH)/(DPH-Xt))  ' division point with projection plane¶
    Zt =FN Yscale((z3*DPH)/(DPH-Xt))  ' scaled¶
  ELSE¶
    Yt = FN Xscale(0)    ¶
    Zt = FN Yscale(0)    ¶
  END IF¶
¶
  IF Yt<0 THEN¶
    Yt=0¶
  END IF¶
  IF Yt>RasterW1% THEN¶
    Yt=RasterW1%¶
  END IF¶
  IF Zt<0 THEN¶
    Zt=0¶
  END IF¶
  IF Zt>RasterH1% THEN¶
    Zt=RasterH1%¶
  END IF¶
END SUB¶
'¶
SUB MinMaxtest(n%,x,y,z) STATIC¶
SHARED DPH,minmax%(),RasterW1%,RasterH1%,Xt,Yt,Zt,XMin%¶
SHARED YMin%,XMax%,YMax%¶
  ' if point preceding projection point => minmax%(n%,0)=-1 => no screen limit¶
  IF minmax%(n%,0)>=0 THEN¶
    CALL Transformmm(x,y,z)¶
    IF Xt>=DPH THEN¶
      minmax%(n%,0)=-1¶
```

```
        minmax%(n%,1)=-1¶
        minmax%(n%,2)=RasterW1%¶
        minmax%(n%,3)=RasterH1%¶
        XMin%=0¶
        XMax%=RasterW1%¶
        YMin%=0¶
        YMax%=RasterH1%¶
      ELSE¶
        IF Yt<minmax%(n%,0) THEN¶
          minmax%(n%,0)=Yt¶
        END IF¶
        IF Yt>minmax%(n%,2) THEN¶
          minmax%(n%,2)=Yt¶
        END IF¶
        IF Zt<minmax%(n%,1) THEN¶
          minmax%(n%,1)=Zt¶
        END IF¶
        IF Zt>minmax%(n%,3) THEN¶
          minmax%(n%,3)=Zt¶
        END IF¶
        IF Yt<XMin% THEN¶
          XMin%=Yt¶
        END IF¶
        IF Yt>XMax% THEN¶
          XMax%=Yt¶
        END IF¶
        IF Zt<YMin% THEN¶
          YMin%=Zt¶
        END IF¶
        IF Zt>YMax% THEN¶
          YMax%=Zt¶
        END IF¶
      END IF¶
    END IF¶
END SUB¶
'¶
InitMinMax:¶
  ' Compute screen section allocated for indivudal objects¶
¶
  ERASE minmax%¶
  DIM minmax%(NumberK,3)¶
¶
  XMin%=RasterW1%¶
  XMax%=0¶
  YMin%=RasterH1%¶
  YMax%=0¶
¶
  FOR n%=1 TO NumberK¶
    minmax%(n%,0)=RasterW1%¶
    minmax%(n%,1)=RasterH1%¶
    minmax%(n%,2)=0¶
    minmax%(n%,3)=0¶
¶
    IF K(n%,0,0)=0 THEN¶
      minmax%(n%,0)=0¶
      minmax%(n%,1)=0¶
      minmax%(n%,2)=RasterW1%¶
      minmax%(n%,3)=RasterH1%¶
      XMin%=0¶
      XMax%=RasterW1%¶
```

```
      YMin%=0¶
      YMax%=RasterH1%¶
    END IF¶
¶
    IF K(n%,0,0)=1 THEN¶
      CALL MinMaxtest(n%,K(n%,1,0),K(n%,1,1),K(n%,1,2))¶
      CALL
MinMaxtest(n%,K(n%,1,0)+K(n%,2,0),K(n%,1,1)+K(n%,2,1),K(n%,1,2)+K(n%,2,2))¶
      CALL
MinMaxtest(n%,K(n%,1,0)+K(n%,3,0),K(n%,1,1)+K(n%,3,1),K(n%,1,2)+K(n%,3,2))¶
    END IF¶
¶
    IF K(n%,0,0)=2 THEN¶
      CALL MinMaxtest(n%,K(n%,1,0),K(n%,1,1),K(n%,1,2))¶
      CALL
MinMaxtest(n%,K(n%,1,0)+K(n%,2,0),K(n%,1,1)+K(n%,2,1),K(n%,1,2)+K(n%,2,2))¶
      CALL
MinMaxtest(n%,K(n%,1,0)+K(n%,3,0),K(n%,1,1)+K(n%,3,1),K(n%,1,2)+K(n%,3,2))¶
      CALL
MinMaxtest(n%,K(n%,1,0)+K(n%,2,0)+K(n%,3,0),K(n%,1,1)+K(n%,2,1)+K(n%,3,1),K(n%,1,2)
+K(n%,2,2)+K(n%,3,2))¶
    END IF¶
¶
    IF K(n%,0,0)>=3 AND K(n%,0,0)<=5 THEN¶
      CALL MinMaxtest(n%,K(n%,1,0)-K(n%,2,0)-K(n%,3,0),K(n%,1,1)-K(n%,2,1)-
K(n%,3,1),K(n%,1,2)-K(n%,2,2)-K(n%,3,2))¶
      CALL MinMaxtest(n%,K(n%,1,0)+K(n%,2,0)-K(n%,3,0),K(n%,1,1)+K(n%,2,1)-
K(n%,3,1),K(n%,1,2)+K(n%,2,2)-K(n%,3,2))¶
      CALL MinMaxtest(n%,K(n%,1,0)-K(n%,2,0)+K(n%,3,0),K(n%,1,1)-
K(n%,2,1)+K(n%,3,1),K(n%,1,2)-K(n%,2,2)+K(n%,3,2))¶
      CALL
MinMaxtest(n%,K(n%,1,0)+K(n%,2,0)+K(n%,3,0),K(n%,1,1)+K(n%,2,1)+K(n%,3,1),K(n%,1,2)
+K(n%,2,2)+K(n%,3,2))¶
    END IF¶
¶
    IF K(n%,0,0)=10 THEN¶
      CALL MinMaxtest(n%,K(n%,1,0)-K(n%,2,0),K(n%,1,1)-K(n%,2,0),K(n%,1,2)-
K(n%,2,0))¶
      CALL MinMaxtest(n%,K(n%,1,0)+K(n%,2,0),K(n%,1,1)-K(n%,2,0),K(n%,1,2)-
K(n%,2,0))¶
      CALL MinMaxtest(n%,K(n%,1,0)-K(n%,2,0),K(n%,1,1)+K(n%,2,0),K(n%,1,2)-
K(n%,2,0))¶
      CALL MinMaxtest(n%,K(n%,1,0)+K(n%,2,0),K(n%,1,1)+K(n%,2,0),K(n%,1,2)-
K(n%,2,0))¶
      CALL MinMaxtest(n%,K(n%,1,0)-K(n%,2,0),K(n%,1,1)-
K(n%,2,0),K(n%,1,2)+K(n%,2,0))¶
      CALL MinMaxtest(n%,K(n%,1,0)+K(n%,2,0),K(n%,1,1)-
K(n%,2,0),K(n%,1,2)+K(n%,2,0))¶
      CALL MinMaxtest(n%,K(n%,1,0)-
K(n%,2,0),K(n%,1,1)+K(n%,2,0),K(n%,1,2)+K(n%,2,0))¶
      CALL
MinMaxtest(n%,K(n%,1,0)+K(n%,2,0),K(n%,1,1)+K(n%,2,0),K(n%,1,2)+K(n%,2,0))¶
    END IF¶
¶
    IF (K(n%,0,0)=20) OR (K(n%,0,0)=21) OR (K(n%,0,0)=24) THEN¶
      IF K(n%,0,0)=20 THEN¶
        Xh%=K(n%,1,0)¶
        Yh%=K(n%,1,1)¶
        Zh%=K(n%,1,2)¶
      ELSE¶
```

```
        Xh%=K(n%,1,0)-K(n%,4,0)¶
        Yh%=K(n%,1,1)-K(n%,4,1)¶
        Zh%=K(n%,1,2)-K(n%,4,2)¶
      END IF¶
      CALL MinMaxtest(n%,Xh%-K(n%,2,0)-K(n%,3,0),Yh%-K(n%,2,1)-K(n%,3,1),Zh%-
K(n%,2,2)-K(n%,3,2))¶
      CALL MinMaxtest(n%,Xh%+K(n%,2,0)-K(n%,3,0),Yh%+K(n%,2,1)-
K(n%,3,1),Zh%+K(n%,2,2)-K(n%,3,2))¶
      CALL MinMaxtest(n%,Xh%-K(n%,2,0)+K(n%,3,0),Yh%-K(n%,2,1)+K(n%,3,1),Zh%-
K(n%,2,2)+K(n%,3,2))¶
      CALL
MinMaxtest(n%,Xh%+K(n%,2,0)+K(n%,3,0),Yh%+K(n%,2,1)+K(n%,3,1),Zh%+K(n%,2,2)+K(n%,3,
2))¶
      Xh%=K(n%,1,0)+K(n%,4,0)¶
      Yh%=K(n%,1,1)+K(n%,4,1)¶
      Zh%=K(n%,1,2)+K(n%,4,2)¶
      CALL MinMaxtest(n%,Xh%-K(n%,2,0)-K(n%,3,0),Yh%-K(n%,2,1)-K(n%,3,1),Zh%-
K(n%,2,2)-K(n%,3,2))¶
      CALL MinMaxtest(n%,Xh%+K(n%,2,0)-K(n%,3,0),Yh%+K(n%,2,1)-
K(n%,3,1),Zh%+K(n%,2,2)-K(n%,3,2))¶
      CALL MinMaxtest(n%,Xh%-K(n%,2,0)+K(n%,3,0),Yh%-K(n%,2,1)+K(n%,3,1),Zh%-
K(n%,2,2)+K(n%,3,2))¶
      CALL
MinMaxtest(n%,Xh%+K(n%,2,0)+K(n%,3,0),Yh%+K(n%,2,1)+K(n%,3,1),Zh%+K(n%,2,2)+K(n%,3
,2))¶
    END IF¶
¶
    IF K(n%,0,0)=22 THEN¶
      CALL MinMaxtest(n%,K(n%,1,0)-K(n%,2,0)-K(n%,3,0),K(n%,1,1)-K(n%,2,1)-
K(n%,3,1),K(n%,1,2)-K(n%,2,2)-K(n%,3,2))¶
      CALL MinMaxtest(n%,K(n%,1,0)+K(n%,2,0)-K(n%,3,0),K(n%,1,1)+K(n%,2,1)-
K(n%,3,1),K(n%,1,2)+K(n%,2,2)-K(n%,3,2))¶
      CALL MinMaxtest(n%,K(n%,1,0)-K(n%,2,0)+K(n%,3,0),K(n%,1,1)-
K(n%,2,1)+K(n%,3,1),K(n%,1,2)-K(n%,2,2)+K(n%,3,2))¶
      CALL
MinMaxtest(n%,K(n%,1,0)+K(n%,2,0)+K(n%,3,0),K(n%,1,1)+K(n%,2,1)+K(n%,3,1),K(n%,1,2)
+K(n%,2,2)+K(n%,3,2))¶
      CALL
MinMaxtest(n%,K(n%,1,0)+K(n%,4,0),K(n%,1,1)+K(n%,4,1),K(n%,1,2)+K(n%,4,2))¶
    END IF¶
  NEXT n%¶
¶
  IF XMin%>XStart% THEN¶
    XStart%=XMin%¶
  END IF¶
  IF XMax%<XEnd% THEN¶
    XEnd%=XMax%¶
  END IF¶
  IF YMin%>YStart% THEN¶
    YStart%=YMin%¶
  END IF¶
  IF YMax%<Yend% THEN¶
    Yend%=YMax%¶
  END IF¶
RETURN¶
'¶
'¶
SUB NormalAngle(Pw,Wi) STATIC¶
SHARED Pi,Pm2¶
  ' => Picture Wi from [ -PI , +PI ] ¶
```

```
  WHILE Wi>Pi¶
     Wi=Wi-Pm2¶
  WEND¶
  WHILE Wi<=-Pi¶
     Wi=Wi+Pm2¶
  WEND¶
  Pw=Wi¶
END SUB¶
'¶
SUB Deltasum3(Pw,w1,w2,w3) STATIC¶
  ' => if light source in triangle: w=2*pi, else w=0¶
  CALL NormalAngle(D1,w2-w1)¶
  CALL NormalAngle(D2,w3-w2)¶
  CALL NormalAngle(D3,w1-w3)¶
  Pw=D1+D2+D3¶
END SUB¶
'¶
SUB Deltasum4(Pw,w1,w2,w3,w4) STATIC¶
  ' => if light source in triangle: w=2*pi, else w=0¶
  CALL NormalAngle(D1,w2-w1)¶
  CALL NormalAngle(D2,w3-w2)¶
  CALL NormalAngle(D3,w4-w3)¶
  CALL NormalAngle(D4,w1-w4)¶
  Pw=D1+D2+D3+D4¶
END SUB¶
'¶
SUB GETxyzlq(Px,Py,Pz,n%,a%,b%,c%) STATIC¶
SHARED K()¶
  ' => Compute  XYZ-coordinates from factors a,b,c¶
  Px=K(n%,1,0)+a%*K(n%,2,0)+b%*K(n%,3,0)+c%*K(n%,4,0)¶
  Py=K(n%,1,1)+a%*K(n%,2,1)+b%*K(n%,3,1)+c%*K(n%,4,1)¶
  Pz=K(n%,1,2)+a%*K(n%,2,2)+b%*K(n%,3,2)+c%*K(n%,4,2)¶
END SUB¶
'¶
SUB GETxyzlqk(Px,Py,Pz,n%,a%,b%,c%) STATIC¶
SHARED K()¶
  ' => Compute XYZ-coordinates for Sphere from factors a,b,c¶
  Px=K(n%,1,0)+a%*K(n%,2,0)¶
  Py=K(n%,1,1)+b%*K(n%,2,0)¶
  Pz=K(n%,1,2)+c%*K(n%,2,0)¶
END SUB¶
'¶
SUB Disttest(x,y,z) STATIC¶
SHARED Qx,Qy,Qz,MinDist¶
  ' => Compute distance  (x,y,z) froml ight source¶
 D=SQR((x-Qx)^2+(y-Qy)^2+(z-Qz)^2)  '  Pythagoream theorem¶
  IF MinDist<0 THEN¶
    MinDist=D¶
  ELSE¶
    IF D<MinDist THEN MinDist=D¶
  END IF¶
END SUB¶
'¶
SUB Arctan(Pw,x1,y1,x2,y2) STATIC¶
SHARED Pi,Pd2¶
  ' Determine pw=arctan((y1-y2)/(x1-x2))¶
  IF x1=x2 THEN¶
    Hw=SGN(y1-y2)*Pd2¶
  ELSE¶
    Hw=ATN((y1-y2)/(x1-x2))¶
```

```
     IF x1<x2 THEN¶
       IF Hw>=0 THEN¶
         Hw=Hw-Pi¶
       ELSE¶
         Hw=Hw+Pi¶
       END IF¶
     END IF¶
   END IF¶
   Pw=Hw¶
END SUB¶
'¶
SUB Calcablq(Pa,Pb,Ainc,Binc,x,y,z) STATIC¶
SHARED Qx,Qy,Qz¶
   ' => a,b = Polar coordinates of light source¶
   ' p.a=angle1 in XY-plane, pb is vertical¶
   CALL Arctan(Ha,y,z,Qy,Qz)¶
   CALL Arctan(Hb,x,z,Qx,Qz)¶
   CALL NormalAngle(Pa,Ha+Ainc)¶
   CALL NormalAngle(Pb,Hb+Binc)¶
END SUB¶
'¶
'¶
SUB Mmlq3Test(n%,x1%,y1%,z1%,x2%,y2%,z2%,x3%,y3%,z3%) STATIC¶
SHARED True,False,Pi,AMin,BMin,AMax,BMax,Ainc,Binc,MinDist¶
   ' => Determine min and max of a and b¶
   ok!=True¶
¶
   RepeatA:¶
     CALL GETxyzlq(x,y,z,n%,x1%,y1%,z1%)¶
     CALL Disttest(x,y,z)¶
     CALL Calcablq(A1,B1,Ainc,Binc,x,y,z)¶
¶
     CALL GETxyzlq(x,y,z,n%,x2%,y2%,z2%)¶
     CALL Disttest(x,y,z)¶
     CALL Calcablq(A2,B2,Ainc,Binc,x,y,z)¶
¶
     CALL GETxyzlq(x,y,z,n%,x3%,y3%,z3%)¶
     CALL Disttest(x,y,z)¶
     CALL Calcablq(A3,B3,Ainc,Binc,x,y,z)¶
¶
     CALL Deltasum3(a,A1,A2,A3)¶
¶
     IF a>Pi THEN¶
       ' => Light source 'within'triangle¶
       AMin=-Pi¶
       AMax=Pi¶
       Ainc=Pi¶
       ok!=True¶
     ELSE¶
       IF A1<AMin THEN AMin = A1¶
       IF A2<AMin THEN AMin = A2¶
       IF A3<AMin THEN AMin = A3¶
       ¶
       IF A1>AMax THEN AMax = A1¶
       IF A2>AMax THEN AMax = A2¶
       IF A3>AMax THEN AMax = A3¶
       ¶
       IF (AMax-AMin>=Pi) AND (Ainc=0) THEN¶
         Ainc=Pi¶
         ok!=False¶
```

```
      ELSE¶
        ok!=True¶
      END IF¶
    END IF¶
¶
    CALL Deltasum3(b,B1,B2,B3)¶
¶
    IF b>Pi THEN¶
      ' => Light source 'within' triangle¶
      BMin=-Pi¶
      BMax=Pi¶
      Binc=Pi¶
    ELSE¶
      IF B1<BMin THEN BMin = B1¶
      IF B2<BMin THEN BMin = B2¶
      IF B3<BMin THEN BMin = B3¶
      ¶
      IF B1>BMax THEN BMax = B1¶
      IF B2>BMax THEN BMax = B2¶
      IF B3>BMax THEN BMax = B3¶
      ¶
      IF (BMax-BMin>=Pi) AND (Binc=0) THEN¶
        Binc=Pi¶
        ok!=False¶
      END IF¶
    END IF¶
¶
  IF ok! <> True GOTO RepeatA¶
END SUB¶
'¶
SUB Mmlq4Test(n%,x1%,y1%,z1%,x2%,y2%,z2%,x3%,y3%,z3%,x4%,y4%,z4%) STATIC¶
SHARED True,False,Pi,Ainc,Binc,AMax,BMax,AMin,BMin,MinDist¶
  ' => Determine  min and max of a and b ¶
  ok!=True¶
  ¶
  RepeatB:¶
    CALL GETxyzlq(x,y,z,n%,x1%,y1%,z1%)¶
    CALL Disttest(x,y,z)¶
    CALL Calcablq(A1,B1,Ainc,Binc,x,y,z)¶
 ¶
    CALL GETxyzlq(x,y,z,n%,x2%,y2%,z2%)¶
    CALL Disttest(x,y,z)¶
    CALL Calcablq(A2,B2,Ainc,Binc,x,y,z)¶
 ¶
    CALL GETxyzlq(x,y,z,n%,x3%,y3%,z3%)¶
    CALL Disttest(x,y,z)¶
    CALL Calcablq(A3,B3,Ainc,Binc,x,y,z)¶
 ¶
    CALL GETxyzlq(x,y,z,n%,x4%,y4%,z4%)¶
    CALL Disttest(x,y,z)¶
    CALL Calcablq(A4,B4,Ainc,Binc,x,y,z)¶
 ¶
    CALL Deltasum4(a,A1,A2,A3,A4)¶
 ¶
    IF a>Pi THEN¶
      ' => Light source 'within' triangle¶
      AMin=-Pi¶
      AMax=Pi¶
      Ainc=Pi¶
      ok!=True¶
```

```
    ELSE¶
      IF A1<AMin THEN AMin = A1¶
      IF A2<AMin THEN AMin = A2¶
      IF A3<AMin THEN AMin = A3¶
      IF A4<AMin THEN AMin = A4¶
      ¶
      IF A1>AMax THEN AMax = A1¶
      IF A2>AMax THEN AMax = A2¶
      IF A3>AMax THEN AMax = A3¶
      IF A4>AMax THEN AMax = A4¶
¶
      IF (AMax-AMin>=Pi) AND (Ainc=0) THEN¶
        Ainc=Pi¶
        ok!=False¶
      ELSE¶
        ok!=True¶
      END IF¶
    END IF¶
¶
    CALL Deltasum4(b,B1,B2,B3,B4)¶
¶
    IF b>Pi THEN¶
      ' => Light source 'within' triangle¶
      BMin=-Pi¶
      BMax=Pi¶
      Binc=Pi¶
    ELSE¶
      IF B1<BMin THEN BMin = B1¶
      IF B2<BMin THEN BMin = B2¶
      IF B3<BMin THEN BMin = B3¶
      IF B4<BMin THEN BMin = B4¶
      ¶
      IF B1>BMax THEN BMax = B1¶
      IF B2>BMax THEN BMax = B2¶
      IF B3>BMax THEN BMax = B3¶
      IF B4>BMax THEN BMax = B4¶
      ¶
      IF (BMax-BMin>=Pi) AND (Binc=0) THEN¶
        Binc=Pi¶
        ok!=False¶
      END IF¶
    END IF¶
  IF ok! <> True GOTO RepeatB¶
END SUB¶
'¶
SUB MmlqKTest(n%,x1%,y1%,z1%,x2%,y2%,z2%,x3%,y3%,z3%,x4%,y4%,z4%) STATIC¶
SHARED True,False,Ainc,Binc,Pi,AMin,AMax,BMin,BMax,MinDist¶
  ' => Determine min and max of a and b¶
  ok!=True¶
¶
  RepeatC:¶
    CALL GETxyzlqk(x,y,z,n%,x1%,y1%,z1%)¶
    CALL Disttest(x,y,z)¶
    CALL Calcablq(A1,B1,Ainc,Binc,x,y,z)¶
¶
    CALL GETxyzlqk(x,y,z,n%,x2%,y2%,z2%)¶
    CALL Disttest(x,y,z)¶
    CALL Calcablq(A2,B2,Ainc,Binc,x,y,z)¶
¶
    CALL GETxyzlqk(x,y,z,n%,x3%,y3%,z3%)¶
```

```
    CALL Disttest(x,y,z)¶
    CALL Calcablq(A3,B3,Ainc,Binc,x,y,z)¶
¶
    CALL GETxyzlqk(x,y,z,n%,x4%,y4%,z4%)¶
    CALL Disttest(x,y,z)¶
    CALL Calcablq(A4,B4,Ainc,Binc,x,y,z)¶
¶
    CALL Deltasum4(a,A1,A2,A3,A4)¶
¶
    IF a>Pi THEN¶
      ' => Light source 'within' triangle¶
      AMin=-Pi¶
      AMax=Pi¶
      Ainc=Pi¶
      ok!=True¶
    ELSE¶
      IF A1<AMin THEN AMin = A1¶
      IF A2<AMin THEN AMin = A2¶
      IF A3<AMin THEN AMin = A3¶
      IF A4<AMin THEN AMin = A4¶
      ¶
      IF A1>AMax THEN AMax = A1¶
      IF A2>AMax THEN AMax = A2¶
      IF A3>AMax THEN AMax = A3¶
      IF A4>AMax THEN AMax = A4¶
¶
      IF (AMax-AMin>=Pi) AND (Ainc=0) THEN¶
        Ainc=Pi¶
        ok!=False¶
      ELSE¶
        ok!=True¶
      END IF¶
    END IF¶
¶
    CALL Deltasum4(b,B1,B2,B3,B4)¶
¶
    IF b>Pi THEN¶
      ' => Light source 'within' triangle¶
      BMin=-Pi¶
      BMax=Pi¶
      Binc=Pi¶
    ELSE¶
      IF B1<BMin THEN BMin = B1¶
      IF B2<BMin THEN BMin = B2¶
      IF B3<BMin THEN BMin = B3¶
      IF B4<BMin THEN BMin = B4¶
      ¶
      IF B1>BMax THEN BMax = B1¶
      IF B2>BMax THEN BMax = B2¶
      IF B3>BMax THEN BMax = B3¶
      IF B4>BMax THEN BMax = B4¶
      ¶
      IF (BMax-BMin>=Pi) AND (Binc=0) THEN¶
        Binc=Pi¶
        ok!=False¶
      END IF¶
    END IF¶
  IF ok!<>True THEN GOTO RepeatC¶
END SUB¶
'¶
```

```
SUB MmlqShpere(n%) STATIC¶
  CALL MmlqKTest(n%,-1,-1,-1,-1,1,-1,1,1,-1,1,-1,-1)¶
  CALL MmlqKTest(n%,-1,-1,-1,-1,1,-1,-1,1,1,-1,-1,1)¶
  CALL MmlqKTest(n%,-1,1,-1,1,1,-1,1,1,1,-1,1,1)¶
  CALL MmlqKTest(n%,1,1,-1,1,-1,-1,1,-1,1,1,1,1)¶
  CALL MmlqKTest(n%,1,-1,-1,-1,-1,-1,-1,-1,1,1,-1,1)¶
  CALL MmlqKTest(n%,-1,-1,1,-1,1,1,1,1,1,-1,1)¶
END SUB¶
'¶
SUB MmlqCylinder(n%) STATIC¶
  CALL Mmlq4Test(n%,-1,-1,0,-1,1,0,1,1,0,1,-1,0)¶
  CALL Mmlq4Test(n%,-1,-1,0,-1,1,0,-1,1,1,-1,-1,1)¶
  CALL Mmlq4Test(n%,-1,1,0,1,1,0,1,1,1,-1,1,1)¶
  CALL Mmlq4Test(n%,1,1,0,1,-1,0,1,-1,1,1,1,1)¶
  CALL Mmlq4Test(n%,1,-1,0,-1,-1,0,-1,-1,1,1,-1,1)¶
  CALL Mmlq4Test(n%,-1,-1,1,-1,1,1,1,1,1,-1,1)¶
END SUB¶
'¶
SUB MmlqCone(n%) STATIC¶
  CALL Mmlq4Test(n%,-1,-1,0,-1,1,0,1,1,0,1,-1,0)¶
  CALL Mmlq3Test(n%,-1,-1,0,-1,1,0,0,0,1)¶
  CALL Mmlq3Test(n%,-1,1,0,1,1,0,0,0,1)¶
  CALL Mmlq3Test(n%,1,1,0,1,-1,0,0,0,1)¶
  CALL Mmlq3Test(n%,1,-1,0,-1,-1,0,0,0,1)¶
END SUB¶
'¶
SUB MmlqEllipsoid(n%) STATIC¶
  CALL Mmlq4Test(n%,-1,-1,-1,-1,1,-1,1,1,-1,1,-1,-1)¶
  CALL Mmlq4Test(n%,-1,-1,-1,-1,1,-1,-1,1,1,-1,-1,1)¶
  CALL Mmlq4Test(n%,-1,1,-1,1,1,-1,1,1,1,-1,1,1)¶
  CALL Mmlq4Test(n%,1,1,-1,1,-1,-1,1,-1,1,1,1,1)¶
  CALL Mmlq4Test(n%,1,-1,-1,-1,-1,-1,-1,-1,1,1,-1,1)¶
  CALL Mmlq4Test(n%,-1,-1,1,-1,1,1,1,1,1,1,-1,1)¶
END SUB¶
'¶
'¶
InitMinmaxLq:¶
  ' => Compute surface interval for shadow computation in polar coordinates¶
  ' a = angle  of X-Axis, b = angle of Y-Axis, mindist = minimum distance to light
source¶
  ERASE minmaxlq¶
  DIM minmaxlq(NumberK,6)¶
¶
  FOR n%=1 TO NumberK¶
    AMin=Pi¶
    AMax=-Pi¶
    BMin=Pi¶
    BMax=-Pi¶
    Ainc=0¶
    Binc=0¶
    MinDist=-1¶
¶
    IF K(n%,0,0)=0 THEN¶
      AMin=-Pi¶
      BMin=-Pi¶
      AMax=Pi¶
      BMax=Pi¶
      MinDist=ABS(Help(n%,0)*(Qx-K(n%,1,0))+Help(n%,1)*(Qy-
K(n%,1,1))+Help(n%,2)*(Qz-K(n%,1,2)))¶
    END IF¶
```

```
¶
    IF K(n%,0,0)=1 THEN¶
      CALL Mmlq3Test(n%,0,0,0,0,1,0,1,0,0)¶
    END IF¶
¶
    IF K(n%,0,0)=2 THEN¶
      CALL Mmlq4Test(n%,0,0,0,0,1,0,1,0,0,1,1,0)¶
    END IF¶
¶
    IF (K(n%,0,0)>=3) AND (K(n%,0,0)<6) THEN¶
      CALL Mmlq4Test(n%,-1,-1,0,-1,1,0,1,-1,0,1,1,0)¶
    END IF¶
¶
    IF K(n%,0,0)=10 THEN¶
      CALL MmlqShpere(n%)¶
    END IF¶
¶
    IF (K(n%,0,0)=20) OR (K(n%,0,0)=21) THEN¶
      CALL MmlqCylinder(n%)¶
    END IF¶
¶
    IF K(n%,0,0)=22 THEN¶
      CALL MmlqCone(n%)¶
    END IF¶
¶
    IF K(n%,0,0)=24 THEN¶
      CALL MmlqEllipsoid(n%)¶
    END IF¶
¶
    minmaxlq(n%,0)=Ainc¶
    minmaxlq(n%,1)=AMin¶
    minmaxlq(n%,2)=AMax¶
    minmaxlq(n%,3)=Binc¶
    minmaxlq(n%,4)=BMin¶
    minmaxlq(n%,5)=BMax¶
    minmaxlq(n%,6)=MinDist¶
  NEXT n%¶
RETURN¶
'END of SHADOW-INIT.asc¶
```

The SHADOWING.ASC module

```
'START of SHADOWING.ASC¶
'¶
'  ********************************¶
'  *        Shadowing             *¶
'  ********************************¶
'¶
SUB IntersectpointPlane(n%,Px,Py,Pz,Rx,Ry,Rz,l) STATIC¶
SHARED Help(),K()            ¶
  ' => l = exact parameter¶
  D=Ry*Help(n%,4)-Rx*Help(n%,3)-Rz*Help(n%,5)¶
  IF D<>0 THEN¶
    l=((Px-K(n%,1,0))*Help(n%,3)-(Py-K(n%,1,1))*Help(n%,4)+(Pz-
K(n%,1,2))*Help(n%,5))/D¶
  ELSE¶
    l=-1¶
  END IF¶
END SUB¶
'¶
SUB IntersectpointTriangle(n%,Px,Py,Pz,Rx,Ry,Rz,l,a,b) STATIC¶
SHARED Help(),K()¶
  ' => l = exact parameter, a,b = area parameter¶
  D=Ry*Help(n%,4)-Rx*Help(n%,3)-Rz*Help(n%,5)¶
  IF D<>0 THEN¶
    l=((Px-K(n%,1,0))*Help(n%,3)-(Py-K(n%,1,1))*Help(n%,4)+(Pz-
K(n%,1,2))*Help(n%,5))/D¶
    IF l>0 THEN¶
      a=FN Det(Px-K(n%,1,0),K(n%,3,0),-Rx,Py-K(n%,1,1),K(n%,3,1),-Ry,Pz-
K(n%,1,2),K(n%,3,2),-Rz)/D¶
      b=FN Det(K(n%,2,0),Px-K(n%,1,0),-Rx,K(n%,2,1),Py-K(n%,1,1),-Ry,K(n%,2,2),Pz-
K(n%,1,2),-Rz)/D¶
      IF a<0 OR b<0 OR a>1 OR b>1 OR a+b>1 THEN¶
        l=-1¶
      END IF¶
    END IF¶
  ELSE¶
    l=-1¶
  END IF¶
END SUB¶
'¶
SUB IntersectpointRectangle(n%,Px,Py,Pz,Rx,Ry,Rz,l,a,b) STATIC¶
SHARED Help(),K()¶
  ' => l = exact parameter, a,b = area parameter¶
  D=Ry*Help(n%,4)-Rx*Help(n%,3)-Rz*Help(n%,5)¶
  IF D<>0 THEN¶
    l=((Px-K(n%,1,0))*Help(n%,3)-(Py-K(n%,1,1))*Help(n%,4)+(Pz-
K(n%,1,2))*Help(n%,5))/D¶
    IF l>0 THEN¶
      a=FN Det(Px-K(n%,1,0),K(n%,3,0),-Rx,Py-K(n%,1,1),K(n%,3,1),-Ry,Pz-
K(n%,1,2),K(n%,3,2),-Rz)/D¶
      b=FN Det(K(n%,2,0),Px-K(n%,1,0),-Rx,K(n%,2,1),Py-K(n%,1,1),-Ry,K(n%,2,2),Pz-
K(n%,1,2),-Rz)/D¶
¶
      IF a<0 OR b<0 OR a>1 OR b>1 THEN¶
```

```
        l=-1¶
      END IF¶
    END IF¶
  ELSE¶
    l=-1¶
  END IF¶
END SUB¶
'¶
SUB IntersectpointCircle(n%,Px,Py,Pz,Rx,Ry,Rz,l,a,b) STATIC¶
  SHARED Help(),K()¶
  ' => l = exact parameter, a,b = area parameter¶
  D=Ry*Help(n%,4)-Rx*Help(n%,3)-Rz*Help(n%,5)¶
  IF D<>0 THEN¶
    l=((Px-K(n%,1,0))*Help(n%,3)-(Py-K(n%,1,1))*Help(n%,4)+(Pz-
K(n%,1,2))*Help(n%,5))/D¶
    IF l>0 THEN¶
      a=FN Det(Px-K(n%,1,0),K(n%,3,0),-Rx,Py-K(n%,1,1),K(n%,3,1),-Ry,Pz-
K(n%,1,2),K(n%,3,2),-Rz)/D¶
      b=FN Det(K(n%,2,0),Px-K(n%,1,0),-Rx,K(n%,2,1),Py-K(n%,1,1),-Ry,K(n%,2,2),Pz-
K(n%,1,2),-Rz)/D¶
¶
      IF a*a+b*b>1 THEN¶
        l=-1¶
      END IF¶
    END IF¶
  ELSE¶
    l=-1¶
  END IF¶
END SUB¶
'¶
'¶
SUB AngleIntervall(l,n%,a,b) STATIC¶
SHARED Pi,Pm2,Pd2,K()¶
  IF a=0 THEN¶
    D=Pd2*SGN(b)¶
  ELSE¶
    D=ATN(b/a)¶
    IF a<0 THEN¶
      D = D+Pi¶
    END IF¶
  END IF¶
  IF D<0 THEN¶
    D = D+Pm2¶
  END IF¶
  IF D<K(n%,5,0) OR D>K(n%,5,1) THEN¶
    l=-1¶
  END IF¶
END SUB¶
'¶
'¶
SUB IntersectpointCircleSector(n%,Px,Py,Pz,Rx,Ry,Rz,l,a,b) STATIC¶
SHARED Help(),K()¶
  ' => l = exact parameter, a,b = area parameter¶
  D=Ry*Help(n%,4)-Rx*Help(n%,3)-Rz*Help(n%,5)¶
  IF D<>0 THEN¶
    l=((Px-K(n%,1,0))*Help(n%,3)-(Py-K(n%,1,1))*Help(n%,4)+(Pz-
K(n%,1,2))*Help(n%,5))/D¶
    IF l>0 THEN¶
      a=FN Det(Px-K(n%,1,0),K(n%,3,0),-Rx,Py-K(n%,1,1),K(n%,3,1),-Ry,Pz-
K(n%,1,2),K(n%,3,2),-Rz)/D¶
```

```
      b=FN Det(K(n%,2,0),Px-K(n%,1,0),-Rx,K(n%,2,1),Py-K(n%,1,1),-Ry,K(n%,2,2),Pz-
K(n%,1,2),-Rz)/D¶
      ¶
      IF a*a+b*b<=1 THEN¶
        CALL AngleIntervall(l,n%,a,b)¶
      ELSE¶
        l=-1¶
      END IF¶
    END IF¶
  ELSE¶
    l=-1¶
  END IF¶
END SUB¶
'¶
SUB IntersectpointCircleRing(n%,Px,Py,Pz,Rx,Ry,Rz,l,a,b) STATIC¶
SHARED Help(),K()¶
  ' => l = exact parameter, a,b = area parameter¶
  D=Ry*Help(n%,4)-Rx*Help(n%,3)-Rz*Help(n%,5)¶
  IF D<>0 THEN¶
    l=((Px-K(n%,1,0))*Help(n%,3)-(Py-K(n%,1,1))*Help(n%,4)+(Pz-
K(n%,1,2))*Help(n%,5))/D¶
    IF l>0 THEN¶
      a=FN Det(Px-K(n%,1,0),K(n%,3,0),-Rx,Py-K(n%,1,1),K(n%,3,1),-Ry,Pz-
K(n%,1,2),K(n%,3,2),-Rz)/D¶
      b=FN Det(K(n%,2,0),Px-K(n%,1,0),-Rx,K(n%,2,1),Py-K(n%,1,1),-Ry,K(n%,2,2),Pz-
K(n%,1,2),-Rz)/D¶
  ¶
      D=SQR(a*a+b*b)¶
      IF (D>=K(n%,4,0)) AND (D<=K(n%,4,1)) THEN¶
        CALL AngleIntervall(l,n%,a,b)¶
      ELSE¶
        l=-1¶
      END IF¶
    END IF¶
  ELSE¶
    l=-1¶
  END IF¶
END SUB¶
'¶
SUB IntersectpointSphere(n%,Px,Py,Pz,Rx,Ry,Rz,l) STATIC¶
SHARED Help(),K(),Threshold¶
  ' => l = exact parameter¶
  D=Rx*Rx+Ry*Ry+Rz*Rz¶
  p=(Rx*(Px-K(n%,1,0))+Ry*(Py-K(n%,1,1))+Rz*(Pz-K(n%,1,2)))/D¶
  q=((Px-K(n%,1,0))^2+(Py-K(n%,1,1))^2+(Pz-K(n%,1,2))^2-K(n%,2,0)*K(n%,2,0))/D¶
  D=p*p-q¶
  IF D>=0 THEN¶
    l=-p+SQR(D)¶
    L1=-p-SQR(D)¶
    IF (L1<l) AND (L1>Threshold) THEN¶
      SWAP l,L1¶
    END IF¶
  ELSE¶
    l=-1¶
  END IF¶
END SUB¶
'¶
'¶
SUB Basistrans(n%,Pxt,Pyt,Pzt,Xt,Yt,Zt,Px,Py,Pz,Rx,Ry,Rz,Original!) STATIC¶
SHARED Help(),K()¶
```

```
  ' Transform (px,py,zy) => (pxt,pyt,pzt), (rx,ry,rz) => (xt,yt,zt)¶
  IF Original! = True THEN¶
    Pxt=Help(n%,10)¶
    Pyt=Help(n%,11)¶
    Pzt=Help(n%,12)¶
  ELSE¶
    Pxt=(Px-K(n%,1,0))*Help(n%,13)-(Py-K(n%,1,1))*Help(n%,14)+(Pz-
K(n%,1,2))*Help(n%,15)¶
    Pyt=(Px-K(n%,1,0))*Help(n%,16)-(Py-K(n%,1,1))*Help(n%,17)+(Pz-
K(n%,1,2))*Help(n%,18)¶
    Pzt=(Px-K(n%,1,0))*Help(n%,19)-(Py-K(n%,1,1))*Help(n%,20)+(Pz-
K(n%,1,2))*Help(n%,21)¶
  END IF¶
  Xt=(Px+Rx-K(n%,1,0))*Help(n%,13)-(Py+Ry-K(n%,1,1))*Help(n%,14)+(Pz+Rz-
K(n%,1,2))*Help(n%,15)-Pxt¶
  Yt=(Px+Rx-K(n%,1,0))*Help(n%,16)-(Py+Ry-K(n%,1,1))*Help(n%,17)+(Pz+Rz-
K(n%,1,2))*Help(n%,18)-Pyt¶
  Zt=(Px+Rx-K(n%,1,0))*Help(n%,19)-(Py+Ry-K(n%,1,1))*Help(n%,20)+(Pz+Rz-
K(n%,1,2))*Help(n%,21)-Pzt¶
END SUB¶
'¶
'¶
SUB IntersectpointCylinder(n%,Px,Py,Pz,Rx,Ry,Rz,l,a,b,c,Original!) STATIC¶
SHARED Threshold¶
  ' => l=exact parameter, a,b,c = transform Intersect point coordinates¶
  CALL Basistrans(n%,Pxt,Pyt,Pzt,Xt,Yt,Zt,Px,Py,Pz,Rx,Ry,Rz,Original!)¶
  D=Xt*Xt+Yt*Yt¶
  IF D<>0 THEN¶
    p=(Pxt*Xt+Pyt*Yt)/D¶
    q=(Pxt*Pxt+Pyt*Pyt-1)/D¶
    D=p*p-q¶
    IF D>=0 THEN¶
      l=-p+SQR(D)¶
      L1=-p-SQR(D)¶
      c=Pzt+l*Zt¶
      D=Pzt+L1*Zt¶
      IF L1<l AND L1>Threshold AND D>=0 AND D<=1 THEN¶
        SWAP l,L1¶
        SWAP c,D¶
      END IF¶
      IF c<0 OR c>1 THEN¶
        l=-1¶
      ELSE¶
        a=Pxt+l*Xt¶
        b=Pyt+l*Yt¶
      END IF¶
    ELSE¶
      l=-1¶
    END IF¶
  ELSE¶
    l=-1¶
  END IF¶
END SUB¶
'¶
SUB IntersectpointCylinderSegm(n%,Px,Py,Pz,Rx,Ry,Rz,l,a,b,c,Original!) STATIC¶
SHARED Threshold ¶
  ' => l=exact parameter, a,b,c = transform  Intersect point coordinates¶
  CALL Basistrans(n%,Pxt,Pyt,Pzt,Xt,Yt,Zt,Px,Py,Pz,Rx,Ry,Rz,Original!)¶
  D=Xt*Xt+Yt*Yt¶
  IF D<>0 THEN¶
```

```
    p=(Pxt*Xt+Pyt*Yt)/D¶
    q=(Pxt*Pxt+Pyt*Pyt-1)/D¶
    D=p*p-q¶
    IF D>=0 THEN¶
      l=-p+SQR(D)¶
      L1=-p-SQR(D)¶
      c=Pzt+l*Zt¶
      C1=Pzt+L1*Zt¶
      IF c>=0 AND c<=1 THEN¶
        CALL AngleIntervall(l,n%,Pxt+l*Xt,Pyt+l*Yt)¶
      ELSE¶
        l=-1¶
      END IF¶
      IF C1>=0 AND C1<=1 THEN¶
        CALL AngleIntervall(L1,n%,Pxt+L1*Xt,Pyt+L1*Yt)¶
      ELSE¶
        L1=-1¶
      END IF¶
      IF (l<-.5) OR (L1<l AND L1>Threshold) THEN¶
        SWAP l,L1¶
        SWAP c,C1¶
      END IF¶
      a=Pxt+l*Xt¶
      b=Pyt+l*Yt¶
    ELSE¶
      l=-1¶
    END IF¶
  ELSE¶
    l=-1¶
  END IF¶
END SUB¶
'¶
SUB IntersectpointCone(n%,Px,Py,Pz,Rx,Ry,Rz,l,a,b,c,Original!) STATIC¶
SHARED Threshold¶
  ' => l=exact parameter, a,b,c = transform Intersect point coordinates¶
  CALL Basistrans(n%,Pxt,Pyt,Pzt,Xt,Yt,Zt,Px,Py,Pz,Rx,Ry,Rz,Original!)¶
  D=Xt*Xt+Yt*Yt-Zt*Zt¶
  IF D<>0 THEN¶
    p=(Pxt*Xt+Pyt*Yt+Zt*(1-Pzt))/D¶
    q=(Pxt*Pxt+Pyt*Pyt-(1-Pzt)^2)/D¶
    D=p*p-q¶
    IF D>=0 THEN¶
      l=-p+SQR(D)¶
      L1=-p-SQR(D)¶
      c=Pzt+l*Zt¶
      D=Pzt+L1*Zt¶
      IF L1<l AND L1>Threshold AND D>=0 AND D<=1 THEN¶
        SWAP l,L1¶
        SWAP c,D¶
      END IF¶
      IF c<0 OR c>1 THEN¶
        l=-1¶
      ELSE¶
        a=Pxt+l*Xt¶
        b=Pyt+l*Yt¶
      END IF¶
    ELSE¶
      l=-1¶
    END IF¶
  ELSE¶
```

```
    l=-1¶
  END IF¶
END SUB¶
'¶
SUB IntersectpointEllipsoid(n%,Px,Py,Pz,Rx,Ry,Rz,l,a,b,c,Original!) STATIC¶
SHARED Threshold¶
  ' => l=exact parameter, a,b,c = transform Intersect point coordinates¶
  CALL Basistrans(n%,Pxt,Pyt,Pzt,Xt,Yt,Zt,Px,Py,Pz,Rx,Ry,Rz,Original!)¶
  D=Xt*Xt+Yt*Yt+Zt*Zt¶
  IF D<>0 THEN¶
    p=(Pxt*Xt+Pyt*Yt+Pzt*Zt)/D¶
    q=(Pxt*Pxt+Pyt*Pyt+Pzt*Pzt-1)/D¶
    D=p*p-q¶
    IF D>=0 THEN¶
      l=-p+SQR(D)¶
      L1=-p-SQR(D)¶
      IF L1<l AND L1>Threshold THEN¶
        SWAP l,L1¶
      END IF¶
      a=Pxt+l*Xt¶
      b=Pyt+l*Yt¶
      c=Pzt+l*Zt¶
    ELSE¶
      l=-1¶
    END IF¶
  ELSE¶
    l=-1¶
  END IF¶
END SUB¶
'¶
'¶
SUB WhichBody (Kp%,Px,Py,Pz,Rx,Ry,Rz,Original!,Shadown!) STATIC¶
SHARED
True,False,minmax%(),NumberK,minmaxlq(),Help(),K(),xb%,yb%,Sx,Sy,Sz,Body%,Ac,Bc,Cc,
la,Threshold¶
  ' => Body% = Nr the body under coordinates xb%,yb%, S(sx,sy,sz)=Intersect point,
la=intersection line¶
  ' => if Typ>=20: (ac,bc,cc) = transform Intersect point coordinates¶
  la=-1¶
  Body%=0¶
¶
  IF Shadown! = True THEN                 ¶
    CALL Calcablq(Anglea,Angleb,0!,0!,Px,Py,Pz)¶
    Dist=SQR(Rx*Rx+Ry*Ry+Rz*Rz)¶
  END IF¶
¶
  FOR n%=1 TO NumberK¶
    IF Original! = True THEN¶
      IF minmax%(n%,0)>xb% THEN¶
        GOTO Nxtk¶
      END IF¶
      IF minmax%(n%,1)>yb% THEN¶
        GOTO Nxtk¶
      END IF¶
      IF minmax%(n%,2)<xb% THEN¶
        GOTO Nxtk¶
      END IF¶
      IF minmax%(n%,3)<yb% THEN¶
        GOTO Nxtk¶
      END IF¶
```

```
END IF¶
¶
IF Shadown! = True THEN¶
  CALL NormalAngle(Wa,Anglea+minmaxlq(n%,0))¶
  CALL NormalAngle(Wb,Angleb+minmaxlq(n%,3))¶
  IF Wa<minmaxlq(n%,1) THEN¶
    GOTO Nxtk¶
  END IF¶
  IF Wa>minmaxlq(n%,2) THEN¶
    GOTO Nxtk¶
  END IF¶
  IF Wb<minmaxlq(n%,4) THEN¶
    GOTO Nxtk¶
  END IF¶
  IF Wb>minmaxlq(n%,5) THEN¶
    GOTO Nxtk¶
  END IF¶
  IF Dist<minmaxlq(n%,6) THEN¶
    GOTO Nxtk¶
  END IF¶
END IF¶
¶
IF K(n%,0,0)=0 THEN¶
  CALL IntersectpointPlane(n%,Px,Py,Pz,Rx,Ry,Rz,l)¶
  GOTO Wkok¶
END IF¶
IF K(n%,0,0)=1 THEN¶
  CALL IntersectpointTriangle(n%,Px,Py,Pz,Rx,Ry,Rz,l,a,b)¶
  GOTO Wkok¶
END IF¶
IF K(n%,0,0)=2 THEN¶
  CALL IntersectpointRectangle(n%,Px,Py,Pz,Rx,Ry,Rz,l,a,b)¶
  GOTO Wkok¶
END IF¶
IF K(n%,0,0)=3 THEN¶
  CALL IntersectpointCircle(n%,Px,Py,Pz,Rx,Ry,Rz,l,a,b)¶
  GOTO Wkok¶
END IF¶
IF K(n%,0,0)=4 THEN¶
  CALL IntersectpointCircleSector(n%,Px,Py,Pz,Rx,Ry,Rz,l,a,b)¶
  GOTO Wkok¶
END IF¶
IF K(n%,0,0)=5 THEN¶
  CALL IntersectpointCircleRing(n%,Px,Py,Pz,Rx,Ry,Rz,l,a,b)¶
  GOTO Wkok¶
END IF¶
IF K(n%,0,0)=10 THEN¶
  CALL IntersectpointSphere(n%,Px,Py,Pz,Rx,Ry,Rz,l)¶
  GOTO Wkok¶
END IF¶
IF K(n%,0,0)=20 THEN¶
  CALL IntersectpointCylinder(n%,Px,Py,Pz,Rx,Ry,Rz,l,a,b,c,Original!)¶
  GOTO Wkok¶
END IF¶
IF K(n%,0,0)=21 THEN¶
  CALL IntersectpointCylinderSegm(n%,Px,Py,Pz,Rx,Ry,Rz,l,a,b,c,Original!)¶
  GOTO Wkok¶
END IF¶
IF K(n%,0,0)=22 THEN¶
  CALL IntersectpointCone(n%,Px,Py,Pz,Rx,Ry,Rz,l,a,b,c,Original!)¶
```

```
      GOTO Wkok¶
    END IF¶
    IF K(n%,0,0)=24 THEN¶
      CALL IntersectpointEllipsoid(n%,Px,Py,Pz,Rx,Ry,Rz,l,a,b,c,Original!)¶
    END IF¶
    Wkok:¶
    ' Work OK!¶
¶
    IF (l>Threshold) AND (la<=0 OR l<la) AND (n%<>Kp% OR K(n%,0,0)>=10) THEN¶
      la=l¶
      Body%=n%¶
      IF K(n%,0,0)>=20 AND Kp%=0 THEN¶
        Ac=a¶
        Bc=b¶
        Cc=c¶
      END IF¶
    END IF¶
    Nxtk:¶
    ' Next body¶
  NEXT n%¶
  ¶
  IF Body%>0 AND Kp%=0 THEN¶
    Sx=Px+la*Rx¶
    Sy=Py+la*Ry¶
    Sz=Pz+la*Rz¶
  END IF  ¶
END SUB¶
'¶
'¶
SUB SetBrightness(n%,Px,Py,Pz,Mirror,Original!) STATIC¶
SHARED Help(),K(),Mat(),Qx,Qy,Qz,Ac,Bc,Cc,Sx,Sy,Sz,Nx,Ny,Nz,Nl,Spx,Spy,Spz,Bright
¶
  ' => Bright=Brightness, SP=Mirror Vector, Mirror=Intensity of LQ-Mirroring¶
¶
  IF K(n%,0,0)<=9 THEN¶
      ' Determine Mirror Vektor SP¶
    Nx=Help(n%,0)¶
    Ny=Help(n%,1)¶
    Nz=Help(n%,2)¶
    IF Original!<>True THEN¶
      IF FN CosinAngle(Nx,Ny,Nz,Px-Sx,Py-Sy,Pz-Sz)<0 THEN¶
        'Normal vector must point to projection point!¶
        Nx=-Nx¶
        Ny=-Ny¶
        Nz=-Nz¶
      END IF¶
    END IF¶
    Dqe=Nx*(Qx-Sx)+Ny*(Qy-Sy)+Nz*(Qz-Sz)¶
¶
    Spx=Sx-Qx+2*Dqe*Nx¶
    Spy=Sy-Qy+2*Dqe*Ny¶
    Spz=Sz-Qz+2*Dqe*Nz¶
¶
    Mirror=FN CosinAngle(Spx,Spy,Spz,Px-Sx,Py-Sy,Pz-Sz)¶
¶
    IF Mirror<0 THEN¶
      Mirror=0¶
    END IF¶
¶
    Bright=FN CosinAngle(Nx,Ny,Nz,Qx-Sx,Qy-Sy,Qz-Sz)¶
```

```
  ELSE¶
      ' Determine mirror vector SP¶
    IF K(n%,0,0)=10 THEN¶
      Nx=Sx-K(n%,1,0)¶
      Ny=Sy-K(n%,1,1)¶
      Nz=Sz-K(n%,1,2)¶
    END IF¶
¶
    IF K(n%,0,0)>=20 AND K(n%,0,0)<24 THEN¶
      Nx=Help(n%,4)*Ac+Help(n%,1)*Bc¶
      Ny=Help(n%,5)*Ac+Help(n%,2)*Bc¶
      Nz=Help(n%,6)*Ac+Help(n%,3)*Bc¶
¶
      IF K(n%,0,0)>=22 THEN¶
        Nl=SQR(Nx*Nx+Ny*Ny+Nz*Nz)¶
        IF Nl<>0 THEN¶
          a=(Ac*K(n%,2,0)+Bc*K(n%,3,0))^2¶
          a=a+(Ac*K(n%,2,1)+Bc*K(n%,3,1))^2¶
          a=(SQR(a+(Ac*K(n%,2,2)+Bc*K(n%,3,2))^2))/Nl¶
          Nx = Nx*a¶
          Ny = Ny*a¶
          Nz = Nz*a¶
          b=SQR(Nx*Nx+Ny*Ny+Nz*Nz)/Help(n%,7)¶
          Nx=K(n%,4,0)*b+Nx/b¶
          Ny=K(n%,4,1)*b+Ny/b¶
          Nz=K(n%,4,2)*b+Nz/b¶
        ELSE¶
          ' If a cone angle:¶
          Nx=K(n%,4,0)¶
          Ny=K(n%,4,1)¶
          Nz=K(n%,4,2)¶
        END IF¶
      END IF¶
    END IF¶
¶
    IF K(n%,0,0)>=24 THEN¶
      Nx=Ac*Help(n%,1)+Bc*Help(n%,4)+Cc*Help(n%,7)¶
      Ny=Ac*Help(n%,2)+Bc*Help(n%,5)+Cc*Help(n%,8)¶
      Nz=Ac*Help(n%,3)+Bc*Help(n%,6)+Cc*Help(n%,9)¶
    END IF¶
¶
    IF FN CosinAngle(Nx,Ny,Nz,Px-Sx,Py-Sy,Pz-Sz)<0 THEN¶
        ' => Normal vector points to projection point¶
      Nx=-Nx¶
      Ny=-Ny¶
      Nz=-Nz¶
    END IF¶
    Nl=SQR(Nx*Nx+Ny*Ny+Nz*Nz)¶
    Nx = Nx/Nl¶
    Ny = Ny/Nl¶
    Nz = Nz/Nl¶
¶
    Dqe=Nx*(Qx-Sx)+Ny*(Qy-Sy)+Nz*(Qz-Sz)¶
¶
    Spx=Sx-Qx+2*Dqe*Nx¶
    Spy=Sy-Qy+2*Dqe*Ny¶
    Spz=Sz-Qz+2*Dqe*Nz¶
¶
    Mirror=FN CosinAngle(Spx,Spy,Spz,Px-Sx,Py-Sy,Pz-Sz)¶
¶
```

```
    IF Mirror<0 THEN¶
      Mirror=0¶
    END IF¶
¶
    Bright=FN CosinAngle(Nx,Ny,Nz,Qx-Sx,Qy-Sy,Qz-Sz)¶
  END IF¶
¶
  IF Mat(K(n%,0,2),4)>0 THEN¶
    Mirror=1.5*Mirror^(30*Mat(K(n%,0,2),4))¶
  END IF¶
END SUB¶
'¶
'¶
SUB StandardFill(x1%,y1%,x2%,y2%,Bright,Col1%,Col2%) STATIC¶
SHARED PatternHS(),PatternS&,NumberPatternS%,RastPort&¶
    ' draw rectangle in standard fill pattern¶
  Min=1E+35¶
  Nr%=0¶
  n%=0¶
¶
  WHILE ABS(Bright-PatternHS(n%))<Min¶
      ' sort in ascending order¶
    Min=ABS(Bright-PatternHS(n%))¶
    Nr%=n%¶
    n% = n% +1¶
    IF n%>=NumberPatternS% GOTO ContinueA¶
  WEND¶
¶
  ContinueA:¶
  CALL SetAPen&(RastPort&,Col1%)¶
  CALL SetBPen&(RastPort&,Col2%)¶
¶
  POKEL RastPort&+8,(PatternS&+Nr%*32)¶
    ' RastPort->AreaPtrn = &(PatternS%(0,Nr%)¶
  ¶
  POKE RastPort&+29,4¶
    ' RastPort->AreaPtSz = 4 (=> 4^2 = 16)¶
¶
  CALL RectFill&(RastPort&,x1%,y1%,x2%,y2%)¶
END SUB   ¶
'¶
SUB ExtendedFill(x1%,y1%,x2%,y2%,Bright,Bright1,Bright2,Col1%,Col2%) STATIC¶
SHARED NumberPatternX%,PatternHX(),PatternX&,RastPort&  ¶
  ' draw rectangle in standard fill pattern¶
  ' binary search for optimal pattern  ¶
  m=(Bright-Bright1)/(Bright2-Bright1)¶
  Min=1E+35¶
  Nr%=0¶
  Ug%=0                  'top limit¶
  Og%=NumberPatternX%*2   'lower limit¶
¶
  Repeat3:¶
    Mitte%=INT((Ug%+Og%)/2)¶
    IF ABS(m-PatternHX(Mitte%))<Min THEN¶
      Min=ABS(m-PatternHX(Mitte%))¶
      Nr%=Mitte%¶
    END IF¶
    IF m>PatternHX(Mitte%) THEN¶
      Ug%=Mitte%+1¶
    ELSE¶
```

```
      Og%=Mitte%-1¶
    END IF¶
  IF (Ug%<=Og%) AND (Min<>0) THEN GOTO Repeat3¶
¶
  CALL SetAPen&(RastPort&,Col1%)¶
  CALL SetBPen&(RastPort&,Col2%)¶
¶
  POKEL RastPort&+8,(PatternX&+Nr%*32)  ' s.o.  ¶
  POKE RastPort&+29,4¶
¶
  CALL RectFill&(RastPort&,x1%,y1%,x2%,y2%)¶
END SUB¶
'¶
SUB SetPoint(x1%,y1%,x2%,y2%,Bright.r,Bright.g,Bright.b) STATIC¶
SHARED MaxColour%,Colour(),RasterH1%,RasterW1%,RastPort&¶
SHARED NumberPatternX%,PatternX&,PatternHX()¶
  IF x2%>RasterW1% THEN x2%=RasterW1%¶
  IF y2%>RasterH1% THEN y2%=RasterH1%¶
¶
  'search colors for simialr color tone:¶
¶
  Min=1E+10¶
  Nr1%=1¶
¶
  'Convert colors to Polar coordinates:¶
¶
  dh=SQR(Bright.r*Bright.r+Bright.g*Bright.g)¶
  IF dh>0 THEN¶
    IF Bright.r>0 THEN¶
      ah=ATN(Bright.g/Bright.r)¶
    ELSE¶
      ah=1.5708¶
    END IF¶
    bh=ATN(Bright.b/dh)¶
    dh=SQR(dh*dh+Bright.b*Bright.b)¶
  ELSE¶
    a=.7854¶
    IF Colour(n%,3)=0 THEN¶
      b=.7854¶
    ELSE¶
      b=1.5708¶
    END IF¶
  END IF¶
¶
  'search for optimim colors:¶
¶
  FOR n%=1 TO MaxColour%¶
    D=SQR(Colour(n%,1)^2+Colour(n%,2)^2)¶
    IF D>0 THEN¶
      IF Colour(n%,1)>0 THEN¶
        a=ATN(Colour(n%,2)/Colour(n%,1))¶
      ELSE¶
        a=1.5708¶
      END IF¶
      b=ATN(Colour(n%,3)/D)¶
      D=SQR(D*D+Colour(n%,3)*Colour(n%,3))¶
    ELSE¶
      a=.7854¶
      IF Colour(n%,3)=0 THEN¶
        b=.7854¶
```

```
      ELSE¶
        b=1.5708¶
      END IF¶
    END IF¶
    h=(a-ah)^2+(b-bh)^2+ABS(D-dh)¶
    IF h<Min THEN¶
      Min=h¶
      Nr1%=n%¶
    END IF¶
  NEXT n%¶
¶
  'Determine best pattern and second color for color combination¶
¶
  Min=1E+10¶
  NrM%=0¶
  Nr2%=1¶
  FOR n%=0 TO NumberPatternX%¶
    FOR Nr%=0 TO MaxColour%¶
      IF Nr%<>Nr1% THEN¶
        h.r=PatternHX(n%)*Colour(Nr1%,1)+(1-PatternHX(n%))*Colour(Nr%,1)¶
        h.g=PatternHX(n%)*Colour(Nr1%,2)+(1-PatternHX(n%))*Colour(Nr%,2)¶
        h.b=PatternHX(n%)*Colour(Nr1%,3)+(1-PatternHX(n%))*Colour(Nr%,3)¶
        h=(Bright.r-h.r)^2+(Bright.g-h.g)^2+(Bright.b-h.b)^2¶
        IF h<Min THEN¶
          Min=h¶
          NrM%=n%¶
          Nr2%=Nr%¶
        END IF¶
        h.r=PatternHX(n%)*Colour(Nr%,1)+(1-PatternHX(n%))*Colour(Nr1%,1)¶
        h.g=PatternHX(n%)*Colour(Nr%,2)+(1-PatternHX(n%))*Colour(Nr1%,2)¶
        h.b=PatternHX(n%)*Colour(Nr%,3)+(1-PatternHX(n%))*Colour(Nr1%,3)¶
        h=(Bright.r-h.r)^2+(Bright.g-h.g)^2+(Bright.b-h.b)^2¶
        IF h<Min THEN¶
          Min=h¶
          NrM%=-n%¶
          Nr2%=Nr%¶
        END IF¶
      END IF¶
    NEXT Nr%¶
  NEXT n%¶
¶
  IF NrM%<0 THEN¶
    NrM%=-NrM%¶
    SWAP Nr1%,Nr2%¶
  END IF¶
¶
  CALL SetAPen&(RastPort&,CINT(Colour(Nr1%,0)))¶
  CALL SetBPen&(RastPort&,CINT(Colour(Nr2%,0)))¶
¶
  POKEL RastPort&+8,(PatternX&+NrM%*32)   ' Address of PatternS¶
  POKE RastPort&+29,4¶
¶
  CALL RectFill&(RastPort&,x1%,y1%,x2%,y2%)¶
¶
END SUB¶
'¶
'¶
SUB ReProjection(xr,yr,zr,x,y,z) STATIC¶
SHARED Sina,Sinb,Sinc,Cosa,Cosb,Cosc,Hx,Hy,Hz¶
  ' 2D->3D¶
```

```
  y1=y*Cosc-z*Sinc          ' Rotation X-Axis¶
  z1=z*Cosc+y*Sinc¶
  x2=x*Cosb-z1*Sinb         ' Rotation Y-Axis¶
  zr=z1*Cosb+x*Sinb+Hz¶
  xr=x2*Cosa-y1*Sina+Hx     ' Rotation Z-Axis¶
  yr=y1*Cosa+x2*Sina+Hy¶
END SUB¶
'¶
Computepoint:  ¶
  ' =>Compute Brightness of the point => stack¶
  StackPtr% = StackPtr% + 1¶
  CALL WhichBody(0,Px,Py,Pz,Rx,Ry,Rz,Original!,False)¶
¶
  IF Body% > 0 THEN¶
    CALL SetBrightness(Body%,Px,Py,Pz,Mirror,Original!) ¶
    RestLght(StackPtr%)=Mat(K(Body%,0,2),4)¶
    ¶
    IF Bright<=0 THEN¶
        ' unlit:    ¶
      Bright.r=Mat(K(Body%,0,2),0)*Mat(K(Body%,0,2),3)¶
      Bright.g=Mat(K(Body%,0,2),1)*Mat(K(Body%,0,2),3)¶
      Bright.b=Mat(K(Body%,0,2),2)*Mat(K(Body%,0,2),3)¶
    ELSE¶
      Kp%=Body%¶
        'Shadow ?¶
      CALL WhichBody(Kp%,Sx,Sy,Sz,Qx-Sx,Qy-Sy,Qz-Sz,False,True)¶
      SWAP Body%,Kp%¶
      IF Kp%>0 AND la<1 THEN¶
          ' in shadow:¶
        Bright.r=Mat(K(Body%,0,2),0)*Mat(K(Body%,0,2),3)¶
        Bright.g=Mat(K(Body%,0,2),1)*Mat(K(Body%,0,2),3)¶
        Bright.b=Mat(K(Body%,0,2),2)*Mat(K(Body%,0,2),3)¶
      ELSE¶
          ' Mirror light source on interface:¶
        Bright=Bright*(1-RestLght(StackPtr%))¶
        IF Bright<Mat(K(Body%,0,2),3) THEN¶
          Bright=Mat(K(Body%,0,2),3)¶
        END IF¶
        Bright.r=Bright*Mat(K(Body%,0,2),0)+Mirror*RestLght(StackPtr%)¶
        Bright.g=Bright*Mat(K(Body%,0,2),1)+Mirror*RestLght(StackPtr%)¶
        Bright.b=Bright*Mat(K(Body%,0,2),2)+Mirror*RestLght(StackPtr%)¶
      END IF¶
    END IF¶
¶
    IF (RestLght(StackPtr%)>0) AND (StackPtr%<MaxStack%) THEN¶
        ' Determine Mirror interface¶
        ' Determine mirror vector to P-S:¶
      Dqe=Nx*(Px-Sx)+Ny*(Py-Sy)+Nz*(Pz-Sz)¶
      Rx=Sx-Px+2*Dqe*Nx¶
      Ry=Sy-Py+2*Dqe*Ny¶
      Rz=Sz-Pz+2*Dqe*Nz¶
¶
      Stack(StackPtr%,0)=Bright.r¶
      Stack(StackPtr%,1)=Bright.g¶
      Stack(StackPtr%,2)=Bright.b¶
¶
      Px = Sx¶
      Py = Sy¶
      Pz = Sz¶
      Original! = False¶
```

```
      GOSUB Computepoint      ' Recursion !!!!¶
       ¶
      Bright.r=Stack(StackPtr%,0)+Stack(StackPtr%+1,0)*RestLght(StackPtr%)¶
      Bright.g=Stack(StackPtr%,1)+Stack(StackPtr%+1,1)*RestLght(StackPtr%)¶
      Bright.b=Stack(StackPtr%,2)+Stack(StackPtr%+1,2)*RestLght(StackPtr%)¶
    END IF¶
  ELSE¶
    IF StackPtr% = 0 THEN¶
      Bright.r=-1¶
      Bright.g=-1¶
      Bright.b=-1¶
    ELSE¶
      Bright.r=0¶
      Bright.g=0¶
      Bright.b=0¶
    END IF¶
  END IF¶
  Stack(StackPtr%,0)=Bright.r¶
  Stack(StackPtr%,1)=Bright.g¶
  Stack(StackPtr%,2)=Bright.b¶
  RestLght(StackPtr%)=0¶
  StackPtr% = StackPtr%-1¶
RETURN¶
'¶
'¶
Shadows:¶
'  Initialization
  Status$ = " Status: Shadows"+CHR$(0)¶
  CALL SetWindowTitles&(NWBase&,SADD(Status$),0)¶
¶
  GOSUB DeleteMenu¶
  ¶
  Status$ = " Status: Init"+CHR$(0)¶
  CALL SetWindowTitles&(NWBase&,SADD(Status$),0)¶
  GOSUB InitShadows¶
¶
  Status$ = " Status: InitMinMax"+CHR$(0)¶
  CALL SetWindowTitles&(NWBase&,SADD(Status$),0)¶
  GOSUB InitMinMax¶
¶
  Status$ = " Status: InitMinMaxLq"+CHR$(0)¶
  CALL SetWindowTitles&(NWBase&,SADD(Status$),0)¶
  GOSUB InitMinmaxLq¶
¶
  CALL Scron¶
¶
  Status$ = " Status: Shadows"+CHR$(0)¶
  CALL SetWindowTitles&(NWBase&,SADD(Status$),0)¶
¶
  XAOff = (BoxW% AND 1)*.5¶
  YAOff = (BoxH% AND 1)*.5¶
¶
    ' Offsets to guarantee correct point size¶
  IF XAOff = .5 THEN¶
    XBOff = .5¶
  ELSE¶
    XBOff = 1¶
  END IF¶
  IF YAOff = .5 THEN¶
    YBOff = .5¶
```

```
   ELSE¶
     YBOff = 1¶
   END IF¶
   ¶
   Body%=0¶
¶
   FOR yb%=YStart%+BoxH%/2 TO Yend%+BoxH%/2 STEP BoxH%¶
     FOR xb%=XStart%+BoxW%/2 TO XEnd%+BoxW%/2 STEP BoxW%¶

       CALL ReProjection(Rx,Ry,Rz,0!,FN Xresc(xb%),FN Yresc(yb%))¶
¶
       Rx = Rx-Px¶
       Ry = Ry-Py¶
       Rz = Rz-Pz¶
¶
       StackPtr% =-1¶
¶
       Px1 = Px¶
       Py1 = Py¶
       Pz1 = Pz¶
       ¶
       Original! = True¶
       GOSUB Computepoint¶
     ¶
       Px = Px1¶
       Py = Py1¶
       Pz = Pz1¶
       ¶
       IF Stack(0,0)>=0 THEN  'If no Intersect point => -1¶
         Bright.r=Stack(0,0)*Qh.r¶
         Bright.g=Stack(0,1)*Qh.g¶
         Bright.b=Stack(0,2)*Qh.b¶
         CALL OSSetPoint&(CLNG(xb%-BoxW%/2+XAOff),CLNG(yb%-
BoxH%/2+YAOff),CLNG(xb%+BoxW%/2-XBOff),CLNG(yb%+BoxH%/2-
YBOff),CLNG(1024*Bright.r),CLNG(1024*Bright.g),CLNG(1024*Bright.b))¶
       END IF¶
     NEXT xb%¶
¶
     IF INKEY$ <> "" THEN¶
       IF yb% < Yend%+BoxH%/2 THEN¶
       ¶
         CALL Scroff¶
         a$="Next line:"+STR$(yb%+BoxH%)¶
         CALL PrintIt(a$,130,False)¶
         CALL DialogBox("Continue",0,True,x1a%,y1a%,x2a%,y2a%,False)¶
         CALL DialogBox("Stop",2,False,x1b%,y1b%,x2b%,y2b%,False)¶
¶
         CALL DoDialog(n%,0,x1a%,y1a%,x2a%,y2a%,-1,-1,-1,-1,x1b%,y1b%,x2b%,y2b%)¶
¶
         CLS¶
         IF n% = 0 THEN¶
       ¶
           CALL Scron¶
          ELSE¶
           GOTO ShadowEnde¶
         END IF¶
       END IF  ¶
     END IF¶
   NEXT yb%¶
¶
```

```
  ShadowEnde:¶
 ¶
  CALL Scroff¶
  CLS¶
  GOSUB MakeMenu  ¶
RETURN¶
'END of SHADOWING.ASC¶
'¶
```

The SERVICE.ASC module

```
'  SERVICE.ASC¶
'  ********************************¶
'  *      'SERVICE' - Module      *¶
'  ********************************¶
'¶
Saver:  ¶
  ' Save array K() to disk¶
  GOSUB Directory¶
¶
  Status$ = " Status: Object Saver"+CHR$(0)¶
  CALL SetWindowTitles&(NWBase&,SADD(Status$),0)¶
  ¶
  LOCATE 3,1¶
  PRINT "  Under what name do you want the object saved?"¶
  PRINT   ¶
  PRINT "      Filename : ";¶
  dn$ = ""¶
  CALL FormInputString (dn$,30!)¶
¶
  CLS¶
  IF dn$<>"" THEN¶
    dn$ = dn$ + ".LIST"¶
    OPEN "O",#1,dn$,1024¶
    PRINT #1,NumberK¶
    FOR n%=1 TO NumberK¶
      FOR p%=0 TO 5¶
        PRINT #1,K(n%,p%,0),K(n%,p%,1),K(n%,p%,2)¶
      NEXT p%¶
    NEXT n%¶
    CLOSE #1¶
'The following will delete icons when included:¶
'    dn$ = dn$+".info"¶
'    KILL dn$¶
  END IF¶
  CLS¶
  GOSUB MakeMenu¶
RETURN¶
'¶
Loader:¶
  ' Load array K() from disk¶
  GOSUB Directory¶
¶
  Status$ = " Status: Object Loader"+CHR$(0)¶
  CALL SetWindowTitles&(NWBase&,SADD(Status$),0)¶
¶
  LOCATE 3,1¶
  PRINT "  Which object do you wish to load?"¶
  PRINT ¶
  PRINT "      Filename : ";¶
  dn$ = ""¶
  CALL FormInputString (dn$,30!)¶
¶
  CLS¶
```

```
  IF dn$ <> "" THEN¶
    dn$ = dn$+".LIST"¶
    OPEN "I",#1,dn$,1024¶
    INPUT #1,NumberK¶
    LOCATE 10,10¶
    PRINT "Total ";NumberK;" Object ("+dn$+")."¶
    PRINT¶
    PRINT "       Maximum number of objects? ";¶
    MaxNumber = NumberK¶
    CALL FormInputInt (MaxNumber,30!,1!,NumberK)¶
¶
    IF NumberK > MaxNumber THEN NumberK = MaxNumber¶
¶
    ERASE K¶
    DIM K(MaxNumber,5,2)¶
    ¶
    FOR n%=1 TO NumberK¶
      FOR p%=0 TO 5¶
        INPUT #1,K(n%,p%,0),K(n%,p%,1),K(n%,p%,2)¶
      NEXT p%¶
    NEXT n%¶
    CLOSE #1¶
    Newone! = True¶
    Start% = 1¶
  END IF¶
  CLS¶
  GOSUB MakeMenu¶
RETURN¶
'¶
Merger:¶
  ' Elements appended to available array K()¶
  IF (MaxNumber-NumberK) <= 0 THEN¶
    Status$ = " Status: Object Merger"+CHR$(0)¶
    CALL SetWindowTitles&(NWBase&,SADD(Status$),0)¶
¶
    a$ = "Insufficent memory for more objects!!!"¶
    CALL PrintIt (a$,100,False)¶
    a$ = "Please select New to create a cleared array K()!"¶
    CALL PrintIt (a$,130,False)¶
    CALL DialogBox("OK",1,True,x1a%,y1a%,x2a%,y2a%,False)¶
  ¶
    CALL DoDialog(n%,1,-1,-1,-1,-1,x1a%,y1a%,x2a%,y2a%,-1,-1,-1,-1)¶
  ELSE ¶
    GOSUB Directory¶
¶
    Status$ = " Status: Object Merger"+CHR$(0)¶
    CALL SetWindowTitles&(NWBase&,SADD(Status$),0)¶
¶
    LOCATE 3,1¶
    PRINT " Which object would you like to merge?"¶
    PRINT¶
    dn$ = "" ¶
    PRINT "       Filename : ";¶
    CALL FormInputString (dn$,30!)¶
¶
    CLS¶
    IF dn$ <> "" THEN¶
      dn$ = dn$ + ".LIST"¶
      OPEN "I",#1,dn$,1024¶
      INPUT #1,x¶
```

```
    ¶
      LOCATE 6,1¶
      PRINT "        Total ";x;" Objects ("+dn$+")."¶
      PRINT ¶
      PRINT "        Sufficent memory for ";MaxNumber-NumberK;" Objects."¶
      PRINT¶
      PRINT "    How many merges? ";¶
      num = x¶
      CALL FormInputInt (num,30!,1!,1000!)¶
¶
      IF x<num THEN num = x¶
      IF MaxNumber-NumberK<num THEN num = MaxNumber-NumberK¶
¶
      IF num>=1 THEN¶
        FOR n%=NumberK+1 TO NumberK+num¶
          FOR p%=0 TO 5¶
            INPUT #1,K(n%,p%,0),K(n%,p%,1),K(n%,p%,2)¶
          NEXT p%¶
        NEXT n%¶
        NumberK = NumberK+num¶
        Newone! = True¶
        Start% = 1¶
      END IF¶
      CLOSE #1¶
    END IF¶
  END IF¶
  CLS¶
  GOSUB MakeMenu¶
RETURN¶
'¶
ArrayInit:¶
  ' Create new array K()  ¶
  Status$ = " Status: New array creation"+CHR$(0)¶
  CALL SetWindowTitles&(NWBase&,SADD(Status$),0)¶
 ¶
  GOSUB DeleteMenu¶
  ¶
  LOCATE 10,1¶
  PRINT "        Maximum number of objects = ";¶
  a = MaxNumber¶
  CALL FormInputInt (a,30!,0!,1000!)¶
 ¶
  IF MaxNumber <> a THEN¶
    MaxNumber = a¶
    NumberK=0¶
    ERASE K¶
    DIM K(MaxNumber,5,2)¶
    Start% = 0¶
  END IF¶
¶
  CLS¶
  GOSUB MakeMenu¶
RETURN¶
'¶
'¶
LoadMat:¶
  GOSUB Directory¶
   ¶
  Status$ = " Status: Material constants loader"+CHR$(0)¶
  CALL SetWindowTitles&(NWBase&,SADD(Status$),0)¶
```

```
¶
  LOCATE 3,1¶
  PRINT "  Which material would you like to load?"¶
  PRINT  ¶
  PRINT "       Filename : ";¶
¶
  dn$ = ""¶
  CALL FormInputString (dn$,30!)¶
¶
  IF dn$<>"" THEN     ¶
    dn$=dn$+".MAT"¶
    OPEN "i",#1,dn$¶
    matptr = 1¶
    INPUT #1,NumberMat¶
    ERASE Mat¶
    DIM Mat(NumberMat,6)¶
    WHILE NOT(EOF(1))¶
      FOR i=0 TO 6¶
        INPUT #1,Mat(matptr,i)¶
      NEXT i¶
      matptr = matptr+1¶
    WEND¶
    CLOSE #1¶
  END IF¶
  CLS¶
  GOSUB MakeMenu¶
RETURN¶
'¶
'¶
ScreenSaver:¶
  GOSUB Directory¶
   ¶
  Status$ = " Status: Screen saver"+CHR$(0)¶
  CALL SetWindowTitles&(NWBase&,SADD(Status$),0)¶
¶
  LOCATE 3,1¶
  PRINT "  Under what name would you like the screen saved?"¶
  PRINT  ¶
  PRINT "       Filename : ";¶
  IFFFile$ = ""¶
  CALL FormInputString (IFFFile$,30!)¶
      ¶
  IF IFFFile$ <> "" THEN¶
     ¶
    Handle& = 0      ' File Handle¶
    Buffer& = 0      ' Buffer memory¶
    ' reserve buffer¶
    Flags& = 65537&     ' MEMF_PUBLIC | MEMF_CLEAR¶
    BufferSize& = 360¶
    Buffer& = AllocMem&(BufferSize&,Flags&)¶
    IF Buffer& = 0 THEN¶
      Dialog$ = "No more memory!!!"¶
      GOTO EndSave¶
    END IF¶
¶
    ColorBuffer& = Buffer&¶
¶
    Null& = 0¶
    PadByte%  = 0¶
    ¶
```

```
    IF RasterW% = 320 THEN¶
      IF RasterH% = 200 THEN¶
        Aspect% = &HA0B¶
      ELSE¶
        Aspect% = &H140B¶
      END IF¶
    ELSE¶
      IF RasterH% = 200 THEN¶
        Aspect% = &H50B¶
      ELSE¶
        Aspect% = &HA0B¶
      END IF¶
    END IF¶
¶
    IFFFile$ = IFFFile$ + CHR$(0)¶
    Handle& = xOpen&(SADD(IFFFile$),1006)¶
    IF Handle& = 0 THEN¶
      Dialog$ = "Can't open the file you wanted!!!"¶
      GOTO EndSave¶
    END IF¶
¶
¶
    ' How many bytes contain IFF-Chunks ?¶
    BMHDSize& = 20¶
    CMAPSize& = MaxColour%*3 + ((MaxColour%*3) AND 1)¶
    CAMGSize& = 4¶
    BODYSize& = (RasterW%/8)*RasterH%*RasterT%¶
    ' FORMsize& = Chunk-Length + 8 Bytes per Chunk-Header + 4 Bytes ("ILBM")¶
    FORMSize& = BMHDSize&+CMAPSize&+CAMGSize&+BODYSize&+36¶
¶
    ' FORM-Header ¶
    Chunk$ = "FORM"¶
    Length& = xWrite&(Handle&,SADD(Chunk$),4)¶
    Length& = xWrite&(Handle&,VARPTR(FORMSize&),4)¶
    ' + ILBM for BitMap-File¶
    Chunk$ = "ILBM"¶
    Length& = xWrite&(Handle&,SADD(Chunk$),4)¶
¶
    IF Length& <= 0 THEN¶
      Dialog$ = "Write error on FORM-Header !!!"¶
      GOTO EndSave¶
    END IF   ¶
¶
    ' BMHD-Chunk ¶
    Chunk$ = "BMHD"¶
    Length& = xWrite&(Handle&,SADD(Chunk$),4)¶
    Length& = xWrite&(Handle&,VARPTR(BMHDSize&),4)¶
    Length& = xWrite&(Handle&,VARPTR(RasterW%),2)¶
    Length& = xWrite&(Handle&,VARPTR(RasterH%),2)¶
    Length& = xWrite&(Handle&,VARPTR(Null&),4)¶
    Temp% = (256 * RasterT%) ' No MASKING¶
    Length& = xWrite&(Handle&,VARPTR(Temp%),2)¶
    Temp% = 0                ' No Packing¶
    Length& = xWrite&(Handle&,VARPTR(Temp%),2)¶
    Temp% = 0¶
    Length& = xWrite&(Handle&,VARPTR(Temp%),2)¶
    Length& = xWrite&(Handle&,VARPTR(Aspect%),2)¶
    Length& = xWrite&(Handle&,VARPTR(RasterW%),2)¶
    Length& = xWrite&(Handle&,VARPTR(RasterH%),2)¶
¶
```

```
    IF Length& <= 0 THEN¶
      Dialog$ = "Write error on BMHD-Chunk !!!"¶
      GOTO EndSave¶
    END IF   ¶
¶
    ' CMAP-Chunk ¶
    Chunk$ = "CMAP"¶
    Length& = xWrite&(Handle&,SADD(Chunk$),4)¶
    Length& = xWrite&(Handle&,VARPTR(CMAPSize&),4)¶
¶
    FOR i%=0 TO MaxColour%-1¶
      Colours% = GetRGB4%(ColorMap&,i%)¶
      blue = Colours% AND 15¶
      Colours% = Colours% - blue¶
      green = (Colours%/16) AND 15¶
      Colours% = Colours%-green*16¶
      red = (Colours%/256) AND 15¶
      POKE(ColorBuffer&+(i%*3)),red*16¶
      POKE(ColorBuffer&+(i%*3)+1),green*16 ¶
      POKE(ColorBuffer&+(i%*3)+2),blue*16¶
    NEXT¶
¶
    Length& = xWrite&(Handle&,ColorBuffer&,CMAPSize&)¶
¶
    IF Length& <= 0 THEN¶
      Dialog$ = "Write error on CMAP-Chunk !!!"¶
      GOTO EndSave¶
    END IF   ¶
¶
    ' CAMG-Chunk ¶
    Chunk$ = "CAMG"¶
    Length& = xWrite&(Handle&,SADD(Chunk$),4)¶
    Length& = xWrite&(Handle&,VARPTR(CAMGSize&),4)¶
    Modes& = PEEKW(Viewport& + 32)¶
    Length& = xWrite&(Handle&,VARPTR(Modes&),4)¶
¶
    IF Length& <= 0 THEN¶
      Dialog$ = "Write error on CAMG-Chunk !!!"¶
      GOTO EndSave¶
    END IF   ¶
    ¶
    ' BODY-Chunk (BitMaps)¶
    Chunk$ = "BODY"¶
    Length& = xWrite&(Handle&,SADD(Chunk$),4)¶
    Length& = xWrite&(Handle&,VARPTR(BODYSize&),4)¶
    BytesPerRow% = RasterW%/8¶
    FOR y1 = 0 TO RasterH%-1¶
      FOR b=0 TO RasterT%-1¶
        Adress& = BitPlanes&(b)+(y1*BytesPerRow%)¶
        Length& = xWrite&(Handle&,Adress&,BytesPerRow%)    ¶
        IF Length& <= 0 THEN¶
          Dialog$ = "Write error  on BODY-Chunk !!!"¶
          GOTO EndSave¶
        END IF      ¶
      NEXT¶
    NEXT¶
  ¶
    Dialog$ = "Saving OK"¶
¶
  EndSave:¶
```

```
    IF Handle& <> 0 THEN CALL xClose&(Handle&)¶
    IF Buffer& <> 0 THEN CALL FreeMem&(Buffer&,BufferSize&)¶
    CALL DialogBox(Dialog$,1,True,x1b%,y1b%,x2b%,y2b%,False)¶
    CALL DoDialog(n%,1,-1,-1,-1,-1,x1b%,y1b%,x2b%,y2b%,-1,-1,-1,-1)  ¶
  END IF¶
  CLS ¶
  GOSUB MakeMenu¶
RETURN¶
'¶
'¶
ScreenLoader:¶
  GOSUB Directory¶
   ¶
  Status$ = " Status: Screen Loader"+CHR$(0)¶
  CALL SetWindowTitles&(NWBase&,SADD(Status$),0)¶
¶
  LOCATE 3,1¶
    PRINT "  Which IFF-File would you like to load?"¶
  PRINT  ¶
  PRINT "      Filename : ";¶
  IFFFile$ = ""¶
  CALL FormInputString (IFFFile$,30!)¶
      ¶
  IF IFFFile$ <> "" THEN¶
¶
    BMHD = False¶
    CMAP = False¶
    CAMG = False¶
    Body = False¶
¶
    Handle& = 0¶
    Buffer& = 0¶
¶
    ' reserve buffer¶
    Flags& = 65537&      ' MEMF_PUBLIC | MEMF_CLEAR¶
    BufferSize& = 360¶
    Buffer& = AllocMem&(BufferSize&,Flags&)¶
    IF Buffer& = 0 THEN¶
      Dialog$ = "No more memory!!!"¶
      GOTO EndLoad¶
    END IF¶
¶
    InputBuffer& = Buffer&¶
    ColorBuffer& = Buffer& + 120¶
¶
¶
    IFFFile$ = IFFFile$ + CHR$(0)¶
    Handle& = xOpen&(SADD(IFFFile$),1005)¶
    IF Handle& = 0 THEN¶
      Dialog$ = "IFF-File can not be opened!!!"¶
      GOTO EndLoad¶
    END IF¶
¶
¶
    Length& = xRead&(Handle&,InputBuffer&,12)¶
    Chunk$ = ""¶
    FOR n% = 8 TO 11¶
      Chunk$ = Chunk$ + CHR$(PEEK(InputBuffer&+n%))¶
    NEXT¶
¶
```

```
    IF Chunk$ <> "ILBM" THEN ¶
      Dialog$ = "Not IFF-Format !!!"¶
      GOTO EndLoad¶
    END IF¶
¶
  ReadLoop:¶
    Length& = xRead&(Handle&,InputBuffer&,8)¶
    Chunkwinlen& = PEEKL(InputBuffer& + 4)¶
    Chunk$ = ""¶
    FOR n% = 0 TO 3¶
      Chunk$ = Chunk$ + CHR$(PEEK(InputBuffer&+n%))¶
    NEXT   ¶
    ¶
    IF Chunk$ = "BMHD" THEN         ' BitMap-Header ¶
      BMHD = True¶
      Length& = xRead&(Handle&,InputBuffer&,Chunkwinlen&)¶
      RDepth%        = PEEK(InputBuffer& + 8)  ¶
      Compression%   = PEEK(InputBuffer& + 10)¶
      RWidth%        = PEEKW(InputBuffer& + 16)¶
      RHeight%       = PEEKW(InputBuffer& + 18)¶
      BytesPerRow%   = RWidth%/8¶
      RMaxColors%    = 2^(RDepth%)¶
¶
      '  IFF-Picture adapted to Display-Screen ?¶
      IF (RWidth% <> RasterW%) OR (RHeight% <> RasterH%) THEN¶
        Dialog$ = "Format error: "+STR$(RWidth%)+" x"+STR$(RHeight%)¶
        GOTO EndLoad¶
      END IF¶
¶
    ELSEIF Chunk$ = "CMAP" THEN  ' Color-Palette¶
      Length& = xRead&(Handle&,ColorBuffer&,Chunkwinlen&)¶
      CMAP = True¶
      ' Color-Palette set up¶
      FOR n% = 0 TO RMaxColors% - 1¶
        red%   = PEEK(ColorBuffer&+(n%*3))/16¶
        green% = PEEK(ColorBuffer&+(n%*3)+1)/16¶
        blue%  = PEEK(ColorBuffer&+(n%*3)+2)/16¶
        dummy = SetRGB4(Viewport&,n%,red%,green%,blue%)¶
                          ¶
        POKEW OSColour&+n%*8+2,red%/15*1024¶
        POKEW OSColour&+n%*8+4,green%/15*1024¶
        POKEW OSColour&+n%*8+6,blue%/15*1024¶
      NEXT¶
¶
    ELSEIF Chunk$ = "BODY" THEN  'BitMap Loader¶
      CALL Scron¶
      Body = True¶
      IF Compression% = 0 THEN  'No compression¶
        FOR y1 = 0 TO RHeight% -1¶
          FOR b = 0 TO RDepth% -1¶
            IF b<RasterT% THEN¶
              Adress& = BitPlanes&(b)+(y1*BytesPerRow%)¶
            ELSE¶
              Adress& = Buffer&¶
            END IF¶
            Length& = xRead&(Handle&,Adress&,BytesPerRow%)    ¶
          NEXT¶
        NEXT¶
¶
    ELSEIF Compression% = 1 THEN  'CmpByteRun1 compression¶
```

```
      FOR y1 = 0 TO RHeight% -1¶
        FOR b = 0 TO RDepth% -1¶
          IF b<RasterT% THEN¶
            Adress& = BitPlanes&(b)+(y1*BytesPerRow%)¶
          ELSE¶
            Adress& = Buffer&¶
          END IF¶
          NumBytes% = 0¶
            ¶
          WHILE (NumBytes% < BytesPerRow%)¶
            Length& = xRead&(Handle&,InputBuffer&,1)¶
            Code% = PEEK(InputBuffer&)¶
            IF Code% < 128 THEN          ' Code%-Bytes take over¶
              Length& = xRead&(Handle&,Adress& + NumBytes%, Code%+1)¶
              NumBytes% = NumBytes% + Code% + 1¶
            ELSEIF Code% > 128 THEN      ' Byte replicates¶
              Length& = xRead&(Handle&,InputBuffer&,1)    ¶
              Byte% = PEEK(InputBuffer&)¶
              FOR n% = NumBytes% TO NumBytes% + 257 - Code%¶
                POKE(Adress&+n%),Byte%¶
              NEXT   ¶
              NumBytes% = NumBytes% + 257 - Code%¶
            END IF¶
          WEND¶
        NEXT¶
      NEXT¶
        ¶
      ELSE¶
        Dialog$ = "Unknown compression procedure!!!"¶
        GOTO EndLoad¶
      END IF¶
    CALL Scroff¶
    ELSE ¶
      ' "Unknown" Chunk-Typ¶
      FOR n = 1 TO Chunkwinlen&¶
        Length& = xRead&(Handle&,InputBuffer&,1)¶
      NEXT¶
      ' Chunks have even numnber of bytes¶
      IF (Chunkwinlen& AND 1) = 1 THEN ¶
        Length& = xRead&(Handle&,InputBuffer&,1)¶
      END IF¶
    END IF¶
¶
    ' All Chunks read?¶
    IF (BMHD = True) AND (CMAP = True) AND (Body = True) THEN¶
      GOTO LoadOK¶
    END IF¶
¶
    ' Read ok, get next Chunk¶
    IF Length& > 0 THEN GOTO ReadLoop¶
¶
    IF Length& < 0 THEN    ¶
      Dialog$ = "Read error!!!"¶
      GOTO EndLoad¶
    END IF   ¶
  ¶
    IF (BMHD=False) OR (CMAP=False) OR (Body=0) THEN¶
      Dialog$ = "Not all necessary ILBM-Chunks found!!!"¶
      GOTO EndLoad¶
    END IF¶
```

```
¶
    LoadOK:¶
      Dialog$ = "Loading OK"¶
¶
    EndLoad:¶
      IF Handle& <> 0 THEN CALL xClose&(Handle&)¶
      IF Buffer& <> 0 THEN CALL FreeMem&(Buffer&,BufferSize&)¶
      CALL DialogBox(Dialog$,1,True,x1b%,y1b%,x2b%,y2b%,False)¶
      CALL DoDialog(n%,1,-1,-1,-1,-1,x1b%,y1b%,x2b%,y2b%,-1,-1,-1,-1)  ¶
  END IF¶
  CLS¶
  GOSUB MakeMenu¶
RETURN¶
'¶
'¶
HardCopy:¶
  Status$ = " Status: Screen hardcopy"+CHR$(0)¶
  CALL SetWindowTitles&(NWBase&,SADD(Status$),0)¶
¶
  GOSUB DeleteMenu¶
¶
  CALL DialogBox("No Printer",0,True,x1a%,y1a%,x2a%,y2a%,False)  ¶
  CALL DialogBox("Printer OK",2,False,x1c%,y1c%,x2c%,y2c%,False)¶
  CALL DoDialog(n%,0,x1a%,y1a%,x2a%,ya2%,-1,-1,-1,-1,x1c%,y1c%,x2c%,y2c%)  ¶
  CLS¶
  IF n% <> 0 THEN¶
    Modes% = PEEKW(Viewport& + 32)¶
¶
    sigBit% =  AllocSignal%(-1)¶
    Flags& = 65537&              ' MEMF_PUBLIC | MEMF_CLEAR¶
    MsgPort& = AllocMem&(40,Flags&)¶
    IF MsgPort& = 0 THEN¶
      Dialog$ = "No 'MsgPort' !!!"¶
      GOTO EndPrinter4¶
    END IF¶
¶
    POKE(MsgPort& + 8), 4 ¶
    POKE(MsgPort& + 9), 0 ¶
    Nam$ = "PrtPort"+CHR$(0)¶
    POKEL(MsgPort& + 10), SADD(Nam$)¶
    POKE(MsgPort& + 14), 0 ¶
    POKE(MsgPort& + 15), sigBit%¶
    SigTask& = FindTask&(0)¶
    POKEL(MsgPort& + 16), SigTask&¶
¶
    CALL AddPort(MsgPort&)  'lsit Port¶
¶
    ioRequest& = AllocMem&(64,Flags&)¶
    IF ioRequest& = 0  THEN¶
      Dialog$ = "No ioRequest !!!"¶
      GOTO EndPrinter3¶
    END IF¶
¶
    POKE(ioRequest& + 8),5 ¶
    POKE(ioRequest& + 9),0 ¶
    POKEL(ioRequest& + 14), MsgPort&¶
¶
¶
    Nam$ = "printer.device"+CHR$(0)¶
    PrinterError& = OpenDevice&(SADD(Nam$),0,ioRequest&,0)¶
```

```
    IF PrinterError& <> 0  THEN¶
      Dialog$ = "No Printer ?!?"¶
      GOTO EndPrinter2¶
    END IF¶
¶
    POKEW(ioRequest& + 28), 11           ' DumpRastport to Printer¶
    POKEL(ioRequest& + 32), RastPort&    ' Print entire screen ¶
    POKEL(ioRequest& + 36), ColorMap&¶
    POKEL(ioRequest& + 40), Modes%¶
    POKEW(ioRequest& + 44), 0¶
    POKEW(ioRequest& + 46), 0¶
    POKEW(ioRequest& + 48), RasterW%¶
    POKEW(ioRequest& + 50), RasterH%¶
    POKEL(ioRequest& + 52), 0&¶
    POKEL(ioRequest& + 56), 0&¶
    POKEW(ioRequest& + 60), &H84¶
¶
    CALL DialogBox("Printing...",1,False,x1a%,y1a%,x2a%,y2a%,False)  ¶
  ¶
    PrinterError& = DoIO&(ioRequest&)¶
    IF PrinterError& <> 0 THEN¶
      Dialog$ = "DumpRPort Error ="+STR$(PrinterError&)+" !!!"¶
      GOTO EndPrinter¶
    END IF¶
¶
    CLS¶
    Dialog$ = "Hardcopy done"¶
  ¶
    EndPrinter:    ¶
      CALL CloseDevice(ioRequest&)¶
¶
    EndPrinter2:¶
      POKE(ioRequest& + 8), &HFF¶
      POKEL(ioRequest& + 20), -1¶
      POKEL(ioRequest& + 24), -1¶
      CALL FreeMem&(ioRequest&,64)¶
¶
    EndPrinter3:¶
      CALL RemPort(MsgPort&)¶
      POKE(MsgPort& + 8), &HFF  ¶
      POKEL(MsgPort& + 20), -1¶
      CALL FreeSignal(sigBit%)¶
      CALL FreeMem&(MsgPort&,40)¶
  ¶
    EndPrinter4:¶
      CALL DialogBox(Dialog$,1,True,x1b%,y1b%,x2b%,y2b%,False)¶
      CALL DoDialog(n%,1,-1,-1,-1,-1,x1b%,y1b%,x2b%,y2b%,-1,-1,-1,-1)  ¶
  END IF¶
  CLS¶
  GOSUB MakeMenu  ¶
RETURN¶
'¶
LoadEditor:¶
  Status$ = " Status: Editor loading"+CHR$(0)¶
  CALL SetWindowTitles&(NWBase&,SADD(Status$),0)¶
¶
  GOSUB DeleteMenu¶
¶
  CALL DialogBox("Cancel,0,True,x1a%,y1a%,x2a%,y2a%,False)  ¶
  CALL DialogBox("Load",2,False,x1c%,y1c%,x2c%,y2c%,False)¶
```

```
  CALL DoDialog(n%,0,x1a%,y1a%,x2a%,ya2%,-1,-1,-1,-1,x1c%,y1c%,x2c%,y2c%)  ¶
  CLS¶
  IF n% = 2 THEN¶
    CHDIR "Tracer:"  ¶
    GOSUB CloseIt¶
    CHAIN "Editor"¶
  END IF¶
  GOSUB MakeMenu  ¶
END¶
'     ¶
ClearScreen:¶
  Status$ = " Status: Clear screen"+CHR$(0)¶
  CALL SetWindowTitles&(NWBase&,SADD(Status$),0)¶
  ¶
  CALL SetRast&(RastPort&,0)¶
  Hg = True¶
  ¶
  GOSUB NOOP¶
RETURN¶
'¶
'¶
Info:¶
  ' Information about free elements of K()¶
  Status$ = " Status: Info"+CHR$(0)¶
  CALL SetWindowTitles&(NWBase&,SADD(Status$),0)¶
¶
  GOSUB DeleteMenu¶
¶
  CALL PrintIt("3D - CAD",60,False)¶
  CALL PrintIt("Original-Version: Peter Schulz (c) 1986",75,False)¶
  CALL PrintIt("Amiga-Version: Bruno Jennrich (c) 1987",90,False)¶
¶
  a$ = "Maximum number of objects : "+STR$(MaxNumber)¶
  CALL PrintIt(a$,105,False)¶
¶
  a$ = "Actual number of objects  : "+STR$(NumberK)¶
  CALL PrintIt(a$,120,False)¶
¶
  GOSUB Pause¶
¶
  CLS¶
  GOSUB MakeMenu¶
RETURN¶
'¶
Help:¶
  ' Which key press for which action¶
  Status$ = " Status: Help"+CHR$(0)¶
  CALL SetWindowTitles&(NWBase&,SADD(Status$),0)¶
¶
  GOSUB DeleteMenu¶
¶
  LOCATE 2,1¶
¶
  PRINT " P rojection point"¶
  PRINT " H Main point"¶
¶
  PRINT " W enter angle"¶
  PRINT " Cursor keys => rotate"¶
  PRINT " R otate (SHIFT,CONTROL)"¶
¶
```

```
  PRINT " D: spacing for main point"¶
  PRINT " +|-|*|/ Enlarge/reduce spacing (SHIFT+|-)"¶
¶
  PRINT " V Enlarge"¶
¶
  PRINT " L oad Object"¶
  PRINT " S ave Object"¶
  PRINT " M erge Object"¶
  PRINT " N ew, clear all objects"¶
  PRINT " B Screen saver"¶
  PRINT " Q => Program end (Quit)"  ¶
¶
  PRINT " F1  => Editor load"¶
¶
  PRINT " F9  => Shadows initialization"¶
  PRINT " F10 => Shadows"¶
  PRINT " <SPACE> => Show picture"¶
  PRINT " C lear screen";¶
¶
  GOSUB Pause¶
  CLS¶
  GOSUB MakeMenu¶
RETURN¶
'¶
'¶
SUB Sky(a%,Col%,num%) STATIC¶
SHARED WScreen&,NWBase&,RasterW%,RasterH%,RasterW1%¶
SHARED RasterH1%,RasterW2%,RasterH2%,RastPort&¶
  CALL Scron¶
    ¶
  CALL SetAPen&(RastPort&,Col%)¶
  CALL SetRast&(RastPort&,0)¶
  ¶
  FOR n%=1 TO num%¶
    RANDOMIZE TIMER¶
¶
    IF a%<4 THEN¶
      IF a% AND 1 THEN¶
        x%=RasterW2%+RasterW2%*RND*RND*SGN(RND-.5)¶
        y%=RasterH2%+RasterH2%*RND*RND*SGN(RND-.5)¶
      ELSE¶
        x%=RND*RasterW1%¶
        y%=RND*RasterH1%¶
      END IF¶
¶
      IF a% AND 2 THEN¶
        IF x%=RasterW2% AND y%=RasterH2% THEN¶
          dummy = WritePixel(RastPort&,x%,y%)¶
        ELSE¶
          x1%=(x%-RasterW2%)*.1+x%¶
          y1%=(y%-RasterH2%)*.1+y%¶
          IF x1%>=0 AND x1%<RasterW% AND y1%>=0 AND y1%<RasterH% THEN¶
            CALL Move&(RastPort&,x%,y%)¶
            CALL Draw&(RastPort&,x1%,y1%)¶
          END IF¶
        END IF¶
      ELSE¶
¶
        IF RND<.9 THEN¶
          CALL WritePixel&(RastPort&,x%,y%)¶
```

```
        ELSE¶
          CALL Move&(RastPort&,x%-1,y%)¶
          CALL Draw&(RastPort&,x%+1,y%)¶
          CALL Draw&(RastPort&,x%,y%-1)¶
          CALL Draw&(RastPort&,x%,y%+1)¶
        END IF¶
      END IF¶
    ELSE¶
¶
      x%=RND*RasterW1%¶
      y%=RND*RasterH1%¶
      CALL Move&(RastPort&,RasterW2%,RasterH2%)¶
      CALL Draw&(RastPort&,x%,y%)¶
    END IF¶
  NEXT n%¶
¶
  CALL SetAPen&(RastPort&,1)¶
¶
  CALL Scroff  ¶
END SUB¶
'¶
SUB Fhg(Colours1%,Colours2%) STATIC¶
SHARED RasterW1%,RasterH1%,Colour(),MaxColour%,WScreen&¶
SHARED NWBase&,RastPort&,OSSetPoint&,OSModus&,OSMaxColour&¶
  ' Produce floating passage between Colours1 and Colours2¶
  CALL Scron¶
   ¶
  red.s=Colour(Colours1%+1,1)¶
  green.s=Colour(Colours1%+1,2)¶
  blue.s=Colour(Colours1%+1,3)¶
  red.e=Colour(Colours2%+1,1)¶
  green.e=Colour(Colours2%+1,2)¶
  blue.e=Colour(Colours2%+1,3)¶
¶
  IF (PEEKW(OSModus&) AND &H800) = &H800 THEN  'HAM¶
¶
 'Background limited to 16 Colors, or else Objects disturbed.¶
¶
    POKEW OSMaxColour&,16¶
    FOR y%=0 TO RasterH1%¶
      red=red.s+(y%/RasterH1%)*(red.e-red.s)¶
      green=green.s+(y%/RasterH1%)*(green.e-green.s)¶
      blue=blue.s+(y%/RasterH1%)*(blue.e-blue.s)¶
'      CALL SetPoint(0,y%,RasterW1%,y%,red,green,blue)¶
      CALL
OSSetPoint&(0,y%,RasterW1%,y%,CLNG(1024*red),CLNG(1024*green),CLNG(1024*blue))¶
    NEXT y%¶
    POKEW OSMaxColour&,64¶
  ELSE¶
    FOR y%=0 TO RasterH1%¶
      red=red.s+(y%/RasterH1%)*(red.e-red.s)¶
      green=green.s+(y%/RasterH1%)*(green.e-green.s)¶
      blue=blue.s+(y%/RasterH1%)*(blue.e-blue.s)¶
'      CALL SetPoint(0,y%,RasterW1%,y%,red,green,blue)¶
      CALL
OSSetPoint&(0,y%,RasterW1%,y%,CLNG(1024*red),CLNG(1024*green),CLNG(1024*blue))¶
    NEXT y%¶
  END IF¶
  CALL Scroff¶
END SUB¶
```

```
'¶
Background:¶
  ' Background Determine¶
  Status$ = " Status: Background selection"+CHR$(0)¶
  CALL SetWindowTitles&(NWBase&,SADD(Status$),0)¶
¶
  GOSUB DeleteMenu¶
  ¶
  CALL DialogBox("Pattern",0,True,x1a%,y1a%,x2a%,y2a%,False)¶
  CALL DialogBox("Load screen",2,False,x1b%,y1b%,x2b%,y2b%,False)¶
  ¶
  CALL DoDialog(n%,0,x1a%,y1a%,x2a%,y2a%,-1,-1,-1,-1,x1b%,y1b%,x2b%,y2b%)¶
  CLS  ¶
¶
  IF n%=2 THEN¶
    GOSUB ScreenLoader¶
    Hg = True¶
  ELSE¶
    CALL DialogBox("Pattern",0,True,x1a%,y1a%,x2a%,y2a%,False)¶
    CALL DialogBox("Sky",1,False,x1b%,y1b%,x2b%,y2b%,False)¶
    CALL DialogBox("Floating",2,False,x1c%,y1c%,x2c%,y2c%,False)¶
¶
    CALL DoDialog(n%,0,x1a%,y1a%,x2a%,y2a%,x1b%,y1b%,x2b%,y2b%,x1c%,y1c%,x2c%,y2c%)
¶
    CLS¶
¶
    IF n% = 0 THEN    ¶
    ¶
      CALL PrintIt("Background = Pattern",40,False)¶
      ¶
      LOCATE 10,1¶
      PRINT "       Number of the pattern (0..34) : ";¶
      a = 0¶
      CALL FormInputInt (Hx,30!,0!,34!)¶
      Xpattern% = a¶
¶
      LOCATE 11,1      ¶
      PRINT "       Foreground pen (APen) : ";¶
      a=APen%¶
      CALL FormInputInt (a,30!,0!,CSNG(MaxColour%-1))¶
      APen% = a¶
¶
      LOCATE 12,1      ¶
      PRINT "       Background pen (BPen) : ";¶
      a = BPen%¶
      CALL FormInputInt (a,30!,0!,CSNG(MaxColour%-1))¶
      BPen% = a¶
¶
      Xpattern% = Xpattern% MOD (NumberPatternS%+NumberPatternX%*2+1)¶
¶
      IF Xpattern% > NumberPatternS% THEN¶
        CALL ExtendedFill(0,0,RasterW1%,RasterH1%,PatternHX(Xpattern%-
NumberPatternS%),0!,1!,APen%,BPen%)¶
       ELSE¶
        CALL StandardFill(0,0,RasterW1%,RasterH1%,PatternHS(NumberPatternS%-
Xpattern%),APen%,BPen%)   ¶
      END IF¶
      CLS¶
      Hg = True¶
    END IF¶
```

```
   ¶
   IF n% = 1 THEN¶
     LOCATE 3,1¶
     PRINT " Sky type:"¶
     PRINT "  0 = Stars (scattered)"¶
     PRINT "  1 = Stars (centered)"¶
     PRINT "  2 = Lines (scattered)"¶
     PRINT "  3 = Lines (centered)"¶
     PRINT "  4 = Lines (middle centered)" ¶
     ¶
     LOCATE 10,1¶
     PRINT " Type   : ";¶
     a = Art%¶
     CALL FormInputInt (a,30!,0!,4!)¶
     Art% = a¶
¶
     LOCATE 11,1¶
     PRINT " Color  : ";¶
     a = 1¶
     CALL FormInputInt (a,30!,0!,CSNG(MaxColour%-1))¶
     HColr% = a¶
            ¶
     LOCATE 12,1¶
     PRINT " Number : ";¶
     a = 100¶
     CALL FormInputInt (a,30!,0!,500!)¶
     num% = a¶
¶
     CLS¶
     CALL Sky (Art%,HColr%,num%)¶
     Hg = True¶
   END IF¶
   ¶
   IF n% = 2 THEN¶
     CLS¶
      ¶
     CALL PrintIt("Floating Background",40,False)¶
     ¶
     LOCATE 10,1¶
     PRINT "         from color: ";¶
     F1 = 0¶
     CALL FormInput (F1,30!,0!,CSNG(MaxColour%-1))¶
     Colours1%=F1¶
     LOCATE 12,1¶
     PRINT "         to color: ";¶
     F2 = 1¶
     CALL FormInput (F2,30!,0!,CSNG(MaxColour%-1))¶
     Colours2%=F2¶
  ¶
     CALL Fhg(Colours1%,Colours2%)¶
     Hg = True¶
   END IF¶
  END IF¶
  CLS  ¶
  GOSUB MakeMenu¶
RETURN¶
```

C. The Editor Program

The following is the complete listing of the editor program found on the optional diskette. The example program that follows contain some BASIC lines that must be entered on one line in AmigaBASIC even though they appear on two lines in this book. Formatting the program listings to fit into this book has caused some long BASIC lines to be split into two lines. To show where a BASIC line is actually ended, an end of paragraph character (¶) will be used. This is not to be entered, it only shows when the <Return> key should be pressed in the BASIC editor. For example, the following line is split into two lines in this book but must be entered as one line in AmigaBASIC:

```
WinDef NWindow, 100, 50, 460, 150, 32+64+512&, 15&+4096&,
0&, Title$¶
```

The ¶ shows the actual end of the BASIC line.

The following pages contain the complete listing of the editor program contained on the optional diskette.

```
'**************************¶
'**  RAY-TRACING-EDITOR  **¶
'**************************¶
¶
GOSUB init 'Initialization all variables and screen configuration¶
WHILE quit=0  'wait until end is signaled by quit=1¶
  a$=INKEY$¶
  IF a$><"" THEN¶
    GOSUB shortcuts  'Get a key and compare with shortcuts¶
  END IF    ¶
WEND¶
GOSUB ende 'Program end¶
END¶
¶
¶
'*************************¶
'**  INITIALIZATION     **¶
'*************************                        ¶
¶
init:¶
  DIM gadgets%(400),gadget%(10,7)¶
  FOR i=0 TO 10      'Clear all gadgets (see below)¶
    gadget%(i,0)=-1¶
  NEXT i  ¶
  nr1%=0  'global gadget pointer to elements used¶
  nr2%=0¶
  nr3%=0¶
  nr4%=0¶
  nr5%=0¶
  nr6%=0¶
  LOCATE 2,1  'Read graphic information of gadgets used¶
  PRINT "  NO  "¶
  LINE (5,5)-(65,20),,b¶
  GET (5,5)-(65,20),gadgets%(200)¶
  LOCATE 2,1 ¶
  PRINT " YES "         ¶
  LINE (5,5)-(45,20),,b¶
  GET (5,5)-(45,20),gadgets%(100)  ¶
  LOCATE 2,1¶
  PRINT " OK "¶
  LINE (5,5)-(35,20),,b¶
  GET (5,5)-(35,20),gadgets%(0)¶
  CLS¶
  DEFINT a-z¶
  FOR i=44 TO 122¶
    legchar$=legchar$+CHR$(i) 'legal characters for text entry¶
  NEXT i  ¶
  grad!=57.29577    'Conversion constants - radian to degree¶
  rad!=.017453      'Conversion constants - degree to radian¶
  empty$=SPACE$(29) 'Empty line¶
  max!=10000        'Upper and lower limits of real values¶
  min!=-max!¶
  ptr=0             'Pointer to current list elements¶
  matptr=0¶
  dir$="libs/"      'current directory¶
  OPEN dir$+"maxnum" FOR INPUT AS 1 'maximum number in bodies and material list¶
  INPUT #1,knum,matnum¶
  CLOSE 1¶
  colour=1           'character color 1=white 3=orange¶
  DIM t(11),tabs(11,1),typ$(24),k!(knum,5,2),mat!(matnum,6)¶
  FOR i=1 TO knum    'combine free lists¶
    k!(i,0,0)=-1¶
```

```
    k!(i,0,1)=i+1¶
  NEXT i¶
  FOR i=1 TO matnum¶
    mat!(i,0)=-1¶
    mat!(i,1)=i+1¶
  NEXT i    ¶
  typ$(0)="Plane"            'arrange by type and name¶
  typ$(1)="Triangle"¶
  typ$(2)="Parallelogram"¶
  typ$(3)="Circle"¶
  typ$(4)="Circle segment"¶
  typ$(5)="Arc"¶
  typ$(10)="Sphere"¶
  typ$(20)="Cylinder"¶
  typ$(21)="Cylinder segment"¶
  typ$(22)="Cone"¶
  typ$(24)="Spheroid"  ¶
  t(1)=0   'Arrange by menu line and type¶
  t(2)=1¶
  t(3)=2¶
  t(4)=3¶
  t(5)=4¶
  t(6)=5¶
  t(7)=10¶
  t(8)=20¶
  t(9)=21¶
  t(10)=22¶
  t(11)=24¶
  xcorrfac!=1.88  'Correction factor for the  horizontal resolution¶
  maxlines=20     'Maximum number of lines available for circle drawing¶
  pi2!=6.283185   '2*3.141592¶
  factor!=1       'Sizing factor¶
  mx!=0           'Position of upper left screen corner¶
  my!=116¶
  mz!=116¶
  quit=0          'Initialize end flag¶
  mox!=0¶
  moy!=0¶
  moz!=0¶
  kfree=1         'Set free pointer to start of list¶
  matfree=1¶
  rp&=WINDOW(8)     'Determine cursor width and height¶
  cw%=PEEKW(rp&+60)¶
  ch%=PEEKW(rp&+58)¶
  File$="objects/" 'contains all Filenames, used by disk operations¶
    ¶
  DECLARE FUNCTION allocmem& LIBRARY  'addition of allocmem and freemem¶
  LIBRARY dir$+"exec.library" 'alloc- and freemem added¶
  LIBRARY dir$+"intuition.library" 'set- and clearpointer added¶
  LIBRARY dir$+"graphics.library" 'add the procedure setdrmd¶
  ¶
  SCREEN 1,640,256,2,2¶
  WINDOW 1,"XY-PLANE",(0,0)-(298,115),7,1¶
  WINDOW 2,"XZ-PLANE",(320,0)-(617,115),7,1¶
  WINDOW 3,"YZ-PLANE",(320,85)-(617,190),7,1¶
  WINDOW 4,"RAY-TRACING-EDITOR",(0,85)-(314,190),22,1¶
¶
  buffer&=allocmem&(68*2,2)  'Memory for mouse pointer¶
  CALL initmaus¶
 ¶
  CALL act1with4  'Menu 1 with 4 active¶
  CALL deactiv5   'Menu 5 deactivated¶
```

```
 ¶
 MENU ON¶
 ON MENU GOSUB choice¶
 ¶
 MOUSE ON¶
 ON MOUSE GOSUB click¶
 ¶
 PRINT"Body  :0"     'Create input window¶
 LOCATE 9,1¶
 PRINT"Segment   :0,116,116"¶
 PRINT"Mouse : 0, 0, 0"¶
 PRINT "Factor:1        Lines :20"¶
 LINE (0,7*ch%+2)-(39*8+3,7*ch%+2)¶
RETURN¶
¶
'***************¶
'**  EEND     **¶
'***************  ¶
   ¶
ende:¶
 MENU OFF       'Close window screen and libraries¶
 MENU RESET¶
 MOUSE OFF¶
 ¶
 WINDOW CLOSE 2¶
 WINDOW CLOSE 3¶
 WINDOW CLOSE 4¶
 SCREEN CLOSE 1¶
 ON ERROR GOTO Problem¶
 WINDOW 1,"Call Tracer " ' AMIGABasic needs WINDOW 1¶
 Problem:                   ' this command checks errors ¶
                            ' it is necessary¶
 CALL freemem&(buffer&,68*2) 'Release memory again¶
 LIBRARY CLOSE¶
 CHAIN "tracer"¶
RETURN¶
¶
'*****************¶
'**  SHORTCUTS  **¶
'*****************¶
¶
shortcuts:¶
  a=ASC(a$) 'ASCII-Value of pressed key¶
  MENU OFF  'Compare with valid keys¶
  IF a=4 THEN¶
    IF mat=0 THEN¶
      CALL deleter(ptr) 'Delete List element¶
    ELSE¶
      CALL deletermat(matptr) 'Delete Material¶
    END IF¶
  END IF¶
  IF a=42 AND mat=0 THEN¶
    CALL factor2(factor!) 'factor=factor*2¶
  END IF¶
  IF a=47 AND mat=0 THEN¶
    CALL factorhalf(factor!) 'factor=factor*0.5¶
  END IF¶
  IF a=114 THEN¶
    IF mat=0 THEN¶
      CALL rights(ptr) 'go to right element¶
    ELSE¶
      CALL rightsmat(matptr)¶
```

```
    END IF¶
  END IF¶
  IF a=108 THEN¶
    IF mat=0 THEN¶
      CALL lefts(ptr) 'go to left element¶
    ELSE¶
      CALL leftsmat(matptr)¶
    END IF¶
  END IF¶
  IF a=11 THEN¶
    IF mat=0 THEN¶
      CALL getelem(ptr) 'correct current element¶
    ELSE¶
      CALL getmat(matptr)¶
    END IF¶
  END IF      ¶
  IF a=115 AND mat=0 THEN¶
    CALL showandwait(ptr) 'show current element on output window¶
  END IF¶
  IF a=18 AND mat=0 THEN¶
    CALL refresh 'redraw screen¶
  END IF¶
  IF a=109 AND mat=1 THEN¶
    CALL matinput(matptr) 'Material input¶
  END IF  ¶
  MENU ON¶
RETURN¶
¶
¶
'*******************¶
'** READ MENU     **¶
'*******************¶
  ¶
choice:¶
  MENU OFF        'select indivual menu items and subroutines¶
  title=MENU(0)¶
  chose=MENU(1)¶
  ¶
  ¶
  IF title=1 THEN    'Transformation¶
    IF chose=1 THEN¶
      CALL rotation(ptr)¶
    END IF¶
    IF chose=2 THEN¶
      CALL translation(ptr)¶
    END IF¶
    IF chose=3 THEN¶
      CALL sizing(ptr)¶
    END IF¶
    IF chose=4 THEN¶
      CALL copier(ptr)¶
    END IF¶
    IF chose=5 THEN¶
      CALL deleter(ptr)¶
    END IF ¶
    IF chose=6 THEN¶
      CALL getelem(ptr)¶
    END IF   ¶
  END IF¶
  ¶
  IF title=2 THEN      'Body¶
    CALL entry(ptr)¶
```

```
  END IF¶
  ¶
  IF title=3 THEN     'Diskette operations¶
    IF chose=1 THEN¶
      CALL loadlist¶
    END IF¶
    IF chose=2 THEN¶
      CALL loadmat¶
    END IF¶
    IF chose=3 THEN¶
      CALL savelist¶
    END IF¶
    IF chose=4 THEN¶
      CALL savemat¶
    END IF¶
  END IF ¶
  ¶
  IF title=4 THEN     'Operation¶
    IF chose=1 THEN¶
      CALL lefts(ptr)¶
    END IF¶
    IF chose=2 THEN¶
      CALL rights(ptr)¶
    END IF¶
    IF chose=3 THEN¶
      CALL liob(mx!,my!,mz!)¶
    END IF¶
    IF chose=4 THEN¶
      CALL setfactor(factor!)¶
    END IF¶
    IF chose=5 THEN¶
      CALL factor2(factor!)¶
    END IF  ¶
    IF chose=6 THEN¶
      CALL factorhalf(factor!)¶
    END IF¶
    IF chose=7 THEN¶
      CALL mateddy¶
    END IF¶
    IF chose=8 THEN¶
      CALL refresh¶
    END IF¶
    IF chose=9 THEN¶
      CALL showandwait(ptr)¶
    END IF¶
    IF chose=10 THEN¶
      CALL setlines(maxlines)¶
    END IF  ¶
    IF chose=11 THEN¶
      CALL finish(quit)¶
    END IF¶
  END IF¶
¶
            ¶
  IF title=5 THEN      'Material editor¶
    IF chose=1 THEN¶
      CALL leftsmat(matptr)¶
    END IF¶
    IF chose=2 THEN¶
      CALL rightsmat(matptr)¶
    END IF¶
    IF chose=3 THEN¶
```

```
      CALL deletermat(matptr)¶
    END IF¶
    IF chose=4 THEN¶
      CALL getmat(matptr)¶
    END IF¶
    IF chose=5 THEN¶
      CALL matinput(matptr)¶
    END IF  ¶
    IF chose=6 THEN¶
      CALL finishmat¶
    END IF¶
  END IF¶
¶
  MENU ON¶
RETURN¶
¶
'******************¶
'** READ MOUSE   **¶
'******************¶
¶
click:¶
  dummy=MOUSE(0)¶
  x!=MOUSE(3)/(factor!*xcorrfac!)  'Get mouse position and compute¶
  y!=MOUSE(4)/factor!¶
  n=WINDOW(0)  'window clicked¶
  oldwindow=WINDOW(1) 'output window¶
  CALL activatewindow&(WINDOW(7))¶
   IF  n<4 THEN  'was projection window clicked?¶
    WINDOW OUTPUT n¶
    LINE (MOUSE(3)-1,MOUSE(4))-(MOUSE(3)+1,MOUSE(4)),3  'Draw circle¶
    LINE (MOUSE(3),MOUSE(4)-1)-(MOUSE(3),MOUSE(4)+1),3¶
    IF n=1 THEN    'compute spatial coordinates¶
      mox!=mx!+x!¶
      moy!=my!-y!¶
    ELSE¶
      IF n=2 THEN¶
        mox!=mx!+x!¶
        moz!=mz!-y!¶
      ELSE ¶
        IF n=3 THEN¶
          moy!=my!-x!¶
          moz!=mz!-y!¶
        END IF¶
      END IF¶
    END IF¶
    mox!=FIX(mox!+.5) 'round¶
    moy!=FIX(moy!+.5)¶
    moz!=FIX(moz!+.5)¶
    WINDOW OUTPUT 4¶
    mo$=STR$(mox!)+","+STR$(moy!)+","+STR$(moz!)¶
    LOCATE 10,8         'delete old mouse values and display new ones¶
    PRINT SPACE$(26)¶
    LOCATE 10,8¶
    PRINT MID$(mo$,1,26) ¶
    WINDOW OUTPUT oldwindow¶
  ELSE¶
    CALL checkgadget  'was a gadget clicked?¶
  END IF¶
RETURN ¶
¶
¶
```

```
'*************¶
'** INPUT   **¶
'*************¶
¶
SUB entry(ptr) STATIC¶
'TASK      :Read data for a new body¶
'PARAMETER:=> ptr points to old body¶
'           <= ptr points to specified body¶
  SHARED k!(),t(),chose¶
  CALL newelem(ptr)¶
  k!(ptr,0,0)=t(chose)¶
  CALL showelem(ptr)¶
  CALL getelem(ptr)¶
  IF k!(ptr,5,2)=1 THEN¶
    CALL drawelem(ptr)¶
  END IF  ¶
END SUB¶
¶
SUB getstring(old$,a$,z$,z,s,inplen)STATIC¶
'TASK      :Reads two strings which can be edited from the input line¶
'           using cursor left/right,backspace and delete.¶
'           In addition the string scrolls when the input extends past¶
'           the screen line ¶
'PARAMETER:=>old$ old value of string to be read¶
'             a$ key pressed ¶
'             z$ valid characters¶
'             z line¶
'             s column¶
'             inplen    Length of input window¶
'           <=old$ specified  string¶
  IF inplen   =1 THEN 'if only one char entered? => no Return¶
    old$=a$¶
    WHILE INSTR(z$,old$)=0¶
      CALL getkey(old$,z,s)¶
    WEND¶
    LOCATE z,s¶
    PRINT old$¶
  ELSE¶
    i=1        'points to current string position¶
    position=1 'points to current screen position¶
    WHILE ASC(a$)><13¶
      IF INSTR(z$,a$)><0 THEN 'valid character?¶
        old$=LEFT$(old$,i-1)+a$+RIGHT$(old$,LEN(old$)-i+1)      ¶
        i=i+1¶
        position=position+1¶
        IF position>inplen    THEN¶
          position=inplen   ¶
        END IF  ¶
      ELSE ¶
        IF ASC(a$)=30 AND i<=LEN(old$) THEN  'Cursor right?¶
          i=i+1¶
          position=position+1¶
          IF position>inplen    THEN¶
            position=inplen   ¶
          END IF  ¶
        ELSE¶
          IF ASC(a$)=31 AND i>1 THEN 'Cursor left?¶
            i=i-1¶
            position=position-1¶
            IF position=0 THEN¶
              position=1¶
            END IF  ¶
```

```
          ELSE¶
            IF ASC(a$)=127 AND i<=LEN(old$) THEN  'delete ?¶
              old$=LEFT$(old$,i-1)+RIGHT$(old$,LEN(old$)-i)¶
            ELSE¶
              IF ASC(a$)=8 AND i>1 THEN  'Backspace ?¶
                i=i-1¶
                position=position-1¶
                IF position=0 THEN¶
                  position=1¶
                END IF¶
                old$=LEFT$(old$,i-1)+RIGHT$(old$,LEN(old$)-i)¶
              END IF¶
            END IF¶
          END IF¶
        END IF¶
      END IF¶
      LOCATE z,s¶
      PRINT MID$(old$+" ",i-position+1,inplen   )  'String output¶
      CALL getkey(a$,z,s+position-1) 'get next key¶
    WEND ¶
  END IF¶
  IF i><position THEN¶
    CALL putstring(old$,z,s,inplen    )¶
  END IF  ¶
END SUB¶
¶
SUB getint(i!,a$,z,s,inplen   ,unt!,ob!) STATIC  ¶
'TASK     :Read integer value¶
'PARAMETER:=>i! old value¶
'           a$ pressed key¶
'           z line¶
'           s column¶
'           inplen    Length of input line¶
'           unt! lower limit¶
'           ob! upper limit¶
'         <=i! specified value¶
  CALL conrealstr(i!,j$)¶
loop:¶
  i$=j$  ¶
  CALL getstring(i$,a$,"1234567890-",z,s,inplen   )¶
  j$=i$¶
  CALL constrreal(i$,i!)¶
  IF i$="" OR i!<unt! OR i!>ob! THEN 'keep searching while input is valid¶
    a$=" "¶
    GOTO loop¶
  END IF¶
END SUB¶
¶
SUB getreal(i!,a$,z,s,inplen   ,unt!,ob!) STATIC¶
'TASK     :Read in real value¶
'PARAMETER:=>i! old value¶
'           a$ pressed key¶
'           z line¶
'           s column¶
'           inplen    length of input line¶
'           unt! lower limit¶
'           ob! upper limit¶
'         <=i! specified value¶
  CALL conrealstr(i!,j$)¶
loop1:   ¶
  i$=j$¶
  CALL getstring(i$,a$,"1234567890-.",z,s,inplen    )¶
```

```
  j$=i$¶
  CALL constrreal(i$,i!)¶
  IF i$="" OR i!<unt! OR i!>ob! THEN¶
    a$=" "¶
    GOTO loop1¶
  END IF¶
END SUB¶
¶
SUB get3real(i1!,i2!,i3!,a$,z,s,inplen   ,unt!,ob!,modus) STATIC¶
'TASK     :read 3 Real values in¶
'PARAMETER:=>i1!,i2!,i3! old value¶
'            a$ key pressed¶
'            z line¶
'            s column¶
'            inplen    Lenght of input line¶
'            unt! lower limit¶
'            ob! upper limit¶
'            modus if=0  no mouse entry¶
'                  if=-1 mouse input  (position vector)¶
'                  if>0  mouse input (Difference vector)¶
'          <=i1!,i2!,i3! specified value¶
  SHARED mox!,moy!,moz!,k!()¶
  CALL con3realstr(i1!,i2!,i3!,j$)¶
  IF a$="" THEN¶
    CALL getkey(a$,z,s)¶
  END IF  ¶
  IF ASC(a$)=13 AND modus><0 THEN¶
    IF modus=-1 THEN¶
      i1!=mox!¶
      i2!=moy!¶
      i3!=moz!¶
    ELSE¶
      i1!=mox!-k!(modus,1,0)¶
      i2!=moy!-k!(modus,1,1)¶
      i3!=moz!-k!(modus,1,2)¶
    END IF¶
    CALL put3real(i1!,i2!,i3!,z,s,26)¶
  ELSE¶
loop2:¶
    i$=j$  ¶
    CALL getstring(i$,a$,"1234567890-.,",z,s,inplen   )¶
    j$=i$¶
    CALL constr3real(i$,i1!,i2!,i3!)¶
    IF i$="" OR i1!<unt! OR i2!<unt! OR i3!<unt! OR i1!>ob! OR i2!>ob! OR i3!>ob!
THEN¶
      a$=" "¶
      GOTO loop2¶
    END IF¶
  END IF¶
END SUB    ¶
¶
SUB getkey(a$,z,s)STATIC¶
'TASK     :Read one character in¶
'PARAMETER:=>z line¶
'            s column¶
'          <=a$ pressed key¶
  CALL setcursor(z,s) ¶
  a$=""¶
  WHILE a$=""¶
    a$=INKEY$¶
  WEND¶
  CALL setcursor(z,s)¶
```

```
END SUB¶
¶
¶
SUB setcursor(z,s) STATIC¶
'TASK      :set cursor at specified position¶
'PARAMETER:=>z line¶
'              s column¶
  SHARED cw%,ch%¶
  CALL setdrmd&(WINDOW(8),2)¶
  LINE (s*cw%-cw%,z*ch%-ch%-1)-(s*cw%,z*ch%-1),3,bf¶
  CALL setdrmd&(WINDOW(8),1)¶
END SUB  ¶
¶
'******************¶
'** DATA ENTRY   **¶
'******************¶
'The following proceures are similar to the ones ¶
'documented earlier.¶
¶
SUB getplane(ptr) STATIC¶
'TASK      :Read the data for one Plane¶
'PARAMETER:=>ptr points to the element to be read¶
  SHARED k!(),tabs(),min!,max!¶
  tabs(0,0)=2  'set tabs for menu¶
  tabs(1,0)=2¶
  tabs(2,0)=3¶
  tabs(3,0)=4¶
  tabs(4,0)=5¶
  tabs(0,1)=10¶
  tabs(1,1)=22¶
  tabs(2,1)=4¶
  tabs(3,1)=4¶
  tabs(4,1)=4¶
  nr=0¶
  WHILE nr<=4 'wait until last line is overwritten¶
    CALL getkey(a$,tabs(nr,0),tabs(nr,1))¶
    IF ASC(a$)=28 THEN 'cursor up?¶
      IF nr>0 THEN¶
         nr=nr-1¶
      END IF   ¶
    ELSE ¶
      IF ASC(a$)=29 THEN 'cursor down?¶
        nr=nr+1¶
      ELSE¶
        IF nr=0 THEN  'can you see it? read it ¶
          CALL getstring(b$,a$,"yn",tabs(nr,0),tabs(nr,1),1)¶
          IF b$="y"THEN   'not input¶
            k!(ptr,5,2)=1¶
          ELSE ¶
            k!(ptr,5,2)=0¶
          END IF¶
        END IF¶
        IF nr=1 THEN  'Read M¶
          CALL getint(k!(ptr,0,2),a$,tabs(nr,0),tabs(nr,1),5,1!,max!)¶
        END IF      ¶
        IF nr=2 THEN  'A read¶
          CALL
get3real(k!(ptr,1,0),k!(ptr,1,1),k!(ptr,1,2),a$,tabs(nr,0),tabs(nr,1),26,min!,max!,
-1)¶
        END IF¶
        IF nr=3 THEN 'B read¶
```

```
          CALL
get3real(k!(ptr,2,0),k!(ptr,2,1),k!(ptr,2,2),a$,tabs(nr,0),tabs(nr,1),26,min!,max!
,ptr)¶
        END IF¶
        IF nr=4 THEN 'C read¶
          CALL
get3real(k!(ptr,3,0),k!(ptr,3,1),k!(ptr,3,2),a$,tabs(nr,0),tabs(nr,1),26,min!,max!,
ptr)¶
        END IF¶
        nr=nr+1¶
      END IF¶
    END IF¶
  WEND¶
END SUB  ¶
¶
SUB getcrseg(ptr) STATIC¶
  SHARED k!(),tabs(),min!,max!,grad!,rad!¶
  tabs(0,0)=2¶
  tabs(1,0)=2¶
  tabs(2,0)=3¶
  tabs(3,0)=4¶
  tabs(4,0)=5¶
  tabs(5,0)=6¶
  tabs(6,0)=6¶
  tabs(0,1)=10¶
  tabs(1,1)=22¶
  tabs(2,1)=4¶
  tabs(3,1)=4¶
  tabs(4,1)=4¶
  tabs(5,1)=4¶
  tabs(6,1)=16¶
  nr=0¶
  WHILE nr<=6¶
    CALL getkey(a$,tabs(nr,0),tabs(nr,1))¶
    IF ASC(a$)=28 THEN¶
      IF nr>0 THEN¶
        nr=nr-1¶
      END IF   ¶
    ELSE¶
      IF ASC(a$)=29 THEN¶
        nr=nr+1¶
      ELSE¶
        IF nr=0 THEN¶
          CALL getstring(b$,a$,"yn",tabs(nr,0),tabs(nr,1),1)¶
          IF b$="y"THEN¶
            k!(ptr,5,2)=1¶
          ELSE ¶
            k!(ptr,5,2)=0¶
          END IF¶
        END IF¶
        IF nr=1 THEN¶
          CALL getint(k!(ptr,0,2),a$,tabs(nr,0),tabs(nr,1),5,1!,max!)¶
        END IF        ¶
        IF nr=2 THEN¶
          CALL
get3real(k!(ptr,1,0),k!(ptr,1,1),k!(ptr,1,2),a$,tabs(nr,0),tabs(nr,1),26,min!,max!,
-1)¶
        END IF¶
        IF nr=3 THEN¶
          CALL
get3real(k!(ptr,2,0),k!(ptr,2,1),k!(ptr,2,2),a$,tabs(nr,0),tabs(nr,1),26,min!,max!
,ptr)¶
```

```
        END IF¶
        IF nr=4 THEN¶
          CALL
get3real(k!(ptr,3,0),k!(ptr,3,1),k!(ptr,3,2),a$,tabs(nr,0),tabs(nr,1),26,min!,max!,
ptr)¶
        END IF¶
        IF nr=5 THEN¶
          k!=k!(ptr,5,0)*grad!¶
          CALL getreal(k!,a$,tabs(nr,0),tabs(nr,1),8,min!,max!)¶
          k!(ptr,5,0)=rad!*k!¶
        END IF  ¶
        IF nr=6 THEN¶
          k!=k!(ptr,5,1)*grad!¶
          CALL getreal(k!,a$,tabs(nr,0),tabs(nr,1),8,min!,max!)¶
          k!(ptr,5,1)=rad!*k!¶
        END IF  ¶
        nr=nr+1¶
      END IF¶
    END IF¶
  WEND ¶
END SUB¶
¶
 ¶
SUB getcrarc(ptr) STATIC¶
  SHARED k!(),tabs(),min!,max!,grad!,rad!¶
  tabs(0,0)=2¶
  tabs(1,0)=2¶
  tabs(2,0)=3¶
  tabs(3,0)=4¶
  tabs(4,0)=5¶
  tabs(5,0)=6¶
  tabs(6,0)=6¶
  tabs(7,0)=7¶
  tabs(8,0)=7¶
  tabs(0,1)=10¶
  tabs(1,1)=22¶
  tabs(2,1)=4¶
  tabs(3,1)=4¶
  tabs(4,1)=4¶
  tabs(5,1)=4¶
  tabs(6,1)=16¶
  tabs(7,1)=4¶
  tabs(8,1)=16¶
  nr=0¶
  WHILE nr<=8¶
    CALL getkey(a$,tabs(nr,0),tabs(nr,1))¶
    IF ASC(a$)=28 THEN¶
      IF nr>0 THEN¶
        nr=nr-1¶
      END IF   ¶
    ELSE ¶
      IF ASC(a$)=29 THEN¶
        nr=nr+1¶
      ELSE¶
        IF nr=0 THEN¶
          CALL getstring(b$,a$,"yn",tabs(nr,0),tabs(nr,1),1)¶
          IF b$="y"THEN¶
            k!(ptr,5,2)=1¶
          ELSE ¶
            k!(ptr,5,2)=0¶
          END IF¶
        END IF¶
```

```
        IF nr=1 THEN¶
          CALL getint(k!(ptr,0,2),a$,tabs(nr,0),tabs(nr,1),5,1!,max!)¶
        END IF        ¶
        IF nr=2 THEN¶
          CALL
get3real(k!(ptr,1,0),k!(ptr,1,1),k!(ptr,1,2),a$,tabs(nr,0),tabs(nr,1),26,min!,max!,
-1)¶
        END IF¶
        IF nr=3 THEN¶
          CALL
get3real(k!(ptr,2,0),k!(ptr,2,1),k!(ptr,2,2),a$,tabs(nr,0),tabs(nr,1),26,min!,max!
,ptr)¶
        END IF¶
        IF nr=4 THEN¶
          CALL
get3real(k!(ptr,3,0),k!(ptr,3,1),k!(ptr,3,2),a$,tabs(nr,0),tabs(nr,1),26,min0!,max!
,ptr)¶
        END IF¶
        IF nr=5 THEN¶
          k!=grad!*k!(ptr,5,0)¶
          CALL getreal(k!,a$,tabs(nr,0),tabs(nr,1),8,min!,max!)¶
          k!(ptr,5,0)=rad!*k!¶
        END IF  ¶
        IF nr=6 THEN¶
          k!=grad!*k!(ptr,5,1)¶
          CALL getreal(k!,a$,tabs(nr,0),tabs(nr,1),8,min!,max!)¶
          k!(ptr,5,1)=rad!*k!¶
        END IF  ¶
        IF nr=7 THEN¶
          CALL getreal(k!(ptr,4,0),a$,tabs(nr,0),tabs(nr,1),8,0!,1!)¶
        END IF  ¶
        IF nr=8 THEN¶
          CALL getreal(k!(ptr,4,1),a$,tabs(nr,0),tabs(nr,1),8,0!,1!)¶
        END IF  ¶
        nr=nr+1¶
      END IF¶
    END IF¶
  WEND ¶
END SUB  ¶
¶
 ¶
SUB getsphere(ptr) STATIC¶
  SHARED k!(),tabs(),min!,max!¶
  tabs(0,0)=2¶
  tabs(1,0)=2¶
  tabs(2,0)=3¶
  tabs(3,0)=4¶
  tabs(0,1)=10¶
  tabs(1,1)=22¶
  tabs(2,1)=4¶
  tabs(3,1)=4¶
  nr=0¶
  WHILE nr<=3¶
    CALL getkey(a$,tabs(nr,0),tabs(nr,1))¶
    IF ASC(a$)=28 THEN¶
      IF nr>0 THEN¶
         nr=nr-1¶
      END IF   ¶
    ELSE ¶
      IF ASC(a$)=29 THEN¶
        nr=nr+1¶
      ELSE¶
```

```
        IF nr=0 THEN¶
          CALL getstring(b$,a$,"yn",tabs(nr,0),tabs(nr,1),1)¶
          IF b$="y"THEN¶
            k!(ptr,5,2)=1¶
          ELSE ¶
            k!(ptr,5,2)=0¶
          END IF¶
        END IF¶
        IF nr=1 THEN¶
          CALL getint(k!(ptr,0,2),a$,tabs(nr,0),tabs(nr,1),5,1!,max!)¶
        END IF        ¶
        IF nr=2 THEN¶
          CALL
get3real(k!(ptr,1,0),k!(ptr,1,1),k!(ptr,1,2),a$,tabs(nr,0),tabs(nr,1),26,-
1000!,1000!,-1)¶
        END IF¶
        IF nr=3 THEN¶
          CALL getreal(k!(ptr,2,0),a$,tabs(nr,0),tabs(nr,1),8,0!,max!)¶
        END IF  ¶
        nr=nr+1¶
      END IF¶
    END IF¶
  WEND ¶
END SUB ¶
¶
 ¶
SUB getcyl(ptr) STATIC¶
  SHARED k!(),tabs(),min!,max!¶
  tabs(0,0)=2¶
  tabs(1,0)=2¶
  tabs(2,0)=3¶
  tabs(3,0)=4¶
  tabs(4,0)=5¶
  tabs(5,0)=6¶
  tabs(0,1)=10¶
  tabs(1,1)=22¶
  tabs(2,1)=4¶
  tabs(3,1)=4¶
  tabs(4,1)=4¶
  tabs(5,1)=4¶
  nr=0¶
  WHILE nr<=5¶
    CALL getkey(a$,tabs(nr,0),tabs(nr,1))¶
    IF ASC(a$)=28 THEN¶
      IF nr>0 THEN¶
        nr=nr-1¶
      END IF   ¶
    ELSE ¶
      IF ASC(a$)=29 THEN¶
        nr=nr+1¶
      ELSE¶
        IF nr=0 THEN¶
          CALL getstring(b$,a$,"yn",tabs(nr,0),tabs(nr,1),1)¶
          IF b$="y"THEN¶
            k!(ptr,5,2)=1¶
          ELSE ¶
            k!(ptr,5,2)=0¶
          END IF¶
        END IF¶
        IF nr=1 THEN¶
          CALL getint(k!(ptr,0,2),a$,tabs(nr,0),tabs(nr,1),5,1!,max!)¶
        END IF        ¶
```

```
        IF nr=2 THEN¶
          CALL
get3real(k!(ptr,1,0),k!(ptr,1,1),k!(ptr,1,2),a$,tabs(nr,0),tabs(nr,1),26,min!,max!
,-1)¶
        END IF¶
        IF nr=3 THEN¶
          CALL
get3real(k!(ptr,2,0),k!(ptr,2,1),k!(ptr,2,2),a$,tabs(nr,0),tabs(nr,1),26,min!,max!,
ptr)¶
        END IF¶
        IF nr=4 THEN¶
          CALL
get3real(k!(ptr,3,0),k!(ptr,3,1),k!(ptr,3,2),a$,tabs(nr,0),tabs(nr,1),26,min!,max!,
ptr)¶
        END IF¶
        IF nr=5 THEN¶
          CALL
get3real(k!(ptr,4,0),k!(ptr,4,1),k!(ptr,4,2),a$,tabs(nr,0),tabs(nr,1),26,min!,max!,
ptr)¶
        END IF¶
        nr=nr+1¶
      END IF¶
    END IF¶
  WEND¶
END SUB  ¶
 ¶
SUB getcylseg(ptr) STATIC¶
  SHARED k!(),tabs(),min!,max!,grad!,rad!¶
  tabs(0,0)=2¶
  tabs(1,0)=2¶
  tabs(2,0)=3¶
  tabs(3,0)=4¶
  tabs(4,0)=5¶
  tabs(5,0)=6¶
  tabs(6,0)=7¶
  tabs(7,0)=7¶
  tabs(0,1)=10¶
  tabs(1,1)=22¶
  tabs(2,1)=4¶
  tabs(3,1)=4¶
  tabs(4,1)=4¶
  tabs(5,1)=4¶
  tabs(6,1)=4¶
  tabs(7,1)=16¶
  nr=0¶
  WHILE nr<=7¶
    CALL getkey(a$,tabs(nr,0),tabs(nr,1))¶
    IF ASC(a$)=28  THEN¶
      IF nr>0 THEN¶
         nr=nr-1¶
      END IF   ¶
    ELSE ¶
      IF ASC(a$)=29 THEN¶
        nr=nr+1¶
      ELSE¶
        IF nr=0 THEN¶
          CALL getstring(b$,a$,"yn",tabs(nr,0),tabs(nr,1),1)¶
          IF b$="y"THEN¶
            k!(ptr,5,2)=1¶
          ELSE ¶
            k!(ptr,5,2)=0¶
          END IF¶
```

```
        END IF¶
        IF nr=1 THEN¶
          CALL getint(k!(ptr,0,2),a$,tabs(nr,0),tabs(nr,1),5,1!,max!)¶
        END IF        ¶
        IF nr=2 THEN¶
          CALL
get3real(k!(ptr,1,0),k!(ptr,1,1),k!(ptr,1,2),a$,tabs(nr,0),tabs(nr,1),26,min!,max!
,-1)¶
        END IF¶
        IF nr=3 THEN¶
          CALL
get3real(k!(ptr,2,0),k!(ptr,2,1),k!(ptr,2,2),a$,tabs(nr,0),tabs(nr,1),26,min!,max!,
ptr)¶
        END IF¶
        IF nr=4 THEN¶
          CALL
get3real(k!(ptr,3,0),k!(ptr,3,1),k!(ptr,3,2),a$,tabs(nr,0),tabs(nr,1),26,min!,max!,
ptr)¶
        END IF¶
        IF nr=5 THEN¶
          CALL
get3real(k!(ptr,4,0),k!(ptr,4,1),k!(ptr,4,2),a$,tabs(nr,0),tabs(nr,1),26,min!,max!,
ptr)¶
        END IF¶
        IF nr=6 THEN¶
          k!=grad!*k!(ptr,5,0)¶
          CALL getreal(k!,a$,tabs(nr,0),tabs(nr,1),26,min!,max!)¶
          k!(ptr,5,0)=rad!*k!¶
        END IF¶
        IF nr=7 THEN¶
          k!=grad!*k!(ptr,5,1)¶
          CALL getreal(k!,a$,tabs(nr,0),tabs(nr,1),26,min!,max!)¶
          k!(ptr,5,1)=rad!*k!¶
        END IF¶
        nr=nr+1¶
      END IF¶
    END IF¶
  WEND¶
END SUB  ¶
 ¶
 ¶
'*************¶
'** OUTPUT  **¶
'*************¶
                                ¶
SUB showelem(ptr) STATIC¶
'TASK      :data output of element ptr¶
'PARAMETER:=>ptr pointer to the specified element¶
  SHARED k!(),typ$(),empty$,grad!,rad!¶
  LOCATE 1,1¶
  FOR i=1 TO 7¶
    PRINT empty$¶
  NEXT i¶
  LOCATE 1,1¶
  PRINT "Body  :"¶
  CALL putreal(ptr*1!,1,8,5)¶
  typ=INT(k!(ptr,0,0))¶
  IF ptr><0 THEN¶
    LOCATE 1,14¶
    PRINT typ$(typ)¶
    LOCATE 2,1¶
    PRINT "visible :";¶
```

```
    IF k!(ptr,5,2)=0 THEN¶
      PRINT "n"¶
    ELSE ¶
      PRINT "y"¶
    END IF¶
    LOCATE 2,13¶
    PRINT "Material:"¶
    CALL putreal(k!(ptr,0,2),2,22,5)¶
    IF typ=10 THEN¶
      LOCATE 3,1¶
      PRINT "M :"¶
      PRINT "r :"¶
      CALL put3real(k!(ptr,1,0),k!(ptr,1,1),k!(ptr,1,2),3,4,26)¶
      CALL putreal(k!(ptr,2,0),4,4,8)¶
    ELSE¶
      LOCATE 3,1¶
      PRINT "M :"¶
      PRINT "A :"¶
      PRINT "B :"¶
      CALL put3real(k!(ptr,1,0),k!(ptr,1,1),k!(ptr,1,2),3,4,26)¶
      CALL put3real(k!(ptr,2,0),k!(ptr,2,1),k!(ptr,2,2),4,4,26)¶
      CALL put3real(k!(ptr,3,0),k!(ptr,3,1),k!(ptr,3,2),5,4,26)¶
      IF typ>=4 THEN¶
        IF typ>=20 THEN¶
          LOCATE 6,1¶
          PRINT "C :"¶
          CALL put3real(k!(ptr,4,0),k!(ptr,4,1),k!(ptr,4,2),6,4,26)¶
          IF typ=21 THEN¶
            LOCATE 7,1¶
            PRINT "sw:"¶
            LOCATE 7,13¶
            PRINT "ew:"¶
            CALL putreal(grad!*k!(ptr,5,0),7,4,8)¶
            CALL putreal(grad!*k!(ptr,5,1),7,16,8)¶
          END IF¶
        ELSE¶
          LOCATE 6,1¶
          PRINT "sw:"¶
          LOCATE 6,13¶
          PRINT "ew:"¶
          CALL putreal(grad!*k!(ptr,5,0),6,4,8)¶
          CALL putreal(grad!*k!(ptr,5,1),6,16,8)¶
          IF typ=5 THEN¶
            LOCATE 7,1¶
            PRINT "ri:"¶
            LOCATE 7,13¶
            PRINT "ra:"¶
            CALL putreal(k!(ptr,4,0),7,4,8)¶
            CALL putreal(k!(ptr,4,1),7,16,8)¶
          END IF¶
        END IF¶
      END IF¶
    END IF¶
  END IF¶
END SUB¶
¶
SUB putstring(s$,z,s,inplen    )STATIC¶
'TASK      :output of a string of a certain length¶
'PARAMETER:=>s$ the string¶
'             z line¶
'             s column¶
'             inplen    Length of output window¶
```

```
  LOCATE z,s           'clear specified range¶
  PRINT SPACE$(inplen   )¶
  LOCATE z,s           'display the string¶
  PRINT MID$(s$,1,inplen   )¶
END SUB¶
¶
      ¶
SUB putreal(i!,z,s,inplen   )STATIC¶
'TASK     :Display real value of predetermined length¶
'PARAMETER:=>i! the real value¶
'           z line¶
'           s column¶
'           inplen    Length of output window¶
  CALL conrealstr(i!,s$)¶
  CALL putstring(s$,z,s,inplen   )¶
END SUB¶
  ¶
SUB put3real(i1!,i2!,i3!,z,s,inplen   )STATIC¶
'TASK     :display  3 Real values of certain length¶
'PARAMETER:=>i1!,i2!,i3! the real values¶
'           z line¶
'           s column¶
'           inplen    Length of the output window¶
  CALL con3realstr(i1!,i2!,i3!,i$)¶
  CALL putstring(i$,z,s,inplen   )¶
END SUB¶
¶
'*******************¶
'** CONVERSIONS   **¶
'*******************¶
¶
SUB conrealstr(i!,i$)STATIC¶
'TASK     :convert real value into string¶
'          rounded to 3 decimal places¶
'PARAMETER:=>i! the real value¶
'          <=i$ the string¶
  i$=STR$(i!)¶
  j!=FIX(1000!*i!+.5*SGN(i!))/1000! 'round¶
  i$=STR$(j!)¶
  IF ABS(j!)>0 AND ABS(j!)<1 THEN  'if 0<j!<1 0 inserted¶
    i$=MID$(i$,1,1)+"0"+MID$(i$,2,LEN(i$))¶
  END IF¶
  IF j!>=0 THEN  'if 0<=j! truncate first place¶
    i$=RIGHT$(i$,LEN(i$)-1)¶
  END IF¶
END SUB¶
¶
SUB constrreal(i$,i!) STATIC¶
'TASK     :convert string into real value¶
'PARAMETER:=>i$ the string¶
'          <=i! the real value¶
'            i$ if conversion error i$=""¶
  i!=VAL(i$)¶
  IF i!>=0 THEN¶
    IF i!>0 AND i!<1 THEN¶
      i$=" "+RIGHT$(i$,LEN(i$)-1) 'insert space and cutoff 0¶
    ELSE  ¶
      i$=" "+i$  'insert space¶
    END IF¶
  END IF¶
  j!=i!-FIX(i!*1000!)/1000! 'round ¶
  IF i$><STR$(i!) OR j!><0 THEN 'Error ?¶
```

```
    i$=""¶
  END IF ¶
END SUB¶
¶
SUB constr3real(i$,i1!,i2!,i3!) STATIC¶
'TASK     :convert one string into 3 real values¶
'PARAMETER:=>i$ the string¶
'          <=i1!,i2!,i3! the real values¶
'            i$ if conversion error i$=""¶
  Problem=0¶
  i$=i$+","¶
  FOR i=1 TO 3¶
    comma=INSTR(i$,",") 'Mark comma position¶
    IF comma<=1 THEN    'Problem ?¶
      Problem=1¶
    ELSE¶
      a$=MID$(i$,1,comma-1) 'truncate string to be converted¶
      i$=RIGHT$(i$,LEN(i$)-comma) 'mark the rest¶
      CALL constrreal(a$,i!(i))   'convert¶
      IF a$="" THEN  'Problem ?¶
        Problem=1¶
      END IF  ¶
    END IF¶
  NEXT i¶
  IF Problem=1 THEN¶
    i$=""    ¶
  ELSE¶
    i$=" "¶
    i1!=i!(1)¶
    i2!=i!(2)¶
    i3!=i!(3)¶
  END IF¶
END SUB      ¶
    ¶
¶
SUB con3realstr(i1!,i2!,i3!,i$) STATIC¶
'TASK     :convert 3 real values into vector string¶
'PARAMETER:=>i1!,i2!,i3! the 3 Real values¶
'          <=i$ the string¶
  CALL conrealstr(i1!,i1$)¶
  CALL conrealstr(i2!,i2$)¶
  CALL conrealstr(i3!,i3$)¶
  i$=i1$+","+i2$+","+i3$¶
END SUB¶
¶
¶
'**************¶
'** GRAPHICS **¶
'**************¶
'Routines to display graphics in the projection windows¶
'the following routines are virtually identical¶
'to one another, hence the lack of comments¶
¶
SUB drawplane(ptr) STATIC¶
  SHARED k!()¶
  mx!=k!(ptr,1,0)¶
  my!=k!(ptr,1,1)¶
  mz!=k!(ptr,1,2)¶
  ax!=k!(ptr,2,0)¶
  ay!=k!(ptr,2,1)¶
  az!=k!(ptr,2,2)¶
  bx!=k!(ptr,3,0)¶
```

```
  by!=k!(ptr,3,1)¶
  bz!=k!(ptr,3,2)¶
  WINDOW OUTPUT 1¶
  CALL setpoint(ax!+mx!,ay!+my!)¶
  CALL drawline(mx!,my!)¶
  CALL drawline(mx!+bx!,my!+by!)   ¶
  WINDOW OUTPUT 2¶
  CALL setpoint(ax!+mx!,az!+mz!)¶
  CALL drawline(mx!,mz!)¶
  CALL drawline(mx!+bx!,mz!+bz!)   ¶
  WINDOW OUTPUT 3¶
  CALL setpoint(ay!+my!,az!+mz!)¶
  CALL drawline(my!,mz!)¶
  CALL drawline(my!+by!,mz!+bz!)    ¶
  WINDOW OUTPUT 4¶
END SUB¶
 ¶
SUB drawtriangle(ptr) STATIC¶
  SHARED k!()¶
  mx!=k!(ptr,1,0)¶
  my!=k!(ptr,1,1)¶
  mz!=k!(ptr,1,2)¶
  ax!=k!(ptr,2,0)¶
  ay!=k!(ptr,2,1)¶
  az!=k!(ptr,2,2)¶
  bx!=k!(ptr,3,0)¶
  by!=k!(ptr,3,1)¶
  bz!=k!(ptr,3,2)¶
  WINDOW OUTPUT 1¶
  CALL setpoint(mx!,my!)¶
  CALL drawline(ax!+mx!,ay!+my!)¶
  CALL drawline(bx!+mx!,by!+my!)¶
  CALL drawline(mx!,my!)                 ¶
  WINDOW OUTPUT 2¶
  CALL setpoint(mx!,mz!)¶
  CALL drawline(ax!+mx!,az!+mz!)¶
  CALL drawline(bx!+mx!,bz!+mz!)¶
  CALL drawline(mx!,mz!)                 ¶
  WINDOW OUTPUT 3¶
  CALL setpoint(my!,mz!)¶
  CALL drawline(ay!+my!,az!+mz!)¶
  CALL drawline(by!+my!,bz!+mz!)¶
  CALL drawline(my!,mz!)                 ¶
  WINDOW OUTPUT 4¶
END SUB¶
                        ¶
¶
SUB drawparall(ptr) STATIC¶
  SHARED k!()¶
  mx!=k!(ptr,1,0)¶
  my!=k!(ptr,1,1)¶
  mz!=k!(ptr,1,2)¶
  ax!=k!(ptr,2,0)¶
  ay!=k!(ptr,2,1)¶
  az!=k!(ptr,2,2)¶
  bx!=k!(ptr,3,0)¶
  by!=k!(ptr,3,1)¶
  bz!=k!(ptr,3,2)¶
  WINDOW OUTPUT 1¶
  CALL setpoint(mx!,my!)¶
  CALL drawline(ax!+mx!,ay!+my!)¶
  CALL drawline(ax!+bx!+mx!,ay!+by!+my!)¶
```

```
    CALL drawline(bx!+mx!,by!+my!)¶
    CALL drawline(mx!,my!)                    ¶
    WINDOW OUTPUT 2¶
    CALL setpoint(mx!,mz!)¶
    CALL drawline(ax!+mx!,az!+mz!)¶
    CALL drawline(ax!+bx!+mx!,az!+bz!+mz!)¶
    CALL drawline(bx!+mx!,bz!+mz!)¶
    CALL drawline(mx!,mz!)                    ¶
    WINDOW OUTPUT 3¶
    CALL setpoint(my!,mz!)¶
    CALL drawline(ay!+my!,az!+mz!)¶
    CALL drawline(ay!+by!+my!,az!+bz!+mz!)¶
    CALL drawline(by!+my!,bz!+mz!)¶
    CALL drawline(my!,mz!)                    ¶
    WINDOW OUTPUT 4¶
END SUB                     ¶
¶
¶
SUB drawcircle(ptr) STATIC¶
    SHARED k!(),pi2!¶
    mx!=k!(ptr,1,0)¶
    my!=k!(ptr,1,1)¶
    mz!=k!(ptr,1,2)¶
    ax!=k!(ptr,2,0)¶
    ay!=k!(ptr,2,1)¶
    az!=k!(ptr,2,2)¶
    bx!=k!(ptr,3,0)¶
    by!=k!(ptr,3,1)¶
    bz!=k!(ptr,3,2)¶
    WINDOW OUTPUT 1¶
    CALL drawellipse(ax!,ay!,bx!,by!,mx!,my!,0!,pi2!)¶
    WINDOW OUTPUT 2¶
    CALL drawellipse(ax!,az!,bx!,bz!,mx!,mz!,0!,pi2!)¶
    WINDOW OUTPUT 3¶
    CALL drawellipse(ay!,az!,by!,bz!,my!,mz!,0!,pi2!)¶
    WINDOW OUTPUT 4¶
END SUB                     ¶
¶
¶
SUB drawcrseg(ptr) STATIC¶
    SHARED k!()¶
    mx!=k!(ptr,1,0)¶
    my!=k!(ptr,1,1)¶
    mz!=k!(ptr,1,2)¶
    ax!=k!(ptr,2,0)¶
    ay!=k!(ptr,2,1)¶
    az!=k!(ptr,2,2)¶
    bx!=k!(ptr,3,0)¶
    by!=k!(ptr,3,1)¶
    bz!=k!(ptr,3,2)¶
    sw!=k!(ptr,5,0)¶
    ew!=k!(ptr,5,1)¶
    WINDOW OUTPUT 1¶
    CALL drawellipse(ax!,ay!,bx!,by!,mx!,my!,sw!,ew!)¶
    CALL setpoint(ax!*COS(sw!)+bx!*SIN(sw!)+mx!,ay!*COS(sw!)+by!*SIN(sw!)+my!)¶
    CALL drawline(mx!,my!)¶
    CALL drawline(ax!*COS(ew!)+bx!*SIN(ew!)+mx!,ay!*COS(ew!)+by!*SIN(ew!)+my!) ¶
    WINDOW OUTPUT 2¶
    CALL drawellipse(ax!,az!,bx!,bz!,mx!,mz!,sw!,ew!)¶
    CALL setpoint(ax!*COS(sw!)+bx!*SIN(sw!)+mx!,az!*COS(sw!)+bz!*SIN(sw!)+mz!)¶
    CALL drawline(mx!,mz!)¶
    CALL drawline(ax!*COS(ew!)+bx!*SIN(ew!)+mx!,az!*COS(ew!)+bz!*SIN(ew!)+mz!) ¶
```

```
  WINDOW OUTPUT 3¶
  CALL drawellipse(ay!,az!,by!,bz!,my!,mz!,sw!,ew!)¶
  CALL setpoint(ay!*COS(sw!)+by!*SIN(sw!)+my!,az!*COS(sw!)+bz!*SIN(sw!)+mz!)¶
  CALL drawline(my!,mz!)¶
  CALL drawline(ay!*COS(ew!)+by!*SIN(ew!)+my!,az!*COS(ew!)+bz!*SIN(ew!)+mz!) ¶
  WINDOW OUTPUT 4¶
END SUB                    ¶
¶
SUB drawcrarc(ptr) STATIC¶
  SHARED k!()¶
  mx!=k!(ptr,1,0)¶
  my!=k!(ptr,1,1)¶
  mz!=k!(ptr,1,2)¶
  ax!=k!(ptr,2,0)¶
  ay!=k!(ptr,2,1)¶
  az!=k!(ptr,2,2)¶
  bx!=k!(ptr,3,0)¶
  by!=k!(ptr,3,1)¶
  bz!=k!(ptr,3,2)¶
  sw!=k!(ptr,5,0)¶
  ew!=k!(ptr,5,1)¶
  ri!=k!(ptr,4,0)¶
  ra!=k!(ptr,4,1)¶
  WINDOW OUTPUT 1¶
  CALL drawellipse(ax!*ra!,ay!*ra!,bx!*ra!,by!*ra!,mx!,my!,sw!,ew!)¶
  CALL drawellipse(ax!*ri!,ay!*ri!,bx!*ri!,by!*ri!,mx!,my!,sw!,ew!)¶
  CALL
setpoint(ax!*ra!*COS(sw!)+bx!*ra!*SIN(sw!)+mx!,ay!*ra!*COS(sw!)+by!*ra!*SIN(sw!)+my
!) ¶
  CALL
drawline(ax!*ri!*COS(sw!)+bx!*ri!*SIN(sw!)+mx!,ay!*ri!*COS(sw!)+by!*ri!*SIN(sw!)+my
!)¶
  CALL
setpoint(ax!*ra!*COS(ew!)+bx!*ra!*SIN(ew!)+mx!,ay!*ra!*COS(ew!)+by!*ra!*SIN(ew!)+my
!) ¶
  CALL
drawline(ax!*ri!*COS(ew!)+bx!*ri!*SIN(ew!)+mx!,ay!*ri!*COS(ew!)+by!*ri!*SIN(ew!)+my
!)¶
  WINDOW OUTPUT 2¶
  CALL drawellipse(ax!*ra!,az!*ra!,bx!*ra!,bz!*ra!,mx!,mz!,sw!,ew!)¶
  CALL drawellipse(ax!*ri!,az!*ri!,bx!*ri!,bz!*ri!,mx!,mz!,sw!,ew!)¶
  CALL
setpoint(ax!*ra!*COS(sw!)+bx!*ra!*SIN(sw!)+mx!,az!*ra!*COS(sw!)+bz!*ra!*SIN(sw!)+m
z!) ¶
  CALL
drawline(ax!*ri!*COS(sw!)+bx!*ri!*SIN(sw!)+mx!,az!*ri!*COS(sw!)+bz!*ri!*SIN(sw!)+mz
!)¶
  CALL
setpoint(ax!*ra!*COS(ew!)+bx!*ra!*SIN(ew!)+mx!,az!*ra!*COS(ew!)+bz!*ra!*SIN(ew!)+mz
!) ¶
  CALL
drawline(ax!*ri!*COS(ew!)+bx!*ri!*SIN(ew!)+mx!,az!*ri!*COS(ew!)+bz!*ri!*SIN(ew!)+mz
!)¶
  WINDOW OUTPUT 3¶
  CALL drawellipse(ay!*ra!,az!*ra!,by!*ra!,bz!*ra!,my!,mz!,sw!,ew!)¶
  CALL drawellipse(ay!*ri!,az!*ri!,by!*ri!,bz!*ri!,my!,mz!,sw!,ew!)¶
  CALL
setpoint(ay!*ra!*COS(sw!)+by!*ra!*SIN(sw!)+my!,az!*ra!*COS(sw!)+bz!*ra!*SIN(sw!)+mz
!) ¶
  CALL
drawline(ay!*ri!*COS(sw!)+by!*ri!*SIN(sw!)+my!,az!*ri!*COS(sw!)+bz!*ri!*SIN(sw!)+mz
!)¶
```

```
  CALL
setpoint(ay!*ra!*COS(ew!)+by!*ra!*SIN(ew!)+my!,az!*ra!*COS(ew!)+bz!*ra!*SIN(ew!)+m
z!) ¶
  CALL
drawline(ay!*ri!*COS(ew!)+by!*ri!*SIN(ew!)+my!,az!*ri!*COS(ew!)+bz!*ri!*SIN(ew!)+m
z!)¶
  WINDOW OUTPUT 4¶
END SUB         ¶
¶
SUB drawsphere(ptr) STATIC¶
  SHARED k!(),pi2!¶
  mx!=k!(ptr,1,0)¶
  my!=k!(ptr,1,1)¶
  mz!=k!(ptr,1,2)¶
  r!=k!(ptr,2,0)¶
  WINDOW OUTPUT 1¶
  CALL drawellipse(r!,0!,0!,r!,mx!,my!,0!,pi2!)¶
  WINDOW OUTPUT 2¶
  CALL drawellipse(r!,0!,0!,r!,mx!,mz!,0!,pi2!)¶
  WINDOW OUTPUT 3¶
  CALL drawellipse(r!,0!,0!,r!,my!,mz!,0!,pi2!)¶
  WINDOW OUTPUT 4¶
END SUB         ¶
¶
¶
SUB drawcone(ptr) STATIC¶
  SHARED k!(),pi2!¶
  mx!=k!(ptr,1,0)¶
  my!=k!(ptr,1,1)¶
  mz!=k!(ptr,1,2)¶
  ax!=k!(ptr,2,0)¶
  ay!=k!(ptr,2,1)¶
  az!=k!(ptr,2,2)¶
  bx!=k!(ptr,3,0)¶
  by!=k!(ptr,3,1)¶
  bz!=k!(ptr,3,2)¶
  cx!=k!(ptr,4,0)¶
  cy!=k!(ptr,4,1)¶
  cz!=k!(ptr,4,2)¶
  WINDOW OUTPUT 1¶
  CALL drawellipse(ax!,ay!,bx!,by!,mx!,my!,0!,pi2!)¶
  CALL setpoint(ax!+mx!,ay!+my!)¶
  CALL drawline(cx!+mx!,cy!+my!)¶
  CALL drawline(mx!-ax!,my!-ay!) ¶
  CALL setpoint(bx!+mx!,by!+my!)¶
  CALL drawline(cx!+mx!,cy!+my!)¶
  CALL drawline(mx!-bx!,my!-by!) ¶
  WINDOW OUTPUT 2¶
  CALL drawellipse(ax!,az!,bx!,bz!,mx!,mz!,0!,pi2!)¶
  CALL setpoint(ax!+mx!,az!+mz!)¶
  CALL drawline(cx!+mx!,cz!+mz!)¶
  CALL drawline(mx!-ax!,mz!-az!) ¶
  CALL setpoint(bx!+mx!,bz!+mz!)¶
  CALL drawline(cx!+mx!,cz!+mz!)¶
  CALL drawline(mx!-bx!,mz!-bz!) ¶
  WINDOW OUTPUT 3¶
  CALL drawellipse(ay!,az!,by!,bz!,my!,mz!,0!,pi2!)¶
  CALL setpoint(ay!+my!,az!+mz!)¶
  CALL drawline(cy!+my!,cz!+mz!)¶
  CALL drawline(my!-ay!,mz!-az!) ¶
  CALL setpoint(by!+my!,bz!+mz!)¶
  CALL drawline(cy!+my!,cz!+mz!)¶
```

```
  CALL drawline(my!-by!,mz!-bz!) ¶
  WINDOW OUTPUT 4¶
END SUB                    ¶
¶
SUB drawcyl(ptr) STATIC¶
  SHARED k!(),pi2!¶
  mx!=k!(ptr,1,0)¶
  my!=k!(ptr,1,1)¶
  mz!=k!(ptr,1,2)¶
  ax!=k!(ptr,2,0)¶
  ay!=k!(ptr,2,1)¶
  az!=k!(ptr,2,2)¶
  bx!=k!(ptr,3,0)¶
  by!=k!(ptr,3,1)¶
  bz!=k!(ptr,3,2)¶
  cx!=k!(ptr,4,0)¶
  cy!=k!(ptr,4,1)¶
  cz!=k!(ptr,4,2)¶
  WINDOW OUTPUT 1¶
  CALL drawellipse(ax!,ay!,bx!,by!,mx!,my!,0!,pi2!)¶
  CALL drawellipse(ax!,ay!,bx!,by!,mx!+cx!,my!+cy!,0!,pi2!)¶
  CALL setpoint(ax!+mx!,ay!+my!)¶
  CALL drawline(ax!+cx!+mx!,ay!+cy!+my!)¶
  CALL setpoint(-ax!+mx!,-ay!+my!)¶
  CALL drawline(cx!-ax!+mx!,cy!-ay!+my!)¶
  CALL setpoint(bx!+mx!,by!+my!)¶
  CALL drawline(cx!+bx!+mx!,cy!+by!+my!)¶
  CALL setpoint(-bx!+mx!,-by!+my!)¶
  CALL drawline(cx!-bx!+mx!,cy!-by!+my!)¶
  WINDOW OUTPUT 2¶
  CALL drawellipse(ax!,az!,bx!,bz!,mx!,mz!,0!,pi2!)¶
  CALL drawellipse(ax!,az!,bx!,bz!,mx!+cx!,mz!+cz!,0!,pi2!)¶
  CALL setpoint(ax!+mx!,az!+mz!)¶
  CALL drawline(ax!+cx!+mx!,az!+cz!+mz!)¶
  CALL setpoint(-ax!+mx!,-az!+mz!)¶
  CALL drawline(cx!-ax!+mx!,cz!-az!+mz!)¶
  CALL setpoint(bx!+mx!,bz!+mz!)¶
  CALL drawline(cx!+bx!+mx!,cz!+bz!+mz!)¶
  CALL setpoint(-bx!+mx!,-bz!+mz!)¶
  CALL drawline(cx!-bx!+mx!,cz!-bz!+mz!)¶
  WINDOW OUTPUT 3¶
  CALL drawellipse(ay!,az!,by!,bz!,my!,mz!,0!,pi2!)¶
  CALL drawellipse(ay!,az!,by!,bz!,my!+cy!,mz!+cz!,0!,pi2!)¶
  CALL setpoint(ay!+my!,az!+mz!)¶
  CALL drawline(ay!+cy!+my!,az!+cz!+mz!)¶
  CALL setpoint(-ay!+my!,-az!+mz!)¶
  CALL drawline(cy!-ay!+my!,cz!-az!+mz!)¶
  CALL setpoint(by!+my!,bz!+mz!)¶
  CALL drawline(cy!+by!+my!,cz!+bz!+mz!)¶
  CALL setpoint(-by!+my!,-bz!+mz!)¶
  CALL drawline(cy!-by!+my!,cz!-bz!+mz!)¶
  WINDOW OUTPUT 4¶
END SUB                    ¶
¶
SUB drawcylseg(ptr) STATIC¶
  SHARED k!()¶
  mx!=k!(ptr,1,0)¶
  my!=k!(ptr,1,1)¶
  mz!=k!(ptr,1,2)¶
  ax!=k!(ptr,2,0)¶
  ay!=k!(ptr,2,1)¶
  az!=k!(ptr,2,2)¶
```

```
  bx!=k!(ptr,3,0)¶
  by!=k!(ptr,3,1)¶
  bz!=k!(ptr,3,2)¶
  cx!=k!(ptr,4,0)¶
  cy!=k!(ptr,4,1)¶
  cz!=k!(ptr,4,2)¶
  sw!=k!(ptr,5,0)¶
  ew!=k!(ptr,5,1)¶
  WINDOW OUTPUT 1¶
  CALL drawellipse(ax!,ay!,bx!,by!,mx!+cx!,my!+cy!,sw!,ew!)¶
  CALL drawellipse(ax!,ay!,bx!,by!,mx!,my!,sw!,ew!)¶
  CALL setpoint(mx!,my!)¶
  CALL drawline(mx!+cx!,my!+cy!)¶
  CALL
drawline(ax!*COS(ew!)+bx!*SIN(ew!)+mx!+cx!,ay!*COS(ew!)+by!*SIN(ew!)+my!+cy!) ¶
  CALL drawline(ax!*COS(ew!)+bx!*SIN(ew!)+mx!,ay!*COS(ew!)+by!*SIN(ew!)+my!)¶
  CALL drawline(mx!,my!)¶
  CALL drawline(ax!*COS(sw!)+bx!*SIN(sw!)+mx!,ay!*COS(sw!)+by!*SIN(sw!)+my!)¶
  CALL
drawline(ax!*COS(sw!)+bx!*SIN(sw!)+mx!+cx!,ay!*COS(sw!)+by!*SIN(sw!)+my!+cy!)¶
  CALL drawline(mx!+cx!,my!+cy!)¶
  WINDOW OUTPUT 2¶
  CALL drawellipse(ax!,az!,bx!,bz!,mx!+cx!,mz!+cz!,sw!,ew!)¶
  CALL drawellipse(ax!,az!,bx!,bz!,mx!,mz!,sw!,ew!)¶
  CALL setpoint(mx!,mz!)¶
  CALL drawline(mx!+cx!,mz!+cz!)¶
  CALL
drawline(ax!*COS(ew!)+bx!*SIN(ew!)+mx!+cx!,az!*COS(ew!)+bz!*SIN(ew!)+mz!+cz!) ¶
  CALL drawline(ax!*COS(ew!)+bx!*SIN(ew!)+mx!,az!*COS(ew!)+bz!*SIN(ew!)+mz!)¶
  CALL drawline(mx!,mz!)¶
  CALL drawline(ax!*COS(sw!)+bx!*SIN(sw!)+mx!,az!*COS(sw!)+bz!*SIN(sw!)+mz!)¶
  CALL
drawline(ax!*COS(sw!)+bx!*SIN(sw!)+mx!+cx!,az!*COS(sw!)+bz!*SIN(sw!)+mz!+cz!)¶
  CALL drawline(mx!+cx!,mz!+cz!)¶
  WINDOW OUTPUT 3¶
  CALL drawellipse(ay!,az!,by!,bz!,my!+cy!,mz!+cz!,sw!,ew!)¶
  CALL drawellipse(ay!,az!,by!,bz!,my!,mz!,sw!,ew!)¶
  CALL setpoint(my!,mz!)¶
  CALL drawline(my!+cy!,mz!+cz!)¶
  CALL
drawline(ay!*COS(ew!)+by!*SIN(ew!)+my!+cy!,az!*COS(ew!)+bz!*SIN(ew!)+mz!+cz!) ¶
  CALL drawline(ay!*COS(ew!)+by!*SIN(ew!)+my!,az!*COS(ew!)+bz!*SIN(ew!)+mz!)¶
  CALL drawline(my!,mz!)¶
  CALL drawline(ay!*COS(sw!)+by!*SIN(sw!)+my!,az!*COS(sw!)+bz!*SIN(sw!)+mz!)¶
  CALL
drawline(ay!*COS(sw!)+by!*SIN(sw!)+my!+cy!,az!*COS(sw!)+bz!*SIN(sw!)+mz!+cz!)¶
  CALL drawline(my!+cy!,mz!+cz!)¶
  WINDOW OUTPUT 4¶
END SUB    ¶
¶
SUB drawspheriod(ptr) STATIC¶
  SHARED k!(),pi2!¶
  mx!=k!(ptr,1,0)¶
  my!=k!(ptr,1,1)¶
  mz!=k!(ptr,1,2)¶
  ax!=k!(ptr,2,0)¶
  ay!=k!(ptr,2,1)¶
  az!=k!(ptr,2,2)¶
  bx!=k!(ptr,3,0)¶
  by!=k!(ptr,3,1)¶
  bz!=k!(ptr,3,2)¶
  cx!=k!(ptr,4,0)¶
```

```
  cy!=k!(ptr,4,1)¶
  cz!=k!(ptr,4,2)¶
  WINDOW OUTPUT 1¶
  CALL drawellipse(ax!,ay!,bx!,by!,mx!,my!,0!,pi2!)¶
  CALL drawellipse(ax!,ay!,cx!,cy!,mx!,my!,0!,pi2!)¶
  WINDOW OUTPUT 2¶
  CALL drawellipse(ax!,az!,bx!,bz!,mx!,mz!,0!,pi2!)¶
  CALL drawellipse(ax!,az!,cx!,cz!,mx!,mz!,0!,pi2!)¶
  WINDOW OUTPUT 3¶
  CALL drawellipse(ay!,az!,by!,bz!,my!,mz!,0!,pi2!)¶
  CALL drawellipse(ay!,az!,cy!,cz!,my!,mz!,0!,pi2!)¶
  WINDOW OUTPUT 4¶
END SUB    ¶
¶
¶
¶
SUB drawellipse(ax!,ay!,bx!,by!,mx!,my!,sw!,ew!)STATIC¶
'TASK     :draw ellipse in current output window¶
'PARAMETER:=>ax!,ay!,bx!,by! span of ellipse¶
'            mx!,my! center point of ellipse¶
'            sw!,ew! the start angle and end angle¶
'                    to be used¶
  SHARED maxlines,pi2!¶
  alpha!=sw!¶
  numlines=ABS(sw!-ew!)*maxlines/pi2! 'Compute number of lines¶
  IF numlines=0 THEN¶
    numlines=maxlines  'if sw!=ew!, draw full ellipse¶
    beta!=pi2!/maxlines¶
  ELSE ¶
    beta!=ABS(sw!-ew!)/numlines  'compute increment angle¶
  END IF¶
  x!=ax!*COS(alpha!)+bx!*SIN(alpha!)+mx! 'compute start point¶
  y!=ay!*COS(alpha!)+by!*SIN(alpha!)+my!¶
  CALL setpoint(x!,y!)  'Start point output¶
  FOR i=1 TO numlines¶
    alpha!=alpha!+beta!  'compute new angle¶
    x!=ax!*COS(alpha!)+bx!*SIN(alpha!)+mx!  'compute new point¶
    y!=ay!*COS(alpha!)+by!*SIN(alpha!)+my!¶
    CALL drawline(x!,y!)  'draw line from old point to new¶
  NEXT i¶
END SUB¶
        ¶
SUB setpoint(x!,y!)STATIC¶
'TASK     :set point in current output window¶
'PARAMETER:=>x!,y! Point coordinate¶
  SHARED mx!,my!,mz!,factor!,xcorrfac!,colour¶
  swindow=WINDOW(1)  ¶
  IF swindow=1 THEN¶
    LINE ((x!-mx!)*xcorrfac!*factor!,(my!-y!)*factor!)-((x!-
mx!)*xcorrfac!*factor!,(my!-y!)*factor!),colour¶
  ELSE¶
    IF swindow=2 THEN¶
      LINE ((x!-mx!)*xcorrfac!*factor!,(mz!-y!)*factor!)-((x!-
mx!)*xcorrfac!*factor!,(mz!-y!)*factor!),colour¶
    ELSE¶
      IF swindow=3 THEN¶
        LINE ((my!-x!)*xcorrfac!*factor!,(mz!-y!)*factor!)-((my!-
x!)*xcorrfac!*factor!,(mz!-y!)*factor!),colour¶
      END IF¶
    END IF¶
  END IF¶
END SUB¶
```

```
¶
SUB drawline(x!,y!)STATIC¶
'TASK      :draw line from last point to specified point¶
'PARAMETER:=>x!,y! Point coordinates¶
  SHARED mx!,my!,mz!,factor!,xcorrfac!,colour¶
  swindow=WINDOW(1)  ¶
  IF swindow=1 THEN¶
    LINE -((x!-mx!)*xcorrfac!*factor!,(my!-y!)*factor!),colour¶
  ELSE¶
    IF swindow=2 THEN¶
      LINE -((x!-mx!)*xcorrfac!*factor!,(mz!-y!)*factor!),colour¶
    ELSE¶
      IF swindow=3 THEN¶
        LINE -((my!-x!)*xcorrfac!*factor!,(mz!-y!)*factor!),colour¶
      END IF¶
    END IF¶
  END IF¶
END SUB¶
¶
'**************¶
'** DISKETTE **¶
'**************¶
                    ¶
SUB loadmat STATIC¶
'TASK      :load the Material list from disk¶
'           WARNING! no test for existing file ¶
  SHARED mat!(),matnum,matptr,legchar$,File$¶
  WINDOW 5,"Load Material",(0,129)-(314,150),0,1¶
  PRINT "Name:"¶
  CALL getstring(File$," ",legchar$,1,6,10) 'get filename¶
  IF File$><"" THEN      'if file$="" then cancel¶
    OPEN File$+".mat" FOR INPUT AS 1¶
    INPUT #1,quantity¶
    WHILE NOT(EOF(1))¶
      CALL newmat(matptr)¶
      FOR i=0 TO 6¶
        INPUT #1,mat!(matptr,i)¶
      NEXT i¶
    WEND  ¶
    CLOSE 1¶
  END IF¶
  WINDOW CLOSE 5¶
  WINDOW OUTPUT 4¶
END SUB¶
¶
SUB savemat STATIC¶
'TASK      :save material list currently in memory to disk¶
  SHARED mat!(),matnum,legchar$,File$¶
  WINDOW 5,"Save Material",(0,129)-(314,170),0,1¶
  PRINT "Name:"¶
  PRINT "from:1"¶
  PRINT "to  :"¶
  mfrom!=1¶
  mto!=matnum¶
  CALL putreal(mto!,3,6,10)  'Read all data¶
  CALL getstring(File$," ",legchar$,1,6,10)¶
  CALL getint(mfrom!," ",2,6,10,1!,matnum*1!)¶
  CALL getint(mto!," ",3,6,10,mfrom!,matnum*1!)¶
  IF File$><"" THEN  'if file$="" then cancel¶
    OPEN File$+".MAT" FOR OUTPUT AS 1¶
    WHILE mfrom!<mto! AND mat!(mto!,0)=-1¶
      mto!=mto!-1¶
```

```
    WEND  ¶
    PRINT #1,mto!-mfrom!+1¶
    FOR ptr=mfrom! TO mto!¶
      FOR i=0 TO 6¶
        IF mat!(ptr,0)=-1 THEN¶

        ELSE  ¶
          PRINT #1,mat!(ptr,i)¶
        END IF¶
      NEXT i¶
    NEXT ptr¶
    CLOSE 1¶
    KILL File$+".MAT.info"¶
  END IF¶
  WINDOW CLOSE 5¶
  WINDOW OUTPUT 4¶
END SUB¶
          ¶
SUB loadlist STATIC¶
'TASK   :See corresponding routine for material list  ¶
  SHARED k!(),knum,ptr,legchar$,File$¶
  WINDOW 5,"Load List",(0,129)-(314,150),0,1¶
  PRINT "Name:"¶
  CALL getstring(File$," ",legchar$,1,6,10)¶
  IF File$><"" THEN¶
    OPEN File$+".list" FOR INPUT AS 1¶
    INPUT #1,quantity¶
    WHILE NOT(EOF(1))¶
      CALL newelem(ptr)¶
      FOR i=0 TO 5¶
        INPUT #1,k!(ptr,i,0),k!(ptr,i,1),k!(ptr,i,2)¶
      NEXT i¶
    WEND  ¶
    CLOSE 1¶
  END IF¶
  WINDOW CLOSE 5¶
  WINDOW OUTPUT 4¶
  CALL showelem(ptr)¶
END SUB¶
¶
SUB savelist STATIC¶
'TASK   :See corresponding routine for material list  ¶
  SHARED k!(),knum,legchar$,File$¶
  WINDOW 5,"Save List",(0,129)-(314,170),0,1¶
  PRINT "Name:"¶
  PRINT "from:1"¶
  PRINT "to  :"¶
  mfrom!=1¶
  mto!=knum¶
  CALL putreal(mto!,3,6,10)¶
  CALL getstring(File$," ",legchar$,1,6,10)¶
  CALL getint(mfrom!," ",2,6,10,1!,knum*1!)¶
  CALL getint(mto!," ",3,6,10,mfrom!,knum*1!)¶
  IF File$><"" THEN¶
    OPEN File$+".LIST" FOR OUTPUT AS 1¶
    quantity=0¶
    FOR i=mfrom! TO mto!    'determine number of elements to be saved¶
      IF k!(i,0,0) ><-1 THEN¶
        quantity=quantity+1¶
      END IF¶
    NEXT i¶
    PRINT #1,quantity    ¶
```

```
    FOR ptr=mfrom! TO mto!¶
      IF k!(ptr,0,0)><-1 THEN  'forget blank elements¶
        FOR i=0 TO 5¶
          PRINT #1,k!(ptr,i,0);",";k!(ptr,i,1);",";k!(ptr,i,2)¶
        NEXT i¶
      END IF¶
    NEXT ptr¶
    CLOSE 1¶
    KILL File$+".LIST.info"¶
  END IF¶
  WINDOW CLOSE 5¶
  WINDOW OUTPUT 4¶
END SUB           ¶
¶
¶
'*********************¶
'** TRANSFORMATION   **¶
'*********************¶
¶
SUB rotation(ptr) STATIC¶
'TASK     :rotate body by three angles¶
'PARAMETER:=>ptr points to the body¶
  SHARED k!(),grad!,rad!,min!,max!¶
  IF ptr><0 THEN¶
    WINDOW 5,"Rotation",(0,129)-(314,170),4,1¶
    vx!=grad!*vx!¶
    vy!=grad!*vy!¶
    vz!=grad!*vz!¶
    LOCATE 2,1¶
    PRINT"V :"¶
    PRINT"q<uit,d<o,c<opy&do :"¶
    CALL put3real(vx!,vy!,vz!,2,4,26)¶
    CALL get3real(vx!,vy!,vz!," ",2,4,26,min!,max!,0)¶
    CALL getstring(a$," ","qcd",3,21,1)¶
    vx!=rad!*vx!¶
    vy!=rad!*vy!¶
    vz!=rad!*vz!¶
    WINDOW CLOSE 5¶
    WINDOW OUTPUT 4¶
    IF a$><"q" THEN¶
      IF a$="c" THEN¶
        CALL copy(ptr)¶
      END IF¶
      IF k!(ptr,0,0)>=20 THEN ¶
        til=4¶
      ELSE¶
        til=3¶
      END IF¶
      FOR i=2 TO til¶
        a!=k!(ptr,i,0)*COS(vz!)-k!(ptr,i,1)*SIN(vz!)¶
        b!=k!(ptr,i,0)*SIN(vz!)+k!(ptr,i,1)*COS(vz!)¶
        c!=a!*SIN(vy!)-k!(ptr,i,2)*COS(vy!)  ¶
        k!(ptr,i,0)=a!*COS(vy!)+k!(ptr,i,2)*SIN(vy!)¶
        k!(ptr,i,1)=c!*SIN(vx!)+b!*COS(vx!)¶
        k!(ptr,i,2)=b!*SIN(vx!)-c!*COS(vx!)¶
      NEXT i¶
      CALL showelem(ptr)  ¶
      IF k!(ptr,5,2)=1 THEN¶
        CALL drawelem(ptr)¶
      END IF  ¶
    ELSE   ¶
      WINDOW CLOSE 5¶
```

```
    END IF¶
  END IF¶
END SUB¶
¶
SUB translation(ptr) STATIC¶
'TASK     :move one body by one vector¶
'PARAMETER:=>ptr points to the body¶
  SHARED k!(),min!,max!¶
  IF ptr><0 THEN¶
    WINDOW 5,"Translation",(0,129)-(314,170),4,1¶
    LOCATE 2,1¶
    PRINT"V :"¶
    PRINT"q<uit,d<o,c<opy&do :"¶
    CALL put3real(vx!,vy!,vz!,2,4,26)¶
    CALL get3real(vx!,vy!,vz!,"",2,4,26,min!,max!,-1)¶
    CALL getstring(a$," ","qcd",3,21,1)¶
    WINDOW CLOSE 5¶
    WINDOW OUTPUT 4¶
    IF a$><"q" THEN¶
      IF a$="c" THEN¶
        CALL copy(ptr)¶
      END IF¶
      k!(ptr,1,0)=vx!¶
      k!(ptr,1,1)=vy!¶
      k!(ptr,1,2)=vz!¶
      CALL showelem(ptr)¶
      IF k!(ptr,5,2)=1 THEN¶
        CALL drawelem(ptr)¶
      END IF  ¶
    ELSE   ¶
      WINDOW CLOSE 5¶
    END IF¶
  END IF¶
END SUB¶
¶
SUB sizing(ptr) STATIC¶
'TASK     :size one body ¶
'PARAMETER:=>ptr points to the body¶
  SHARED k!(),min!,max!¶
  IF ptr><0 THEN¶
    WINDOW 5,"Sizing",(0,129)-(314,170),4,1¶
    LOCATE 2,1¶
    PRINT"V :"¶
    PRINT"q<uit,d<o,c<opy&do :"¶
    CALL put3real(vx!,vy!,vz!,2,4,26)¶
    CALL get3real(vx!,vy!,vz!," ",2,4,26,min!,max!,0)¶
    CALL getstring(a$," ","qcd",3,21,1)¶
    WINDOW CLOSE 5¶
    WINDOW OUTPUT 4¶
    IF a$><"q" THEN¶
      IF a$="c" THEN¶
        CALL copy(ptr)¶
      END IF¶
      IF k!(ptr,0,0)>=20 THEN ¶
        til=4¶
      ELSE¶
        til=3¶
      END IF¶
      FOR i=2 TO til  ¶
        k!(ptr,i,0)=vx!*k!(ptr,i,0)¶
        k!(ptr,i,1)=vy!*k!(ptr,i,1)¶
        k!(ptr,i,2)=vz!*k!(ptr,i,2)¶
```

```
      NEXT i¶
      CALL showelem(ptr)¶
      IF k!(ptr,5,2)=1 THEN¶
        CALL drawelem(ptr)¶
      END IF  ¶
    ELSE    ¶
      WINDOW CLOSE 5¶
    END IF¶
  END IF  ¶
END SUB¶
¶
¶
'*********************¶
'** SYSTEM ROUTINES **¶
'*********************¶
¶
¶
SUB copy(ptr) STATIC¶
'TASK     :copy one body¶
'PARAMETER:=>ptr points to the body¶
  SHARED k!()¶
  IF ptr><0 THEN  'not the starting element¶
    old=ptr       'save pointer¶
    CALL newelem(ptr)  'create new space¶
    FOR i=0 TO 5       'copy¶
      FOR j=0 TO 2¶
        k!(ptr,i,j)=k!(old,i,j)¶
      NEXT j¶
    NEXT i¶
  END IF¶
END SUB¶
¶
SUB copier(ptr) STATIC¶
'TASK     :copies a body and displays its data¶
'PARAMETER:=>ptr points to the body¶
  IF ptr><0 THEN¶
    CALL copy(ptr)¶
    CALL showelem(ptr)¶
  END IF¶
END SUB   ¶
¶
SUB deleter(ptr) STATIC¶
'TASK     :delete one body¶
'PARAMETER:=>ptr points to the body¶
  SHARED k!(),kfree¶
  IF ptr><0 THEN 'not the starting element¶
    FOR i=0 TO 5 'Delete¶
      FOR j=0 TO 2¶
        k!(ptr,i,j)=0¶
      NEXT j¶
    NEXT i    ¶
    k!(ptr,0,0)=-1     'Add body to free list¶
    k!(ptr,0,1)=kfree¶
    kfree=ptr¶
    CALL lefts(ptr)¶
  END IF  ¶
END SUB¶
¶
SUB lefts(ptr) STATIC¶
'TASK     :get element to left of current elememt¶
'PARAMETER:=>ptr points to current body¶
  SHARED k!()¶
```

```
  IF ptr><0 THEN ¶
    ptr=ptr-1¶
  END IF¶
  WHILE k!(ptr,0,0)=-1¶
    ptr=ptr-1¶
  WEND¶
  CALL showelem(ptr)¶
END SUB         ¶
                ¶
SUB rights(ptr) STATIC¶
'TASK     :get element to right of current element¶
'PARAMETER:=>ptr pointer to current body¶
  SHARED k!(),knum¶
  old=ptr¶
  IF ptr<knum THEN¶
    ptr=ptr+1¶
  END IF¶
  WHILE k!(ptr,0,0)=-1 AND ptr<knum¶
    ptr=ptr+1¶
  WEND¶
  IF k!(ptr,0,0)=-1 THEN¶
    ptr=old      ¶
  ELSE¶
    CALL showelem(ptr)¶
  END IF¶
END SUB¶
¶
¶
¶
SUB liob(mx!,my!,mz!) STATIC¶
'TASK     :read coordinates of upper left hand corner¶
'PARAMETER:=>mx!,my!,mz! old coordinates¶
'          <=mx!,my!,mz! new coordinates¶
  SHARED min!,max!¶
  CALL get3real(mx!,my!,mz!,"",9,12,26,min!,max!,-1)¶
END SUB¶
¶
SUB setfactor(f!) STATIC¶
'TASK     :read the new sizing factor¶
'PARAMETER:=>f! old factor¶
'          <=f! new factor¶
  CALL getreal(f!," ",11,8,8,.015625,64!)¶
END SUB¶
¶
SUB factor2(f!)STATIC¶
'TASK     :multiply factor! by 2¶
'PARAMETER:=>f! old factor¶
'          <=f! new factor¶
  IF f!<=32 THEN¶
    f!=f!*2¶
    CALL putreal(f!,11,8,8)¶
  END IF  ¶
END SUB¶
¶
SUB factorhalf(f!)STATIC¶
'TASK     :multiply factor! with 0.5¶
'PARAMETER:=>f! old factor¶
'          <=f! new factor¶
  IF 1/f! <=32 THEN¶
    f!=f!*.5¶
    CALL putreal(f!,11,8,8)¶
  END IF¶
```

```
END SUB¶
¶
SUB setlines(maxlines) STATIC¶
'TASK      :read max number of lines allowed for drawing a circle¶
'PARAMETER:=>maxlines old value¶
'           <=maxlines new value¶
  i!=maxlines¶
  CALL getint(i!," ",11,24,3,1!,50!)¶
  maxlines=i!¶
END SUB  ¶
¶
SUB showandwait(ptr) STATIC¶
'TASK      :display data for a body then moves the upper left ¶
'           corner so that it appears in the middle of the screen¶
'           or the body appears on the screen in color¶
'PARAMETER:<=ptr points to desired body¶
  SHARED knum,k!(),factor!,mx!,my!,mz!,colour,xcorrfac!¶
  IF ptr><0 THEN¶
    WINDOW 5,"Show",(0,129)-(314,170),4,1¶
    LOCATE 2,1¶
    PRINT"Body   :"¶
    PRINT"D<ata,M<iddle,C<olor :"¶
    CALL putreal(ptr*1!,2,9,10)¶
    p!=ptr¶
    CALL getreal(p!," ",2,9,10,1!,knum*1!)¶
    CALL getstring(a$," ","dmc",3,23,1)¶
    WINDOW CLOSE 5¶
    WINDOW OUTPUT 4¶
    IF k!(p!,0,0)><-1 THEN¶
      IF p!><ptr THEN¶
        ptr=p!¶
        CALL showelem(ptr)¶
      END IF ¶
      IF a$><"d" THEN¶
        IF a$="m" THEN¶
          mx!=k!(ptr,1,0)-149/xcorrfac!/factor!  'compute new upper left corner
          my!=k!(ptr,1,1)+57/factor!¶
          mz!=k!(ptr,1,2)+57/factor!¶
          CALL put3real(mx!,my!,mz!,9,12,26)  'and display¶
        ELSE¶
          colour=3¶
          CALL drawelem(ptr)¶
          a$=""¶
          WHILE a$=""¶
            a$=INKEY$¶
          WEND¶
          colour=1¶
          CALL drawelem(ptr)¶
        END IF¶
      END IF¶
    END IF      ¶
  END IF         ¶
END SUB¶
¶
SUB refresh STATIC¶
'TASK      :Refresh screen¶
  SHARED k!(),knum¶
  FOR i=1 TO 3¶
    WINDOW OUTPUT i¶
    CLS¶
  NEXT i¶
  FOR i=1 TO knum¶
```

```
    IF k!(i,5,2)=1 AND k!(i,0,0)><-1 THEN¶
      CALL drawelem(i)¶
    END IF¶
  NEXT i ¶
  WINDOW OUTPUT 4 ¶
END SUB¶
¶
SUB drawelem(ptr) STATIC¶
'TASK      :draw current body¶
'PARAMETER:=>ptr points to the body¶
  SHARED k!(),mx!,my!,mz!¶
  IF ptr><0 THEN¶
    CALL busymouse¶
    typ=k!(ptr,0,0)¶
    IF typ=0 THEN¶
      CALL drawplane(ptr)¶
    END IF¶
    IF typ=1 THEN¶
      CALL drawtriangle(ptr)¶
    END IF¶
    IF typ=2 THEN¶
      CALL drawparall(ptr)¶
    END IF¶
    IF typ=3 THEN¶
      CALL drawcircle(ptr)¶
    END IF¶
    IF typ=4 THEN¶
      CALL drawcrseg(ptr)¶
    END IF¶
    IF typ=5 THEN¶
      CALL drawcrarc(ptr)¶
    END IF¶
    IF typ=10 THEN¶
      CALL drawsphere(ptr)¶
    END IF¶
    IF typ=20 THEN¶
      CALL drawcyl(ptr)¶
    END IF¶
    IF typ=21 THEN¶
      CALL drawcylseg(ptr)¶
    END IF¶
    IF typ=22 THEN¶
      CALL drawcone(ptr)¶
    END IF¶
    IF typ=24 THEN¶
      CALL drawspheriod(ptr)¶
    END IF¶
    CALL lazymouse¶
  END IF¶
END SUB¶
¶
SUB getelem(ptr) STATIC¶
'TASK      :Read the necessary body data¶
'PARAMETER:ptr points to the specified body¶
  SHARED k!()¶
  typ=k!(ptr,0,0)¶
  IF typ<=3 AND ptr>0 THEN ¶
    CALL getplane  (ptr)¶
  END IF ¶
  IF typ=4 THEN¶
    CALL getcrseg(ptr)¶
  END IF¶
```

```
  IF typ=5 THEN¶
    CALL getcrarc(ptr)¶
  END IF¶
  IF typ=10 THEN¶
    CALL getsphere(ptr)¶
  END IF¶
  IF typ=20 OR typ=22 OR typ=24 THEN ¶
    CALL getcyl(ptr)¶
  END IF¶
  IF typ=21 THEN¶
    CALL getcylseg(ptr)¶
  END IF¶
  IF k!(ptr,5,2)=1 THEN¶
    CALL drawelem(ptr)¶
  END IF  ¶
END SUB¶
¶
SUB finish(quit) STATIC¶
'TASK     :Confirms quitting program¶
'PARAMETER:=>quit =0¶
'          <=quit =0 =>no cancel ¶
'                 =1 => cancel¶
  SHARED gadget%()¶
  WINDOW 5," QUIT ",(0,129)-(314,150),0,1¶
  PRINT "Really ? "¶
  CALL initgadget(110,3,15,30,1,5,nr1%,100,-1)¶
  CALL initgadget(160,3,15,60,1,5,nr2%,200,-1)¶
  WHILE gadget%(nr1%,4)><0 AND gadget%(nr2%,4)><0¶
  WEND¶
  IF gadget%(nr1%,4)=0 THEN¶
    quit=1¶
  END IF¶
  WINDOW CLOSE 5 ¶
  CALL deletegadget(nr1%)¶
  CALL deletegadget(nr2%)¶
END SUB¶
¶
SUB newelem(ptr) STATIC¶
'TASK     :get address of free place in list¶
'PARAMETER:<=ptr points to this area¶
  SHARED kfree,k!(),knum¶
  IF kfree<knum THEN¶
    ptr=kfree¶
    kfree=k!(ptr,0,1)¶
    k!(ptr,0,0)=0¶
    k!(ptr,0,1)=0¶
    k!(ptr,0,2)=1¶
  END IF  ¶
END SUB¶
¶
      ¶
SUB act1with4 STATIC¶
'TASK   :activate Menu 1 to 4¶
  CALL busymouse ¶
  MENU 1,0,1,"Transform.  "¶
  MENU 1,1,1,"Rotation    "¶
  MENU 1,2,1,"Translation "¶
  MENU 1,3,1,"Enlarge     "¶
  MENU 1,4,1,"Copy        "¶
  MENU 1,5,1,"Delete    ^D"¶
  MENU 1,6,1,"Correction ^K"¶
     ¶
```

```
  MENU 2,0,1,"Body          "¶
  MENU 2,1,1,"Plane         "¶
  MENU 2,2,1,"Triangle      "¶
  MENU 2,3,1,"Parallelogram "¶
  MENU 2,4,1,"Circle        "¶
  MENU 2,5,1,"Circle segment"¶
  MENU 2,6,1,"Arc           "¶
  MENU 2,7,1,"Sphere        "¶
  MENU 2,8,1,"Cylinder      "¶
  MENU 2,9,1,"Cylinder seg. "¶
  MENU 2,10,1,"Cone          "¶
  MENU 2,11,1,"Spheroid      "¶
  ¶
  MENU 3,0,1,"Disk     "¶
  MENU 3,1,1,"Load List"¶
  MENU 3,2,1,"Load Mat "¶
  MENU 3,3,1,"Save List"¶
  MENU 3,4,1,"Save Mat "¶
  ¶
  MENU 4,0,1,"Operations "¶
  MENU 4,1,1,"Left      L"¶
  MENU 4,2,1,"Right     R"¶
  MENU 4,3,1,"Segment    "¶
  MENU 4,4,1,"Factor     "¶
  MENU 4,5,1,"Factor*2  *"¶
  MENU 4,6,1,"Factor/2  /"¶
  MENU 4,7,1,"Mat.editor "¶
  MENU 4,8,1,"Refresh  ^R"¶
  MENU 4,9,1,"Show      S"¶
  MENU 4,10,1,"Lines      "¶
  MENU 4,11,1,"Quit       "¶
  CALL lazymouse¶
END SUB¶
¶
SUB entact1with4 STATIC¶
'TASK   :deactivate MENU 1 TO 4¶
  CALL busymouse  ¶
  ¶
  MENU 1,0,0,"Transform   "¶
  MENU 1,1,1,"Rotation    "¶
  MENU 1,2,1,"Translation "¶
  MENU 1,3,1,"Enlarge     "¶
  MENU 1,4,1,"Copy        "¶
  MENU 1,5,1,"Delete n  ^D"¶
  MENU 1,6,1,"Correction ^K"¶
    ¶
  MENU 2,0,0,"Body          "¶
  MENU 2,1,1,"Plane         "¶
  MENU 2,2,1,"Triangle      "¶
  MENU 2,3,1,"Parallelogram "¶
  MENU 2,4,1,"Circle        "¶
  MENU 2,5,1,"Circle segment"¶
  MENU 2,6,1,"Arc           "¶
  MENU 2,7,1,"Sphere        "¶
  MENU 2,8,1,"Cylinder      "¶
  MENU 2,9,1,"Cylinder seg. "¶
  MENU 2,10,1,"Cone          "¶
  MENU 2,11,1,"Spheroid      "¶
  ¶
  MENU 3,0,0,"Disk     "¶
  MENU 3,1,1,"Load List"¶
  MENU 3,2,1,"Load Mat "¶
```

```
  MENU 3,3,1,"Save List"¶
  MENU 3,4,1,"Save Mat "¶
  ¶
  MENU 4,0,0,"Operations "¶
  MENU 4,1,1,"Left      L"¶
  MENU 4,2,1,"Right     R"¶
  MENU 4,3,1,"Segment    "¶
  MENU 4,4,1,"Factor     "¶
  MENU 4,5,1,"Factor*2  *"¶
  MENU 4,6,1,"Factor/2  /"¶
  MENU 4,7,1,"Mat.editor "¶
  MENU 4,8,1,"Refresh  ^R"¶
  MENU 4,9,1,"Show      S"¶
  MENU 4,10,1,"Lines     "¶
  MENU 4,11,1,"Quit      "¶
  CALL lazymouse¶
END SUB¶
¶
SUB akt5 STATIC¶
'TASK   :activate Menu 5¶
  CALL busymouse  ¶
  MENU 5,0,1,"Mat.editor  "¶
  MENU 5,1,1,"Left       L"¶
  MENU 5,2,1,"Right      R"¶
  MENU 5,3,1,"Delete    ^D"¶
  MENU 5,4,1,"Correction^K"¶
  MENU 5,5,1,"Material   M"¶
  MENU 5,6,1,"Quit        "¶
  CALL lazymouse¶
END SUB  ¶
¶
SUB deactiv5 STATIC¶
'TASK   :deactivate Menu 5¶
  CALL busymouse  ¶
  MENU 5,0,0,"Mat.editor  "¶
  MENU 5,1,0,"Left       L"¶
  MENU 5,2,0,"Right      R"¶
  MENU 5,3,0,"Delete    ^D"¶
  MENU 5,4,0,"Correction^K"¶
  MENU 5,5,0,"Material   M"¶
  MENU 5,6,0,"Quit        "¶
  CALL lazymouse¶
END SUB  ¶
¶
'*********************¶
'** MATERIAL-EDITOR **¶
'*********************¶
SUB mateddy STATIC¶
'TASK   :configure window for material editor¶
  SHARED matptr,mat,nr1%,nr2%,nr3%,nr4%,nr5%,nr6%¶
  CALL entact1with4¶
  CALL akt5¶
  mat=1¶
  WINDOW 5,"Material-Editor",(0,85)-(314,190),16,1¶
  CALL showmat(matptr)¶
  CALL deletegadget(nr1%) 'active gadget must be deactivated¶
  CALL deletegadget(nr2%)¶
  CALL deletegadget(nr3%)¶
  CALL deletegadget(nr4%)¶
  CALL deletegadget(nr5%)¶
  CALL deletegadget(nr6%)¶
END SUB¶
```

```
¶
SUB newmat(matptr) STATIC¶
'TASK   :See corresponding routine for the body list¶
  SHARED matfree,mat!(),matnum¶
  IF matfree<matnum THEN¶
    matptr=matfree¶
    matfree=mat!(matptr,1)¶
    mat!(matptr,0)=0¶
    mat!(matptr,1)=0¶
  END IF   ¶
END SUB¶
¶
SUB finishmat STATIC¶
'TASK   :See corresponding routine for the body list¶
  SHARED mat,gadget%()¶
  WINDOW 6," QUIT ",(0,129)-(314,150),0,1¶
  PRINT "Really ? "¶
  CALL initgadget(110,3,15,30,1,6,nr1%,100,-1)¶
  CALL initgadget(160,3,15,60,1,6,nr2%,200,-1)¶
  WHILE gadget%(nr1%,4)><0 AND gadget%(nr2%,4)><0¶
  WEND¶
  IF gadget%(nr1%,4)=0 THEN¶
    mat=0¶
    WINDOW CLOSE 5¶
    WINDOW CLOSE 6¶
    CALL deactiv5¶
    CALL act1with4¶
    PALETTE 2,0,0,0¶
  ELSE¶
    WINDOW CLOSE 6 ¶
  END IF¶
  CALL deletegadget(nr1%)¶
  CALL deletegadget(nr2%)¶
END SUB¶
¶
SUB deletermat(matptr) STATIC¶
'TASK   :See corresponding routine for the body list¶
  SHARED mat!(),matfree¶
  IF matptr><0 THEN¶
    FOR i=0 TO 6¶
      mat!(matptr,i)=0¶
    NEXT i    ¶
    mat!(matptr,0)=-1¶
    mat!(matptr,1)=matfree¶
    matfree=matptr¶
    CALL leftsmat(matptr)¶
  END IF  ¶
END SUB¶
¶
SUB leftsmat(matptr) STATIC¶
'TASK   :See corresponding routine for the body list¶
  SHARED mat!(),nr1%,nr2%,nr3%,nr4%,nr5%,nr6%¶
  IF matptr><0 THEN ¶
    matptr=matptr-1¶
  END IF¶
  WHILE mat!(matptr,0)=-1¶
    matptr=matptr-1¶
  WEND¶
  CALL showmat(matptr)¶
  CALL deletegadget(nr1%)¶
  CALL deletegadget(nr2%)¶
  CALL deletegadget(nr3%)¶
```

```
  CALL deletegadget(nr4%)¶
  CALL deletegadget(nr5%)¶
  CALL deletegadget(nr6%)¶
END SUB          ¶
                          ¶
SUB rightsmat(matptr) STATIC¶
'TASK   :See corresponding routine for the body list¶
  SHARED mat!(),matnum,nr1%,nr2%,nr3%,nr4%,nr5%,nr6%¶
  old=matptr¶
  IF matptr<matnum THEN¶
    matptr=matptr+1¶
  END IF¶
  WHILE mat!(matptr,0)=-1 AND matptr<matnum¶
    matptr=matptr+1¶
  WEND¶
  IF mat!(matptr,0)=-1 THEN¶
    matptr=old       ¶
  ELSE¶
    CALL showmat(matptr)¶
    CALL deletegadget(nr1%)¶
    CALL deletegadget(nr2%)¶
    CALL deletegadget(nr3%)¶
    CALL deletegadget(nr4%)¶
    CALL deletegadget(nr5%)¶
    CALL deletegadget(nr6%)¶
  END IF¶
END SUB¶
¶
SUB matinput(matptr) STATIC¶
'TASK   :See corresponding routine for the body list¶
  SHARED mat!()¶
  CALL newmat(matptr)¶
  CALL getmat(matptr)¶
END SUB¶
¶
SUB getmat(matptr) STATIC¶
'TASK   :see corresponding routine for the body list¶
  SHARED mat!(),gadget%(),nr1%,nr2%,nr3%,nr4%,nr5%,nr6%¶
  CALL showmat(matptr)¶
  WHILE gadget%(nr6%,4)><0¶
    PALETTE 2,gadget%(nr1%,4)/100,gadget%(nr2%,4)/100,gadget%(nr3%,4)/100¶
  WEND ¶
  mat!(matptr,0)=gadget%(nr1%,4)/101¶
  mat!(matptr,1)=gadget%(nr2%,4)/101¶
  mat!(matptr,2)=gadget%(nr3%,4)/101¶
  mat!(matptr,3)=gadget%(nr4%,4)/101¶
  mat!(matptr,4)=gadget%(nr5%,4)/101¶
  CALL deletegadget(nr1%)¶
  CALL deletegadget(nr2%)¶
  CALL deletegadget(nr3%)¶
  CALL deletegadget(nr4%)¶
  CALL deletegadget(nr5%)¶
  CALL deletegadget(nr6%)¶
END SUB ¶
¶
SUB showmat(matptr) STATIC¶
'TASK   :See corresponding routine for the body list¶
  SHARED mat!(),nr1%,nr2%,nr3%,nr4%,nr5%,nr6%¶
  CLS¶
  PRINT "Material:"¶
  CALL putreal(matptr*1!,1,10,10)¶
  IF matptr ><0 THEN¶
```

```
    LOCATE 1,20¶
    PRINT "R+G+B="¶
    PALETTE 2,mat!(matptr,0),mat!(matptr,1),mat!(matptr,2)¶
    LINE (250,0)-(260,7),2,bf¶
    PRINT "Red        :"¶
    PRINT ¶
    PRINT "Green      :"¶
    PRINT ¶
    PRINT "Blue       :"¶
    PRINT ¶
    PRINT "Shadow     :"¶
    PRINT ¶
    PRINT "Mirroring :"¶
    w1%=mat!(matptr,0)*101¶
    w2%=mat!(matptr,1)*101¶
    w3%=mat!(matptr,2)*101¶
    w4%=mat!(matptr,3)*101¶
    w5%=mat!(matptr,4)*101    ¶
    CALL initgadget(110,8,10,102,w1%,5,nr1%,-1,-1)¶
    CALL initgadget(110,24,10,102,w2%,5,nr2%,-1,-1)¶
    CALL initgadget(110,40,10,102,w3%,5,nr3%,-1,-1)¶
    CALL initgadget(110,56,10,102,w4%,5,nr4%,-1,-1)¶
    CALL initgadget(110,72,10,102,w5%,5,nr5%,-1,-1)      ¶
    CALL initgadget(110,88,15,30,1,5,nr6%,0,-1)¶
  END IF¶
END SUB¶
¶
'***************¶
'**  GADGETS  **¶
'***************¶
SUB checkgadget STATIC¶
'TASK   :test whether a gadget has been clicked  ¶
  SHARED gadget%(),gadgets%()  ¶
  dummy=MOUSE(0)¶
  ax=MOUSE(3) 'Mouse position¶
  ay=MOUSE(4)¶
  i=0¶
  WHILE i<=10  'search entire array¶
   x%=gadget%(i,0)     'get values from array ¶
   y%=gadget%(i,1)¶
   h%=gadget%(i,2)¶
   l%=gadget%(i,3)¶
   valu%=gadget%(i,4)¶
   wind%=gadget%(i,5)¶
   yes%=gadget%(i,6)¶
   none%=gadget%(i,7)  'Mouse over gadget ?¶
   IF x%<ax AND x%+l%>ax AND y%<ay AND y%+h%>ay AND x%>=0 AND WINDOW(0)=wind% THEN¶
      old=WINDOW(1) 'reserve output window¶
      WINDOW OUTPUT wind%   'delete old slider draw new one¶
      IF yes%=-1 THEN¶
        LINE (valu%+x%+1,y%+1)-(valu%+x%+1,y%+h%-1),0¶
        valu%=ax-x%-1¶
        LINE (valu%+x%+1,y%+1)-(valu%+x%+1,y%+h%-1),3¶
        gadget%(i,4)=valu%  'get new value¶
      ELSE¶
        IF none%=-1 THEN¶
          IF valu%=1 THEN  'first time, invert it¶
            gadget%(i,4)=0¶
            LINE (x%,y%)-(x%+l%,y%+h%),0,bf¶
            PUT (x%,y%),gadgets%(yes%),PRESET¶
          ELSE  ¶
            gadget%(i,4)=1  'else return ¶
```

```
          LINE (x%,y%)-(x%+l%,y%+h%),0,bf¶
          PUT (x%,y%),gadgets%(yes%)¶
        END IF¶
      ELSE    ¶
        IF valu%=1 THEN  'first time, display no output¶
          gadget%(i,4)=0¶
          LINE (x%,y%)-(x%+l%,y%+h%),0,bf¶
          PUT (x%,y%),gadgets%(none%)¶
        ELSE  ¶
          gadget%(i,4)=1 'else yes output¶
          LINE (x%,y%)-(x%+l%,y%+h%),0,bf¶
          PUT (x%,y%),gadgets%(yes%)¶
        END IF¶
      END IF¶
    END IF¶
    WINDOW OUTPUT old   'old output window active¶
    i=10    ¶
  END IF¶
  i=i+1¶
 WEND¶
END SUB     ¶
¶
SUB initgadget(x%,y%,h%,l%,valu%,wind%,nr%,yes%,none%)STATIC¶
'TASK     :place a new gadget in the gadget array gadget%()¶
'PARAMETER:=>x%,y% Position of upper left corner¶
'             h%,l% border height and lenght¶
'             valu% Start value¶
'             wind% Output window¶
'             yes%,none% if yes%=-1,then slider¶
'                        if none%=-1,gadgets inverts when clicked¶
'                        else display another gadget¶
'                        yes% and none% supply the indices for graphic information¶
'                        of the array gadgets ¶
'           <=nr% Position of the gadgets in array ¶
  SHARED gadget%(),gadgets%()¶
  IF x%>=0 AND y%>=0 AND h%>=2 AND l%>=3 AND valu%>=0 AND valu%<l% AND wind%>0
THEN¶
    MOUSE OFF¶
    old=WINDOW(1)¶
    WINDOW OUTPUT wind%¶
    IF yes%=-1 THEN¶
      LINE  (x%,y%)-(x%,y%+h%)¶
      LINE -(x%+l%,y%+h%)¶
      LINE -(x%+l%,y%)¶
      LINE -(x%,y%)¶
      LINE (valu%+x%+1,y%+1)-(valu%+x%+1,y%+h%-1),3¶
    ELSE¶
      IF valu%=1 THEN¶
        PUT (x%,y%),gadgets%(yes%)¶
      ELSE¶
        PUT (x%,y%),gadgets%(none%)¶
      END IF¶
    END IF¶
    nr%=0¶
    WHILE gadget%(nr%,0)><-1 AND nr%<=9 ¶
      nr%=nr%+1¶
    WEND¶
    IF gadget%(nr%,0)=-1 THEN    ¶
      gadget%(nr%,0)=x%¶
      gadget%(nr%,1)=y%¶
      gadget%(nr%,2)=h%¶
      gadget%(nr%,3)=l%¶
```

```
        gadget%(nr%,4)=valu%¶
        gadget%(nr%,5)=wind%¶
        gadget%(nr%,6)=yes%¶
        gadget%(nr%,7)=none%¶
      END IF  ¶
      MOUSE ON¶
      WINDOW OUTPUT old¶
    END IF¶
  END SUB¶
    ¶
  SUB deletegadget(i) STATIC¶
  'TASK      :delete a gadget¶
  'PARAMETER:=>i Index of  gadgets in array  ¶
    SHARED gadget%()¶
    IF i>=0 AND i<=10 THEN¶
      gadget%(i,0)=-1¶
    END IF¶
  END SUB   ¶
  ¶
  '******************¶
  '** MOUSE POINTER**¶
  '******************¶
  ¶
  SUB busymouse STATIC¶
  'TASK     :the mouse pointer in busy mode¶
    SHARED buffer&¶
    FOR i=1 TO 4¶
      WINDOW OUTPUT i¶
      CALL setpointer&(WINDOW(7),buffer&,15,16,-8,-7)¶
    NEXT i  ¶
  END SUB¶
  ¶
  SUB lazymouse STATIC¶
  'TASK     :Change mouse pointer to cross hair¶
    SHARED buffer&¶
    FOR i=1 TO 4¶
      WINDOW OUTPUT i¶
      CALL setpointer&(WINDOW(7),buffer&+68,15,16,-8,-7)¶
    NEXT i¶
  END SUB¶
  ¶
  SUB initmaus STATIC¶
  'TASK     :save two mouse pointers¶
    SHARED buffer&¶
  mousedata:¶
    DATA 0,0¶
    DATA  0, 1, 0,-32767, 0,-18751, 0,-1, 0,-18751, 0,-32767¶
    DATA  14016,-32767, 14016,-14017, 14016,-32767, 0,-32767¶
    DATA  13848,-18919, 13848,-1, 13848,-18919, 0,-32767, 0¶
    DATA -32767¶
    DATA 0,0¶
    DATA 0,0¶
    DATA  256, 0, 256, 0, 256, 0, 256, 0, 256, 0, 256, 0, 256, 0¶
    DATA -258, 0, 256, 0, 256, 0, 256, 0, 256, 0, 256, 0, 256, 0¶
    DATA  256, 0¶
    DATA 0,0¶
    RESTORE mousedata¶
    FOR i=0 TO 67¶
      READ valu%¶
      POKEW buffer&+i*2,valu%¶
    NEXT i¶
  END SUB¶
```

D. The SetPoint Program

The `SetPoint` machine language program used by the tracer program is listed here. The program appears here in machine language source code and as a BASIC loader, for those of you who do not have the ***AssemPro*** assembler.

```
;SetPoint.ASM
;Output one rectangle in one  Rastport (screen)

;Calculate  from the existing colour word the desired combination
; for the desired color word.

_LVOOpenLibrary   = -552
_LVOCloseLibrary  = -414
_LVOReadPixel     = -318
_LVORectFill      = -306
_LVOSetAPen       = -342
_LVOSetBPen       = -348

HAM          = $800
rp_AreaPtrn = 8
rp_FgPen     = 25
rp_BgPen     = 26
rp_AreaPtSz = 29

;Offsets for the parameter of the stack: All longwords

NumPattern = 11
sinc=15*4
xl=4+sinc
yl=8+sinc
xr=12+sinc
yr=16+sinc
red=22+sinc
green=26+sinc
blue=30+sinc

CALLSYS:MACRO $\1
 JSR _LVO\1(A6)
 ENDM

OpenGfx:

;open libraries

 MOVEM.L D0/D1/A0/A1/A6,-(SP)

 MOVEQ #0,D0
 LEA GfxName,A1
 MOVE.L 4,A6
 CALLSYS OpenLibrary
 LEA GfxBase,A0
 MOVE.L D0,(A0)

 MOVEM.L (SP)+,D0/D1/A0/A1/A6
```

```
 RTS

CloseGfx:

;close libraries

 MOVEM.L D0/D1/A0/A1/A6,-(SP)

 MOVE.L GfxBase,D0
 BEQ.S \R
 MOVE.L D0,A1
 MOVE.L 4,A6
 CALLSYS CloseLibrary
\R:
 MOVEM.L (SP)+,D0/D1/A0/A1/A6
 RTS

SetPoint:

;output one rectangle. Parameter:

; (xl,yl,xr,yr,red,green,blue)

 MOVEM.L D0-A6,-(SP)

 MOVE.L GfxBase,D0
 BEQ \R
 MOVE.L D0,A6

 MOVE Modus,D0
 ANDI #HAM,D0
 BEQ \NORMAL
;Determine color of last  pixel:

 MOVEM.L xl(SP),D0/D1
 SUBQ #1,D0
 BCC.S \HAM1
 MOVEQ #0,D0          ;If Pixel = first in line => background color
 BRA.S \HAM2
\HAM1:
 MOVE.L RastPort,A1
 CALLSYS ReadPixel
 TST D0
 BMI \R
\HAM2:                    ;D0= Color number

;Copy additional HAM-Colors  in array:

 LSL #3,D0
 LEA Colour,A0
 LEA 2(A0,D0),A1        ;^ oldcolor
 MOVEM (A1),D3-D5       ;red,green,blue
 ADD #128,A0            ;Start the list for HAM-Colors: 128=16*8

 MOVEQ #$10,D1          ;ColorNr: blue
 MOVEQ #16,D0           ;16 Steps
 MOVEQ #0,D5            ;blue-Intensity=0
 BRA.S \SHIB
\SHLB:
 MOVE D1,(A0)+
 ADDQ #1,D1
 MOVEM D3-D5,(A0)
```

```
 ADDQ.L #6,A0
 ADD #64,D5
\SHIB:
 DBRA D0,\SHLB
 MOVE 4(A1),D5          ;old blue-Intensity

 MOVEQ #0,D3            ;red-Intensity=0
 MOVEQ #16,D0
 BRA.S \SHIR
\SHLR:
 MOVE D1,(A0)+
 ADDQ #1,D1
 MOVEM D3-D5,(A0)
 ADDQ.L #6,A0
 ADD #64,D3             ;64=1024/16
\SHIR:
 DBRA D0,\SHLR
 MOVE (A1)+,D3

 MOVEQ #16,D0           ;ColorNr=$30! :Green
 MOVEQ #0,D4
 BRA.S \SHIG
\SHLG:
 MOVE D1,(A0)+
 ADDQ #1,D1
 MOVEM D3-D5,(A0)
 ADDQ.L #6,A0
 ADD #64,D4
\SHIG:
 DBRA D0,\SHLG

;Now all 64 possible colors are calculated => all normal
;additional.

\NORMAL:

;Seacrh first for the color, in one pass:

 LEA Colour,A0
 MOVE MaxColour,D0
 MOVEQ #-1,D7           ;Minimum
 MOVE.L A0,A1
 BRA.S \IN1
\LP1:

 MOVE 2(A0),D1
 SUB red(SP),D1
 MULS D1,D1
 MOVE 4(A0),D2
 SUB green(SP),D2
 MULS D2,D2
 ADD.L D2,D1
 MOVE 6(A0),D2
 SUB blue(SP),D2
 MULS D2,D2
 ADD.L D2,D1

 CMP.L D1,D7
 BLS.S \NXT1
  MOVE.L D1,D7
  MOVE.L A0,A1
```

```
 \NXT1:
  ADDQ.L #8,A0
 \IN1:
  DBRA D0,\LP1

 ;Search now the color, in the second pass:

  LEA Colour,A0
  MOVE MaxColour,D0
  MOVEQ #-1,D7          ;Minimum
  MOVE.L A0,A2
  BRA.S \IN2
 \LP2:

  BSR \COMPARE_Colour
  BEQ.S \NXT2

  MOVE 2(A0),D1
  SUB red(SP),D1
  MULS D1,D1
  MOVE 4(A0),D2
  SUB green(SP),D2
  MULS D2,D2
  ADD.L D2,D1
  MOVE 6(A0),D2
  SUB blue(SP),D2
  MULS D2,D2
  ADD.L D2,D1

  CMP.L D1,D7
  BLS.S \NXT2
   MOVE.L D1,D7
   MOVE.L A0,A2

 \NXT2:
  ADDQ.L #8,A0
 \IN2:
  DBRA D0,\LP2

 ;Search pattern for optimal approximation:

  BSR.S \SEARCH_PATTERN
  MOVE.L D7,D3
  MOVE.L A3,A4

 ;Is equal again with inverse Pattern:

  EXG A1,A2 BSR.S \SEARCH_PATTERN
  CMP.L D3,D7
  BLO.S \RECT
  EXG A1,A2 MOVE.L A4,A3          ;Old value was better!
 \RECT:

 ;A1^ ColorNr1, A2^ ColorNr2, A3^ Pattern

  MOVE (A1),D7
  MOVE (A2),D0
  MOVE.L RastPort,A1
  MOVE.L A3,rp_AreaPtrn(A1)
  MOVE.B #4,rp_AreaPtSz(A1)
  MOVE.L A1,-(SP)
  CALLSYS SetAPen
```

```
 MOVE.L (SP),A1
 MOVE D7,D0
 CALLSYS SetBPen
 MOVE.L (SP)+,A1

;Clipping:

 MOVEM.L x1(SP),D0-D3
 MOVEM RasterW1,D4/D5
 CMP D4,D0
 BHI.S \R
 CMP D5,D1
 BHI.S \R
 CMP D4,D2
 BLS.S \R1
 MOVE D4,D2
\R1:
 CMP D5,D3
 BLS.S \R2
 MOVE D5,D3
\R2:
 CALLSYS RectFill

\R:
 MOVEM.L (SP)+,D0-A6
 RTS

\SEARCH_PATTERN:

;A1 ^ Color1, A2 ^ Color2. => A3 ^ Pattern.

 LEA PATTERN,A0
 LEA 2(A0),A3
 MOVEQ #-1,D7
 MOVEQ #NumPattern-1,D0
\LPM:
  MOVE (A0),D1
  MOVE #1024,D2
  SUB D1,D2           ;1-BkgkPattern

  MOVE 2(A1),D6
  BEQ.S \E1
  MULU D2,D6          ;Color1.red*(1-BkgnPattern)
  DIVU #1024,D6
\E1:
  MOVE 2(A2),D5
  BEQ.S \E2
  MULU D1,D5          ;Color2.red*BkgnPattern
  DIVU #1024,D5
\E2:
  ADD D5,D6           ;Color.red
  SUB red+4(SP),D6    ;Difference
  MULS D6,D6          ;The quadrant

  MOVE 4(A1),D4
  BEQ.S \E3
  MULU D2,D4          ;Color1.green*(1-BkgnPattern)
  DIVU #1024,D4
\E3:
  MOVE 4(A2),D5
  BEQ.S \E4
  MULU D1,D5          ;Color2.green*BkgnPattern
```

```
  DIVU #1024,D5
\E4:
  ADD D5,D4            ;Color.green
  SUB green+4(SP),D4
  MULS D4,D4
  ADD.L D4,D6

  MOVE 6(A1),D4
  BEQ.S \E5
  MULU D2,D4           ;Color1.blue*(1-BkgnPattern)
  DIVU #1024,D4
\E5:
  MOVE 6(A2),D5
  BEQ.S \E6
  MULU D1,D5           ;Color2.blue*BkgnPattern
  DIVU #1024,D5
\E6:
  ADD D5,D4            ;Color.blue
  SUB blue+4(SP),D4
  MULS D4,D4
  ADD.L D4,D6          ;distance between desired and current Color

  CMP.L D6,D7
  BLS.S \NXTM
    LEA 2(A0),A3
    MOVE.L D6,D7
    BEQ.S \FND

\NXTM:
 ADD #34,A0
 DBRA D0,\LPM

\FND:
 RTS

\COMPARE_Colour:

;A1^ Color1, A0^ Color2

 CMP.L A1,A0
 BEQ.S \CFR
 MOVE 2(A1),D1
 CMP 2(A0),D1
 BNE.S \CFR
 MOVE 4(A1),D1
 CMP 4(A0),D1
 BNE.S \CFR
 MOVE 6(A1),D1
 CMP 6(A0),D1
\CFR:
 RTS

GfxName:DC.B 'graphics.library',0
 ALIGN
GfxBase:DC.L 0

RastPort:DC.L 0
MaxColour:DC.W 0
Modus:DC.W 0
RasterW1:DC.W 320
RasterH1:DC.W 200
```

```
PATTERN:
 DC.W 0
 DC.W $0000
 DC.W $0000
 DC.W $0000
 DC.W $0000
 DC.W $0000
 DC.W $0000
 DC.W $0000
 DC.W $0000
 DC.W $0000
 DC.W $0000
 DC.W $0000
 DC.W $0000
 DC.W $0000
 DC.W $0000
 DC.W $0000
 DC.W $0000

 DC.W 4
 DC.W $8000
 DC.W $0000
 DC.W $0000
 DC.W $0000
 DC.W $0000
 DC.W $0000
 DC.W $0000
 DC.W $0000
 DC.W $0000
 DC.W $0000
 DC.W $0000
 DC.W $0000
 DC.W $0000
 DC.W $0000
 DC.W $0000
 DC.W $0000

 DC.W 8
 DC.W $8000
 DC.W $0000
 DC.W $0000
 DC.W $0000
 DC.W $0000
 DC.W $0000
 DC.W $0000
 DC.W $0000
 DC.W $0080
 DC.W $0000
 DC.W $0000
 DC.W $0000
 DC.W $0000
 DC.W $0000
 DC.W $0000
 DC.W $0000

 DC.W 16
 DC.W $8080
 DC.W $0000
 DC.W $0000
 DC.W $0000
 DC.W $0000
 DC.W $0000
```

```
DC.W $0000
DC.W $0000
DC.W $8080
DC.W $0000
DC.W $0000
DC.W $0000
DC.W $0000
DC.W $0000
DC.W $0000
DC.W $0000

DC.W 32
DC.W $8080
DC.W $0000
DC.W $0000
DC.W $0000
DC.W $0808
DC.W $0000
DC.W $0000
DC.W $0000
DC.W $8080
DC.W $0000
DC.W $0000
DC.W $0000
DC.W $0808
DC.W $0000
DC.W $0000
DC.W $0000

DC.W 64
DC.W $8888
DC.W $0000
DC.W $0000
DC.W $0000
DC.W $8888
DC.W $0000
DC.W $0000
DC.W $0000
DC.W $8888
DC.W $0000
DC.W $0000
DC.W $0000
DC.W $8888
DC.W $0000
DC.W $0000
DC.W $0000

DC.W 128
DC.W $8888
DC.W $0000
DC.W $2222
DC.W $0000
DC.W $8888
DC.W $0000
DC.W $2222
DC.W $0000
DC.W $8888
DC.W $0000
DC.W $2222
DC.W $0000
DC.W $8888
DC.W $0000
```

```
DC.W $2222
DC.W $0000

DC.W 256
DC.W $AAAA
DC.W $0000
DC.W $AAAA
DC.W $0000
DC.W $AAAA
DC.W $0000
DC.W $AAAA
DC.W $0000
DC.W $AAAA
DC.W $0000
DC.W $AAAA
DC.W $0000
DC.W $AAAA
DC.W $0000
DC.W $AAAA
DC.W $0000

DC.W 384
DC.W $AAAA
DC.W $1111
DC.W $AAAA
DC.W $4444
DC.W $AAAA
DC.W $1111
DC.W $AAAA
DC.W $4444
DC.W $AAAA
DC.W $1111
DC.W $AAAA
DC.W $4444
DC.W $AAAA
DC.W $1111
DC.W $AAAA
DC.W $4444

DC.W 448
DC.W $AAAA
DC.W $5555
DC.W $AAAA
DC.W $4444
DC.W $AAAA
DC.W $5555
DC.W $AAAA
DC.W $4444
DC.W $AAAA
DC.W $5555
DC.W $AAAA
DC.W $4444
DC.W $AAAA
DC.W $5555
DC.W $AAAA
DC.W $4444

DC.W 512
DC.W $AAAA
DC.W $5555
DC.W $AAAA
DC.W $5555
```

```
 DC.W $AAAA
 DC.W $5555
 DC.W $AAAA
 DC.W $5555
 DC.W $AAAA
 DC.W $5555
 DC.W $AAAA
 DC.W $5555
 DC.W $AAAA
 DC.W $5555
 DC.W $AAAA
 DC.W $5555

Colour:
 DS.B 64*8    ;ColorNr,red,green,blue

                  END
```

The following program is the BASIC loader used to create `SetPoint.B` on a disk named `Tracer`. The example program that follows contain some BASIC lines that must be entered on one line in AmigaBASIC, even though they appear on two lines in this book. Formatting the program listings to fit into this book has caused some long BASIC lines to be split into two lines. To show where a BASIC line is actually ended, a ¶ will be used. This is not to be entered, it only shows when the <Return> key should be pressed in the BASIC editor.

```
'SetPoint.BAS¶
OPEN "tracer:SetPoint.B" FOR OUTPUT AS 1¶
FOR i=1 TO  1528¶
READ a$¶
        a%=VAL("&H"+a$)¶
        PRINT #1,CHR$(a%);¶
        NEXT¶
CLOSE 1¶
KILL "Tracer:SetPoint.B.info"¶
¶
datas:¶
DATA 48,E7,C0,C2,70,0,43,FA,2,58,2C,78,0,4,4E,AE,FD,D8,41,FA¶
DATA 2,5E,20,80,4C,DF,43,3,4E,75,48,E7,C0,C2,20,3A,2,4E,67,A¶
DATA 22,40,2C,78,0,4,4E,AE,FE,62,4C,DF,43,3,4E,75,48,E7,FF,FE¶
DATA 20,3A,2,34,67,0,1,68,2C,40,30,3A,2,34,2,40,8,0,67,0¶
DATA 0,80,4C,EF,0,3,0,40,53,40,64,4,70,0,60,E,22,7A,2,14¶
DATA 4E,AE,FE,C2,4A,40,6B,0,1,3E,E7,48,41,FA,3,86,43,F0,0,2¶
DATA 4C,91,0,38,D0,FC,0,80,72,10,70,10,7A,0,60,E,30,C1,52,41¶
DATA 48,90,0,38,5C,88,DA,7C,0,40,51,C8,FF,F0,3A,29,0,4,76,0¶
DATA 70,10,60,E,30,C1,52,41,48,90,0,38,5C,88,D6,7C,0,40,51,C8¶
DATA FF,F0,36,19,70,10,78,0,60,E,30,C1,52,41,48,90,0,38,5C,88¶
DATA D8,7C,0,40,51,C8,FF,F0,41,FA,3,26,30,3A,1,A4,7E,FF,22,48¶
DATA 60,2C,32,28,0,2,92,6F,0,52,C3,C1,34,28,0,4,94,6F,0,56¶
DATA C5,C2,D2,82,34,28,0,6,94,6F,0,5A,C5,C2,D2,82,BE,81,63,4¶
DATA 2E,1,22,48,50,88,51,C8,FF,D2,41,FA,2,E8,30,3A,1,66,7E,FF¶
DATA 24,48,60,32,61,0,1,20,67,2A,32,28,0,2,92,6F,0,52,C3,C1¶
DATA 34,28,0,4,94,6F,0,56,C5,C2,D2,82,34,28,0,6,94,6F,0,5A¶
DATA C5,C2,D2,82,BE,81,63,4,2E,1,24,48,50,88,51,C8,FF,CC,61,5C¶
DATA 26,7,28,4B,C5,49,61,54,BE,83,65,4,C5,49,26,4C,3E,11,30,12¶
DATA 22,7A,1,C,23,4B,0,8,13,7C,0,4,0,1D,2F,9,4E,AE,FE,AA¶
DATA 22,57,30,7,4E,AE,FE,A4,22,5F,4C,EF,0,F,0,40,4C,BA,0,30¶
DATA 0,EE,B0,44,62,14,B2,45,62,10,B4,44,63,2,34,4,B6,45,63,2¶
```

```
DATA 36,5,4E,AE,FE,CE,4C,DF,7F,FF,4E,75,41,FA,0,D0,47,E8,0,2¶
DATA 7E,FF,70,A,32,10,34,3C,4,0,94,41,3C,29,0,2,67,6,CC,C2¶
DATA 8C,FC,4,0,3A,2A,0,2,67,6,CA,C1,8A,FC,4,0,DC,45,9C,6F¶
DATA 0,56,CD,C6,38,29,0,4,67,6,C8,C2,88,FC,4,0,3A,2A,0,4¶
DATA 67,6,CA,C1,8A,FC,4,0,D8,45,98,6F,0,5A,C9,C4,DC,84,38,29¶
DATA 0,6,67,6,C8,C2,88,FC,4,0,3A,2A,0,6,67,6,CA,C1,8A,FC¶
DATA 4,0,D8,45,98,6F,0,5E,C9,C4,DC,84,BE,86,63,8,47,E8,0,2¶
DATA 2E,6,67,8,D0,FC,0,22,51,C8,FF,82,4E,75,B1,C9,67,1C,32,29¶
DATA 0,2,B2,68,0,2,66,12,32,29,0,4,B2,68,0,4,66,8,32,29¶
DATA 0,6,B2,68,0,6,4E,75,67,72,61,70,68,69,63,73,2E,6C,69,62¶
DATA 72,61,72,79,0,0,0,0,0,0,0,0,0,0,0,0,0,0,1,40¶
DATA 0,C8,0,0,0,0,0,0,0,0,0,0,0,0,0,0,0,0,0,0¶
DATA 0,0,0,0,0,0,0,0,0,0,0,0,0,0,0,0,0,4,80,0¶
DATA 0,0,0,0,0,0,0,0,0,0,0,0,0,0,0,0,0,0,0,0¶
DATA 0,0,0,0,0,0,0,0,0,0,0,8,80,0,0,0,0,0,0,0¶
DATA 0,0,0,0,0,0,0,0,0,80,0,0,0,0,0,0,0,0,0,0¶
DATA 0,0,0,0,0,10,80,80,0,0,0,0,0,0,0,0,0,0,0,0¶
DATA 0,0,80,80,0,0,0,0,0,0,0,0,0,0,0,0,0,0,0,20¶
DATA 80,80,0,0,0,0,0,0,8,8,0,0,0,0,0,0,80,80,0,0¶
DATA 0,0,0,0,8,8,0,0,0,0,0,0,0,40,88,88,0,0,0,0¶
DATA 0,0,88,88,0,0,0,0,0,0,88,88,0,0,0,0,0,0,88,88¶
DATA 0,0,0,0,0,0,0,80,88,88,0,0,22,22,0,0,88,88,0,0¶
DATA 22,22,0,0,88,88,0,0,22,22,0,0,88,88,0,0,22,22,0,0¶
DATA 1,0,AA,AA,0,0,AA,AA,0,0,AA,AA,0,0,AA,AA,0,0,AA,AA¶
DATA 0,0,AA,AA,0,0,AA,AA,0,0,AA,AA,0,0,1,80,AA,AA,11,11¶
DATA AA,AA,44,44,AA,AA,11,11,AA,AA,44,44,AA,AA,11,11,AA,AA, 44,44¶
DATA AA,AA,11,11,AA,AA,44,44,1,C0,AA,AA,55,55,AA,AA,44, 44,AA,AA¶
DATA 55,55,AA,AA,44,44,AA,AA,55,55,AA,AA,44,44,AA,AA,55,55, AA,AA¶
DATA 44,44,2,0,AA,AA,55,55,AA,AA,55,55,AA,AA,55,55,AA,AA,55,55¶
DATA AA,AA,55,55,AA,AA,55,55,AA,AA,55,55,AA,AA,55,55,0,0,0,0¶
DATA 0,0,0,0,0,0,0,0,0,0,0,0,0,0,0,0,0,0,0,0¶
DATA 0,0,0,0,0,0,0,0,0,0,0,0,0,0,0,0,0,0,0,0¶
DATA 0,0,0,0,0,0,0,0,0,0,0,0,0,0,0,0,0,0,0,0¶
DATA 0,0,0,0,0,0,0,0,0,0,0,0,0,0,0,0,0,0,0,0¶
DATA 0,0,0,0,0,0,0,0,0,0,0,0,0,0,0,0,0,0,0,0¶
DATA 0,0,0,0,0,0,0,0,0,0,0,0,0,0,0,0,0,0,0,0¶
DATA 0,0,0,0,0,0,0,0,0,0,0,0,0,0,0,0,0,0,0,0¶
DATA 0,0,0,0,0,0,0,0,0,0,0,0,0,0,0,0,0,0,0,0¶
DATA 0,0,0,0,0,0,0,0,0,0,0,0,0,0,0,0,0,0,0,0¶
DATA 0,0,0,0,0,0,0,0,0,0,0,0,0,0,0,0,0,0,0,0¶
DATA 0,0,0,0,0,0,0,0,0,0,0,0,0,0,0,0,0,0,0,0¶
DATA 0,0,0,0,0,0,0,0,0,0,0,0,0,0,0,0,0,0,0,0¶
DATA 0,0,0,0,0,0,0,0,0,0,0,0,0,0,0,0,0,0,0,0¶
DATA 0,0,0,0,0,0,0,0,0,0,0,0,0,0,0,0,0,0,0,0¶
DATA 0,0,0,0,0,0,0,0,0,0,0,0,0,0,0,0,0,0,0,0¶
DATA 0,0,0,0,0,0,0,0,0,0,0,0,0,0,0,0,0,0,0,0¶
DATA 0,0,0,0,0,0,0,0,0,0,0,0,0,0,0,0,0,0,0,0¶
DATA 0,0,0,0,0,0,0,0,0,0,0,0,0,0,0,0,0,0,0,0¶
DATA 0,0,0,0,0,0,0,0,0,0,0,0,0,0,0,0,0,0,0,0¶
DATA 0,0,0,0,0,0,0,0,0,0,0,0,0,0,0,0,0,0,0,0¶
DATA 0,0,0,0,0,0,0,0,0,0,0,0,0,0,0,0,0,0,0,0¶
DATA 0,0,0,0,0,0,0,0,0,0,0,0,0,0,0,0,0,0,0,0¶
DATA 0,0,0,0,0,0,0,0,0,0,0,0,0,0,0,0,0,0,0,0¶
DATA 0,0,0,0,0,0,0,0,0,0,0,0,0,0,0,0,0,0,0,0¶
DATA 0,0,0,0,0,0,0,0¶
```

E. Tracer Error Messages

While the program is running, different errors can occur. The most frequent error is an input/output error, which arises when, for example, you try to access a nonexistent file, or when the disk has a read/write error.

Such errors are processed in the tracer routine `ErrorHandling`. Also, when the modules are merged incorrectly, errors are handled in this routine.

Errors occuring during the transfer of IFF graphics to and from disk are not processed by this routine. `ErrorHandling` is activated by `ON ERROR`.

`ScreenLoad` and `ScreenSave` use the library commands to access the disk. Errors such as a full disk are trapped in these routines that (for example, `..-Chunk cannot be saved!!!`) allow you to return to the program.

Error messages when starting the program (`No free Chip mem!!!`) are caused by insufficient memory. Here little tricks, like working with a very small AmigaDOS window help. You must also close or delete less important programs running in the background. Unfortunately it can also happen that the computer or AmigaBASIC will ignore the lack of memory. This can occur with a large `K` array (200+ elements) on a 512K machine.

Errors can also be encountered during the initilization of the shadowing process: When the basis of an object is not a basis at all, you are informed. (A basis consists of three independent, linear vectors. A vector is not presented as a multiple of the other two vectors). These errors occur when the vectors a, b, and c span no space of an ellipsoid, cone, or cylinder or when they are coplanar or colinear.

When you present one of the three vectors by using the other two vectors (for example a = x*b + y*c), only one plane or one line and no space is spanned causing an error.

Index

A

AC/BASIC compiler 193
Addition theorem 55
Algorithm 10,167,179
AmigaBASIC 19,193
Angles 184
Arc 17,149
ASCII format 51

B

B-splines 167
Background 73,157
Bezier 167
Brightness 9

C

Cartesian coordinates 45,58
Circle 13,148
Color 10,173
Compiling 194
Components 181
Cone 14,151
Coordinates 12,181
Cosine 53
Cray 48
Cylinder 14,150

D

Data structure 16
Determinant 23,188
Difference vectors 179
Direction vector 37
Display 11

E

Editor 74-75,145-159, 167,179,302-344
Editor data manipulation 94
Editor instructions 145-159
Editor sample run 78
Ellipsoid 14
Enhanced objects 167
Enlargement 58,94,160,174
Equal vectors 179
Error messages 356
Exiting tracer program 159

F

File manipulation 154

G

Gadgets 77
Graph paper 173

H

HAM mode 40,173
Hardcopy 117
Hidden line algorithms 7
Hidden surface algorithms 7

I

Interchange File Format (IFF) 114,117, 169,193
Intersection point 22,187

K

Keyboard shortcuts 126,163

L

Light rays 9
Light source 8,161,170,174
Loading Materials 157

M

Main point 52
Material editor 152
Memory management 93
Menus 84
Modules 75
Multiple light sources 170

O

Object data 146
Object rotation 168
Objects 7,146,167
Optimization 44
Optional disk 78,193

P

Parallelogram 11,148
Perception 19
Perpendicular 13
Perspective 55
Pixel size 161
Pixels 8,161,174
Plane 11,147,182
Planning graphics 173
Point of view 174
Polar coordinates 14
Printing graphics 158
Projection point 22,174
Pythagorean theorem 185

R

Ray tracer program—*see Tracer*
Ray tracing 7
Ray tracing algorithms 7
Rectangle 22,160
Recursion 10
Reference point 94
Reflection 9
Requester 131
Resolution 173
Rotation 52,55

S

Saving graphics 158
Scalar 22
SetPoint program 193,345-355
Shading 173
Shadow 7,160
ShowILBM program 193
Sine 53
Smooth shading 168
Sphere 14,150,182
Spheroid 151

T

Tangent 53
Tracer 19,104,119,145-163,167,179,207-301
Tracer instructions 155-163
Tracer menus 155-163
Tracer modules 203-206
Transparency 10,169
Triangle 7,147,167
Tricks and tips 173
Two dimensional objects 14

V

Vectors 22,179
Visual rays 9

W

Wire model 51,104,160,174
Word processor 74

X

X coordinate 51

Y

Y coordinate 51

Z

Z coordinate 51

Companion Diskette Offer

For your convenience, the program listings contained in this book are available on an Amiga format floppy disk. You should order the diskette if you want to use the programs, but don't want to type them in from the listings in the book.

The companion diskette for **Amiga 3D Graphic Programming in BASIC** includes BASIC source code for the editor program, ASCII sources of the tracer program modules, and compiled, ready to run versions of the tracer and editor programs. Also included are a set of 3D wire model graphics and their matching materials, ready for calculation.

All programs on the diskette have been fully tested. You can change the programs to suit your particular needs. The diskette is available for $14.95 plus $2.00 ($5.00 foreign) for shipping and handling.

When ordering by mail, please give your name and shipping address. Enclose a check, money order or credit card information. Mail your order to:

5370 52nd Street SE
Grand Rapids, MI 49512

Or for fast service (credit card orders only)
call **616-698-0330** (orders within Michigan)
or **1-800-451-4319** (orders outside of Michigan).

One Good Book deserves another and another, and another, and

Amiga C for Advanced Programmers

-contains a wealth of information from the pros: how compilers, assemblers and linkers work, designing and programming user friendly interfaces using Intuition, combining assembly language and C codes, and more. Includes complete source code for text editor.

ISBN 1-55755-046-8 400 pp **$34.95**

Amiga C for Beginners

-an introduction to learning the popular C language. Explains the language elements using examples specifically geared to the Amiga. Describes C library routines, how the compiler works and more.

ISBN 1-55755-045-X 280 pp **$19.95**

Amiga 3-D Graphic Programming in BASIC

-shows you how to use the powerful graphic capabilities of the Amiga. Details the techniques and algorithms for writing three-dimensional graphic programs: ray tracing in all resolutions, light sources and shading, saving graphics in IFF format and more.

ISBN 1-55755-044-1 300 pp **$19.95**

Amiga Disk Drives Inside & Out

-is the most in-depth reference available covering the Amiga's disk drives. Learn how to speed up data transfer, how copy protection works, computer viruses, Workbench and the CLI DOS functions, loading, saving, sequential and random file organization, more.

ISBN 1-55755-042-5 360 pp **$29.95**

Amiga For Beginners *

-the first volume in our Amiga series, introduces you to Intuition (Amiga's graphic interface), the mouse, windows, the CLI, and Amiga BASIC and explains every practical aspect of the Amiga in plain English.

ISBN 1-55755-021-2 184 pp **$16.95**

Includes Workbench 1.3 Info

AmigaBASIC Inside & Out

-THE definitive step-by-step guide to programming the Amiga in BASIC. Every AmigaBASIC command is fully described and detailed. Topics include charts, windows, pulldown menus, files, mouse and speech commands.

ISBN 0-916439-87-9 554 pp **$24.95**

Includes Workbench 1.3 Info

Amiga Tricks & Tips

-follows our tradition of other Tricks and Tips books for CBM users. Presents dozens of tips on accessing libraries from BASIC, custom character sets, AmigaDOS, sound, important 68000 memory locations, and much more!

ISBN 0-916439-88-7 348 pp **$19.95**

AmigaDOS Inside & Out

-covers the insides of AmigaDOS from the internal design up to practical applications. Includes detailed reference section, tasks and handling, DOS editors ED and EDIT, how to create and use script files, multitasking, and much more.

ISBN 1-55755-041-7 280pp **$19.95**

Includes Workbench 1.3 Info

Amiga Machine Language

-is a comprehensive introduction to 68000 assembler machine language programming and is THE practical guide for learning to program the Amiga in ultra-fast ML. Also covers 68000 microprocessor address modes and architecture, speech and sound from ML and much more.

ISBN 1-55755-025-5 264 pp **$19.95**

Amiga System Programmer's Guide

-comprehensive guide to what goes on inside the Amiga in a single volume. Only a few of the many subjects covered include the EXEC structure, I/O requests, interrupts and resource management, multitasking functions and much, much more.

ISBN 1-55755-034-4 442 pp **$34.95**

AmigaDOS Quick Reference *

-an easy-to-use reference tool for beginners and advanced programmers alike. You can quickly find commands for your Amiga by using the three handy indexes designed with the user in mind. All commands are in alphabetical order for easy reference. *Includes Workbench 1.3 Info*

ISBN 1-55755-049-2 128 pp **$9.95**

Save Time and Money!-Optional program disks are available for many of our Amiga reference books. All programs listed in the books are on each respective disk and will save you countless hours of typing! **$14.95**

(* Optional Diskette Not Available for these Titles)

Abacus

Dept. B8, 5370 52nd Street S.E.
Grand Rapids, MI 49512
(616) 698-0330

See your local Dealer or Call Toll Free 1-800-451-4319

Add $4.00 Shipping and Handling per Order
Foreign add $12.00 per item

New Software

All Abacus software runs on the Amiga 500, Amiga 1000 or Amiga 2000. Each package is fully compatible with our other products in the Amiga line

The *Ideal* AMIGA wordprocessor

TextPro
AMIGA

TextPro AMIGA upholds the true spirit of the AMIGA: it's powerful, it has a surprising number of "extra" features, but it's also very easy to use. **TextPro AMIGA**—the Ideal AMIGA word processor that proves just how easy word processing can be. You can write your first documents immediately, with a minimum of learning—without even reading the manual. But **TextPro AMIGA** is much more than a beginner's package. Ultra-fast onscreen formatting, graphic merge capabilities, automatic hyphenation and many more features make **TextPro AMIGA** ideal for the professional user as well. **TextPro AMIGA** features:

- High-speed text input and editing
- Functions accessible through menus or shortcut keys
- Fast onscreen formatting
- Automatic hyphenation
- Versatile function key assignment
- Save any section of an AMIGA screen & print as text
- Loading and saving through the RS-232 interface
- Multiple tab settings
- Accepts IFF format graphics in texts
- Extremely flexible printer adaptations. Printer drivers for most popular dot-matrix printers included
- Includes thorough manual
- Not copy protected

TextPro AMIGA sets a new standard for word processing packages in its price range. So easy to use and modestly priced that any AMIGA owner can use it—so packed with advanced features, you can't pass it up.

Suggested retail price: $79.95

More than word processing...

BeckerText
AMIGA

This is one program for serious AMIGA owners. **BeckerText Amiga** is more than a word processor. It has all the features of **TextPro AMIGA**, but it also has features that you might not expect:

- Fast WYSIWYG formatting
- Calculations within a text—like having a spreadsheet program anytime you want it
- Templates for calculations in columns
- Line spacing options
- Auto-hyphenation and Auto-indexing
- Multiple-column printing, up to 5 columns on a single page
- Online dictionary checks spelling in text as it's written
- Spell checker for interactive proofing of documents
- Up to 999 characters per line (with scrolling)
- Many more features for the professional

BeckerText AMIGA is a vital addition for C programmers—it's an extremely flexible C editor. Whether you're deleting, adding or duplicating a block of C source-code, **BeckerText AMIGA** does it all, automatically. And the online dictionary acts as a C syntax checker and finds syntax errors in a flash.

BeckerText AMIGA. When you need more from your word processor than just word processing.

Suggested retail price: **$150.00**

Imagine the <u>perfect</u> database

DataRetrieve

AMIGA

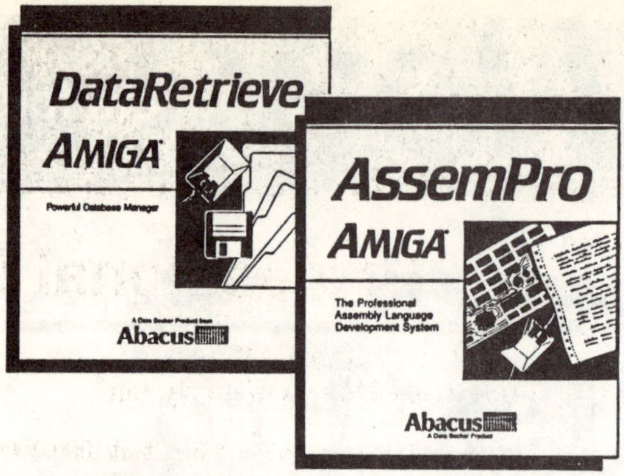

Imagine, for a moment, what the perfect database for your AMIGA would have. You'd want power and speed, for quick access to your information. An unlimited amount of storage space. And you'd want it easy to use—no baffling commands or file structures—with a graphic interface that does your AMIGA justice.

Enter **DataRetrieve AMIGA**. It's unlike any other database you can buy. Powerful, feature-packed, with the capacity for any business or personal application—mailing lists, inventory, billing, etc. Yet it's so simple to use, it's startling. **DataRetrieve AMIGA**'s drop-down menus help you to define files quickly. Then you conveniently enter information using on-screen templates. **DataRetrieve AMIGA** takes advantage of the Amiga's multi-tasking capability for *optimum* processing speed.

DataRetrieve AMIGA features:

- Open eight files simultaneously
- Password protection
- Edit files in memory
- Maximum of 80 index fields with variable precision (1-999 characters)
- Convenient search/select criteria (range, AND/OR comparisons)
- Text, date, time, numeric and selection fields, IFF file reading capability
- Exchange data with other software packages (for form letters, mailing lists, etc.)
- Control operations with keyboard or mouse
- Adjustable screen masks, up to 5000 x 5000 pixels
- Insert graphic elements into screen masks (e.g., rectangles, circles, lines, patterns, etc.)
- Screen masks support different text styles and sizes
- Multiple text fields with word make-up and formatting capabilities
- Integrated printer masks and list editor.
- Maximum filesize 2 billion characters
- Maximum data record size 64,000 characters
- Maximum data set 2 billion characters
- Unlimited number of data fields
- Maximum field size 32,000 characters

DataRetrieve AMIGA —it'll handle your data with the speed and easy operation that you've come to expect from Abacus products for the AMIGA.

Suggested retail price: **$79.95**

Not just for the experts

AssemPro

AMIGA

AssemPro AMIGA lets every Amiga owner enjoy the benefits of fast machine language programming.

Because machine language programming isn't just for 68000 experts. **AssemPro AMIGA** is easily learned and user-friendly—it uses Amiga menus for simplicity. But **AssemPro AMIGA** boasts a long list of professional features that eliminate the tedium and repetition of M/L programming. **AssemPro AMIGA** is the complete developer's package for writing of 68000 machine language on the Amiga, complete with editor, debugger, disassembler and reassembler. **AssemPro AMIGA** is the perfect introduction to machine langage development and programming. And it's even got what you 68000 experts need.

AssemPro AMIGA features:

- Written completely in machine language, for ultra-fast operation
- Integrated editor, debugger, disassembler, reassembler
- Large operating system library
- Runs under CLI and Workbench
- Produces either PC-relocatable or absolute code
- Macros possible for nearly any parameter (of different types)
- Error search function
- Cross-reference list
- Menu-controlled conditional and repeated assembly
- Full 32-bit arithmetic
- Debugger with 68020 single-step emulation
- Runs on any AMIGA with 512K and Kickstart 1.2.

Suggested retail price: **$99.95**

Abacus Products for *Amiga* computers

Professional DataRetrieve

The Professional Level
Database Management System

Professional DataRetrieve, for the Amiga 500/1000/2000, is a friendly easy-to-operate professional level data management package with the features most wanted in a relational data base system.
Professional DataRetrieve has complete relational data mangagement capabilities. Define relationships between different files (one to one, one to many, many to many). Change relations without file reorganization.

Professional DataRetrieve includes an extensive programming laguage which includes more than 200 BASIC-like commands and functions and integrated program editor. Design custom user interfaces with pulldown menus, icon selection, window activation and more.
Professional DataRetrieve can perform calculations and searches using complex mathematical comparisons using over 80 functions and constants.

Professional DataRetrieve is a friendly, easy to operate programmable RELATIONAL data base system. **PDR** includes PROFIL, a programming language similar to BASIC. You can open and edit up to 8 files simultaneously and the size of your data fields, records and files are limited only by your memory and disk storage. You have complete interrelation between files which can include IFF graphics. NOT COPY PROTECTED. ISBN 1-55755-048-4

MORE features of **Professional DataRetrieve**

Easily import data from other databases....file compatible with standard **DataRetrieve**....supports multitasking...design your own custom forms with the completely integrated printer mask editor....includes PROFIL programming language that allows the programmer to custom tailor his database requirements...

MORE features of PROFIL include:

Open Amiga devices including the console, printer, serial and the CLI.
Create your own programmable requestors
Complete error trapping.
Built-in compiler and much, much more.

Suggested retail price: $295.00

Features

- Up to 8 files can be edited simultaneously
- Maximum size of a data field 32,000 characters (text fields only)
- Maximum number of data fields limited by RAM
- Maximum record size of 64,000 characters
- Maximum number of records disk dependent (2,000,000,000 maximum)
- Up to 80 index fields per file
- Up to 6 field types - Text, Date, Time, Numeric, IFF, Choice
- Unlimited number of searches and subrange criteria
- Integrated list editor and full-page printer mask editor
- Index accuracy selectable from 1-999 characters
- Multiple file masks on-screen
- Easily create/edit on-screen masks for one or many files
- User-programmable pulldown menus
- Operate the program from the mouse or the key board
- Calculation fields, Data Fields
  IFF Graphics supported
- Mass-storage-oriented file organization
- Not Copy Protected, NO DONGLE; can be in stalled on your hard drive

Books for the AMIGA

AmigaDOS Quick Reference Guide

AmigaDos Quick Reference Guide is an easy-to-use reference tool for beginners and advanced programmers alike. You can quickly find commands for your Amiga by using the three handy indexes designed with the user in mind. All commands are in alphabetical order for easy reference. The most useful information you need fast can be found- including:

- All AmigaDOS commands described, including Workbench 1.3
- Command syntax and arguments described with examples
- CLI shortcuts
- CTRL sequences
- ESCape sequences
- Amiga ASCII table
- Guru Meditation Codes
- Error messages with their corresponding numbers

Three indexes for quick information at your fingertips! The AmigaDOS Quick Reference Guide is an indispensable tool you'll want to keep close to your Amiga.

Suggested retail price US $9.95 ISBN 155755-049-2

Abacus Amiga Books

Vol. 1	Amiga for Beginners	1-55755-021-2	$16.95
Vol. 2	AmigaBASIC Inside & Out	0-916439-87-9	$24.95
Vol. 3	Amiga 3D Graphic Programming in BASIC	1-55755-044-1	$19.95
Vol. 4	Amiga Machine Language	1-55755-025-5	$19.95
Vol. 5	Amiga Tricks & Tips	0-916439-88-7	$19.95
Vol. 6	Amiga System Programmers Guide	1-55755-034-4	$34.95
Vol. 7	Advanced System Programmers Guide	1-55755-047-6	$34.95
Vol. 8	AmigaDOS Inside & Out	1-55755-041-7	$19.95
Vol. 9	Amiga Disk Drives Inside & Out	1-55755-042-5	$29.95
Vol. 10	Amiga C for Beginners	1-55755-045-X	$19.95
Vol. 11	Amiga C for Advanced Programmers	1-55755-046-8	$34.95
Vol. 12	More Tricks & Tips for the Amiga	1-55755-051-4	$19.95
Vol. 13	Amiga Graphics Inside & Out	1-55755-052-2	$34.95
Vol. 14	Amiga Desktop Video Guide	1-55755-057-3	$19.95
	AmigaDOS Quick Reference Guide	1-55755-049-2	$ 9.95